SALLY RIDE

AMERICA'S FIRST WOMAN IN SPACE

LYNN SHERR

SIMON & SCHUSTER
New York   London   Toronto   Sydney   New Delhi

90

Simon & Schuster
1230 Avenue of the Americas
New York, NY 10020

First Simon & Schuster hardcover edition June 2014

SIMON & SCHUSTER and colophon are registered trademarks of
Simon & Schuster, Inc.

For information about special discounts for bulk purchases,
please contact Simon & Schuster Special Sales at 1-866-506-1949
or business@simonandschuster.com.

The Simon & Schuster Speakers Bureau can bring authors to your live event. For
more information or to book an event, contact the Simon & Schuster Speakers
Bureau at 1-866-248-3049 or visit our website at www.simonspeakers.com.

Interior design by Joy O'Meara
Jacket design by Jackie Seow
Jacket photographs: (front) courtesy of NASA; (back) by Randy Taylor; and
(spine) by Shutterstock

Manufactured in the United States of America

10   9   8   7   6   5   4   3   2   1

Library of Congress Cataloging-in-Publication Data
Sherr, Lynn.
   Sally Ride : America's first woman in space / Lynn Sherr.
      pages   cm
   Includes bibliographical references and index.
   1. Ride, Sally.   2. Women astronauts—United States—Biography.
3. Astronauts—United States—Biography.   I. Title.
   TL789.85.R53S54   2014
   629.450092—dc23
   [B]   2013039647

ISBN 978-1-4767-2576-5
ISBN 978-1-4767-2578-9 (ebook)

CONTENTS

For Tyler, Tessa, Riley and Sammy: our future.

SALLY RIDE

INTRODUCTION

The man in the spacesuit drifted down the ladder, a ghostly image on the surface of the Moon. A quarter-million miles away, on a steamy, hot night during Earth's midsummer, an eighteen-year-old college student stared at the TV screen in awe, fighting off the sleep she needed for the next day's tennis tournament.

"That's one small step..." began Neil Armstrong, etching the first human footprint into lunar soil.

Sally Ride was mesmerized. She could not know that the same forces that had propelled the astronaut to the Moon would one day shape the trajectory of her own life; that she, too, would make cosmic history; and that their paths would eerily converge. That night, it was unimaginable. Anyway, she had a match to play.

—July 20, 1969

"Who was Sally Ride?"

A flurry of little hands shoots skyward, urgently beating the air to get my attention. The long answer is complicated—elusive, to many of her friends—but I'm going for the obvious here, posing the question to a group of fifth graders in New Jersey who are bursting to show off what they've learned. Sort of.

I point to a girl with neat cornrows taming her hair, dressed in the yellow shirt and navy pants that is the school uniform.

"The first woman to walk on the Moon?"

"Not quite," I tell her. "Anyone else?"

"The first lady to step in space?" This from a slim, studious-looking fellow with a voice deeper than his years.

"Nope. But close," I say, thrilled that they're thinking galaxy. "Next?"

"A great scientist?"

Well, yes, but . . .

I am about to end the exercise when an insistent youngster with pearly studs punctuating her earlobes lowers her arm, looks at me calmly and announces with confidence, "The first American woman in space."

Bingo.

Never mind that these two dozen preteens were born nearly two decades after she soared into their history books, and that this is their first hands-on science class. Sally Ride is on their radar (or near enough) because she made the unimaginable possible, bringing outer space to their inner-city classroom. Long after her own trip off the planet, she created a program that takes them to the Moon—through their laptops—where they can act like science tourists, ordering custom snapshots of its mysterious, gray terrain by keying in coordinates that will be relayed to cameras on twin satellites orbiting the lunar surface. Tomorrow their carefully chosen images will be delivered: real-time close-ups of craters and mountains as accessible as the Grand Canyon, ready to study, frame and slap onto the refrigerator door. The project is called MoonKAM, a unique opportunity for young Earthlings to expand their futures by clicking into the ancient heavens; a close encounter with the solar system that not only keeps them focused for a solid hour and a half but ignites their dreams and can change their lives.

Just ask Genesis Santos, the optimistically named twelve-year-old daughter of a Puerto Rican mother and Honduran father. She participated in the program last year and has stopped by to offer the more grown-up perspective of a sixth grader. I ask how taking pictures with MoonKAM has affected the way she regards the big yellow ball hanging over her Jersey City neighborhood at nighttime. "Well," she confides, "I used to think that the Moon just illuminated the sky. Now I see a dif-

ferent view. It makes me want to float in space and walk on the Moon."
By focusing beyond Earth, Genesis discovered herself. She wants to be
a scientist.

Which pretty much sums up the arc and the impact of Sally Ride's
own life.

Her place in history will forever be secure as the plucky, thirty-two-
year-old physicist with the winning grin who rocketed through the celestial glass ceiling to prove that women, too, could have the right stuff.
On June 18, 1983, well into the social revolution that enabled women
to start taking their equal place throughout the rest of society, she de-
fied the institutional gravity of American spaceflight and zoomed into
the national psyche. Sally Ride was not the first woman in orbit—two
Russians had gotten there before her—but she was the first *American*
woman in space, with the attendant publicity and allure of the free
world. She also remains the youngest American ever launched. Her
achievement, and the celebrity that resulted, captivated and inspired
several generations of admirers. She was, briefly, the most famous person on the planet.

Being first at anything guarantees headlines, at least temporarily. We
honor pioneers; we crave heroes; we count on explorers of every di-
mension to peek beyond the edges of our neighborhoods, our nations
and our understanding to tell us what's out there. And when "out there"
is outer space, news becomes legend. What's up—as in thumbs or the
stock market or our outlook—is good. Brightness and beauty are measured by the sun and the stars, righteousness by heaven. Progress means
breaking through ceilings, not floors; astonishment is otherworldly.
The mystery of the universe, with its infinite horizons and limited access, and the fiery risk of riding two giant Roman candles to get there,
magnified Sally Ride's entry into what had long been an all-male cowboy
culture, into a potent, can-do symbol. Many women, especially young
women, translated her bold journey into their own tickets to success. If
that door was open, they reasoned, so is everything else.

But while flying in space defined her public image, and would always anchor her public service, it never circumscribed Sally's view of herself. Being an astronaut was her adventure, not her vocation. She spent only nine years at NASA. For the next quarter century she mastered a succession of careers that grew out of her earliest convictions and built upon each other. As a teen, she tasted, then rejected a life in professional tennis but assimilated the lessons of teamwork and grace under pressure. As a retired astronaut, she did research on arms control and taught physics to university students, increasingly motivated by the fragility of Earth that she'd seen from space. In Washington, DC, she advised two presidents, testified before committees of Congress, and regularly refused political office, too private to belong to the public. Once the bright new face of NASA, she also became its conscience, repeatedly agreeing to help get the agency back on track or chart its future. And wherever she found herself, she championed programs to advance the status of women and fought against stereotypes that dampened children's dreams, barriers to success that had never stopped her. There was no master plan, just pieces she kept fitting together as she refined her vision.

Her trust in science led to her conviction that a scientifically literate nation is our only hope. It all coalesced in the company she founded, Sally Ride Science, whose purpose was to get and keep eight- to twelve-year-olds, especially girls, interested in and committed to math and science. The message, relayed through innovative educational products and programs for both students and teachers, and sometimes partnered with NASA (like the orbiting cameras focused on the Moon) echoed her own fantastic voyage: Science is cool and gender no obstacle to rocketing into space or sequencing the genome of a tropical frog. The grander goal was implicit: with proper encouragement and support, kids can be who, and what, they want. Even the sky is no limit. That was her passion and her focus when she died of cancer in 2012, too young at age sixty-one.

I met Sally Ride in 1981 when, as a correspondent for ABC News, I was asked to join the team covering NASA's upcoming new space shuttle program. My first assignment, on my first trip to the Johnson Space Center in Houston, was to profile some of the so-called new breed of astronauts—the women and minorities and male civilian scientists ushering in an era of more routine rocketry. Sally was one of the newbies NASA offered up. A self-described astrophysicist who spoke in English, not technotalk, she hooked me in our first interview with her direct manner and her determination. "Why do you want to go into space?" I asked, expecting the cocksure response of the dominant astronaut culture. "I don't know," she answered. "I've discovered that half the people would love to go into space, and there's no need to explain it to them. The other half can't understand, and I couldn't explain it to them. If someone doesn't know why, I can't explain it." In a fraternity of uptight crew cuts, she was a breath of fresh feminism, acknowledging unequivocally that the women's movement had made her selection possible; that NASA, with its twenty-year heritage of white male fighter pilots, was finally doing the right thing. We became friends immediately.

As the program developed and I wound up anchoring ABC's space coverage, Sally and I continued to spend time together. We bonded over cold shrimp and funny stories at a variety of local dives, at least one of which promised mud wrestling, which we somehow avoided. We shared a healthy disregard for the overblown egos and conservative intransigence of both our professions. And beneath her unemotional demeanor that some called icy, I found a caring friend with an impish wit. When she married fellow astronaut Steve Hawley, their home became my beer-and-pizza hangout during other folks' shuttle missions. They were friends as well as stories, and none of us betrayed our bosses. In fact, given NASA's longstanding distrust of the press—we were the dreaded diggers who could unmask a space hero as a mere mortal—I think we all enjoyed having a pal in the other camp. I knew that Sally avoided most reporters, that she kept her private life more private than most, but in those days before the maw of 24/7 cable chatter devoured every scrap of a celebrity's existence, the tidbits I picked up seemed irrelevant. Our off-the-grid conversations informed my on-the-air coverage. And

Sally got as good as she gave, relishing her entrée into the back story of network news and thanking the editors and producers who helped put her story on the air.

On the eve of her famous first flight (a time when, to avoid stray germs, astronauts were quarantined from human contact and off-limits to reporters) Sally telephoned me while I was working on that night's script at the ABC workspace.

"Hi there!" came a familiar, cheery voice. "In five minutes, why don't you walk outside your trailer and look down towards the parking lot."

I put down the phone and stepped out into the fading Florida sun. There she stood, about twenty-five yards away, wearing shorts and a tee-shirt and waving to me from a car parked off the main drive. I wasn't allowed to get closer—and she knew I wouldn't jeopardize the flight—but it was reassuring to see her in such good spirits. I could report exclusively on the air that night that the woman most in demand at the Kennedy Space Center at that moment was doing just fine. And pushing the envelope, as she always did, with a playful, anti-authoritarian attitude—up to a point. Sally liked to break rules she found dumb, which made her great fun as a friend. But she was also a reliable team player, who could line up with her crew crossing the tarmac behind her commander and take orders like a trooper.

When her flight ended, and her face adorned every major magazine on the newsstand, my husband, Larry, and I became her refuge in New York. She and Steve visited us in the city and at the beach. After she flew again the following year—taking small items aloft for both Larry and me in the strictly limited space of her personal kit—they joined us on a tropical Christmas vacation.

Sally was fine company, always up for a word game, interested in everything. Her celebrity never got in the way of her humility or her good humor. It's not that she had no ego—she did, and it was healthy. But it didn't enter the room before she did, either in private or in public. And it certainly didn't get in the way of our friendship.

Then, in January 1986, *Challenger* exploded, and the scales dropped from all of our eyes. Some of NASA's managers and contractors—heirs to those who had put a dozen men on the Moon and brought Apollo 13 home safely, who had made the Shuttle the bright new hope—were caught in their own carelessness. Sally joined the Rogers Commission investigating the accident, and I covered it daily, as the grim revelations emerged. For a time she was posted to NASA Headquarters in Washington, helping plot a new direction for the space agency. And then we both moved on. Sally got divorced, retired from NASA, returned to California and academia. I transferred to *20/20*, where, despite my best efforts, space was never regarded as a ratings grabber.

Our friendship endured—long dinners and visits when we found ourselves in the same city; breezy phone conversations, amusing little notes, then emails. Plus her usual apologetic requests when the inevitable documentary or awards dinner required a quote from someone who knew her when. And while she might dine with Prince Charles or take meetings in the Oval Office, I often found Sally flopped on the floor of my living room, shoeless, legs draped over the coffee table, watching TV.

But over her last few years, I hardly saw her. And while we stayed in touch, I was unaware that beyond the zone of privacy that gave her room to breathe—the zone where I hung out and thought I knew her— a barrier of secrecy had concealed essential pieces of Sally's self.

I did not realize the psychic price she had paid for being the first American woman in space. I did not know she had been diagnosed with cancer that would take her life in just seventeen months. And I did not know for sure, as was revealed in the last line of her obituary, that she had been in a loving and committed relationship with a woman for the past twenty-seven years.

Sally was very good at keeping secrets.

If Sally Ride had written this book, it would be a thin one, lean as its subject (5′5½″, 110 pounds), with no literary version of body fat. Or excess emotion. In grammatical terms—totally appropriate for the

Stanford graduate with a dual major in English and physics—Sally was never an adjective, pausing to embellish; she was a verb, an action verb. Her headline-ready name was a sentence, maybe a command. She did, performed, carried out; after NASA, she used her considerable clout to reset frontiers, pushing gently against anything that might stop her forward momentum. Sally always looked ahead, never back. But even that vision had limits: "I'm not a goal-oriented person," she told one reporter, articulating an often-repeated sentiment. "I don't look out into the future and say, 'Five or ten years from now, this is what I want to be doing, there is where I want to be.' I'm very much a person who lives in the moment and gets very, very involved in whatever I happen to be doing now."

That *carpe diem* mentality may also explain why she never wanted the story of her own life confined between two covers, insisting even after she owned the made-for-marketing title—First American Woman in Space!—that she hadn't yet done enough. Later, when by any measure she had, there were just too many things competing for her time.

And a few she did not want to make known.

"I'm not ready and may never *be* ready to write the book that publishers want me to write," she said in 1986, without amplification. That was after publication of the only book she did write about her blastoff from the planet and into history—a children's book, because, according to coauthor and childhood friend Susan Okie, she liked kids' enthusiasm. "They asked the questions that everybody wanted to know the answers to, but that adults were too embarrassed to ask," Okie recalls. Like, how do you go to the bathroom in space? Sally had no problem with queries like that. Far more irritating were what her father, Dale Ride, called the "monumentally insipid questions" from (mostly) male reporters, epitomized by the breathtakingly flat-footed, "When you get angry, do you weep?" Sally was mindful of her responsibility to the public as the beneficiary of a government program, but there were some things she was just not interested in, or capable of, sharing. It's not who she was.

So who was she?

That's what this book seeks to describe. I'm writing it because Tam O'Shaughnessy, her partner in love and business, decided within days of her death that it was time for a proper biography. That the obituaries, fine as many were, didn't capture the richness or the nuance of her life. And that the helicopters circling overhead and the reporters ringing the doorbell meant that the collective gasp over her newly revealed sexual orientation needed to be addressed with a full appreciation of the life she shared with Tam. In short, that in the interest of honesty it was time to lift the veil of privacy Sally had guarded so tenaciously. In the process, the family—Tam, along with Sally's sister, Bear Ride; and her mother, Joyce Ride—would make themselves exclusively available to the author to tell their stories. When Tam laid this all out to her agent, Esther Newberg, and asked about an author, Esther called me. The offer was bittersweet: back when Sally decided to write her first children's book, she had asked me to recommend an agent and I'd connected her with Esther. Our friendship had come full circle.

So yes, I bring bias to this project, but I have not checked my journalism credentials at the door. Writing Sally's life without her participation has made me, like any biographer, part detective, part historian, part arbiter of divergent tales, often piecing together fragments very reluctantly divulged. I have also tried to view her story against the backdrop of the times and attitudes that shaped sweeping changes in American behavior. Because I lived through and reported on both the social revolution that enabled her flight and the extraordinary impact of the mission itself, I've been able to draw on my own stories, notes and memories. Much of her NASA history, of course, is public, and Sally's responses to thousands of questions from other reporters, as well as from the legislators who sought her wisdom, not to mention the many articles and op-eds she wrote herself, can be as enlightening as they are repetitive. Her voice rings throughout much of this book. But on occasion, she changed her version of events, an annoying trait that confounds the facts and confuses the historical record. Just for instance, she did not grow up wanting to be an astronaut, and except for a few offhand quips, never considered the possibility until she was twenty-six. But in later years— out of boredom? making mischief? because she thought it would be easier to understand?—she sometimes reimagined herself to audiences as a little girl with rocket dreams. That kind of harmless inconsistency was easy enough to correct here.

Far more difficult has been defining the mind-set that shielded her privacy behind often unscalable walls, trying to hear what her mother (who never heard them either) calls Sally's "internal conversations." She was resolutely guarded and a superb compartmentalizer, able to shut off various rooms in her mind until she needed to visit them. No doubt it was a survival technique that often served her well. But in the process, she also kept those of us who knew her from knowing her completely. As her friend, I am saddened that I missed the chance to share the happiness of her life with Tam, and to say a proper good-bye at the end. As a reporter who covered countless stories exploring the human side of the gay rights movement, I can't help wondering whether a few more questions might have cracked the code. Although, as both friends and family lament, there's no guarantee I would have gotten any answers. "There is a part of her," admits Tam, "no one will ever know."

Sally's family has filled in many blanks, with recollections, artifacts and correspondence. That was a start. In her childhood diary, I saw early hints of the singular woman she would become. In letters home and to close friends (preserved, in some cases, for more than four decades; what does *that* say about her impact?), I found a late-blooming teen starting to come to grips with unfamiliar stirrings. And while her grownup journals are sparse, with a maddening preference for abbreviated bullet points rather than revealing paragraphs, some of Sally's handwritten comments express tender vulnerabilities. I have also gained access to her files, from her college transcripts to her days at NASA through her role as CEO of her company. And I have unearthed many pages of documents related to Sally's NASA career, including her application and the essay she wrote on why she wanted to be an astronaut. In addition, I have listened with fascination to hours of previously undisclosed audio journals that Sally recorded about her first trip to space and its aftermath, including the spine-tingling details of her forbidden encounter with a Soviet cosmonaut. I have also conducted several hundred interviews with friends, romances and colleagues, triangulating their accounts to verify decades-old memories. The recollections are theirs; the conclusions, mine.

The story is Sally's: the all-too-human tale of a smart, witty, daring optimist who loved deeply—both men and women—and cared passionately—for the minds of girls and boys and for the future of planet Earth—beneath an image of cool detachment. She was that, too: at heart, a scientist, often happiest at her desk or in front of the chalkboard, quietly figuring out "the way and the wonder of the world around us," according to one of her students. And how to make it more wonderful.

"Imagine this room in space," she would tell an auditorium filled with a thousand youngsters, "and you could do thirty-five somersaults in a row. My favorite thing about space was being weightless. There's not even a close second."

This is also the story of a particular time in a particular place and a woman who had the brains and agility to seize the moment. When Sally Ride was born in 1951, outer space was science fiction and women's rights were marginal. The social advances and lucky timing that would enable both to intersect with the life of a gifted young scientist make hers an inspiring lesson in modern American history. She took full advantage of the ever-widening definition of "woman's place," and spent much of her life making sure it was everywhere. That she could not, or would not, openly identify herself as a gay woman, reflects not only her intense need for privacy, but the shame and fear that an intolerant society can inflict even on its heroes. And the consequences of that secrecy on many of those close to her.

Today, with the evolution in attitudes that has made same-sex marriage legal in many states and inching towards full recognition by the federal government, the need for such caution is waning. With a majority of Americans supporting the idea of a woman as US president, and with the International Space Station orbiting overhead—meaning that humans, often female humans, permanently occupy the heavens—the idea that Sally and her peers were feminist pioneers may seem antiquated, even ridiculous. If only. As first females know well, every small step by one is a giant leap for us all.

A note about logistics: the sequence of this book is mostly chronological, as Sally lived her life, with occasional time shifts to accommodate history and to deal with the episodic nature of her career. In referring to the characters in Sally's life, I've followed my own rules. Most are called by their last names, usually without titles, in the contemporary journalistic style so many of us fought for back in the days when a woman could be identified only by her marital status (Miss or Mrs.). In some special cases, however—notably, Sally's family and close friends—I've used first names to avoid confusion.

That's also true for Sally herself. Her PhD made her Dr. Ride, and she was rightfully proud of that. But I'll be calling her Sally because that's how I knew her. It's also the way she chose to be remembered when she donated her sky blue flight suit to the Smithsonian National Air and Space Museum. Every astronaut gets a set of Velcro-backed, leather name patches: first name, last name, title, whatever. The one Sally chose for the museum—the one you can see on display by the space shuttle exhibit on the first floor—reads simply, Sally.

That's also her ID as the fictional protagonist of a video game called *Sally Saves the Alphabet*. Sally and Tam, along with some potential business partners, cooked it up to help kids learn their ABCs, an animated adventure in which an intrepid little astronaut takes a spacewalk from the Shuttle to corral twenty-six letters, scattered by a gust of solar wind into aimless orbit above Earth. Although the game was never produced, the description of its star is fetchingly familiar: "Sally is a likable character, somewhere between 8 and 10 years old . . . She is independent and spunky, and should have the demeanor of an encouraging, adventurous older sister. She can be surprised, but not frightened; and should have a sense of humor. . . ."

As one of her high school classmates described the real-life Sally, "The adult she became was the kid that she was."

Specifically, an introvert who spent much of her life on the public stage. A fiercely private individual who once agreed to autograph a trout. A wonk with a twinkle, a physicist who loved Shakespeare, a world-renowned space traveler who saw herself as an educator. NASA was her launchpad, not her apogee, and no challenge matched the thrill of sensing the neurons firing to make new connections in a young girl's brain.

At a time when celebrity is cheap and romance an internet blip, Sally Ride stood for something of value. In a world that has increasingly Tweeted its innermost feelings to strangers, she protected most of hers. And buried others.

Sally worked hard to control her own narrative, and in many ways it was both authentic and exemplary. One would do well to follow her tracks. But as her mother observed when Sally quit tennis, "she couldn't always make the ball go where she wanted." So too, with her life. In the end, with no time left to elaborate, she came to accept that. And while she neither contributed to, nor controlled the creation of this biography, I like to think she would appreciate the chance to set the record straight, to remove—finally—the burden of secrecy and burnish her image with truth. I only wish she could have done so while she lived.

"I'm so glad you are writing this book," many of her friends told me eagerly. "I can't wait to see how you connect the dots."

"Me too," I told them honestly.

I'll start where she did, in the place on Earth where Sally always felt at home.

1

CALIFORNIA GIRL

MAY 1951–JUNE 1968

California, 1970.

During her interview before the committee selecting new NASA astro-nauts, twenty-six-year-old graduate student Sally Ride, a native of Los Angeles, breezed through the standard questions about her college major, her PhD research, her interest in space. Her poise impressed everyone. Then they asked, "What do you like to do for fun?" Sally's cool self-confidence brimmed over. "Ride down the freeway, with the radio blaring," she said, grinning, "volume at full speed." NASA's Dr. Carolyn Huntoon, the only woman among the interrogators, quickly recognized a smart, attractive personality who enjoyed life, and jotted down— approvingly—"California girl."

ROOTS

The brilliant sun and laid-back living of Southern California were unimaginable to her forebears, generations of God-fearing farmers and preachers and shopkeepers and craftsmen who prospered amidst the frigid snows of Northern Europe and the often rigid confines of social custom. That modern descendants found their way to the wide open American West reflects the grit, idealism, and recurrent strains of rebellion on both parents' sides. Not to mention a preference for keeping warm. Sally would inherit much of that spirit.

The Ride family name reaches back nearly four hundred years to Derbyshire, a rural, inland county as close to the center of England and as far from the ocean as it's possible to get. Which, according to an early geographer, "made it for many centuries more or less inaccessible." It was, however, known for its beauty: craggy mountains in the north yielding to gentle hills and broad plains further south, with abundantly flowing rivers to keep it all very green. Swift horsemen hunted fox across the tall hedges and lush fields; tenant farmers tilled the rich land surrounding great estates where some Rides would be employed. Think Downton Abbey, but more remote, less manicured and a century older. Even older genealogically. In the tiny parish of Mugginton, within the thick-walled Church of All Saints—whose Romanesque, square stone tower dates back to the Norman Conquest—entries for Rides are among the earliest in the register, and the graveyard is thick with stones of ancient relatives.

One of the first to seek another destiny was John Ride, a young man of "passionate and ungovernable temper," according to a contemporary, so captivated by the fiery sermon of an itinerant Primitive Methodist preacher (a revivalist faction at odds with the mainstream church), John fell to his knees in his father's frozen pasture and shouted, "Glory to God! He has pardoned all my sins!" To which his father (also John) responded, "The Methodists have driven my poor boy mad!" That was in 1807. Soon both converted to the new faith, and John Jr. became a traveling preacher himself. But hostility towards the daring new evangelists sent John and his family packing, making him the first Ride to reach American shores in 1820. His stay was brief, and after returning to England John Ride relocated to Australia. The Rides were on the move, progenitors of the "fierce spirit of independence" that would later characterize their California namesakes.

Three generations later, through the offspring of John's brother William, the trek to America was repeated, this time for good. In 1880, at the age of twenty, William's great-grandson William Ride sailed off, leaving behind the Wesleyan Chapel by the beechnut trees, the old wooden pump where he drank from the spout, and the blacksmith shop, touchstones of a community where mail was delivered by a boy on a pony. He also left his friends and family: hairdressers, domestic servants, wheelwrights, tailors, and undertakers like his brother, Sam, known for estimating villagers' coffin size when he visited them on their sickbeds.

"It was a brave move for a young man at a time when foreign travel was practically unheard of," reported a local newspaper of Will's journey. "But he . . . believed a better life beckoned him in Pennsylvania."

After a successful career as a carpenter and cabinetmaker in Jackson Center, a small Pennsylvania mill town near the Ohio border, William crossed the Rockies to Colorado, where he became a farmer in the early 1900s. Then he and his wife, Alice Irene Vernam, headed for the Pacific, settling on a small ranch in Escondido, just north of San Diego. California "is a fine place to live," he wrote to a childhood friend back in Derby. "It seldom freezes, never snows, a wonderful place for old folk and children." William Ride was sixty-eight, thankful for safe harbor as the

Great Depression began in November 1929. "This is a very extravagant country," he told his village pal. "People live well, dress well, and do a lot of riding around. Automobiles are very common, nearly every family has one or more. You hardly ever see a horse on the road and seldom see anybody on foot. We have wonderful paved roads and thousands of miles of them, mostly made out of cement."

William's son, Thomas Vernam Ride, was by then living in Santa Monica with his wife, Jennie Mae Richardson. Her ancestors, who had left England even earlier for the New World, included a distant link to Robert E. Lee and direct ties to two patriots from the American Revolution, later making Sally eligible for membership in the Daughters of the American Revolution (DAR), a straitlaced affiliation her liberal mother would preemptively reject. Tom and Jennie's first child was a boy, Dale Burdell Ride, born in 1922.

THE NORTHERN ROUTE

Through her maternal grandmother, Sally was descended from several generations of Dutch Mennonites: German-speaking Protestant dissidents who roamed Europe in search of a place to practice their faith without persecution. They found refuge in Russia when Catherine the Great offered the Mennonites land and security in what is now Ukraine. But in 1878, faced with conscription into the czar's army—the same threat that powered great waves of immigrants from other parts of Eastern Europe—Wilhelm Rempel II, thirty-two, a prosperous grain farmer, and his wife, Anna Harder Rempel, sturdy folks with a severe demeanor, fled to America and made their way to Butterfield, Minnesota, near the state's southern border, a dot placed on the map by the railroad line to help develop the prairie. With the population barely breaking three digits (the town's first store had been razed several years earlier due to lack of customers), Wilhelm lured them in with hammer and nails, owning and operating the hardware store on Main Street. It flourished, as did his family, after a fashion.

Wilhelm and Anna's daughter Anna (Sally's ancestors on both sides recycled names the way she would later recycle cans of 7UP) fell in love with Sylvester Sulem, the son of nearby homesteaders from Lom, Norway, a quiet village in a verdant valley of arresting majesty: immense, snowy peaks, gentle reindeer, brilliant wildflowers. With dim prospects for the future, the Sulems had skied to the coast and steamed across the ocean to join countrymen in Minnesota. Problem was, Sylvester, thirty-eight, was nearly twice the age of Anna, twenty; worse yet to the strict Mennonite Rempels, he was Lutheran. When neither church would marry them, the couple sent a horse and buggy to Mankato, nearly fifty miles away, to find a justice of the peace, and held the ceremony in Sylvester's sister's home in St. James. He wore a snappy waistcoat, she a flowing veil. They later got even by helping found the local Presbyterian Church.

They also opened a dry goods emporium across the street from the hardware store owned by the Rempels, who refused to speak with their rebel daughter or new son-in-law. The family squabble did not extend to their ten children, the recitation of whose names, in birth order, would become one of the favorite parlor tricks of Sally and her sister: Ada, Ethel, John, Willard, Myrtle, Pearl, Martha, Marie, Chester, Vivian. Ada Sulem left school in tenth grade to change her siblings' diapers and work in the family store. Then she married Andy Anderson, the son of another Norwegian farming family, from Stavanger on Norway's west coast. When Andy didn't want his wife to work, she gave up her career as a Registered Nurse. They moved upstate to Detroit Lakes, the tourist town (with 425 lakes that swelled the population tenfold in summer) where he prospered as the owner of a bowling alley, a chain of movie theaters, and a golf course that remains popular today. Their older daughter, (Carol) Joyce Anderson, played saxophone in the high school marching band and skied or tobogganed all winter long from their house atop a hill. Andy retired early, at forty-seven, and tired of chilly Minnesota, moved his family to Santa Monica in 1941. That's where Joyce met Dale Ride on a blind date in 1948.

"He had this gorgeous dark red hair," Joyce recalls today. "Very appealing." She was twenty-four, a diminutive brunette with a quick smile, a clever (if infrequently motivated) tongue, and a recent psychology degree from UCLA. He was twenty-six, a six-foot-tall, rangy World War II veteran who had landed at Marseilles to help liberate Eastern France, then crossed into Germany, Bavaria and Austria. The perilous trail of Dale's combat with the 928th Field Artillery Battalion of the 103rd Infantry Division, like that of the entire war, had been tracked by his family with clippings pasted into a scrapbook: NAZIS CHASED OUT OF ALSACE, MANNHEIM FALLS, GOERING SURRENDERS. And finally, a triumphant strip of yellowed newsprint pasted diagonally across the entire page: GERMANY SURRENDERS. Dale came home with a Purple Heart, and got his degree from Haverford College, in Pennsylvania, on the GI Bill. Joyce met him when he returned to get his master's in education at UCLA. Was it love at first sight? "I think so," she recalls, which for her is very enthusiastic. They married six months later in a church ceremony with tossed rice, long, white gloves and flirty veils, the bride barely reaching the groom's chin, even in high heels. Tradition stopped there: she wore neither white nor a long train.

That duality—dollops of nonconformity bubbling beneath the aura of custom—would characterize the Rides and their children into the next century. The rebellion of their ancestors and their search for new opportunities recombined beneath the Pacific sun to produce a family that would make its own distinctive way into postwar America. The newlyweds moved into a small starter apartment in Santa Monica, certified members of the Greatest Generation eager to live their version of the American Dream. Two years later, on May 26, 1951, they made their first contribution to the national baby boom. It was a girl. A California girl. They named her Sally Kristen.

You don't remember Crusader Rabbit? *To understand Sally, you must! She was the Rabbit and I was Rags the Tiger, his sidekick. She was like*

*that—the fearlessness. Throw yourself into danger's way and your hap-
less sidekick will help out. Someone's got to save the world!*

—Bear Ride, Sally's younger sister

CHILDHOOD

As a child of the television age, it is more than appropriate that one of
Sally Ride's earliest heroes appeared in the first made-for-TV cartoon—
a black-and-white series starring a bunny in knight's armor who charged
across the plains (or the sea, or the jungle) to make the planet a better
place. Some of his causes: battling Texans who wanted to rid the state of
jackrabbits by shipping them to the North Pole; rescuing tigers whose
stripes were being stolen to make India ink; foiling a plot by bloodthirsty
pirates to rob New York City of its silverware. And always, aided and
abetted by his loyal helpmate. The clever little Crusader was the perfect role model for a pragmatic child with an emerging sense of irony:
he was tiny in size but took on gigantic missions; he had guts, but not
superpowers. He couldn't fly or stop trains, but he could run really fast.
And he oozed the sort of upbeat optimism that moves mountains. Swap
the shining armor for a flight suit, add even more focused brainpower,
and you've got the real-life mind-set of Sally Ride. She also wanted to
save the world—quietly—with plenty of best buddies along the way.

As an infant, she was both sunny and willful, from her pure blue eyes
and corn silk Nordic hair to the tireless little legs that never seemed to
stop moving. "Sally was a child who knew what she wanted," Joyce says.
"Her first word was 'No.'" Contrast that to her sister, Karen, who came
along just over two years later: brown bob, equally bright smile, but "My
first word was 'thank you,'" she says.

The siblings got off to a rocky start when Joyce was nursing the baby.
"Sally came over and bonked me on the head with the telephone," Joyce
says; she was so jealous, Joyce soon stopped nursing. Earlier, when she
was pregnant, "Sally would run at me and say, 'Pick Sassy up!'" Little
"Sassy," as she called herself, also had trouble pronouncing "Karen" as a

child, so morphed "Kar" into "Pear," and then finally "Bear." The name stuck and the pattern of their sisterhood was set.

"Sally loved being in control," Bear says, without rancor. "She always dictated what the game was going to be and what the television show was going to be, and it was fine." Also, "she'd always win. She liked to win, and I learned how to be a gracious loser." Bear shrugs off the role she was assigned, steering me to another favorite TV cartoon, *Rocky and Bullwinkle*, with an intrepid flying squirrel and a loyal backup moose. "I think it was just the prerogative of being the older sibling. And having a younger sibling who would go along with it. Sally always struck me as being much braver and much smarter, so she should be Rocky to my Bullwinkle."

It took a special sister to permit—and laugh off—such dominance; special parents, too. After Sally's first spaceflight, a colleague approached Dale and asked, "Aren't you proud of your daughter?" "Which one?" he responded. Bear would take her own road less traveled, inheriting her ancestors' churchgoing bent to become a Presbyterian minister. Her gift for connecting the spiritual to the mundane was evident to everyone, including her mother, whose highest compliment tended to be, "That wasn't half bad." Joyce did much better in a letter to Sally some years later, writing about Bear, "Preaching I can take or leave, but she's good."

Bear also remembers being with her dad as a child when a friend asked, "Are you the tennis player?"—meaning Sally. Dale answered, "No, she's the saxophone player." Sally may have been the golden child, but the Rides always shared the glow equally. "Absolutely," Bear says, "I never doubted that they loved me as much as Sally."

By all accounts, love infused the Ride household. It just wasn't something anyone talked about. Or had to validate. Sally later described her relationship with Bear this way: "The two of us always got along very well and we enjoyed each other's company, but we were not real close as sisters." Bear says it wasn't a traditional closeness, but that they shared "an intuitive way of being connected. With one word or one look, we'd totally get what the other was thinking." Bear also lays it on the old country.

"Closeness is not a word that is often used to describe relationships in our family," she explains, citing the DNA of her Norwegian forebears. "My maternal grandmother used to call our family 'tight lipped.' Our people were not overly demonstrative nor given to excessive chatter. I come from a long line of intuitive introverts whose conversations were by and large internal." Joyce chalks it up to "generations of distant parents." Her mother and father, Ada and Andy, she tells me, "did nothing but argue, and they never showed any affection to each other or to me, so I was not a terribly affectionate mother." It is a stark confession, a rare moment of self-analysis and as close as I get to a "Rosebud" moment to explain Sally's guarded manner. But Joyce says it evenly, with no apparent regrets, which is how things worked in their family.

None of Sally's friends remembers a lot of kissing and hugging in her house. Or any at all. And no one ever heard anyone say, "I love you." That wasn't the way they communicated. "I taught more by example than by words," Joyce tells me. Bear calls it "wordlessness, a lack of social skills, or something like that. Sally just picked it up, and I did too, to some extent, but I broke out of it. But I always assumed that my parents loved me."

In a culture that took its cues from television, the Rides were neither the warm and fuzzy Nelsons nor the outwardly cozy Andersons, whose Father always knew Best. (Although Sally, as a high school senior, would have a single blind date with actor Jerry Mathers, the star of TV's iconically perfect family in *Leave it to Beaver*. Bear peered out the window when Mathers arrived, announcing, "It's the Beave!") They were, however, good-natured, good-humored and undeniably loving—a "happy house," one regular visitor recalls, where the girls felt cared for and where a solid, middle-class family enjoyed the peace and prosperity of the Eisenhower years.

With yet another difference.

Sally's parents were free-thinking, open-minded, risk-taking individuals who raised their children to be citizens of the world, like the international visitors who often stayed at their house because Dale and Joyce were on a State Department list to host foreigners. An array of guests of various skin colors and ethnicities were also invited to the regular Saturday night parties where Dale would tend the bar and cook the desserts. "Sally grew up assuming that everyone was a potential friend," Joyce says.

Dale, after teaching junior high school social studies and earning his EdD specializing in adult education, became a political science professor at Santa Monica Community College (SMCC). He was gregarious, genial, athletic and a committed Republican. Joyce likes quoting the reporter who described Dale's "pleasantly ruffled face and tousled white hair. He sunburned easily," she says. "Sally worshiped him and channeled his happy outlook, literally following him around everywhere." He was the family extrovert.

Joyce, still succinct and arch at ninety, is both witty and guarded, favoring one-word answers. Sally fully appreciated Joyce's quirky humor (her favorite holiday is Groundhog Day) and absorbed both her unorthodox approach to life and her politics. "I cheerfully went out and canceled Dale's vote every time," boasts Joyce. "I never voted Republican." At UCLA, where she worked in the personnel office after graduating, she refused to sign the 1950 Loyalty Oath, an anti-Communist excess like many sweeping the country during the "Red Scare" tactics of the McCarthy Era (when red was the color of Communism, not Republican states). "I thought it was stupid," she says today. When she left UCLA, she directed her considerable energy towards a variety of volunteer progressive causes, working mostly with women, especially the incarcerated, for the next half century. "Yes," sighs Bear, "I told my own children: Grandma's in prison again! She continues to be my hero."

The family dynamic, says Bear, was simple: "Sally got my dad, I got my mom." Joyce agrees. "Bear always knew where I was coming from and I always knew where she was coming from," she tells me. As for Sally: "We were on a very friendly basis." The casual—or removed—

nature of their relationship is evident in lines from two letters Joyce wrote to her older daughter. 1996: "There must be something new in your mundane life." 1998: "All I really need to know is how's your life, and as usual, I don't know what to ask or where to start . . . I figure you're taking care of the planet. Heavy responsibility."

But for all the lack of intimacy, there was a loving strategy.

"We wanted our daughters to excel, not conform," Joyce told a reporter. "We never patronized them or treated them like they were inferior to us. We never talked baby talk to them. We gave birth to persons, not possessions." She calls it benign neglect. "We just let them develop normally," Dale explained. "We might have encouraged, but mostly we let them explore."

Theirs was an unusually enlightened approach during the *Mad Men* mentality of the 1950s. At a time when girls were supposed to get married, have a family and cook dinner every night in a kitchen with avocado-colored appliances, the Rides raised their daughters without preconceptions or gender constraints. "I guess I was oblivious to the fact that men were in any way superior," explains Joyce drily. "Dale was good about giving a hand up to women on the faculty at SMCC. I just assumed that we were equal, and he failed to disabuse me of the fact."

In 1985, after Sally's two flights, Dale was offended by a print ad for financial aid to the nation's colleges. It showed a picture of a little boy dressed in a spacesuit. "Help him get America's future off the ground," read the headline. Dale fired off a letter to the sponsor, lambasting the "unconscious (I assume) bias we have in education. . . . As a parent of the first US woman astronaut, I know firsthand that girls also aspire to math and science and we should encourage *her* [emphasis added] to 'get America's future off the ground.' "

That is one very hip dad, and the gift of equality from both her parents helped guarantee Sally a boundless future. Born into a world that paid women just over half of what men earned—for the same work—Sally saw her prospects through a positive lens. Or maybe the blinders of the invincible. "There was absolutely no sense—through all the years growing up—that there was any limit to what I could do or what I could pursue," she said.

VAN NUYS

Life was good for the two little girls growing up in their new house on the pie-shaped lot on quiet Gerald Avenue in Van Nuys. Both sets of grandparents lived within babysitting range. Tom and Jennie—Dale's parents—were in Santa Monica, in the stucco house with the Spanish tile roof that Tom had built himself in 1925 with lumber hauled on a donkey cart before Wilshire Boulevard was paved. He grew berries, kept bees and let the girls collect eggs from a coop full of chickens. Andy and Ada lived one community over, in Brentwood, where they played cards with the girls, and became Grap and Gada from their shorthanded names on the scorecard.

At home, Sally mastered the backyard trampoline and was "a terror on a tricycle," according to Bear, rolling through the early years on an array of strollers, wagons, bikes and other modes of travel. "Any way she could get out and about," explains Bear. Sally also swam, fished, skied, skated, kayaked, sledded and rode a pony, dressed in everything from snow pants to frilly dresses and one spiffy red gingham romper suit. One early photo that captures her climbing out of her crib makes you understand the futility of ever trying to fence her in. Or hold her back. As Mighty Mouse, Bear recalls, she would "launch herself from the front seat to the back" of the family Plymouth, Bear recalls, crying, "Here I come to save the day!"

Competition came with the territory. Dale helped football and basketball players transfer from SMCC to UCLA, adding coaches from all the teams to his wide circle of friends and bringing his daughters to practice sessions. He and Joyce were both diehard, miss-no-games UCLA Bruins fans, with season tickets for both the football and the basketball teams, the latter even before John Wooden made them champions. Sally inherited their love of the Bruins and would later cherish a copy of Wooden's famous Pyramid of Success that she bought at auction. After hers became a household name, Wooden, by then a close family friend, absent-mindedly told a sports reporter that he once held little Sally Rand (the popular blonde stripper who both scandalized and enthralled audiences) as a baby—a slip of the tongue he quickly corrected: "No, no, no! . . . I meant to say Sally Ride, you know, the astronaut." The Rand/Ride mixup was so common, Sally early included it in her own joke repertoire.

Sally also revered the Los Angeles Dodgers, those more recent immigrants to California, who became her personal obsession (she had boxes full of baseball cards) and an early thwarted career ambition. Playing shortstop for the Dodgers, Joyce would later say, was the only thing she told Sally that she could not do simply because she was a girl.

At five, Sally raced her father to the newspaper each morning to check the box scores, having learned to read from comic strips. At eight, she commemorated the Dodgers' 3–2 victory over the San Francisco Giants during a tight pennant race ("tighter than a pair of slacks on Aunt Fanny," according to one colorful columnist firmly rooted in the '50s) with a crayon drawing of pitcher Don Drysdale (wearing blue) facing down all the Giants in the field (wearing red). The players, including Willie Mays and Orlando Cepeda, are neatly labeled. Bear is convinced that Sally's habit of analyzing batting averages and pitching statistics, which she memorized, got her hooked on math early.

At Hayvenhurst public school, followed by Gault Street Elementary, science and math came more easily than speaking out. "I was a quiet kid when I was growing up," Sally said in 2006, "and so I didn't really like to be called on in class. I think that my most stressful moments were probably sitting in class, huddled down, hoping that the teacher didn't notice me and call on me. Whether I knew the answer or not, that was irrelevant." She wondered whether she was "an introvert by nature." Her mother says all the females in the family were, and that Sally was definitely "an 'I' [for Introversion] on the Myers-Briggs" psychological scale, the once-standard measure of personality types.

Introverts gather energy by being alone. They recharge their batteries by turning inward and prefer the company of a small group of people. Their opposites are extroverts, who rev up in social situations, thrive in large crowds and tend to be more talkative and excitable. Being an introvert explains much of Sally's behavior as an adult. As a child it certainly didn't affect her academically. She skipped a year in grammar school and supplemented her education with a ravenous appetite for reading. Among the favorites: the *Nancy Drew* series (solving just about anything), *Danny Dunn and the Anti-Gravity Paint* (among others) and bedtime tales of Damon Runyon, because the vivid characters "kind of tickled" Joyce.

The Rides valued education highly but not conventionally. "[T]hey made sure," Sally said later in an interview, "that I spent plenty of time studying, but also trying to make it fun and trying to make it entertaining and trying to make me appreciate that it was a good way to get ahead in the world."

EUROPE

In 1960, when Sally was nine and Bear seven, Dale and Joyce turned his sabbatical into a yearlong tour of Europe, global education on a grand scale. They pulled the girls out of school (with permission from the principal), sold the house on Gerald Avenue along with most of the furniture, then flew to New York and sailed to Holland on the S.S. *Rotterdam*. In Bremen, Dale bought a white Borgward Combi station wagon to explore the land of their forebears and the cities he had help liberate in the war. Along with the authorized schoolroom lessons that Joyce brought along, the girls were assigned hobbies and tasks to keep them focused. Both started stamp collections—animals for Bear; sports and Olympics for Sally, whose four albums would one day contain five hundred stamps and hold her attention long into adulthood. The girls were also directed to keep diaries of the trip. Sally's, in red leatherette, is a charming (if succinct) exercise by an astute (and often funny) young observer that begins the day they arrived:

Sept. 17 1960. Rotterdam (rain).

It could be an entry in the notebook of the grown-up Sally more than two decades later, a preview of her shorthand style, complete with her lifelong allergy to proper spelling. She writes of visiting the Hage, and the Hauge, never quite getting it right. And she records her first ferryboat ride in Denmark, her first snowfall (and snowman) in Austria, her first ski lesson in the Alps, where they spent Christmas. That's also where she taught Bear the truth about Santa Claus. "She dared me to stay awake to watch, and I did," Bear recalls, still amused. Sally also revealed the identity of the Tooth Fairy by telling Bear to look at the handwriting on the note and compare it to their father's.

In Germany, Sally wrote, "I met Wienersnitzel." No clarification, no adjectives. She meant dinner, not a person, because her first encounter with a breaded veal cutlet was ambrosia to her little palate, setting off years of seeking out German restaurants back home to repeat the thrill.

She also acted like a proper tourist.

Oct. 2. Oslo. Looked around.

Really, how much more do you need? Oslo was the gateway to Lom, where Sally met her Norwegian relatives for the first time. The next day, in Copenhagen, her parents picked out the elegant Danish modern furniture for their new California home.

It was, by all accounts, an outstanding trip to worlds present and past. In England, Sally and Bear obediently donned their itchy wool Norwegian outfits and posed for a photo in front of the Russell and Ride Memorial Chapel, dedicated to the memory of great-great-great-great Uncle John Ride. They kept the home fires burning, too. Sally regularly tuned in the Dodgers games on Armed Forces Radio (or Yankees, if that was the only alternative) and tore open Grap's letters with newspaper clippings from the sports pages. She also managed to find a bat and ball at the home of family friends in Paris.

In Spain that spring, Joyce Ride made a connection with life-changing consequences. She put her nine-year-old daughter on a clay court and taught her how to play tennis. Sally liked it immediately—better than the two weeks of piano lessons she'd had in Vienna. For the rest of the trip, "I had her squeezing tennis balls and exercising her right wrist to make it strong," Joyce recalls, rotating her hand to demonstrate. It was not the only harbinger of her future.

During the long road trips, Sally occupied the front seat of the Borgward with a map, the family's official navigator. Bear and Joyce sat in back and sang, filling the car with lyrics of the catchy, child-friendly tune that Bing Crosby had made famous: "Would you like to swing on a star?"

Dale and I raised Sally with a lot of help from our collie, Tsigane. The kids were her sheep, and nobody had better raise a hand to them. I tried once, when I was really angry. Tsigane gently took my wrist and said, "We don't do that."

—Joyce Ride

ENCINO

Back home in California, the Rides moved into a three-bedroom, two-bathroom ranch house on a quiet cul-de-sac in Encino, in the San Fernando Valley, the one that gave Valley Girls their name. For $35,500 they were now authentic, middle-class suburbanites, and they had the barbecue, the hammock and the Rambler to prove it. Sally's bedroom at 4926 Texhoma overlooked a backyard fragrant with a rose garden, a vegetable patch and a small grove of orange and lemon trees. Movie legend John Wayne lived a few streets over; TV star Dick Van Dyke lived around the corner. It may have been a development, but it was, after all, California.

It was September 1961, and while an ocean had separated them from some major US developments during their European sojourn—the election of President Kennedy, the launch of America's first astronaut, the disastrous Bay of Pigs invasion of Cuba—they plunged right back into the Left Coast's embrace of civil rights and the counterculture. Joyce taught her Sunday school class to sing "We Shall Overcome," and "was hauled before the church session to explain herself," Bear says proudly. She later taught English as a second language to immigrants and got her class of Japanese students to sing "Red River Valley."

Joyce also acquired the family collie, inspired by a dog they'd seen catching snowballs in the former Yugoslavia. The girls were so besotted, they adopted the dog's name, Tsigane, which means "gypsy." (With no idea that it was also the name of a dog launched, and recovered, on a Soviet rocket in 1951, the year Sally was born.) Sally and Bear were devoted to Tsigane, playing, wrestling and sleeping with her; as an adult, Sally would use "Tsigane" as her email address and password—usually dropping the "e," a misspelling that I have corrected for consistency. With the dog in residence, Joyce ordered a collie-colored carpet to reduce her vacuuming time. And she was only kidding about sharing the discipline with Tsigane. "The girls behaved," she tells me.

Sally and Bear were not raised to deal with conflict and never learned the consequences of fighting, Bear says, because their parents (unlike Joyce's own) didn't argue. As with most households of the early 1960s, their own little Camelot revolved around the mammoth hi-fi cabinet in the living room, where, starting at five each evening, Dale and Joyce would listen to Dixieland jazz during martini hour while nibbling on nuts or Triscuits. As Daddy graded blue books, Sally and Bear would spread out on the floor to do their homework, one hand on Tsigane's rump. Dinner was some iteration of "Mom's special tuna glop" or Swanson's chicken pot pies. Or whatever anyone wanted, usually consumed in the living room. They rarely gathered around the dining room table, but when they did, grace was said. Then they'd reconvene in the living room to watch Walter Cronkite or Huntley and Brinkley deliver the news at seven. The girls had their own appointment shows: reruns of

Groucho Marx's *You Bet Your Life*, *I Love Lucy*, *Get Smart*. Over and over again. TV was important. As an adult, Sally's ringtone for Tam on her iPhone would be the sexy music from *Perry Mason*.

Weekends meant UCLA home basketball games, or Bruins football. Or occasional trips to Disneyland, where Sally appropriated most of the E tickets in the packet—the hottest rides on the fastest machines. She was one of the kids tucked into the toboggan at Tomorrowland when the Matterhorn roller coaster was new.

On Sundays, the Rides headed across the commercial corridor of Ventura Boulevard to the First Presbyterian Church of Encino, where Dale and Joyce both taught and served as elders. That's when Bear embraced the church and decided to make it her life's work.

Sally, on the other hand, announced in junior high school that she was done with church. Weekend junior tennis tournaments were a handy excuse, and no one objected. "Church is no good if you have to force someone to go," Joyce explains. She'd so disliked Saturday morning Lutheran church school during her Minnesota childhood, she once found a "Quarantine: Measles" sign and hung it on the church door. There was no class that morning.

As a nine-year-old, Sally had visited a German Sunday school and pronounced it "just a place to keep kids!" As an astronaut, she deflected every effort by reporters to turn her into an evangelist from orbit. Here's Tom Brokaw coming up against the indomitable Ride sisters before Sally flew:

> Brokaw: Are you particularly religious?
> Sally: My sister got most of the religion in the family.
> Bear: She's her own person and she certainly has her own belief system
>   and it doesn't have to fit into mine.
> Brokaw: Will you see this flight in any spiritual way?
> Bear: No [Laughter].
> Brokaw: A triumph of man and technology?
> Bear: Of woman and technology.

After Sally's flight, it got worse.

"There are a lot of people who have asked me since I've come back whether I found religion in space," Sally told Gloria Steinem in a TV interview, "or whether I had any mystical experiences up there. And no!"

She attended Encino Elementary, then Gaspar De Portola Junior High, where she barely stomached seventh-grade home ec classes ("Can you imagine cooking and eating tuna casserole at eight a.m.?") but gulped down more math and science. "People who like math like knowing that equations are going to balance. That something equals something," explains one of Sally's later physics colleagues. "It's an interesting kind of truth." Thanks to some gifted teachers, she also learned about her aptitude for long math equations, for the elements of physics, for the brain teasers in *Scientific American* magazine. Sally soon had her own subscription to *Scientific American.*

And a new favorite hero: James Bond, the dashing spy created by Ian Fleming during the Cold War with the Soviet Union. Fear of atomic bombs led to a rash of backyard fallout shelters, where families thought they'd be safe. At school, Sally hid beneath her desk during duck-and-cover drills, and built a model of an atom out of wire and Styrofoam balls. Like every other kid in 1960s America, when the teacher wheeled a black-and-white TV into the classroom and adjusted the rabbit-ear antennae, she watched the snowy screen with fascination as the early astronauts launched us into the space age.

Her parents bought her a telescope—a 16-inch-long Bushnell Sky Rover as powerful as the one Galileo used to discover the moons of Jupiter three centuries earlier. As a young teen, Sally would carry the black and silver instrument out to the front lawn at night and focus in on Orion, her favorite constellation (because "I can find it so easily! It's prominent in the sky," she'd later explain). Or she'd locate Saturn and point out the rings to Bear. The telescope was a more successful present than the microscope, which went largely unused. The chemistry set, however, produced, as Bear recalls, "something stinky. We would have fun dramatically setting up chemistry experiments, and we'd call ourselves 'mad scientists.' Apparently we didn't blow anything up."

Sally spent most of her time on the ball field—any ball, any field. The house on Texhoma dead-ended into a perfect spot for football and baseball, where Sally headed every day after school to play with neighborhood boys. She tossed a pigskin better than most of them. And when the kid next door tried to steal second while she was pitching, she threw the ball so hard to get him out, it broke his nose.

She was a gifted, graceful athlete who ran on her toes and always pushed harder. But do not make the mistake of calling her a tomboy. "I really don't like that term," Sally told a reporter many years later. "Tomboy, when applied to a girl, means a girl acting like a boy. As opposed to a girl acting like a girl." And the only problem with being a girl, she would say, was that girls' basketball was a half-court game with only three dribbles.

The sport that most engaged her was the one she'd learned in Europe. Joyce hired Alice Marble, the power-hitting Wimbledon and US Open tennis champion, to give Sally a few lessons at the Deauville Country Club in nearby Tarzana. It was not a match based on love. "Alice Marble found it hard to control Sally," according to Dale. "Sally's not controllable." Adds Joyce: "I remember Alice Marble saying, 'I'm fifty years old!' Because Sally was hitting the ball too hard." Marble's penchant for hyperbole—or her frustration with the independent-minded preteen whose athleticism she admired—seemed to grow in retrospect. From her retirement home in Palm Desert many years later, she claimed that Sally had tried to bat her in the head with the ball. "I had to duck like crazy. It wasn't that she mis-hit the ball. She had perfect aim. I was terribly amused she was chosen to be an astronaut," Marble said. "I think she probably had these aggressive feelings all her life." No one who really knew Sally saw her aggression as anything but spirited concentration on the athletic field. But a number of adults had the same reaction. Joyce, who usually beat Dale, stopped playing with her daughter when she realized, "I wasn't seeing the ball go by." The headmaster at

Sally's high school would recount the first—and last—mistake he made by showing off with her. "She looked at me, smiled rather malevolently and then fired . . . three successive drives aimed right between the eyes."

Sally was soon playing in tournaments, in the pre-commercial world when racquets were wood and the balls white, the same color as their outfits. Girls' junior tennis was both competitive and fun, a way of life that would produce Sally's closest pals, her deepest love, her eternal support group. Some of us were lucky enough to go to summer camp, where we forged our best friendships and enjoyed our earliest athletic victories; some found adolescent outlets at the beach or in the mountains or maybe just the local YMCA. The girls on the tennis circuit learned about life while traveling the United States on muscles and speed. Every weekend during the school year, then all summer long, they played at public parks and tony clubs—in Los Angeles or around the country—stayed in affluent homes and sometimes fancy mansions made available by wealthy CEOs and governors and other supporters, and swung their racquets to advance to the next rung and take home yet another silver tray or trophy or double-handled cup. They spent day after day in each other's company, practicing and playing and sharing victories and losses, whiling away the downtime over gin rummy. Off the court, Sally often landed at the home of Ann Lebedeff in San Marcos, where she and the other fourteen- and fifteen-year-olds would put on the record player and merrily dance to Russian folksongs or the Beatles. "Sally was a bit shy, so one of us would grab her hand and make her dance with us," Tam recalls. "But once she got started Sally got into it and had fun, too."

In an era long before Title IX would level the playing fields and open up opportunity, scholarships and purse money for female athletes, tennis was Sally's entrée to the world beyond the San Fernando Valley. Her partners and opponents were the stars of Southern California girls' and women's tennis. They rubbed shoulders with tennis royalty: Pancho Gonzalez, Maria Bueno, Rod Laver, Billie Jean King. "Tennis," says Tam, who was a top-ranked teen, "made us immune to celebrity."

Sally learned well, a serve-and-volley player with a wicked backhand, a sneaky drop shot, and a forehand that always needed work. "Start low, racket shaft parallel to ground, butt of racket (as in 'M' or 'W') pointing toward oncoming ball," Sally wrote in a ringed green notebook, using the shorthand of those playing with Wilson racquets. But the lessons only went so far. Sally bluntly said her forehand stunk, which may be more a comment on her own standards than on her ability. Whitney Grant, her first doubles partner and close friend, says she and Sally devised a unique system of hand signals. The net player would "alert the server of her intent to poach, to fake a move, or stay still," whatever. They wrote up their rules in a limited edition of two reference manuals, bound in pink ribbon. "The final statement of the booklet said that we were sworn to keep our signals secret, and if either of us broke that promise we would be required to eat the book!" Whitney can't find hers, and Sally's has disappeared, but it is the sort of collaboration that Sally would enjoy forever, on and off the court. She always had a best friend, and she always preferred playing team sports like doubles to singles.

In 1963, when she was starting eighth grade, Sally was ranked number 20 in Southern California Tennis for Girls 12 and under. A year later, Whitney's father, who informally coached Sally, suggested that she join his daughter at the private and prestigious Westlake School for Girls in Holmby Hills, where she could play serious tennis, get an excellent education and a major start on whatever future she chose. Mr. Grant helped arrange a partial tennis scholarship when Sally entered as a sophomore in 1965, to be supplemented by a class taught by Dale. It is hard to overstate the door this opened to Sally. In a trait that would carry her throughout life, she was ready and willing to sail through.

Tennis Team Captain . . . sixteen and single . . . She thinks; there-
fore she is, or is she? . . . takes everything with a grain of salt . . . gross
underachiever . . .

—Sally Kristen Ride, from her senior year
self-portrait in the Westlake yearbook, 1968

WESTLAKE

"I used to think that Westlake was going to last forever," confessed her
best friend, Sue Okie, in the handwritten, two-page, yearbook farewell
like those teenage girls have been inscribing to their closest pals forever.
"I have never felt so . . . at home . . . [as I do] with you." Sally's inscription in Okie's yearbook was considerably less impassioned. "I won't be
sentimental because it's not in my character," she began unnecessarily,
sliding into her usual set of verbal winks and quips.

Sally and Okie joined forces the day they met. "She had a blinding
smile, glinty blue eyes and gorgeous white teeth," Okie tells me. "I found
her really open and . . . no, not open. Sally could never be described as
an open person. But she was very friendly and engaging, a no-nonsense
person." They were a Mutt and Jeff pairing (Sue was 6-feet tall) of super
smart girls who each found comfort in another outsider among their
privileged classmates.

The Westlake School for Girls, then an exclusive single-sex institution (and now the coed Harvard-Westlake), was an academically elite
prep with a roster of famous alums, including Candice Bergen and
Shirley Temple. The Spanish-style mansion with a great hall, elegant
stairways and rich lawns, contained fewer than a dozen girls in a classroom; Sally's graduating class numbered only fifty. Sally and Okie car-
pooled daily from the un-chic Valley, gossiping and giggling up and over
Mulholland Drive and down the winding roads into lush Holmby Hills
as somebody's parent drove. A year later, when a third Valley classmate
was old enough to drive her own car, they cranked up the radio with
the Supremes or Jefferson Airplane (the scene she would describe to

the NASA board) and purposely took detours to get lost in the winding roads or to visit the swans at the Hotel Bel-Air. Anything to be late
to assembly. They were California cool—nonchalant, irreverent, carefully cultivating a sense of irony. When Sally and her lab partner had
to dissect a fetal pig, they named the cadaver Sir Francis Bacon. Sally's
yearbook photograph—posed like Rodin's *The Thinker*—was accompanied by Jean-Paul Sartre's absurdist riff on Descartes: "I do not think;
therefore I am a moustache."

Determinedly blasé, Sally sometimes put off studying until the car
ride to school. "She could have gotten A's in every subject," Okie recalls,
"but she didn't work to get A's in every subject. If she liked a teacher,
she would work. But she could look really snide and roll her eyes, and
the teachers could tell that she was kind of making fun of them. I mean,
she could be obnoxious. She wouldn't come out and challenge them so
much but she would, you know, just give this look." Bear calls it the Ride
Glower.

Nearly a decade later, in college, one of her professors would give
Sally an A on a paper with the added note, "your class participation was
not sufficient to warrant more than a B."

Most of Sally's classmates recall her as an energetic, buoyant teen
with total devotion to the school. As seniors, in their white blouses and
navy suits, saddle shoes tied neatly, Sue and Sally were among a small
group of students handpicked to take early-morning classes at UCLA
to stretch their minds. As juniors, they reveled in Dr. Elizabeth Mommaerts's Human Physiology class, an unusually advanced course taught
by a luminous scientist.

Mommaerts, born and educated in Hungary, was one of the few
female PhDs in science, and brought her outrage over the unequal
opportunities for women to her job at Westlake. She also brought
a college-level examination of the human body—as a set of systems
wondrously intertwined. When she taught the eye, she explained the
chemical and neurological processes behind it. When she taught the
endocrine system, she told the girls to imagine they were on a date,

sweating nervously. "What are the physical reactions?" "Are you getting colder?" "How did that happen?" The lesson on human reproduction meant lectures on love and emotional satisfaction. "She was just starry-eyed about the process of discovery," Susan Okie tells me. "She'd talk about the kidney, and osmosis and how salts go through membranes and how the kidney works and what a miracle it is. And it wasn't just, 'Memorize the parts of a kidney.' It was, 'You have to understand what's going on here and you have to be able to explain it.' She was demanding."

Mommaerts was especially fond of Sally and Sue, who, she said, had "glowing potential." "My mother had a great admiration for people with a very clear-thinking brain," says Edina Weinstein, Mommaerts's daughter, "which in her mind was a very scientific brain. Sally and Sue were students who she thought were not only bright, but had the kind of brain that meant they could do something about scientific thinking. She wanted to impart a sense of appreciation for their potential and talent."

Still, Mommaerts needled Sally, Okie recalls, because of Sally's casual approach to exams. One test required students to draw a nephron—the functional unit of a kidney—and describe how it works. "And Sally could not remember what a nephron looked like. But she drew a circle and then another circle and then a bunch of little polka dots in the middle, and labeled it Nephron." Okie, laughing at her bravura, recalls that Mommaerts never let Sally hear the end of it, saying, "Sally, that's ridiculous, how could you forget what a nephron is?!"

Later, as a college freshman, Sally made sure Mommaerts knew about a dinner where "I was the only one at a table of seven Swarthmore students who was able to explain the structure and function of (would you believe) a nephron—I may not remember anything else from physiology, but I'll never forget nephrons."

Sally brought Mommaerts little intellectual puzzles that her teacher polished off instantly. "She could solve anything," Okie says. "On the morning of the final exam we brought her the toughest puzzle that we could come up with"—a kind of Rubik's Cube—"and she had it all done before we were halfway through the test." Mommaerts also hosted a series of Saturday night dinners for favorite students, introducing them to soufflés and ratatouille and other sophisticated food. "We were all just totally gaga over her," says Okie. Sally called her "my ideal." She was, Sally said, "the kind of person that I wanted to pattern my life after. She was very logical, seemed to be in control of her life and of her emotions and was just a brilliant person."

Decades later, Sally would write an article that began, "Thank you, Dr. Mommaerts . . . If you hadn't taken a personal interest in me in high school, who knows what career path I might have followed. . . . She challenged me to be curious, ask questions, and think for myself."

One other teacher captured Sally's attention: Janet Mennie, a newly minted Mount Holyoke graduate who taught Westlake's first physics and calculus classes and would remain a close friend. She and Mommaerts "*were* the science department," Sally later pointed out, having excelled with both. "Sally's genius," Mennie (now Janet Schroeder) tells me, "was in writing exactly one sentence for a chemistry essay."

Sally attributed much of her ability as an excellent student to being at a single-sex school. "A lot of the things that can kind of come into play when you're a fifteen-, sixteen-year-old girl with boys in the school and boys in the classroom just didn't happen at Westlake," she said. "It was easier to focus on academics." Thanks to her teachers there, and a few others from her coed public junior high school, Sally would also say, "I didn't succumb to the stereotype that science wasn't for girls. I got encouragement from my parents. I never ran into a teacher or a counselor who told me that science was for boys."

There was one, however, who said it wasn't for her. According to several of her classmates, a certain senior-year English teacher, not one of the girls' favorites, would occasionally go around the room telling students what was wrong with them. When she landed on Sally, she decreed, "far too science-oriented. No creativity." For a teenager who was prepared to devote her life to physics, it must have been very painful. Sally started to cry. So did many in the class when the teacher singled them out. Some months later, the teacher went at it again, this time telling Sally that she had a "first-rate mind, wasted in science." The tears coursed down Sally's face. Whatever sensitive nerve that touched, whatever vulnerability the teacher triggered, it is the only time any of her high school friends remembers seeing her cry. Few would ever see her do so again.

Sally had already decided she would major in physics—specifically, astrophysics, which made least one friend's mother wrinkle her nose ("Astrophysics?! What are you ever going to do with that?") and baffled her pals. Sally was undeterred. When a friend asked what it meant, Sally said simply, "It's about space." Which was not where she wanted to travel, not then. It was more about the big picture, says Okie, who shared her bff's science passion and never questioned her choice. She and Sally used to have long discussions about "what's out there" after sleepover dates watching *The Twilight Zone* and *Star Trek*. "What do you think happened at the beginning of the universe? How far is far?" they asked each other. " 'What does it mean that you go back in time when you are looking at the stars?' She liked the abstract concepts."

As captain of the Westlake tennis team, Sally also continued her education on the court. "Tennis taught me a lot about self-control," she often said. "Self-discipline. How to maintain a kind of relatively cool demeanor even when you're winning or losing by a lot—to be able to control my emotions and to kind of keep a cool head." Bear remembers their father yelling "Don't choke!" at the matches. Dale was the parent who took her to the tournaments, driving her around California and putting her on the planes that deposited her at the next court. He also dropped coins in a big jar at home to save up for her entry fees and plane fares. Several friends think Dale's enthusiasm for Sally's ascent up the tennis ladder pushed her harder than she liked. "I think there were always more rungs that he wanted her to climb," Ann Lebedeff tells me. Another recalls Sally's story about the day she and a girlfriend went surfing. "Her father said that she should have been playing tennis instead."

Susan Okie witnessed the dynamic. "You'd go over to the house and Sally would be sprawled on the living room carpet with Tsigane, watching TV, and her father would say, 'Why don't you go run around the block?'" Okie pauses to chuckle. "Sometimes she would, but she kind of actively resisted working quite as hard as her father wanted her to. It was part of their relationship. She'd never talk about it, and you could tell she loved her father but there was a sort of a rebellious streak about how hard he was pushing her, and she didn't want to completely knuckle under him, to do everything he'd say to the nth degree."

Dale was also responsible for piling Sally's tennis trophies onto the living room hi-fi set, an act of paternal pride that led to a typically eccentric *pas de deux* between him and Joyce. The cups and bowls and statuettes mounted up, cramming the furniture and leading Joyce, unimpressed with the second- and third-place knickknacks, to start removing the offending objects. Gradually, Sally said, "I started noticing trophies turning up as soap dishes, candy trays, flower vases, book ends and paperweights." Sally, amused, would move them back; Joyce, unannounced, would relocate them to the bathroom or kitchen. The game went on. At one point Sally went east on the Junior Tennis Circuit. When she returned to California, all seventy-four trophies had been shunted away to the garage. Sally wrote to a friend that she found it very funny. When I ask Joyce the point of her clean-up exercise she says simply, "Ostentation."

COLLEGE BOUND

In June 1968, as the world mourned the murder of Robert F. Kennedy, following the April assassination of Martin Luther King Jr., Sally was graduated from Westlake with honors in science. Because Sue had gotten interested in Swarthmore College, a top-ranked, small, coed Quaker institution outside of Philadelphia, Sally had applied, too. She interviewed with Fred Hargadon, the dean of admissions, who was visiting the West Coast. As they sat in her yard in the California twilight, Sally pointed out the stars that she'd observed through her telescope. "It didn't give me any sense at the time about Sally's future," Hargadon says now. He was, however, impressed with her mind, as well as her performance on the tennis court. She was accepted to Swarthmore with a full financial scholarship. Dean Hargadon followed up with a letter to Dale: "Sally might also be interested in knowing that an alumnus has just agreed to foot the bill for resurfacing our entire field house. This will give us four indoor tennis courts."

And one fine tennis player. The California girl was headed east.

2

40–LOVE, SALLY

SUMMER 1968–JANUARY 1977

Sally Ride, an 18-year-old sophomore at Swarthmore College, may one day be the first woman astronaut but for the moment she is the number one woman college tennis player in the East. She acquired this status by winning the recent Eastern Women's Intercollegiate Tennis Championships ... About the astronaut business: Sally is a physics stu-

dent who plans to specialize in astrophysics and would like to work some-
day for NASA. She hopes she has what it takes to make a space team.

—Delaware County (PA) *Daily Times*, November 1969

SWARTHMORE

The prophetic article, nearly fourteen years before the fact, always bemused Sally. While she basked in the attention—and proudly sent the
newspaper clipping home—she had no recollection of mentioning any
NASA goals to the reporter. Certainly the science part was true; also the
tennis trophy. But Sally's ambitions in that last unliberated decade were
grand in a more down-to-Earth way.

"Sally wanted to be famous," recalls Susan Okie. "She said she
wanted to be famous. But she wanted to win the Nobel Prize." And that
was just for starters. "I suggest you keep this letter," she wrote playfully
to her former chemistry teacher, Janet Mennie Schroeder, "as it may
become a collectors' item and worth millions of dollars when I become
famous (as an astrophysicist-tennis player)."

She was on track to achieve both.

After graduation from Westlake in June 1968, she and Sue took an
advanced math class at Santa Monica Community College, where Sally
used a computer for the first time and learned to design simple programs using punched cards, at least one of which worked. In July she
joined her family on a car trip to Colorado and Minnesota to visit relatives, stopping off for a tennis tournament in South Dakota and flying
east for the USLTA Junior Invitational in Philadelphia. "I hate grass," she
reported after losing (on a grass court) in the third round to the number 7 girl in the nation. "I should have won."

Grass of another variety was absorbing much of the rest of the country during that turbulent summer of 1968. In Chicago, Vice President
Hubert Humphrey was nominated for president by a Democrat party
torn by riots over the Vietnam War. Hippies and yippies took to the

streets, and marijuana moved from the fringes of the urban ghetto to college campuses. Richard Nixon was the Republican standard-bearer and would easily be elected to the White House. The culture wars had begun, but Sally had other things on her mind.

On September 18, 1968, she began her freshman year at Swarthmore College and took a few uncharacteristic moments to smell the roses.

"I love the school so far," she wrote Janet a few weeks later, in one of the many handwritten, chatty missives to family and close friends that would detail the next few years of her life. "The campus is beautiful . . . Being from Los Angeles, I'm not used to all these trees. I've been doing most of my studying (if you can call it that) under a huge oak, flanked by 2 rare Japanese cherry trees . . . Most campuses have dandelions, Swarthmore has lilacs and other strange purple things sprouting up between the semi-cobblestone paths."

Her botanical observations were matched by her sketches of Swarthmore's lively, coed social scene, an exotic revelation to the graduate of an all-girls' prep school.

> I think there is an all-campus undercover plot to devise so many interesting and diverse activities, that the freshmen won't have time to study, and will flunk out, making the lunch lines much shorter. Last week there were 2 fraternity desserts; 1 mixer; a production of The Knack (excellent) by a campus group; 2 movies; parts 1 and 2 of Flash Gordon; a folk singing session around a bonfire; a refugee professor from Charles U. in Prague speaking on the Czech liberalization drive (also excellent); dessert at the home of a faculty member (a math teacher who was the spitting image of ensign Parker on "McHale's Navy"); a square dance; and, of course, the student center.

The letters are impressionistic, skating over the surface rather than digging into the soul. But for someone who kept so much of her private life private, they are both revealing and entertaining. Sally was bursting with the exuberance of a maturing young adult, eager to discover the rest of the world and starting to find herself, although self-examination was not an obvious priority. Mostly her correspondence sparkles with trenchant asides, carefully composed commentary on everything and everyone she encountered. One professor struck her as "a nervous, hyperthyroid hummingbird"; one beau, "a good ping-pong player—i.e., I don't have to throw points to lose (usually)." She was equally sardonic about herself, but usually framed the story so she came out ahead. When she tried out for Swarthmore's field hockey team—a game she had neither played nor watched—she wrote that she "confidently strode onto the field without ever having seen a hockey stick (paddle? Racket? Mallet? Club?), and knowing none of the rules. If you can imagine an eskimo or African native one day deciding he'd like to learn how to play baseball, and going to try out for the Dodgers without ever having seen a bat, you've got the general picture of me the first day. I've since improved to the point where I might start varsity, but it requires at least three 1½ hr sessions per week, not including games. It's ruining my golf swing." Notice the offhand shrug—the hockey team she's trying out for pales in comparison to her golf. But oh yes, she "might" make varsity. Of course she did, or it's unlikely she would have mentioned it in the first place.

Things usually turned out well in Sally's world. Perhaps it came from her parents, who told her she could do or be anything. Or perhaps it was a defensive maneuver, to abolish anything that didn't satisfy the rosy glow of her usual self-confidence. Either way, it would become her trademark. As an adult, the only tennis photograph she put on the shelf was of a match she won. In these letters home, she generally came out ahead.

She also sprinkled in references to Darwin, Hobbes and her beloved Shakespeare. And she could turn herself into the Seinfeld of letter writers, scribbling page after page that said absolutely nothing, in the wisecracking mode of the moment: "I've never hit a good volley in my life—no, wait—I remember now—in 1965 at Ojai—I hit a forward volley in the court. My father fainted." Or a rare burst of politics: "And remember . . . as we anti-war canvassers are told . . . 'Show me Lenin's grave, and I'll show you a Communist plot.' "

Sally wrote on anything she could find—school stationery, sheets of onionskin paper, letterheads she'd stockpiled from the nation's fanciest tennis clubs, even an exam blue book liberated from the classroom. Her indifference towards the paper was echoed by the breezy image she affected: *I'm cool, I'm unmoved by all this, don't sweat the small stuff.* It was reinforced by the speed writer's favorite traffic sign: the dash. Even there Sally flaunted the rules. "The dash is the lazy man's punctuation mark," she often wrote, quoting the unpopular Westlake English teacher. Then she'd insert a dash. Halfway through her sophomore year at Swarthmore she streamlined her handwriting, turning the childlike cursive into a simpler, bolder statement, with an almost-printed initial "S" and "R" for her signature. "I'm sure this has incredible Freudian overtones," she announced to her family, "which I'd rather not know about." She also adopted a sign-off that merged her preferred score on the tennis court with at least the illusion of emotion: "40–love, Sally."

The collie got her own greeting. "Woof to Tsigane," she'd add in the postscript.

But as much as she avoided introspection, the "gross underachiever" of her high school yearbook couldn't always hide her passion, especially for the classes that fired her brain and fed her immense curiosity. As a freshman she got into the honors sections of both chemistry and calculus, and proudly reported that she'd aced an exam in the former. Although she declared her major in physics early in her first semester, one class was tougher than she expected, and she confessed to some serious doubts about making it, about being "petrified" during an exam. But the "period of black depression" vanished and she regained her confidence. "I really *love* physics," she wrote to Gada and Grap about a later course. "We had our first lab last week, and it lasted for 6 hours. We were studying collisions, and got to use a strobe light and a really cool World War II press camara [sic]—which we learned to use and develop film for." Another course in mechanics and wave motion clinched it. "It's a really good feeling, because we're doing things I've never had before," she wrote Janet Mennie Schroeder, "using methods in math I never knew existed, and although I really have to study, I can understand what's going on (you may never again hear me admit that I study occasionally)." She did repeat it, to her sister, in a rundown of her courses: "The only one I have to work at is physics, but I really have to work at that."

Sally's sudden candor spilled over to her non-science studies. In African American history and political science, she wrote, "I've said more in 2 classes here than I did in English all last year." She also tossed a lighthearted dig at her father, the political science professor: "I calculated that I spent about 25–30 hours (no, not consecutively) studying for Political Science, as opposed to about 1½ hours for Chemistry. I think that shows something about where my natural ability, or lack of same, lies; it also says something about the failure of some hereditary process somewhere—I seem to have inherited Daddy's inability to spell, and nothing else."

Not quite true. She was now totally in sync with Dale's drive for her tennis game, barely masking her ambition with this only slightly sarcastic tour of the facilities at Swarthmore: "a magnificent library (complete with thick red carpeting and chandeliers), a dining hall, which strangely resembles a ski lodge, a modern health center, and last but certainly not least—4 indoor tennis courts: the ultimate in luxury; the final goal of any college." Just as Fred Hargadon had promised. She stopped by his office one day to see if he wanted to hit some balls, and the speedy little freshman wiped the unsuspecting dean of admissions off the court— even after slowing down her game. "From that point," confessed the latest adult victim, "I decided just to watch Sally play."

In her first year of competition for Swarthmore, she won all six varsity matches and took the Eastern Intercollegiate Women's Singles Championship for the first time. With her long, straight hair tied into bunches, and her toned legs whipping by, she was unbeatable. "I couldn't figure out what she was doing there," recalls one upperclassman who was awed by her grace on the court as he walked to the dining hall each day. "She was way too good for the school." Fitting her matches into East Coast weather patterns took some juggling, but Sally maintained a tough schedule off-campus, in tournaments from Santa Monica to Philadelphia. "I've been playing a lot and I'm playing really well," she wrote home, also reporting that she'd ordered an aluminum racquet (one of the earliest) and was practicing several hours a day. She told one reporter why tennis so engaged her inquisitive mind: "Because it takes a lot more thinking than any other sport. You can have all the strokes, stamina and speed, but still you must always out-think your opponent to win."

In May 1969, she retained her Eastern Intercollegiate championship with a 6–1, 6–1 victory, dominating her opponent, according to *The New York Times*, "with deep, forceful hitting." That July, she found herself yawning through a big match in Wilmington, Delaware, the morning after the Moon landing she'd watched avidly on television. Sally didn't get very far in the tennis that day, and the men of Apollo 11 didn't spark any astronaut goals of her own. "I just assumed there would never be a place for women," she later said. "When I saw them on TV they all seemed to be Navy or Air Force test pilots. I suppose I just took it for granted that it was pretty much a closed club."

She did purchase three posters of lunar photographs for the "astronomy corner" in her dorm room that fall, four flights up in Parrish Hall, which also housed Swarthmore's administrative and admissions office. "It was a cheerful room," recalls her sophomore roommate, Sherri Davis, with twin beds separated by bookcases for privacy (an upperclass improvement over the bunk beds of her freshman year) and covered, in enduring student style, with Indian print spreads. Thanks to a cash infusion from Gada and Grap, they also had an armchair beneath the Moonscapes. The day they moved in that September of 1969, Sally and Sherri opened the window, blasted their new Blood, Sweat and Tears album on the hi-fi, and sat on the wide sill shouting greetings to friends as they drifted back to campus across the lawn. Later that semester, the large central room often served as the gathering place for folk-singing and late-night conversations. Simon and Garfunkel and the Beatles were the ones that made Sally's heart sing.

She added badminton (that's "badmitton" in the Sally spelling book) to her athletic repertoire, along with ice skating. When a snowstorm brought the entire California contingent outdoors, she sledded down the hill on a cafeteria tray. Her family sent UCLA football clippings and *Peanuts* cartoon strips in the mail, and she had her subscriptions to *MAD* magazine and *Scientific American* transferred to the campus post office box. A string of boyfriends with no identifying last names turned her head. There was Chuck, about whom the only thing known is that she traveled to New Haven and Washington, DC with him; Jed, the football punter, with whom she watched a horror film on Hallowe'en and then sang pumpkin carols; Bill, who introduced her to wine and cheese that she actually liked; Gary, a 6'11" sports editor. She supplemented her allowance by working in the admissions office and the library ($1.40 an hour), giving tours, and finally grading physics papers ($1.75 an hour).

Sally had not participated in the social protests that rocked the Swarthmore campus her freshman year. But she joined several busloads of Swarthmoreans to travel to Washington, DC, for the November 15, 1969, Moratorium to End the War in Vietnam, a gathering of some half a million demonstrators at the Washington Monument, across from the White House. Sally flashed the peace sign, tried unsuccessfully to buy an "effete snob against the war" button (co-opting the words of Vice President Spiro Agnew), and listened to speeches by George McGovern and Coretta Scott King, music from Richie Havens and Peter, Paul and Mary. Then she joined half a million demonstrators swaying to the beat as Pete Seeger led them singing "Give Peace a Chance." The moratorium was a moment of truth for many young Americans; Sue Okie was moved to write, "I've never felt as much a part of my own generation." Sally, as usual, revealed nothing about her feelings. But there is obvious delight in her account of dancing her way out of the crowd and winding up between a poster of Ho Chi Minh and a North Vietnamese flag at the

Justice Department, just as some demonstrators threatened to disrupt the peace. "When the first bottle flew," she wrote, "I cleared out fast."

Sally seemed satisfied—challenged by her physics classes, sweeping opponents off the tennis courts, surrounded by new friends, living her life in tune with the times. True, college tennis in those pre–Title IX days was not up to the caliber that her peers were playing on the tour. But Sally appeared to be having fun. For Christmas vacation in 1969, she tapped into her inner Crusader Rabbit and enlisted Bear, then a Westlake sophomore, on an elaborate secret plot to surprise her parents by returning home a day earlier than they expected. So it shocked everyone when she returned to campus in January 1970 and, after three semesters at Swarthmore, announced that she was dropping out of school and going back to California.

"I decided, 'What was I thinking?' " Sally later explained. " 'I should have been a professional tennis player.' I had this very, very strong feeling that I had something in me that I hadn't really explored, and it was, 'How good a tennis player could I be? Could I be good enough to be a professional tennis player? There is no way I am going to find this out at Swarthmore College, and if I wait until after I graduate, it will likely be too late.' So I thought about it for several weeks pretty seriously, . . . [and] I . . . packed my bags and headed home."

Tennis balls don't bounce in the snow.
—Joyce Ride's explanation of why Sally left Swarthmore

Californians tend to miss California.
—Bear Ride's explanation

UCLA

In mid-January 1970, Sally moved back to Encino. Two months later, she wrote a letter to her ex-roommate in freezing Pennsylvania saying that it was sunny and warm, that her tennis was back up to the level of the past summer, and that she and Bear were the new owners of a sporty new red Toyota Corolla. Her ancestors had had the right idea.

In most accounts of Sally's life, her year and a half at Swarthmore is a parenthetical, a detour on her route to future fame. It's not even mentioned in her official biographies. But from the letters she wrote and the recollections of people I interviewed, I think it represented much more—a chance to find herself, to experiment, to cement her love of physics, to consider tennis seriously. And to recognize how rooted she was on the West Coast.

Sally had missed California more than she realized. Now she basked in its bounty, slipping into shorts instead of snow pants, eating fresh oranges from her backyard trees instead of frozen juice in the school cafeteria, playing tennis outdoors on hard, green, predictable courts instead of the faster indoor surfaces where the ball skidded. She enrolled at nearby UCLA and joined its team; she teamed up with an old doubles partner and registered for tournaments from Seattle to New Mexico. Could she make it in the pros?

The truth hit her like a wicked slice down the line. On one warm August day, she played three separate matches; the next morning, she noted, "all of the muscles in my body have formed a union, and gone on strike for shorter hours." That's all it took. "I didn't quite have the discipline it takes to practice tennis eight hours a day," Sally later explained. "I discovered that very quickly." A future in tennis was over. For the rest of her life, when asked what kept her from a professional career, she'd smile—not quite ruefully—and say, consistently, "My forehand." She also said, "I realized finally and for certain, what I had realized but waffled on in the past: that my education, science, was more important to me than tennis was." It wouldn't keep her from playing—and usually winning—over the next decade, but it would refocus her attention on physics. Sally pivoted and moved on.

"Even in tough tennis matches, she didn't brood over losses," Dale would later say. "She'd be discouraged for a very short period of time, but she's not one to have taken a loss home with her. It was the same in school. She did very well, but if there was a disappointment, she'd just handle it and move on to the next problem. She's not one to get down on herself or blame someone else for whatever happens."

Sally had prepared for the tennis verdict, signing up for two classes at UCLA during the spring semester—Shakespeare and Elementary Quantum Mechanics. She got A's in both, complaining that she'd "never studied so hard in her life" for the latter. That's also where she met her first real romance.

"You can guess how many attractive young women there were in an undergrad physics class at that time," explains John Tompkins, the volunteer teaching assistant [TA] for the class. "Sally was the only one. Actually, she was the only woman." Tompkins's comment reflects a cultural cliché of the 1970s, quickly eclipsed by his appreciation of Sally's "absolutely unstated demand to be treated as an equal. Anybody that knew that wouldn't mess around." They hit it off instantly: the long-haired, bespectacled, twenty-four-year-old grad student and the longer-haired, nineteen-year-old tennis bum (her term); two kindred souls turning each other's heads over the structure of the atom. "We were very much alike," Tompkins tells me, "both very competitive," although he is quick to add that Sally "was much smarter than I was, and certainly a better athlete. And quite fearless. I never lost so many ping-pong games! I did beat her in basketball." Like Sally, John was living at home ("Yeah, we were a couple of nerds!"), which meant a lot of time driving his white Mustang from Pacific Palisades to Encino, over the Sepulveda pass into the Valley. That's where she annihilated him over table tennis on the Ride family patio and where they compared notes on her collie and his two borzois. They joked that their shared Scandinavian roots (his mother's side was Swedish) explained their mutual reticence. And they embarked, he says, on a real romance—"physical but not sexual. We were both slow starters. But it was very intense. Sally was not trivial or superficial. We spent an awful lot of time together in a relatively short period."

Short, because that September John Tompkins flew to Moscow, to join cutting-edge research on a subatomic particle called the pion. John's trip to the Institute for High Energy Physics in Protvino, working with what was then the world's highest energy proton accelerator—as big as a circus arena—was as exotic as the mission itself: with the Cold War still raging and President Nixon in the White House, student exchanges with the then–Soviet Union were rare in 1970. John was part of an unusual collaboration between the UCLA physics department and a Soviet group. Sally was pining for him before he landed.

"This is going to be a very long 6 months," she wrote him one Friday evening from Encino. "The night you left I just felt kind of numb and empty." One day later: "I miss you too much. Maybe you could sabotage the experiment . . ." Over the course of the next year or so, in between her usual clever commentary and meticulously detailed play-by-play recaps of Bruins and Lakers games, she would pour out her heart to her new best pal, discovering strange new feelings.

> I always seem to end letters by saying either that I miss you, or that I love you—or both. I guess that's because both of those are more important to me than anything else I have to say—so I won't write any more in this letter.
>
> I miss you.
> I love you.
> Love,
> Sally.

Rash words for someone who had grown up without ever saying them.

Sally focused on her own next chapter. She had decided to transfer to Stanford University, where, in another of the happy coincidences of timing that smoothed her life, she was readily accepted by the same man who had welcomed her to Swarthmore. Now dean of admissions at Stanford, Fred Hargadon found himself reading her college application for the second time. And, he recalls, "there was another tennis coach delighted at the prospect of Sally's enrolling." Years later, when Hargadon invited her to address a conference of college counselors and admissions officers, he says Sally joked "that I had admitted her twice because I didn't want to admit I'd made a mistake the first time."

On a cool September morning in 1970, long before the sun illuminated Joyce's rose bushes on Texhoma Avenue, Sally took sole possession of the red Toyota and drove north to Palo Alto. She arrived before noon and dove into the nearest glass of ice tea. Sally was exhausted, exhilarated and facing a significant new stage in her life. For a moment, the detached irony of the college sophisticate evaporated. Her letter to Moscow that night was exuberant: "Dear John . . . I'm at Stanford!!"

"Well! A girl physics major! I've been waiting to see what you'd look like—I haven't seen one for years!"
— Dr. Melvin Schwartz, Sally's physics advisor at Stanford, 1970

STANFORD

In 1988, Dr. Melvin Schwartz shared the Nobel Prize in Physics for his earlier work (while at Columbia) on the subatomic neutrino particle. He is one of more than fifty Nobel laureates associated, at some point in their career, with Stanford University. Long one of the nation's elite institutions with a highly competitive physics department, Stanford polished its reputation in the 1960s with the Stanford Linear Accelerator Center (SLAC), a federally funded, super high-tech facility that attracted researchers from around the globe. When Sally arrived on campus in 1970, physics was considered by many the most exciting and exacting of the sciences, luring the brightest students with the sharpest minds (although not always the most socialized) at a university with no ego problems in any department. How many Stanford students does it take to screw in a lightbulb? One to hold it up, went the joke, and then the world revolves around him.

When it came to physics, the operative word was "him." In 1970, only some 6 percent of all US bachelor's degrees in physics were awarded to women; the percentage of female doctoral candidates was about half that. At Stanford that year, you could count the number of female physics majors on one thumb. Nor were there any women teaching physics there. As one of Sally's later colleagues tells me, "being in physics means there's never a line at the ladies' room." When women did get in, they often faced more than black holes and charged particles. One male Stanford professor (another star physicist) reportedly stood up in class and said, "What are these girls doing here? You are taking jobs away from men!"

Sally Ride—junior transfer student, declared physics major, wannabe Nobelist, unshakable optimist—sized up her "friendly, neighborhood advisor," Melvin Schwartz, as "a rather large, tan, jolly fellow with a good sense of humor." Still, she reported his greeting in a letter to John with mock panic: "Help!!!" When Schwartz told her about the phenomenal 60 percent dropout rate in his class on electricity and magnetism (a class she'd signed up for, with some anxiety), "he managed to scare me." But she didn't quit, didn't protest, didn't file a sex discrimination lawsuit, which, in any case, wasn't available. She walked out of his office and went apartment hunting.

"She was very smart, very independent, and she was a competitor," Tompkins says now. "I think she was twenty years ahead of her time in her absolutely unstated demand to be treated as an equal. She didn't carry placards or signs or use jargon or trite phrases, she just asserted herself in a way that said, 'I'm here and I'm capable and I'm doing it.' Her view of piloting that world at that time was just to do it better than men or anyone else."

For the next eight years, that is exactly how she would do it at Stanford. She had chosen the quintessential California campus—eight thousand acres, some twenty times the size of little Swarthmore, with more than five times the undergrads—with its pale yellow sandstone buildings and graceful Spanish-style arcades, located in the heart of what would become yet another famous valley, Silicon. Never enamored of East coast ivy or ice storms, Sally was back in the land of palm trees and blue skies, soaking up the good vibrations. "Stanford was a little bit more suited to my personality," she said. "Particularly the California side of my personality." More than a decade later, she would enjoy Stanford from a loftier perspective, picking out its distinctive red tile roofs through the window of the space shuttle.

Her academic home was the physics department, where she slaked her growing thirst for the fundamental structure of the universe. "Physics is the basis for everything," another scientist tells me. "If you understand physics, then in principle you understand everything else." And if you woke up Sally Ride in the middle of the night and asked her what one word best described her (a question I often pose to size someone up), she would say, according to everyone who knew her best, "Physicist." She liked that fact that only ninety-some naturally occurring elements comprise everything from a grain of sand to the furthest star; that physics means being precise, not arbitrary; that it dwells in the real world with natural law. These were Sally's most comfortable coordinates.

Her later focus on high-energy physics was, according to a physics colleague, "a quest to get to the highest level of understanding of the universe."

Her grades were good, not perfect. As an undergraduate she made many straight A's, not only in the first semester of the dreaded Electricity and Magnetism, but in Atomic Structure, Kinetic Theory, Quantum Mechanics, Statistical Mechanics. There were four physics B's. One was in the second semester of Electricity and Magnetism; then she fell to a C. That course would always bedevil but never impede her progress. In 1973 she got her BS in physics.

She also got a BA in English literature—a rare double major—in which she graduated with distinction. That's better than she did in physics. Her honors essay analyzed the theme of grace in Shakespeare's *Hamlet* and *The Tempest*. On one final exam, the teacher gave her an A and wrote, "A superb job. I hope you're as successful with physics as with literature, in which you are very fine indeed." So much for the Westlake English teacher who had belittled her lack of creativity with a mind "wasted in science."

Sally juggled both disciplines with ease. In one notebook, she recorded her physics lectures front to back, then flipped the notebook and turned it upside down to write her *Richard II* notes, back to front. That's how Sally solved many problems. If the rules didn't work, she rewrote them.

Or just moved on. Uncertain about her next step after graduation, she combined her interests to apply for a Fulbright Fellowship to London, where she wanted to study the "Impact of Science on Elizabethan Thought": how British literature responded to the radical new concepts of Copernicus and "other pre-Galilean astronomical advances." Her recommending professor from the history department at Stanford called her "an unusually competent and mature student . . . [who] refuses to be intimidated or discouraged by difficult topics (as might be expected of a combination English-Physics major)."

But when Sally was accepted for graduate work at Stanford, she plunged into science full-time and got her master's degree in physics. As she honed her focus to astrophysics (the physics of astronomy), she also served as a teaching assistant to an astronomy class, where one student remembers her as "a kid in sneakers. She was so small! And we were building the Stanford Observatory, up in the foothills, working on the darkroom and the mount for the telescope. It was the greatest lab I ever had."

Sally's research centered on the free electron laser, a beam of highly charged particles—only recently invented—with a pinpoint blast, like her own. "She was very comfortable in details," says a colleague. "She saw big pictures, but could focus narrowly."

For her doctorate, she was the first student to be advised by Dr. Arthur B. C. Walker, a noted astrophysicist who invited Sally to join him in modeling the interaction of x-rays and the gas surrounding the stars, known as the interstellar medium. Walker taught science as a team project, right up Sally's alley from her tennis doubles days. She liked working collaboratively. And finding answers. The day she finished her dissertation, she later told Tam, "she sat back and realized that she knew something that no one else in the world knew." That, she thought, was the real dividend of doing research, the real joy of doing science.

MOLLY

Shortly after she arrived at Stanford in September 1970, Sally pulled on a tee-shirt and a pair of cutoff jeans, grabbed her tennis racquet, and knocked on the door of the dorm where Molly Tyson, whom she knew from the teen circuit, had just moved in. "Hi!" she said when Molly answered the door, "Wanna hit some?"

Molly, who thought Sally was still at Swarthmore, was startled. "What are you doing here?" she asked.

"I missed the sunshine," Sally quipped.

Molly stammered a bit, saying that she was out of shape, hadn't been playing. She was also slightly intimidated by Sally, who was not only a year older, but had always been a better player. Molly still had a clipping in her high school scrapbook where Sally was ranked number 9 (in the Girls 18 and under division) and she was only number 19 (in Girls 16 and under). They weren't even particularly close friends.

Sally persisted. "You're the only one here I know, so come on!"

They walked across campus to Stanford's bright green, hard-surfaced courts and started to hit, just as they would every day from that moment on, an afternoon ritual when they didn't have class. Occasionally they played under the lights at 11:00 p.m., two slim, sporty, long-haired athletes—Molly the blonde, Sally the brunette—who rarely kept score, just thwacked the ball back and forth, keeping a rally going for hundreds of shots. Sometimes they bet pomegranate seeds on who would miss first, 500 at a clip. At one point, Sally was 3,500 pomegranates ahead. The goal was to keep the ball in play, not to hit a winner. "I'm not sure how much exercise we got playing that way," Molly says today, "but it was fun."

Then they joined the tennis team. When the coach tried to pair Sally, who was ranked number 1 at Stanford, with the number 2 player for doubles, Sally shook her head. "No, I'm going to play with Molly [who was number 6]," she insisted, in a take-it-or-leave-it manner. And that was that. "I felt like I was getting a privilege that I didn't deserve," Molly recalls. "But it was pretty exciting. I'd just look over my shoulder and there she was." Molly played forehand, Sally, backhand. "She was a wonderful competitor," Molly says, with a wicked drop shot and the precision to lob the ball over your head. "She could just outthink you and anticipate what would happen." On weekends, they piled into Sally's car and traveled to tournaments in Fresno, Bakersfield, San Diego, Phoenix, once finding their own chaperone and paying their own way to a tournament in Ojai, 350 miles away, when the phys ed department wouldn't authorize the funds.

Sally knew that tennis was neither top rank nor a priority at Stanford, where winning a tournament was less important than "general improvement," and she ultimately quit the team to protest the school's refusal to join the competitive Pac-8 conference. "It's not only not good practice, it's bad practice to play against girls who can't even serve," she told the university newspaper. But she didn't stop playing. With college athletic scholarships not yet available for women, she and Molly taught tennis on campus during the summer to earn money. Every day during lunch break, along with some other tennis teachers, they raced to a TV to catch the soap opera *All My Children*. During the school year, they were partial to *Star Trek* reruns, when they weren't playing killer volleyball.

They also started writing a long, involved children's book on big rolls of butcher paper, an allegory about good and evil. Creating the characters and the bad puns sent both women into peals of laughter. They illustrated it with, among other silliness, Sally's sketch of the "Black & Blueberry"—a wrinkled, Yoda-like blueberry wrapped in bandages and leaning on a crutch. "We just wanted to spend time together," Molly says.

Molly was an English major, a "staunch science hater," according to Sally, who took courses like Physics for Poets to fulfill her science requirement but listened with fascination to Sally's clear explanation of the scientific world. "She could make science interesting, even to me," Molly says. "She could turn astrophysics lectures into science fiction thrillers." Sally's tastes and talents ranged even wider. She added literature courses to her own schedule—just for balance, she said, a "sanity class" or two to mitigate all the hard physics. Also, she could borrow Molly's notes. Shakespeare became a parlor game. On road trips, Molly and Sally would memorize obscure Shakespeare quotations and then work them into conversations. It became a running joke. For instance, Molly explains, if someone said, "Lynn *seems* trustworthy," the other would launch into Hamlet's " 'Seems,' madam? Nay, it is; I know not 'seems,' " or some other appropriate line from another play. Molly remembers all of them.

Molly and Sally spent vacation time in Tulsa, where Molly's family had moved. Sally took Molly down to Encino, for visits with the Rides. And she wrote to John Tompkins about their friendship. "Molly and I are taking the university by storm," she announced about their tennis. "We entered the all-university women's doubles tournament and have convincingly swept our way into the semi-finals." She told him they'd gone to a church service—"a very rare occurance [sic]"—to hear Yale's William Sloane Coffin, the antiwar activist. "We decided that if we're going to satirize everything in sight, we should at least know something about the things we're satirizing." The women were so close and their friendship so easy, Molly scrawled her greetings to John (whom she'd not met) on the envelope, with her own little drawing from the work-in-progress.

Sally, who always had a best buddy, now had two.

JOHN

One day in November Sally sat down with, of all things, an exam blue book ("graciously donated by the Stanford physics department"), and tried to explore her feelings to her physicist beau in Moscow. It is a remarkably candid document—maybe not for any other college girl accustomed to baring her soul—but for Sally, who preferred looking out, to faraway galaxies, not inward. "I'm not used to analyzing my feelings and emotions—much less used to trying to communicate them," she started out to John, "so please forgive my clumsiness: being serious is very hard for me." She then talked about how much she'd been missing him while he was in the Soviet Union, how their letters (which had now gone on longer than their in-person relationship) might have distorted things.

> I told you I loved you—and I'm very sorry I did because at the time I knew subconsciously that it wasn't true. I'd better explain that ... I've come to realize that I'm physically, mentally, and emotionally incapable of loving someone who I don't know very, very, very well. "Love at first sight" would be impossible for me, because I'm not an emotional person—I don't get "carried away" with anything. I just never thought about it before, and "I love you" seemed like the thing to say, especially with you repeating it so often. I remember the first time you said it to me—the first time anyone had directly—and how much it meant to me ...

Sally, at nineteen, was apparently encountering her hormones for the first time, at least in print. Whether she was struggling with her feelings about John, or about herself, is impossible to know. She was clearly attached to him, but utterly unfamiliar with the sensation, or what to do about it. "I feel very sure that some day . . . I'll know," she wrote, more hopeful than convinced. Then she withdrew the toe she'd stuck into the turbulent waters and retreated to the safe, glib ground of physics.

> I'm very sure that I'm only a very short quantum jump from love, and that a very little transfer of energy this April will bring me there—I'm existing in a stable state until then, and waiting patiently.

She signed it "Love, Sally."

John doesn't recall the "blue book" letter, and there's no evidence of his response. He was, after all, on his own journey of discovery in the Soviet Union. Sally continued to write him letters, although back to her breezy self. But after John returned and Sally went away for the summer, he broke up with her, in a letter. Sally was furious. "I'm not going to let you break things off by mail," she wrote. "You'll have to do it in person . . . Give me a chance, John . . ." At the bottom of the page she added, "Written 'in a countenance more in sorrow than in anger . . .' *Hamlet*, Act I, Scene 2."

"I think I did it sort of passively," Tompkins says now. "Just sort of drifted away. I changed a bit after having never been out of the country before, and never living on my own, and I'd come to the realization that we were different. First she felt pressure, then I felt pressure as well." He adds something common to all of Sally's beaux: "It was very difficult for me to be too open emotionally at the time. With hindsight, we were probably too much alike."

MOLLY AND SALLY

"That's when our physical relationship started."

Molly has never talked about this publicly.

"When Sally and John split, she seemed pretty sad. She was in a vulnerable state, and I'd never seen her show any vulnerability before," Molly says. She and Sally had been spending more and more time together in the year since Sally showed up, playing bridge, teaching tennis, taking car trips. Now it became a romance.

"I think it's possible Sally and I were obsessed with each other for a long time before we had anything physical," she says. Before, in fact, either of them had been physical with any other woman.

"Eventually it dawned on us that something was going on. But when it became a relationship, it felt like an extension of the friendship." It was 1971, and homosexuality was still mostly closeted—still a crime in many states, including California. Although the Stonewall riots had taken place two years earlier at a New York City bar—widely considered the beginning of the American gay rights movement—Greenwich Village and San Francisco (up the peninsula from Stanford) saw far more activism than other parts of the country. The campaign had not yet caught on nationally the way the women's movement had, on the heels of the civil rights movement. Across America, feminists were marching for their rights wearing buttons that proclaimed, "Sisterhood Is Powerful" and "Uppity Women Unite." At Stanford, Sally joined the newly formed National Organization for Women.

But if you were gay, says a friend who is, "you were considered a sexual freak." In fact, a Gay Students Union had been founded at Stanford the year before, but early meetings were held off-campus, and many who attended in search of support, still preferred anonymity. Sally and Molly knew of no other gay couples on campus. If they had, it wouldn't have mattered. "In our ignorance, we probably would have put them in the category of, Those Icky People," Molly says. "They were not like us. We didn't want to be associated with our idea of what gay people were like." Anyway, they weren't looking for a peer group.

"It's a pretty familiar story that with a person's first relationship, you're absolutely certain that this does not mean you're gay, that it has nothing to do with being gay," Molly says, explaining the mind-set of some who grew up in an era when homosexuals were regarded as social deviates. "You are in love with a particular person, and you're not generalizing it to say, 'Oh, okay, I've now learned something about myself.' Both Sally and I had been in relationships with men before then, so we were just thinking, okay, this is interesting. It's just you that I'm attracted to." They discussed it, Molly says, and "It seemed like an anomaly. We didn't want this to be a label that was attached to us forever."

I ask Molly if she was in love with Sally.

"Yes."

Was she in love with you?

"Yes."

Did you think it would last forever?

"No. I thought it would end when college ended. I was counting on that. Because then I'd go off and get married and have kids."

Molly was nineteen; Sally, twenty. "There was a lot of fumbling around in the dark," Molly tells me about their physical relationship. "We did the best we could. But we were clueless people coming up against a pretty formidable taboo. Kissing felt incredibly daring, sleeping in the same bed felt incredibly daring. But nobody was swinging from the chandeliers. It's safe to say that sex was not the driving force. It was this emotional intimacy, a connectedness. We knew how to finish each other's sentences. In hindsight it was not a very sexual relationship, but it felt huge because of all the barriers we were crossing."

Sally and Molly moved in together, a two-bedroom house decorated, student-style, with brick-and-board bookcases, posters from Shakespeare festivals, and a bust of Julius Caesar from the San Jose flea market. Supernovae posters covered the kitchen wall and a solar system mobile hung from the living room ceiling. They took pride in living cheaply, with lots of frozen spinach at nineteen cents a box. Sally made a wicked guacamole and a very good strawberry pie. When her parents came to town, they contributed jars of cashews. Both women worked at odd jobs to pay the rent: Sally cleaned house, taught tennis, TA'd classes. And they hit the books, hard. No more pretense that Sally didn't study:

she was putting in sixteen-hour days, her focus as intense as the lasers she was exploring. She could, colleagues say, burn through to a subject's core. "Sally could study through a whistling tea kettle and not hear it," Molly remembers. She could also turn a ten-page Shakespeare assignment into a three-page paper that the teacher would call "Brilliant!"

As far as the world knew, they were roommates, just like anyone else, with Sally the quieter, more serious one and Molly the outgoing, funny one, "a real kick." But there weren't that many people who might have known. "We pretty much kept to ourselves," Molly says. It was Sally's trademark social group: small and tight, no outsiders. When they did interact, "This was not something that we wanted to share with anyone." Their love affair was a secret, but they never made rules about keeping it. "It was just sort of a given," Molly says, "at that time, for people like us."

There were some adjustments. "You continue to communicate with your parents but you stop using pronouns," Molly explains. "You become very vague. You know, *I* went to the San Jose flea market, *I* went to the Shakespeare Festival. As far as they know, you're by yourself. Now, because this is about Sally it's going to get some attention, but this is a very familiar story."

In retrospect, it seems impossible that Sally felt no *angst* from hiding their relationship. With Molly she had found the love that eluded her with John: not "something that just happens," Sally had written him, "but it grows slowly, probably imperceptibly, from little things, special memories, and shared experiences and feelings—but more than anything, from close and constant association." They were inseparable. Sally was smitten. But she couldn't share it with anyone except Molly.

"It's a very uncomfortable feeling to be completely in love with somebody and think, 'This is so wrong,' " Molly says.

Because society says it's wrong?

"Yes."

Molly agonized over the secrecy. But if Sally did, it wasn't obvious. "There was never any sign that she was troubled about her relationship with me or anything else," Molly says, still amazed. "That's what's so attractive about her: she is the loosest. She'd be joking in the most stressful kind of situation."

And, of course, she was also a superb compartmentalizer.

Physics (and Shakespeare) kept her busy in class, and tennis still claimed a large chunk of her life. During the summers of 1971 and 1972, she and Molly worked as counselors at Dennis Van der Meer's TennisAmerica camp in Lake Tahoe, Nevada, a joint venture with superstar Billie Jean King, the four-time Wimbledon champion, and her husband, Larry King. Bear Ride worked in the pro shop. Sally and Molly were not only smart, accomplished athletes; they were the kind of fun-loving leaders campers wanted to hang out with, writing lyrics to silly camp songs with Molly strumming on the guitar.

"Sally and Molly were the heart of the camp," says Gordon Kent, another counselor at the time who now runs his own tennis camps. "They patiently went through all the step-by-step progressions to teach the basic strokes. They were great—understanding, patient, fun. And Sally was so attractive. I had a big crush on her."

Jan Graham was a camper, a self-described awkward adolescent. "The Sally and Molly I remember were smart," she writes on her blog. "And gentle. And inclusive. And worldly . . . without being snotty or blasé about it. They shared a lot of 'grown-up' observations in a casual way, as though we were mature enough to appreciate it." Graham remembers the day "Molly broke her arm tripping over a tennis ball and had to get a cast. Sally washed Molly's hair in the sink and goofed for the camera (not mine, sadly), pretending she was in a Prell commercial. Both of them helped us write tennis-camp specific parodies of Simon and Garfunkel songs for the 'talent' show." Graham tells me that as her counselors, they were "just those great sort of role models who seemed to understand that teens struggle, and that a bit of warmth and kindness and a kick-ass sense of humor goes a long way."

More importantly for Graham, "Molly and Sally seemed to honor their friendship as something important and integral, not something to pass the time until the right guy came long. I didn't have many friends. I wore the wrong clothes, had the wrong haircut, didn't know how to be a proper 'girl' even had I wanted to, which I wasn't all that sure I did. (This was not yet a time when 'alternative lifestyles' were condoned.) Yet Sally and Molly made me feel . . . totally okay about who I was. So Sally was a role model for at least one anxious, confused, self-doubting dweeb who is forever grateful."

Graham, who came out as a lesbian sometime later, had no idea about Sally and Molly's relationship. No one did. They were, says Molly, very discreet.

One day in August 1972, as the Watergate scandal unfolded in Washington, DC, Billie Jean stopped by TennisAmerica in Nevada after her latest Wimbledon victory. The campers and counselors had cheered her success when it was announced over the camp PA system. Now they were thrilled at her appearance; awed, too, by the scars from her latest knee surgery. Even more exciting, King would participate in an exhibition mixed doubles match. To her utter delight, Sally (considered the best female player in residence) was asked to be the fourth, partnering with Van der Meer against King and camp director Dick Peters before a crowd of two hundred cheering campers, parents and other spectators. It was an elite crowd. The ballboys, both campers, were Martin Luther King III and his brother Dexter.

Sally's entertaining recap of the event in a letter to John Tompkins (they were friends by then, as all of her serious romances would become) barely disguises her excitement:

> I got to rally with BJK in the warmup and (hold onto your seat) didn't miss a shot—on the other hand, she didn't either. Dennis served first, and imagine my surprise when, 4 points later, we changed sides ahead 1–0 (after I won a point off a mildly difficult volley, and bowed to the wild applause). 8 games later, I held serve to put us ahead 6–3 . . . unfortunately, we decided to play an 8 game pro set (first team to eight),

so instead of winning the set, we ended up losing 8–7. I played nothing short of spectacular (for me), got in all kinds of pictures, and even got to sign a couple of autographs while BJK was being besieged by pen and paper . . . why . . . SHE even told me I have a good backhand, and fair reflexes . . . so I've decided to quit tennis, and retire my racket, shoes, socks, and sweatsuit. See you at the ping-pong table.

Anyway, my illustrious career has reached its climax—I'm afraid it's all downhill once you've played the #1. We may schedule a rematch for tomorrow, but she doesn't seem overly eager. I should probably quit while I'm not too far behind.

For Sally, the unexpected match created an important mentor and friend. A year later, she would interrupt a qualifying test for her doctoral degree to watch King, the world's top female tennis player, take on Bobby Riggs, formerly the world's number 1 male tennis player, in a battle of the sexes witnessed by some ninety million TV viewers. Riggs had boasted to King that since no woman was as strong as a man, of course he could beat her. King trounced him in straight sets, breathing air under the wings of women—including Sally—on and off the court. Billie Jean, who transformed women's tennis into a big-money, big-time sport, remained Sally's hero.

The admiration was mutual, but while King remembers seeing Sally play in Junior Tennis, she has no specific recollection—as has frequently been cited—of urging her to turn pro. "She was a very smart tennis player," King tells me, "with a really good backhand. But she wasn't really powerful because she wasn't really big." King suspects she advised Sally that if she had any interest in playing professionally, she should "at least try, because you don't want to look in the mirror in your sixties and say, 'Oh, I never tried.' "

By the time of the camp match in Lake Tahoe, Sally had tried and rejected the possibility. Now her professional sights were set on science. After they played, Billie Jean King asked what she was majoring in at Stanford. Sally said astrophysics. She also said she'd be the first woman on the Moon. At least, that's how King remembers it.

BILL

Back at Stanford, a couple of years later, Sally and Molly widened their little circle to include two more physics grad students: Rich Teets, a tall, slim Coloradan with shoulder-length blond hair and a quick wit; and Bill Colson, a tall, slim Michigander from "a nice wholesome community" who had never seen a play or read a wine label before he got to California. Body size mattered because the new foursome spent hours playing volleyball, a campus-wide addiction of pickup games that they played indoors and out, endlessly. The women were the "setters," the men the "spikers," with excellent results. "We became known as a volleyball power on campus—the physics department!" Colson notes. "In California, that's pretty good." They also spent hours playing bridge together, canoeing on the Russian River, and joining the party when Dale and Joyce came to town, a fun-loving quartet of "mad scientists" (Colson's term) who once made Baked Alaska by putting the ice cream in liquid nitrogen so it wouldn't melt in the oven. The frozen brick that resulted was inedible for hours.

Bill was ready for new friends. His marriage was breaking up and he had moved out of his house, sometimes sleeping in his office like any other obsessed graduate student. He and Sally would consult on physics questions, later collaborating on a number of papers about free electron lasers. They were colleagues in an unusually close and supportive group of what Teets describes as "somewhat liberal agnostics with our noses buried in the lab." Sally and Bill were friends. Just friends. Which is how it always started with her.

Bill found himself attracted to Sally and wondered why she seemed so distant. Finally, he worked up the courage to ask her. Sitting on the green couch near the front door of the house on College Avenue she shared with Molly, he got his answer. "She said she was in love with somebody," he recalls. "I said, 'Okay.' And that answered a lot of questions." Then Sally said, "This is really hard." She had a difficult time of it, but she told him she was in love with Molly. "It's as if she expected I'd say, 'Oh, you're homosexual,' and walk out the door," Colson tells me.

His impression was very different from Molly's. "She was afraid of what people thought about her." The next day Molly sat with him out on the front lawn and confirmed their relationship. I ask him how he reacted.

"That's an interesting question for a dumb kid from Michigan," he says. "I think it was as much a relief as anything else, so I could move on. It wasn't, 'You're a jerk and I don't want to spend time with you.' It answered the behavior. I still liked this person, so I said 'Okay, I guess so.' It wasn't something I told anybody else about. It didn't seem to be their business. I didn't even tell Rich, and I was quite close to Rich." The foursome remained intact.

Sometime in 1975, Molly wanted out. She'd been feeling uncomfortable for a long while, thought the relationship was strained, hated living in what she saw as Sally's shadow. "It wasn't her fault," Molly says now. "She was a better athlete, a better scholar, and a more confident person. It was actually a great relief when she was chosen for the astronaut program and eventually chosen to be the first American woman astronaut, because I didn't have to compare myself to a mere mortal. Although Sally never cast me in the role of sidekick, I saw myself that way and it probably contributed to my need to get away."

Molly also felt trapped by the secrecy. "If you have to live in a bunker or a closet or a box with somebody, you can't get anyone better than Sally," she says. "But I wanted to bust loose. I was very burdened by this secret. If you're always worried that people are going to find out, you're not relaxed. I don't think Sally cared about pleasing people. I do. And I did. And I felt that I was hiding a big part of myself. I wanted to be out."

They had been together nearly five years. Molly left for New York, to work as an editor at *womenSports* magazine. It broke Sally's heart. "It was excruciatingly difficult to leave the relationship, and Sally must have felt really hurt," Molly says. "Not to flatter myself, but the only mean thing I think she ever said to me was, 'You won't be able to write without me editing your stuff.' I took that to mean that I'd really hurt her. But once I make a decision, I don't look back."

She had no regrets about her relationship with Sally. "I want to make it clear that it was a very fun time," Molly volunteers. "And I want the bad guy in your story to be a world that makes it so hard for people who love each other to be together. Thankfully, that is changing."

Sally later told Tam that it took her several years to get over Molly, an eternity for someone with a deep need for an anchor in her life. Then again, she lived in the moment, one day at a time. So when Bill Colson, who was by then divorced, found out about the breakup some time later, what happened next was probably inevitable. "I think we would both say we fell in love at that point," Colson says confidently. "She told me that, I told her that." And while he admits, "I might have gotten Sally on the rebound," he does not think it was any kind of trial period. "I think she was jumping in with both feet."

I ask about their sexual relationship.

"It was very good," he tells me without hesitation. "She was a willing and fully participating partner."

Sally and Bill became an item, a picture-perfect grad school couple in their jeans and plaid shirts, with his beard and her long hair surrounding a face untouched by cosmetics. They never again discussed Sally's time with Molly, and Bill never tried to define it. "It just didn't register one way or the other to categorize Sally," he explains. "Whatever the label is, she's more complicated than that. It was about intimacy, not sexual orientation. I think she found that it was about being with the right person. If she was interested in being with Molly, sex was part of it, and the same thing happened to me."

Once, Bill says, when they briefly broke up and he showed up at a volleyball game with another woman, Sally came to his office and announced, "I'm jealous." Bill was stunned. "Because Sally doesn't let down her guard like that," he tells me, "she has a lot of pride." They got back together. I ask if they spoke about getting married. "Not specifically. Her relatives talked about marriage more than we did. But we talked about moving in together."

They lived on peanut butter sandwiches, put their heads together in her living room over the thesis each was writing. And talked about what they would do with their doctoral degrees. "We thought were going to be physics professors together and go off and have a life," Colson says.

Deep into her research and completely engrossed with the science that had fixated her since childhood, Sally figured she'd go for a postdoc, probably in laser physics, at some university. She felt at home in academia and was looking forward to teaching.

It was January 1977. Jimmy Carter was headed for the White House, outgoing President Gerald Ford said he had no regrets about pardoning Richard Nixon, sideburns and moustaches decorated the faces of hip men, and the first-ever snow fell in Miami, Florida. For Sally, it was time to start writing the next set of graduate school applications. One morning, she was sitting in the student union with a cinnamon roll and coffee, trying to wake up before class. She picked up a copy of *The Stanford Daily* and never got beyond the front page. The headline was just above the fold: "NASA to Recruit Women."

Sally's future had just landed in her lap.

WAIT!

OCTOBER 1957–JUNE 1978

The cartoon appeared just after she died, wry commentary on the power of progress. In a bedroom bursting with science textbooks and space shuttle knick-knacks, a tee-shirted teen sits at her desk, eyes widened in disbelief. It's not so much what she sees on her computer—the familiar face alongside the newspaper headline mourning "Sally Ride, 1951–2012"—as her shock at the back story. "Wait," she says to her mother, hovering behind her in mom-jeans. "Are you saying there was a time when women weren't astronauts?!"

SPUTNIK

Listen up, kids.

America entered the space age in 1958. It would take another quarter century to let a woman do the job. The struggle to open that door reflects the social upheaval and political pressures that would transform almost every segment of traditional culture. The world was spinning far beyond its geophysical axis, tugging NASA along with it.

It began with a beep. Make that "beep-beep-beep," the eerie transmission from the shiny metal sphere lofted into the sky by the Soviet Union on October 4, 1957. "This is Radio Moscow," came the startling announcement from our Cold War adversary. "The first artificial Earth satellite in the world . . . was today successfully launched . . ." It was no bigger than a beach ball and could do nothing besides circle the globe. But the stunning achievement introduced a new word to the language— "Sputnik," or "fellow traveler"—along with an icy terror: someone was up there, and it wasn't us. Today, with several thousand satellites reliably delivering everything from Jon Stewart to Words with Friends, it is hard to grasp the impact of 184 pounds of hardware on the American psyche. But at the time it was scary, a dramatic wake-up call that threatened our presumed supremacy. Our archenemies, the "godless Commies" (the ones we disparaged as our technological inferiors), had a platform for weapons that could annihilate us, plus rockets powerful enough to launch them. We, with all our vaunted scientific know-how, had nothing close. Sputnik taunted Americans as it girded the planet, a mini-moon in what once was an empty sky.

As a teenager in suburban Philadelphia, I bundled up against the early autumn frost one night and watched Sputnik cross the autumn darkness above me, like a tiny star dancing over the horizon. I was in high school, where the implications of the Soviet achievement became an object lesson in American unpreparedness. Almost overnight, Russian language classes were introduced into the classroom, along with more math and science. Technology was how you avoided being either dead or Red.

In Washington, Republican President Dwight D. Eisenhower, the five-star general who had led the allied victory in Europe, refused to panic. He saw space as a place for peace and was determined to prevent its militarization. Or bust the federal budget. "They have put one small ball into the air," he said dismissively. But Democratic senator Lyndon Baines Johnson, the Senate Majority Leader, who would became the US space program's biggest booster, disagreed and seized the political moment for his party. A month later, when the USSR launched a second Sputnik—carrying a dog named Laika, which inevitably led the American press to rechristen the spacecraft "Muttnik"—Johnson scheduled hearings on the issue. The testimony was more convincing than the satellite, which did not return the dog to Earth. "Control of space means control of the world," LBJ concluded. In 1958, after the US got its first satellite aloft, Ike gave in. He replaced the outdated National Advisory Committee for Aeronautics (NACA), which had focused only on airplanes (and where space travel was disdained as "Buck Rogers nonsense"), with the National Aeronautics and Space Administration (NASA), pointedly making it a civilian entity. He also authorized a program to put a human in space. The race was on.

THE RIGHT STUFF

The new gods of the sky wore suits of silver.

They were instant heroes, flesh-and-blood Flash Gordons who would zoom us into the future, seven supermen with the otherworldly new title, Astronaut. Like much of the country, Sally Ride knew all their names: Scott Carpenter, Gordon Cooper, John Glenn, Gus Grissom, Wally Schirra, Alan Shepard, Deke Slayton—an All-American front line of square-jawed, white Protestant husbands and fathers. At the press conference introducing them—an event so stuck in a time warp, three of the new stars casually smoked cigarettes—the usually cynical press corps stood up and applauded. The astronauts were such immediate portraits of virtue (having done nothing more heroic than show up to be announced), the supreme arbiter of American values, *Life* magazine, paid them $500,000, to be divided equally, for exclusive rights to their stories, which were carefully sanitized and spun out like modern fairy tales.

Like the Greek and Roman idols for whom the program itself was named—Mercury, the fleet messenger of the gods with his winged sandals, for the single-man capsules that would get us into space quickly; Gemini, the twins, for the two-man capsules that would flex NASA's maneuvering muscles; and Apollo, the god of prophecy and light, to carry us to the Moon with a crew of three—the astronauts inhabited their own pantheon. With their own mythology. Author Tom Wolfe called it "The Right Stuff," a dashing brew of confidence, courage and "aw shucks" cool that was rooted in the cockpits where they'd earned their wings. Never mind that the other, equally fearless test pilots they left behind at Edwards Air Force Base in California (epitomized by Chuck Yeager, the man who first flew faster than sound) denigrated them as "spam in a can"—mere passengers in flying pods. The nation's first astronauts leapfrogged to the top of the heap, viewed by a hungry public as sole possessors of the patriotic moxie that would catapult America to its righteous command of the skies.

That was the hope, despite a dizzying succession of embarrassments under the next president, John F. Kennedy. On April 12, 1961, Soviet cosmonaut Yuri Gagarin became the first human in space, orbiting Earth one extraordinary, revolutionary time. A week later, the United States suffered a humiliating defeat at the Bay of Pigs in Cuba, at the hands of Fidel Castro, the USSR's man. Finally, on May 5, the US launched its first astronaut, Alan Shepard, a grand achievement that lifted national spirits and made everything—in the new space idiom—"A-O.K!" But Shepard's fifteen-minute flight was suborbital, just on the fringes, up and down. Moscow was literally flying circles around us. "The Communists," said one reporter, "seem to be putting us on the defensive."

Still, Shepard's success emboldened the new young president. Less than three weeks later, the United States stopped looking over its shoulder and chose to lead what Kennedy would call "the greatest and most complex exploration" in human history. He gave the newborn space program its purpose and expansive vision, dramatically regaining the high ground on May 25, 1961, when he announced to a joint session of Congress, "I believe that this nation should commit itself to achieving the goal, before this decade is out, of landing a man on the Moon and returning him safely to the Earth." It was audacious, it was electrifying, and better yet, it was funded by Congress with almost no debate. With an unprecedented fusion of brain power, guts and deep pockets, the United States would shoot for the Moon and the pendulum would swing back to the West. It was all about beating the Russians. "To be sure, we are behind, and will be behind for some time in manned flight," President Kennedy announced a year later. "But we do not intend to stay behind, and in this decade, we shall make up and move ahead."

If the American space program was triggered largely by the fear of "going to bed each night by the light of a Communist moon," as LBJ put it, it was also energized by the wonder of the unknown. Kennedy, who would not live to see the realization of the force he'd unleashed (but whose name would identify the site from which its missions were launched), softened his Cold Warrior stance with an exuberant metaphor. "This nation has tossed its cap over the wall of space," he said on the day before he was assassinated, "and we have no choice but to follow it." That confident spirit infected millions, who saw the mission and its missionaries as saviors of the American dream.

No one exemplified it better than John Glenn, the freckle-faced Marine and stalwart family man whose small-town charm and fighter-pilot fortitude made him a sentimental favorite. On February 20, 1962, the third Mercury mission, he climbed 162 miles into the sky to become the first American to reach orbit, circling the globe three times as the entire nation rode with him. Glenn came home to a star-spangled welcome that certified the growing might of US rockets and celebrated his own valor.

In time, the Mercury Seven would all prove their mettle, their swashbuckling self-assurance toughened by years in uniform. They wore suits and ties now, but all were members of the military, as directed by President Eisenhower when he reluctantly signed off on the program.

In an effort to catch up quickly to the Soviets, Ike had ditched the idea of open applications for the first astronauts and restricted NASA to the pool of military test pilots, reasoning that the nation's high-performance fliers, battle-hardened to screeching brakes, steep climbs, nose dives and eject buttons, were already cleared for national security and accustomed to dealing with danger.

And they faced very real dangers. They were sitting atop the world's biggest firecrackers, smaller versions of which, without human cargo, had exploded on the pad—sensationally, with the world looking on. The modified missiles were such volatile cannons, their missions were called "shots"—space shots. Moreover, the first people to step into the black void were no surer of their fate than the first fish that crawled ashore. It would take raw gumption to ride an untested rocket into the void . . . and then what? Would weightlessness make it impossible to swallow? Would eyeballs float out from an astronaut's sockets? A year before the first astronauts were chosen, a *New York Times Magazine* article asked about a hypothetical human flier, "Will he need bones of steel and powerful muscles to resist rocket thrust . . . a mighty heart, the aplomb of an acrobat . . . ?" The article was entitled, "Portrait of the Ideal Space Man."

Make no mistake, the only humans considered for space travel were men—white men, no taller than 5'11" at first, so they could fold inside the blunt-nosed cones. Race was not mentioned, but no pilots of color were selected. And at a time when newspaper Help Wanted ads were legally separated into "Male" and "Female" columns, NASA hadn't bothered to stipulate gender in the search for its first space travelers. It wasn't necessary: the military and its jet aircraft were strictly off-limits to women, guaranteeing that none could even apply.

ASTRONETTES

American women had been piloting planes in increasing numbers since the 1920s. Amelia Earhart, the first female to fly solo across the Atlantic

Ocean (1932), was just the most famous. Equally intrepid women performed vital roles in World War II, ferrying bombers across the seas and
training male pilots for battle command, as bona fide members of the
Women Airforce Service Pilots, or WASPs. But the women were uncer-
emoniously sent home when the war ended, banned from jets until the
1970s, officially forbidden from combat roles until 2013. They weren't
even awarded veterans' benefits until two female members of Congress
interceded. The bias continued in peacetime, when the closest women
got to commercial cockpits was, at first, as stewardesses, that quaint
combination of hostess, nurse, safety officer and sex symbol, to usher in
the air travel business.

Space travel gave women new hope. While the new Mercury astronauts were training for flight, a group of female pilots underwent some
of the same grueling medical exams that had gotten the men selected
in the first place. Dr. Randy Lovelace, a NASA consultant in aerospace
medicine, recognized that women would one day be part of space-based
communities. How might they fare, he wondered, taking the same tough
tests he'd devised for the men? With funding from Jacqueline Cochran,
who led the WASPs during wartime and was the first woman to break
the sound barrier in 1953, Lovelace invited some highly skilled aviators
to be guinea pigs, including Jerrie Cobb, a decorated and record-setting
pilot and aviation executive, and Jane Hart, a pioneering aviator and
outspoken feminist. They were among the so-called Mercury 13—an
after-the-fact label never used by the women themselves—who had icy
water squirted into their ear canals, barium enemas shot through their
intestines, and all senses deprived in a dark tank of water. "We were
x-rayed in places we didn't know we had places," said one of the volunteers. The women did splendidly, but when a final test was scheduled
at a US Navy facility, the program was abruptly canceled. The women
were furious.

Lovelace had never promised them NASA's approval or acceptance—
his research was independent—but the women kept pressing for their
chance to fly. On March 15, 1962, Cobb and pilot Jane Hart took their

case to Lyndon Johnson, now vice president. During a meeting in his office across from the Senate, the man who ran the National Aeronautics and Space Council told them the matter was out of his hands. What he did not tell them was that his executive assistant, the resourceful Liz Carpenter, had drafted a noncommital letter from her boss to the NASA administrator, in which Johnson agreed "that sex should not be a reason for disqualifying a candidate for orbital flight" and asked for clarification of the criteria. Carpenter suggested LBJ show it to the women to give them "some encouragement" and get some "good press" for himself. He did not. Instead, after Cobb and Hart left, Johnson scrawled his decision across the signature line in inch-high letters: "Let's stop this now!" And directed that the paper be filed away. The unsent letter remains the only known written proof that women were purposely grounded for twenty-five years.

Four months later, Cobb and Hart appeared before a House subcommittee to settle "once and for all," according to a New York congressman, "this problem about women astronauts." The women pointed out their physiological and intellectual readiness, and noted the prestige factor of getting a woman in space before the Soviets. "[W]e women pilots . . . are not trying to join a battle of the sexes," Cobb said in her opening statement. "We seek, only, a place in our nation's space future without discrimination." One member was strongly sympathetic; the rest, barely tolerant. Celebrity witness John Glenn, still enjoying the full glamour and glory of his triumphal flight earlier that year, spelled out the status quo. "I think this gets back to the way our social order is organized," he said. "The men go off and fight the wars and fly the airplanes and come back and help design and build and test them. The fact that women are not in this field is a fact of our social order. It may," he added, "be undesirable."

Glenn testified on the second and last day of the hearings, which were summed up by Ohio Democrat Walter H. Moeller. "[I]f today our priority . . . is getting a man on the Moon," he intoned, "maybe we should ask the good ladies to be patient and let us get this thing accomplished first and then go after training women astronauts." It was the same patronizing reply that women had heard for centuries, as they demanded everything from the right to vote to the need for equal pay: *Wait—until we're ready to let you in.*

SCIENCE

Space

THE VICE PRESIDENT
WASHINGTON
March 15, 1962

Dear Jim:

I have conferred with Mrs. Philip Hart and Miss Jerrie Cobb concerning their effort to get women utilized as astronauts. I'm sure you agree that sex should not be a reason for disqualifying a candidate for orbital flight.

Could you advise me whether NASA has disqualified anyone because of being a woman?

As I understand it, two principal requirements for orbital flight at this stage are: 1) that the individual be experienced at high speed military test flying; and 2) that the individual have an engineering background enabling him to take over controls in the event it became necessary.

Would you advise me whether there are any women who meet these qualifications?

If not, could you estimate for me the time when orbital flight will have become sufficiently safe that these two requirements are no longer necessary and a larger number of individuals may qualify?

I know we both are grateful for the desire to serve on the part of these women, and look forward to the time when they can.

Sincerely,

Lets stop this now!

Lyndon B. Johnson

File

Mr. James E. Webb
Administrator
National Aeronautics and Space Administration
Washington, D. C.

So the exclusionary treatment continued. When half a dozen women applied for training in the second astronaut selection, in 1962, NASA disqualified them because none had jet test-pilot experience; several, management said, also lacked the educational requirements and another was too old. The response was the same even as the prerequisites became less stringent. In 1963, the test-pilot requirement was removed; in 1965 and 1967, you didn't even have to know how to fly. NASA was seeking non-pilot astronaut scientists, and gender wasn't specified. Still, NASA turned down the two women who sought pilot jobs in 1963, the four women who sought scientist-astronaut jobs for the third group in 1965, and the seventeen accomplished female scientists who applied for the 1967 selection. "No Girls Allowed" was the message clearly scrawled on the NASA clubhouse, because they'd set the bar way beyond women's access. Candidates were required to have a degree in engineering, or certain technical abilities, at a time when few women qualified for science or engineering doctoral programs. "The US government isn't going to have women astronauts for two thousand years," grumbled spurned applicant Janett Rosenberg Trubatch, one of the first female graduates of the Polytechnic Institute of Brooklyn. "NASA thinks the American ideal is for women to marry, have kids and stay home."

Meanwhile, the Russians beat us again. On June 16, 1963, Valentina Tereshkova became the first female and the sixth cosmonaut to fly in space, orbiting Earth forty-eight times over three days. American space leaders brushed off the event as propaganda, belittling Tereshkova's background as an assembly worker in a textile factory and an amateur skydiver. US journalists commented condescendingly about her plump charm and dimpled chin, with "her feminine curves hidden in a clumsy space suit." *Life* magazine ran a suspiciously posed photo of a grim Tereshkova getting her dark blonde hair combed out by a hairdresser, "primping for orbit." Whatever the Soviet motivation, it was not necessarily equal rights. Tereshkova never flew again, and the Soviets didn't send up another woman for twenty years.

Nor did Tereshkova's flight advance the public dialogue in the United States, with its winks and one-liners. A 1958 editorial in the *Los Angeles Times* had welcomed women on interplanetary flights as mere "feminine companionship" for the "red-blooded space cadet," to "break up the boredom" and produce "a new generation of 'space children.' " But, asked the writer, what if the "feminine passenger" (the concept of coworker was not yet on the radar) was incompatible? "Imagine hurtling tens of millions of miles accompanied by a nagging back-seat rocket pilot." *Look* magazine, *Life*'s popular, photocentric competitor, framed the debate more soberly (but no more hopefully) in 1962, with a cover story entitled, "Should a Girl Be First in Space?" Answer: "[W]omen will follow men into space."

As "cosmonaut" and "astronaut" became concrete career goals, culture goddesses from Lucille Ball's "Lucy" to Mattel's "Barbie" slithered into space suits, with the predictable emphasis on comedy and curves. But the "problem that had no name," described by Betty Friedan in her 1963 book, *The Feminine Mystique*, had not yet lured many women to liberation, and the clenched fists of the modern women's movement would not be raised en masse until the next decade. In 1965, newspaper columnist Dorothy Roe declared, "Girls who are clamoring for equal rights as astronettes [I swear, she wrote "astronettes"] should consider all the problems of space travel. How, for instance, would they like to wear the same space suit without a bath or a change of clothes for six weeks? . . . How will a girl keep her hair curled in outer space?" A Wisconsin editorial writer fantasized, "We want our gals to look their best when they meet up there with those Martians and Venusians."

Earthlings married to astronauts also had to dress for success. News about the men and their machines was worshipful; stories about their wives worshipped what they wore to church. "Jane Conrad . . . is dressed in intense canary yellow and a matching headscarf," NBC's Aline Saarinen breathlessly reported—LIVE!—in August 1965, while Jane's husband, Pete, flew on Gemini 5. Women remained support players in the drama hanging overhead, the big round Moon still ripe for plucking by the Russian enemy unless we got there first.

On July 20, 1969, that is spectacularly what happened. Neil Armstrong and Buzz Aldrin alit on the Sea of Tranquility, emerging from the *Eagle* to explore the mythic disc of so many dreams. For the first time, humans set foot on another heavenly body. In full view of this world, the rest of the universe seemed a bit smaller, the new possibilities, infinite. The space race was over, and the winners planted a US flag on the Moon. The message on the plaque they left behind was more inclusive: "We came in peace for all mankind."

As five more spacecraft deposited ten more men on the lunar surface, the women behind them also went under the microscope, with their own oppressive code of conduct. "Astronauts' wives were to be back home in Houston, running the household and smiling for photographers," writes Eugene Cernan, the commander of Apollo 17 and the last man to leave his footprints on the Moon. In an unusually candid confession, Cernan calls the lack of attention to wives by both hard-driving astronauts and clueless NASA management, "a dreadful oversight." When he came home for a weekend, he writes, "all I wanted to talk about was our training and the program. It was, 'My God, let me tell you what I did,' rather than asking, 'What did you do this week?' Looking back now, I realize my family suffered because of my tunnel vision." Cernan, like the majority of his astronaut colleagues, subsequently got divorced.

No one reported on the extramarital activities of the country's most celebrated hunks, and no wife complained out loud. For them, as one explained, having the right stuff meant looking the other way. Some of the wives also opposed the idea of sharing their men with women in the cockpit, for the same reasons male police officers' wives early fought against allowing female partners to ride shotgun in the front seat.

What they saw as a threat their marriage was viewed by some of their husbands as a threat to their manhood. Space was no place for "the weaker sex," they said, because the suits wouldn't fit and the women wouldn't fit in; stress was too high and the danger too great. Danger, one might ask, to whom? "Had we lost a woman back then," said Mercury flight director Chris Kraft many years later, "we would have been castrated." And when all else failed, someone invariably brought up personal hygiene. How to cope with privacy issues for mixed genders in spaceships so confining, the joke went, you didn't fit into them but put them on? Eileen Collins, the air force colonel who would become the first female commander of the space shuttle in 1999, saw some of the same limp excuses regarding women in the military. While the vast majority of her male colleagues were supportive, she says, there were a few with attitude, for whom it was all about the male ego. "Occasionally, I would run across a man who thought, 'If a woman can do it, then apparently I'm not as good as I think I am.'"

"It never occurred to American decision makers to seriously consider a woman astronaut," writes historian Margaret Weitekamp. "In the late 1950s and early 1960s, NASA officials and other American space policy makers remained unconscious of the way their calculations implicitly incorporated postwar beliefs about men's and women's roles. Within the civilian space agency, the macho ethos of test piloting and military aviation remained intact. The tacit acceptance that military jet test pilots sometimes drank too much (and often drove too fast) complemented the expectation that women wore gloves and high heels—and did not fly spaceships."

Behind the scenes, it was just as bad. In 1964, only 1 percent of those working at GS-12 or higher positions at NASA (the better paying jobs) were women. When Dr. Carolyn Huntoon arrived four years later as a postdoctoral student studying biochemical changes in astronauts' bodies, she was not permitted to finish her experiments on the recovery ships when the astronauts splashed down because the Navy didn't allow women on their vessels. NASA wouldn't intercede. "I had to hire male lab technicians to go and process the samples," she tells me. "All my *compadres* were guys. They all went, and would send me postcards from Hawaii and pester me." I ask if it made her crazy. "No, it just irritated me," she says calmly. Huntoon, whose soft southern accent and firm resolve make you wonder how anyone could ever refuse her anything, says the attitude persisted in other visible ways. "I believe that people tend to support people like themselves, so when it came to hiring, giving awards and promotions—particularly with guys ten years older than me—they always went to the guys. And I've talked with people in other fields, they said the same thing: If there is no woman in the room, women don't have opportunities. Unless someone there is their champion."

On the other hand, she added, "once the rules were made in the federal government that they were not going to discriminate against women, the rules were followed."

PROGRESS

In 1972, the Equal Employment Opportunity Act was passed—technically, an amendment to the Civil Rights Act of 1964, validating the illegality of discrimination on the basis of sex. Every government agency was ordered to comply, although the path could be steep. In 1973, the woman hired to run NASA's equal opportunity programs, Ruth Bates Harris, told the administrator that the agency's effort was a "near total failure" for blacks and women. Minorities comprised just over 5 percent of its employees, compared to some 20 percent for the federal government as a whole. And nearly 88 percent of the agency's women were stuck in the lowest pay grades. In a report coproduced with two senior EEO staff members Harris wrote, "During an entire generation—from 1958 until the end of this decade—NASA will not have a woman or a minority astronaut in training." She included a comment that would have been funny if it didn't ring true: "There have been three females sent into space by NASA. Two are Arabella and Anita—both spiders. The other is Miss Baker—a monkey." Harris was fired, then rehired (at a salary increase) after a public outcry and congressional hearings, during which one senator lamented that the agency's "space age bureaucracy" was stuck "in the Middle Ages when it comes to minority employment."

But the winds of change swirling around the country were beginning to stir NASA. There were studies to test women's ability to withstand space travel, actual drawings of a toilet that could accommodate female members of a space crew. The armed services opened jets and test pilot schools to women in the 1970s and '80s.

At the same time, space travel as America knew it was coming to an end. With both public interest and federal funding waning, the last men left the Moon just before Christmas 1972. The next two programs—one with the Russians, who were becoming our friends; then Skylab, the first US space station—ended the run. America had won the space race but lost its motivation. Just as NASA started thinking seriously about female and minority astronauts, there was nowhere to fly them.

SHUTTLE

President Nixon viewed the Apollo program he inherited as a useful foreign policy tool; the reflected glory from the astronauts worked on the home front, too. But his drive to reduce the price tag, and replace large-scale "leaps" with more "normal" space activities, effectively curtailed space exploration. Nixon turned down a proposal for a mission to Mars, approving instead the less ambitious—and far less sexy—plan to create a shuttle fleet for low Earth orbit. It was called the Space Transportation System, and it was planned to go up routinely, fly around the planet to deliver payloads and execute other tasks in low Earth orbit, then return to launch again. In those budget-minded times, it would, as the president said, "take the astronomical costs out of astronautics." In fact, Shuttle costs far outran the original estimate, and customers complained about the many compromises required to fit their payloads into its cargo hold. With production of expendable launchers suspended, the private sector and the Defense Department, along with NASA, would now deploy all satellites, or anything else they wanted launched, from the new spacecraft. The US military was especially concerned about putting all of our space eggs into the Shuttle basket.

But the unthinkably complicated machine with the overly ambitious schedule also gave America a chance to redeem its image after the emotionally and financially draining Vietnam War and to regain its technological edge. It was a new kind of vehicle for a new generation of Americans that would launch like a rocket, orbit like a spacecraft and land like an airplane—actually, more like a glider. Its centerpiece, the orbiter, or shuttle, looked like a snub-nosed DC-9 jetliner, with a 60-foot-long cargo hold (the payload bay) back where a commercial passenger section would be. Up front was the cockpit, or flight deck, and one flight below, the middeck living quarters, a 13-by-10-foot compartment where astronauts would work, cook and sleep—in effect, a split-level apartment with more space for spacefarers.

To get off the pad, a bulbous fuel tank that looked like a fifteen-story silo (and which, if you laid it down horizontally, was just slightly longer than the distance of the Wright Brothers's first flight) fed the orbiter's three main engines with a mixture of liquid oxygen and hydrogen. Two solid rockets (safer to store and cheaper than the liquid-fueled rockets of old), poised on the pad like twin white crayons, provided the serious launch boost, to break the earthly bonds and punch through to the sky. And it was all controlled by computers—five onboard machines constantly assessing the situation, the first fly-by-wire spacecraft. Americans would now go into space on a stream of little ones and zeroes.

Unlike the small, ballistic capsules of the earliest explorers—throw-away projectiles to get to the Moon and back—the roomier shuttle was designed to be refurbished and reused. The external tank was the only component that would be ditched when empty. The spent rockets would be retrieved from the sea, to refill and reignite, and the shuttle itself would bring the crew home and then relaunch. Instead of trying to pass through the harsh elements of an alien environment on our way to another world, it would work within the space surrounding this world. It marked, as astronaut Joe Allen put it, a "fundamental shift in the goals of manned space flight from exploration to operation—from testing the means of getting into space to using the resources found there." From exploring to doing.

NASA was downplaying the exotic and accentuating the ordinary: the shuttle was a truck, they said, a workhorse to deliver satellites and spare parts into space, to conduct experiments and, in time, to serve as a kind of commuter plane to the planned space station. And commuters looked more like you and me. NASA created a new category of astronaut to work alongside the pilots: the mission specialist, a scientifically trained individual who would specialize in whatever the mission demanded. The commander and pilot (mostly drawn from the ranks of military pilots) would fly the shuttle; the mission specialist (with no military experience required) would tend to what was being flown. Either could be any gender and any color. "We needed to recognize that the world was changing and the nation was changing," explains NASA's George Abbey, who would head up the board making the astronaut selection. "And we had some qualified women and minorities that we had to give opportunities to."

Not everyone could adjust. At one meeting to discuss the new agenda, astronaut Deke Slayton, who supported more traditional recruitment criteria, "stood up and said, 'I want no part of this,' and walked out." He would not participate in the selection of new astronauts for the shuttle program.

MISSION SPECIALIST

NASA issued the new call for candidates on July 6, 1976, just as the three military academies—West Point, Annapolis, and the US Air Force Academy—also prepared for their first females.

The rules for mission specialists were the most relaxed yet. Candidates required no flying experience and just a single degree in engineering, physical science, mathematics or biological science. Advanced degrees were "desired." Good health was critical, which a NASA physical (less exacting in terms of eyesight than for pilots) would ensure. And NASA welcomed folks between 5'0" and 6'4". Here was the job description:

> Shuttle missions could include deploying and retrieving satellites, servicing satellites in orbit, operating laboratories for astronomy, Earth sciences, space processing and manufacturing, and developing and servicing a permanent space station.
>
> Mission specialist astronauts will be responsible for the coordination of overall orbiter operations in the areas of flight planning, consumables usage and other activities affecting payload operations. At the discretion of the payload sponsor, the mission specialist may assist in the management of payload operations, and may, in specific cases, serve as the payload specialist. They will be able to continue in their chosen fields of research and to propose, develop and conduct experiments.

Minority and female candidates were "encouraged to apply."

The notice went out to news organizations around the country, from *The New York Times* to *Ebony* magazine to *La Luz*. Technical publications were contacted, at organizations like the Society of Women Engineers. NASA personnel took to the road to make the appeal in person. "Everyone was asking, 'Is NASA really serious, or is this just window dressing?' " recalls Carolyn Huntoon, elevated to the Astronaut Selection Board now that women were being recruited to join the astronaut corps. "So I went to Lions Clubs, high schools, colleges, clubs, even retirement communities, just telling them that it would be a broader program, that we were including minorities and women." The only African American on the board, Dr. Joseph D. Atkinson Jr., went to California to find potential applicants at NASA contractors and other sites. "Were we always reaching the individual applying?" Huntoon wonders. "Maybe not, but I was reaching their parents, grandparents, uncles and aunts, to make sure people knew that we were serious about including minorities and women in the next class." She said that at one Lions Club gathering, a woman told her, "I can't imagine any woman wanting to be an astronaut." And Huntoon replied, "Well maybe you don't, but your daughter, your granddaughter might." As a result, she says, "a lot of people applied who wouldn't have thought it's what they wanted to do, because they didn't know they could."

NASA also stretched into the sci-fi future to enlist Nichelle Nichols, the African American actor who played the brainy Lt. Uhura on *Star Trek*, to help spread the word. She was fitted with a tailored flight suit and given abbreviated astronaut training to help counter the skepticism. "Women didn't believe them," Nichols tells me. "Because for six previous recruitments they would say, 'Yes, you can apply,' and then suddenly nobody was qualified that was female." So she too went on tour—to TV stations and to meetings of black engineers—to pitch the program. Her presence, and the model she'd provided in her TV role, generated a swarm of requests for information.

At Stanford University, Sally Ride was finishing up her graduate studies in astrophysics, unaware of both the twenty-year effort to integrate the astronaut corps and the six-month-old campaign to attract female scientists like herself. NASA, casting an ever-wider net, had recently expanded its appeal to minority and women's organizations, especially targeting college campuses. Just after Christmas, the director of Stanford's Center for Research on Women was contacted and asked to recommend potential applicants. Instead, she called the campus newspaper, which published an interview with her on January 12, 1977. That's the Page One article that caught Sally's eye.

The Stanford Daily

♦ Wednesday, January 12, 1977
Stanford, California
Volume 170, Number 57

p chase, manhunt in two arrests

(article text largely illegible)

Senate reviews Carter choices

Washington — The men picked to fill the top national security and legal posts in the Carter administration underwent close question by yesterday about their past roles and the positions they would pursue once in office. Four Carter choices for secretary of agriculture won quick committee approval.

(remaining article text largely illegible)

Where'd they go?

Police officials examine the getaway car used in yesterday's robbery of a Woodside branch of the Wells Fargo Bank. Two suspects were arrested late last night when they walked into a police dragnet set up after the pair ditched their car at Alpine Road following a high-speed chase and gun battle. Police shooting at the car in an attempt to flush out a suspect made eight bullet holes.

CROW asked for names

NASA to recruit women

By Will Nixon

The National Aeronautics and Space Administration (NASA) has contacted Margaret Collins, director of the Center for Research on Women here, in its effort to recruit women to become astronauts in its space shuttle program. Collins has not recommended any specific person, but she has forwarded the request to other people and organizations.

"We are using a sex blind selection process," said a public information officer at the Lyndon B. Johnson Space Center in Houston, Texas. NASA is conducting a year-long search ending June 30, 1977 for applicants to its astronaut training program. To date they have received more than 1000 applications. Roughly 10 per cent of these have been from women.

A spokesman for Ames Research Center in Mountain View said that an experiment conducted there in September 1973 indicated that women could serve on the space shuttle flights.

He said that 12 nurses ages 21-35 underwent two weeks of tests with a bedrest facility which simulates space flight. These nurses suffered from physiological deterioration but not any more than men would under similar tests. These tests indicate that women of similar physical condition would be able to go along on a shuttle flight as scientists or passengers, said the spokesman.

Stanford scientists involved

Donald Harrison and Richard Papp, professors of cardiology at the Medical Center, worked as collaborators on this experiment. Ames knew of no other similar tests involved.

NASA has never had a woman as an astronaut. The Russians had one

female cosmonaut, Valentina Tereshkova. She flew a mission, Vostok Six, on June 16, 1963. No women have gone into space since.

The space shuttle flights for which NASA is stepping up its recruitment of women will carry a crew of three NASA trained people: a commander, a pilot and a mission specialist. NASA will choose at least 15 people for pilot training and at least 15 for the mission specialist position.

Three different jobs

Pilots will fly the shuttle and be responsible for its maintenance. Mission specialists will coordinate the command of the shuttle with the particular project of each flight. The shuttle will be used to perform missions ranging from the upkeep of satellites to the performing of experiments in many fields of science.

According to Fred Crawford, electrical engineering professor here, who NASA consulted about the space shuttle program, experiments to be done on shuttle flights are still in the planning stages. One to four people will be on each flight to operate these projects. These people will need only limited training, probably a few months, said Crawford.

Crawford forecasts the first shuttle flights will be in 1979 or 1980. Successful applicants for the astronaut positions will begin training in July 1978, according to NASA. They will train for two years after which pilots and mission specialists will be chosen for the different flights.

However, the federal government has not made any final commitment or budgetary allocations for future space programs.

Student loan defaults hit $46,000 in 1975

By Beth Stern

Stanford lost $46,000 to defaulted student loans in 1975, and the loss in 1976 could be twice as much, according to Joseph Jedd, manager of student accounting.

"At present, a person can acquire an education by borrowing $10,000, and for a fee of $500, clear himself of all debt," according to Jedd.

Bankruptcy declarations involving students here and at other universities have increased greatly over the past few years.

In addition to students defaulting on their loans, colleges across the country are having problems with delinquent repayment of loans.

Jedd said that Stanford presently faces an 11 per cent delinquency rate for every $100 loaned, only $89 is collected on time. Some delinquent loans are eventually repaid, said Jedd, since the university continues collection efforts for 20 years, but much of the money is written off as lost.

Taxpayers pay

Most of that written-off money is paid for by the taxpayers, said Jedd. Government loans, which account for 60 per cent of all Stanford loan funds, are 90 per cent financed by the

kruptcy was usually undertaken as a last desperate move.

Today, according to Jedd, people simply want to clear their slate of obligations. Jedd said he felt that colleges instead of dealing with students who are truly unable to pay, are dealing with students who are simply unwilling to pay.

"We try to prevent it," said Jedd. "We write them letters, we plead with them. When everything else fails, we turn to an outside collection agency."

Stronger collection

Intensifying collection efforts was a main discussion topic at the November meeting of the Consortium of Financing Higher Education, a group of universities including Stanford. As a result of this meeting, recommendations for strengthening bankruptcy collections at Stanford have been sent to President Richard Lyman for approval.

These include placing holds on registration materials and academic records until the obligation is cleared. Also, a student who has had a bad credit record (for example, one who consistently pays tuition after the due date) ...

roposes energy unit

(article text largely illegible)

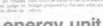

THE APPLICATION

"I just had this 'Wow!' feeling," Sally later said. "I read through the list of requirements for mission specialist and said to myself, "I could do that." She ripped the article from the paper and went in search of stationery. On a letterhead from the Institute of Plasma Research (no blue books for NASA), she printed, by hand, a neat, brief request:

INSTITUTE FOR PLASMA RESEARCH
STANFORD UNIVERSITY
VIA CRESPI, STANFORD, CALIFORNIA 94305

To whom it may concern,

I am a PhD candidate in Astrophysics at Stanford University, & am interested in the space shuttle program. Please send me the forms necessary to apply as a "Mission Specialist" candidate.

Thank you.

Sally Ride

Sally Ride
c/o Physics Dep't
Stanford University
Stanford, CA
94305

JAN 27 1 44 PM 1977

The application arrived by return mail, a standard government document that was disappointingly spare. "There was no room on it to convince them I was exactly the person that they wanted," she said later, in droll protest. When I dig up Sally's application and see it myself—probably the first time in more than thirty years that anybody has looked—I find myself agreeing. It's lean. Sally did her best, listing her résumé, her medical history ("good; tonsils out at about 7"), her academic record (grade point averages: 3.67 out of 4 undergraduate, 4 out of 4 graduate). To the question, "Have you ever been convicted of an offense against the law?" Sally wrote, "(1) traffic ticket (about $30, for speeding) and (2) Trespassing violation (1972)." What she trespassed remains a mystery. She also attached her transcripts and her Graduate Record Exam scores (700, 740).

But it gets more interesting. Sally was asked to list several references. Here are the names she put down: Molly Tyson, Bill Colson, John Tompkins. When I spot this on her application, I am startled. Granted that everyone calls on friends to put in a good word, it still seems pretty bold to name three lovers (including two with a secret that would never fly at NASA in 1977) as recommenders for the job of a lifetime. True, John had been her TA at UCLA, and Bill knew her work in astrophysics at UCLA. And all three certainly fit the amorphous requirement for non-relatives with "definite knowledge of your qualifications and fitness for the position for which you are applying" (as if anyone had any idea what made someone fit to be an astronaut). For anyone else it might indicate either a very small cohort of friends or a desire to live on the edge. For Sally, who lived in the moment without guile or regret, it seems more likely that she just picked the people who knew her best, with complete trust in their confidence, and perhaps a touch of naiveté. Anyway, who would think then to ask about love between two women?

On January 30, 1977, just over two weeks after she'd spotted the article, Sally mailed the application to the Johnson Space Center in Houston. A form postcard confirmed its receipt and advised her that no decisions would be made until December 31.

THE PROCESS

Nearly 25,000 people received the same government forms that Sally filled out. By June 30, 1977, the deadline, 8,079 had filled them in and sent them back. By far the majority wanted to be mission specialists. Preliminary screening of them (for US citizenship, educational levels, the right major, which included astrophysics) identified 5,680 (including 1,251 women) who qualified for further evaluation. Another eight women (among 659 total) qualified in the first round as pilots. Now NASA had to winnow the applicants to a manageable pool of candidates. They started with the individuals listed as references. Sally's came through splendidly.

Bill Colson called her "an excellent graduate student and researcher of the highest regard at Stanford U." On the printed questionnaire, where he was asked to check off rankings about certain qualities, he crossed out all the masculine pronouns (as in, "Quality of His Professional Background") and replaced them with "her" or "she," giving Sally the best marks for everything. He did not mention that he was her boyfriend.

Molly Tyson ignored the form, saying their relationship had "not been professional," but typed up a letter on the stationery of *women-Sports*, the magazine she was editing in New York, and gave Sally "a very high character rating," calling her "one of my most trusted friends." Molly wrote that Sally "was a good enough tennis player that several pros (among them Billie Jean King) urged her to delay her physics career in favor of a career in professional tennis. That Sally chose physics over the more glamorous, potentially lucrative tennis circuit is an unusual, but convincing piece of evidence to her interest in science." Molly also noted Sally's double major in English and praised "her way with words."

Molly's letter, like Bill's recommendation, is a tribute to the deep loyalty Sally engendered in so many of her friends. They protected her all of her life, unasked. "There was a kind of unwritten, nondisclosure statement that you signed up for," says one colleague of several decades.

"She never asked you to. It was more of a trust factor that you weren't going to do anything to embarrass her, or reveal personal stuff. She never told you what you could or couldn't say. But I can tell you that if people crossed the line, they were out of the inner circle."

Expulsion was never a risk for Molly. She was, however, surprised not only by the request from NASA, but by the government agent— "maybe he had a trench coat"—who showed up at her office to do a background check on Sally. Molly found the encounter so bizarre, she recounted his questions in a sardonic article for *womenSports*, the magazine she was editing in New York:

> Did the candidate drink, smoke, or take drugs? Was she a good leader, a good follower? How did she react to stress, to emergencies? Did she keep her room neat, hair combed? I got flustered only once—trying to explain how Sally could be simultaneously a good leader and a good follower; otherwise I was a model witness, and I only lied once. But I figured that dust and dirty dishes wouldn't accumulate in a space capsule the way they had in our apartment.

When I ask Molly whether the guy in the trench coat asked about sexual orientation, she says, "I don't recall any questions that required me to lie about our personal life."

No one I spoke to remembers any such queries. Homosexuality could—and did—get people fired for security reasons back in 1977, due to the possibility of blackmail in a closeted era. But NASA wasn't asking.

The agency did, however, seek out its own sources, getting in touch with people who might provide a more unbiased view of each applicant. Arthur Walker, Sally's doctoral advisor, called her "very bright . . . with *some* originality—not as much as others . . . can work independently (to some degree) once problem is defined; very thoughtful and analytical . . . even-tempered." Then, in a phrase that may well have sealed the deal, Walker, who had directed the big team projects she had worked on at Stanford, called her "good at working with difficult people."

Teamwork was critical to the Selection Board. "You've got to be able to work well with others," says George Abbey, who, as the head of Flight Operations, also ran the board. "It's not a place for someone who wants to be a star unto himself or herself." They were, he says, looking for people with "a good education, well disciplined, who did things over and above their area of interest. Someone who had worked under stress." In short, not just accomplished scientists or engineers, but generalists, people who also worked, say at a sport. Duane Ross, the personnel manager who functioned as head of the Astronaut Selection Office, adds, "We definitely had an interest in women and minority candidates."

NASA narrowed the field to 208 finalists, just over half of whom were applicants for mission specialists. Of the latter, 21 were female. All were invited to Houston for the next step, in ten separate groups over as many weeks.

THE INTERVIEW

Sally, still at Stanford, still plugging away at her thesis, got the call late in September 1977. Could she come to the Johnson Space Center on October 2—all expenses paid—for a week of medical tests and interviews for the astronaut selection program? A follow-up mailgram instructed her to bring gym clothes and running shoes, and advised her to avoid food, alcohol and caffeine for twenty-four hours prior to the physical exam. Sally telephoned Susan Okie with the news. "She was really excited," Okie says. "She said that this was a big deal, and she was going to call back when she got the word."

Sally was more than excited. She was apprehensive. "I didn't know whether they were going to throw us into a centrifuge or hang us from the ceiling by our toes," she later confessed. But there were no ice water drips, no spinning chairs, no inkblot tests. Instead, along with nineteen starry-eyed young men—Sally was the only female in her group—she got her first look at the Johnson Space Center and sat through a series of briefings on the shuttle and its operation. She posed for what look like posture pictures in her bra and shorts (front, side and center) with her jaw clenched in a "when will this be over?" look. Doctors examined her eyes, her ears and her brain; she carried a blue flight bag containing a jar for the urine that had to be collected for twenty-four hours. NASA would find no foul substances in her body. Except for a mild caffeine addiction (at least four cups of coffee a day), Sally indicated that she drank only a few glasses of beer a week, only two glasses of wine a month. Her squeaky clean regime was confirmed several years earlier when, on a trip to Berkeley with a friend, she wandered around drug-friendly Telegraph Avenue "graciously declining offers of speed, hash and acid." Sally's addiction of choice that day was a hot fudge sundae.

At NASA, she told physicians that she jogged more than twenty miles a week, acing the NASA cardio test on the treadmill. She stayed on the machine at maximum effort for a record seventeen pounding minutes—far more than most people can manage—only stopping when her legs started to cramp. "One of the best TM [treadmill] performances by a female candidate seen at this lab so far," wrote the astonished doctor.

She was quizzed, for about forty-five minutes each, by two psychiatrists whose roles have been described by every astronaut I know as a good-shrink-bad-shrink tag team. Psych 1, as they called him, asked friendly questions: "Tell me about your sister." "Tell me about yourself." "Do you love your mother?" Everyone liked Psych 1. Psych 2 was there to rattle them. "Count backwards by seven." "Name five American presidents." When Sally recited the list from George Washington onward, he said, "That would be very good. Now what about the one you left out?" "Huh?" she asked. "Left out?" The process was unsettling, on purpose. A nervous candidate from another group remembers being asked, " 'Do you want a Coke?' And I remember thinking, do I want a

Coke? How should I answer that? If I say 'Yes' and he brings me a Coke, should I offer to pay for it? So in the end I said I didn't want a Coke." The memory still makes him laugh. He was also asked, " 'What would you do if you found a letter on the street as you were walking by?' And I think I asked him, 'Is there a stamp on it?' He said, 'Yeah.' So I said, 'Probably mail it.' "

The psychiatrists "were just there to see if we were crazy or not. It was a pass-fail system," explains one of the astronauts who made it through. She was asked what kind of animal she'd be if she were reincarnated. A dolphin, she said. Most of the men said, "stallions." Another woman was asked what she'd like to come back as, if she were run over by a garbage truck. "In the selection process, you can't really test for normal people," Huntoon says. "You look for abnormal things. We were looking for anyone with, really, problems that would prevent them from doing the job." It's called screening out, as opposed to screening in, "to identify those applicants most likely to perform effectively under the stress of spaceflight."

There was another, more obvious stress test. Sally was zipped into a yard-wide fabric ball—a prototype "rescue sphere" that might be used to transfer astronauts from one shuttle to another. She had oxygen but no light, and no indication how long she'd be enclosed. Afterwards, probably no more than fifteen minutes or so, she was asked to detail her reaction. "Although there was more room than I expected," she wrote in her placid, postbubble appraisal, "I was glad I'm not a couple of inches taller—after about 5 minutes it got a little cramped. The climate inside was fairly comfortable, but started getting stuffy toward the end."

She was also asked to write a one-page essay on why she wanted to go into space, an assignment that must have seemed scarier than a blue book. Sally steered a safe course around her qualifications, with barely a hint of her excitement.

I'm very much a product of the media's fascination with the early space flights and lunar landings, and I suspect that everyone who watched

Walter Cronkite's enraptured accounts from "the cape" has dreamt of trading places with the astronaut. . . . I've been fascinated with space ever since those early telecasts, but never really thought it would be possible for me to become an astronaut—my chances of getting certification as a test pilot appeared pretty slim then. Going up in space didn't look feasible, but studying it from the ground did. . . . Now that the space program has evolved to the point where (a) astronauts are being selected from the scientific community, and (b) women are being considered, I feel that I'm being offered an incredible opportunity. Further, I think that my background (the scientific training in general, and astrophysics experience in particular) qualifies me to contribute as much to the program as I expect to get out of it.

The final hurdle was the hour-long interview with the Selection Committee. This was the one that counted—the one that was impossible to prepare for. "There weren't any right or wrong answers. It was just how they went about responding and handling themselves," explains Carolyn Huntoon. She says the questions were as bland as " 'What did you do on your summer vacation? Do you have siblings? How do you get along?' One of the issues we used to look at is, were people willing to make changes? Anybody that was willing to take a chance and do something different." They also wanted scientists who had not yet gotten too far down a path of research or teaching, "because it would be very hard for them to give it up. Assessing applicants' operational skills was very important."

Nothing was gender-specific. Humor was appreciated—to a point. One candidate, asked why he wanted to be an astronaut, said, "My father was an astronaut. My grandfather was an astronaut. My great-grandfather was an astronaut. It's a tradition in my family." The panel laughed, and turned him down. And there was at least one trick question. "We knew they all talked to each other, so we'd put in a question and then change it," George Abbey said. "Like something about the Panama Canal. Then when another candidate came in and we didn't ask the question, he said, 'You were supposed to ask about Panama.' We flunked him in intelligence."

THE WAIT

Sally returned to her studies at Stanford more eager than she'd imagined after playing astronaut-for-a-week. She'd grown close to her fellow candidates, connecting more than competing. And laughing off the fact that some of the meetings had started with, "You guys will . . . ah . . . you guys and Miss . . . ah Ms. Ride." She also noticed that while they were being interviewed, workmen were adding a women's locker room to the astronaut gym. Would she be back to use it? Before applying to NASA, she had never considered flying in space; now, it was all she wanted to do.

One day in October, she drove down to the Mojave desert near Los Angeles to join some of her fellow candidates at Edwards Air Force Base watching the test landing of *Enterprise*, a prototype of the 75-ton shuttle. With no engines for acceleration, but with two pilots at the controls—a dead-stick landing, just like the real thing—*Enterprise* was dropped from the back of a Boeing 747 to glide down to the runway on Earth. Britain's Prince Charles, a pilot himself, was also there to witness the touchdown—unusually bumpy with three unplanned bounces. "Up until this morning I wasn't afraid at all," Sally admitted in a letter to Molly. "It never entered my mind that there were actual risks involved. But seeing that landing this morning, knowing that they couldn't pull up for another try—that scared me."

She got over it. In San Francisco, she and Bill took his young sons to see *Star Wars*, the first in the series, and Sally hung a poster from the movie on her office wall, right next to a map of the heavens. As she sat beneath both and tried to complete the calculations for her thesis, she fretted about the outcome. "I had trouble finishing writing my dissertation," she later said, "because a group of us that had been down there interviewing were all the time calling each other saying, 'Have you heard anything? When do you think they're going to make the decision?' "

Waiting to learn her future, Sally cast a rare glimpse into her past. She attended a Westlake reunion at Don the Beachcomber's in Marina Del Rey, turning a cynical eye towards some of her conspicuously consuming classmates. No longer democratized by their navy blue uniforms, they seemed more focused on their fingernails and their wealth. It was an event Sally had been avoiding—"subconsciously," she suspected—because she hadn't gotten over the awful shock that Elizabeth Mommaerts, her idol, her beloved physiology professor, had succumbed to manic-depression and taken her own life. Janet Mennie Schroeder had called Sally with the news, which left her "crushed. There was a long silence when I told her." Mommaerts's daughter, Edina Weinstein, speculates that Sally, like her mom, was "aware of how unacceptable it was to mom" to go through a mental breakdown, to no longer be logical and brilliant. After the Westlake reunion, Sally shared her sorrow with Sue Okie. "I think that's going to stay with me for a long time," she wrote. She told Sue that she'd been rereading the high school yearbook, and found Mommaerts's inscription to her "absurdly appropriate: 'Without words we always understood each other. Such a comfort in a noisy life.' " Sally appended the only curse word I ever knew her to utter. "Damn."

Then she pulled herself together and finished the letter with her own obsession. "I'll fill you in on the astronaut business later (although I guess by the time you get this NASA will have either accepted or rejected me)."

In Houston, Sally's application was working its way through the hierarchy. "She was young and didn't have a lot of experience, but she looked like she had a lot of potential," George Abbey tells me. He was especially taken with her tennis experience, that she "had worked well with people and had done science with others." Carolyn Huntoon remembers her confidence in talking to the board. "We had some people come in who couldn't look at any of us, or who mumbled." Not Sally. Besides, Huntoon says, "She didn't do any sucking up. Some candidates would flatter you and say, 'I know all about your work.' Sally was very direct."

In December, the decisions were made. "I chaired the Selection Board and we always met and deliberated as a group," Abbey explains. "We discussed the strengths and weaknesses of the various candidates. I perhaps guided the discussion, but the board agreed," he says modestly. That includes the selection of the six women. Then, Abbey presented the selections to Chris Kraft, the Johnson Space Center director, who was known as the father of the Mission Control Center. "And he bought off on it and that was it." Abbey finalized the list at twenty pilots, twenty mission specialists, which is how Kraft submitted it to Dr. Robert Frosch, the NASA administrator, in Washington, DC, for official approval. The plan was to announce the new choices that month, and all the candidates had supplied telephone numbers where they'd be reachable through Christmas vacation. But everything was delayed when Frosch questioned the number of pilots. He wondered if there might be too many military members. Maybe, Frosch says now, "they over interpreted" his question—meaning, maybe JSC overreacted by trimming the list. JSC saw it as a mandate. "They wanted us to cut it down to thirty-five," George Abbey recalls. A few weeks later, there were five fewer pilots (all white males), who were told to reapply next time. The longest and largest astronaut selection process in NASA history was complete. Now they just had to tell the new astronauts.

THE PHONE CALL

The call jolted Sally out of a deep sleep in the front bedroom of her house on College Avenue at Stanford. It was George Abbey, who tended to make major pronouncements in a maddeningly oblique manner. The conversation that January 16, 1978, went something like this:

"Remember that job you applied for? You still interested in that?"

"Yes sir!"

"Well, we'd love to have you come join us."

It took Sally a minute to figure out what he was telling her. "I was asleep until halfway through the call," she said. "I woke up in a hurry."

And then started jumping up and down. Sally called her parents, her sister, her old friend, Sue, who tells me, "The first thing she said was, 'Hi! This is your friendly local astronaut.' And that became her greeting whenever she called. She was really on Cloud Nine." Before she knew it, she was also on television and in print, getting her first introduction to the insatiable, often ill-mannered, press. At a hastily called news conference arranged by Stanford ("My gosh, I was a PhD physics student. Press conferences were not a normal part of my day"), Sally faced a phalanx of cameras and an army of inane questions from reporters who had apparently slept through the liberation of the American work force. "Aren't you afraid of being in orbit with all those men?" asked one. "What's the highest you've ever been before?" tried another. No, she said patiently to a third, "I don't expect to run into any UFOs." Photographers crowded into her cluttered office, climbing over astrophysics texts and computer printouts, a pile of faded jogging suits in the corner. Sally, even-tempered as ever, was accommodating. "They wanted me to go out running. So I went out and ran."

Sally was ecstatic, every inch the graduate student-turned-adventurer with her black turtleneck, slim jeans and shiny bangs flopping over her forehead. She understood fully the opportunity she had been handed. "Thirty years from now," she told a reporter, "when they're selling round-trip tickets to Mars, this might not be glamorous, but right now it's your basic once-in-a-lifetime opportunity."

Her parents shared the glory in their own idiosyncratic way. "My father, who hasn't got a scientific bone in his body, never understood what I did as an astrophysicist," Sally said. "Now that I'm an astronaut, his problem is solved!" Her mother spun it differently. With Sally going to space and her sister Bear studying to be a minister at a theological seminary, Joyce Ride said, "One of the two of them is going to heaven!"

```
MAILGRAM SERVICE CENTER          western union Mailgram®        UNITED STATES POSTAL SERVICE
MIDDLETOWN, VA. 22645                                            U.S. MAIL
                                                                 ★★★★★★

    1=127320U016006 01/16/78 ICS WA12139          SFOA
    01501 MLTN VA 01/16/78


▶   MS. SALLY K. RIDE
    PHYSICS DEPT
    STANFORD UNIVERSITY
    STANFORD, CA  94305



    UNCLAS AHX/JSC0117 0161558Z JAN 78
    I CONGRATULATE YOU ON HAVING BEEN SELECTED FOR THE ASTRONAUT
    CANDIDATE PROGRAM.

    THERE WILL BE AN ORIENTATION SESSION AT THE JOHNSON SPACE CENTER
    ON JANUARY 30, 31, AND FEBRUARY 1.  INFORMATION ON TRAVEL ASSOCIATED
    WITH THIS WILL BE PROVIDED SHORTLY.

    YOU ARE SCHEDULED TO REPORT FOR DUTY AT THE JOHNSON SPACE CENTER ON
    JULY 10, 1978.  YOU WILL BE APPOINTED AS A GS=12, SALARY $21,883
    PER ANNUM.  INFORMATION ON YOUR MOVE TO HOUSTON WILL BE PROVIDED
    LATER BY OUR PERSONNEL OFFICE.

    WE ARE LOOKING FORWARD TO SEEING YOU AGAIN IN HOUSTON.  IN THE
    MEANTIME, SHOULD YOU HAVE QUESTIONS, YOU MAY CALL DUANE ROSS AT
    713=483=5067.

    SINCERELY,
    JACK R. LISTER
    PERSONNEL OFFICER
    NASA JSC HOUSTON TX

    (ARS RUCHNVM 1=16=01=012544)
    22118 EST

    MGMCOMP MGM
```

For Bear Ride, the exciting news was both a harbinger of her sister's changed life and a rerun of their childhood roles. Several months later, facing her oral exams before the presbytery—the governing body for her ordination as a minister—she was full of anxiety, "sweating bullets, wanting to be as smart as possible," she tells me. The committee, in her home presbytery, knew her (and her family) well, but Bear was anticipating "weird theological questions" to test her studies over four years. "And I walked in and the chair of the committee said, 'Welcome. We're so glad to see you. Just one question: What's it like to be Sally Ride's sister?" To her credit, Bear finds the episode amusing. "On the one hand,

I was pleased not to have to translate the Hebrew scriptures for them," she says. "On the other hand, it was just so bizarre!" Bear was ordained shortly afterwards. The family dynamic was secure.

The first new astronaut class in nearly ten years—only the eighth since the US committed to human spaceflight—was huge news. NASA had selected fifteen pilots and twenty mission specialists—the largest group yet. But the real headline was the inclusion of six women and four minority men: three African Americans, one Asian American. After nearly two decades and seventy-three white men, the space agency looked like an affirmative action poster, eager to claim bragging rights. "We have selected an outstanding group of men and women who represent the most competent, talented and experienced people available to us today," said a very pleased Administrator Frosch at the official announcement later that day in Washington. Chris Kraft added, "We had no problem finding minorities that were totally competitive." When ABC's Jules Bergman pressed him on why no females had been selected sooner, Kraft said, "It was difficult to choose women because of their lack of qualification. I think that in the last few years, because of the women's movement frankly, women are much more qualified." When asked about the rumor that the list had been trimmed from twenty pilots to fifteen "so that perhaps a woman or more women or ethnic minorities could fulfill that role," Kraft answered firmly, "Negative."

Two weeks later, Sally met the rest of her classmates when they were summoned back to Houston to be presented formally to the public. Thirty-five mostly young, largely ill-at-ease astronauts-to-be were called up to the stage, then introduced by name, military rank (if any), residence and current occupation or school. The men and women alike looked like actors in a high school pageant, dressed in a less-than chic range of plaid pants and three-piece polyester suits. There were lots of sideburns. No one smoked. Sally took her seat in a molded plastic chair, alphabetically, between another female mission specialist named Judy Resnik, and a pilot named Dick Scobee. They would become close friends.

After another round of press interviews, Sally flew back to California to finish her dissertation. Despite (or perhaps because of) her euphoria, she struggled with the friend's computer on which she was writing it, deleting the entire first chapter when she pressed the wrong key. From then on, she kept five copies on a disk. On June 1, 1978, at 3:15 p.m., she defended her work at oral examinations. During a ten-minute break, she was interrupted by a phone call from a reporter who had somehow broken through the protective screen set up by her colleagues in the physics department. Sally explained that she was mid-exam, and that she only had ten minutes. "That's okay," he said, "ten minutes is all I need."

Sally's house was packed up and waiting for NASA's designated movers; her cartons were piled in the living room, along with the boxes of books and clothes that Bill Colson had brought over from his own house. They were still a couple—it had been almost two years now—and he was moving with her, having taken the trouble to secure a research grant at Rice University so they could be together. The rest of the country may have been caught up in more global events—with Jimmy Carter in the White House, John Travolta taking over the role of Doody in *Grease* on Broadway, Proposition 13 starting to cut property taxes in California and the cartoon strip *Garfield* making its first appearance. Sally was focused on her own moment of change. She and Bill loaded their hand luggage into Sally's green VW Rabbit and headed for Houston.

4

THIRTY-FIVE NEW GUYS

JULY 1978–MARCH 1982

The TFNG logo.

I had no idea what to expect. I mean, what do you do when you're an astronaut? Who knows? I don't even remember having specific goals, other than to fly in space!

—Sally Ride

REPORTING FOR DUTY

There wasn't even a spacecraft.

In July 1978, when Sally Ride drove down NASA Road 1 towards the Johnson Space Center in Houston, *Columbia*, the first orbiter, was still moving down the assembly line in Palmdale, California. Sally and her multicultural colleagues were about to train for a program that hadn't gotten off the ground, so they could fly in a spacecraft that still wasn't built, at an agency where testosterone and cigars were still essential gear for the white, male fighter jocks Sally and her classmates idolized.

They were the first generation of astronauts to grow up watching their predecessors on TV. The first to go through school studying space travel as both science fiction and career fact. Many had reaped the benefits of the surge to science after Sputnik; now they were part of it, whatever "it" was going to be. That was part of the thrill: to help model the program that would operate the shuttle that was still taking shape.

Formally, they were the class of 1978, thirty-five would-be space-farers from twenty-six states and twenty-seven different undergraduate institutions holding three MDs, eleven PhDs and infinite dreams of discovery. Twenty-one were military officers, of whom nineteen had served in Vietnam, a war ended only three years earlier. Most of them were the pilots. Sally, who had linked arms with antiwar activists at the Moratorium nearly a decade before, would now risk her life with men who had flown combat missions against the Viet Cong. Richard "Mike" Mullane, an Air Force captain, was unapologetically skeptical of scientists like her: "These were men and women who, until a few weeks ago, had been star-gazing on mountaintop observatories and whose greatest fear had been an A– on a research paper. Their lives were light-years apart from those of the military men of the group. . . . In our work a mistake wasn't noted by a professor in the margin of a thesis, but instead brought instant death."

What they would all learn in the next few years was that preparing for space travel was a great leveler; that just as career soldiers who had spent their lives in uniformed, all-male societies could reenter a world where civilians of both genders were their equals, so too could left-leaning demonstrators learn to accept pilots—not, in the words of Sally's classmate Robert "Hoot" Gibson, as "air pirates and baby killers, but people who had a job to do and did it." It would just take time. As one candidate said during the interview process, when asked how he'd feel about flying with a woman, "I'd fly with little green men if it meant getting a chance in space."

That's the drive I discovered several years later, when I arrived at JSC as a rookie space reporter. Covering NASA was like a trip through a brainy amusement park: on the one hand, an instant education, with layers of brilliant engineers and technicians eager to share their latest gadgetry or theories, to be sure you got the circuitry of the satellite or the composition of the medical kit just right. The gadgets were splendid. On the other hand, if you pushed too hard, or tried to get beyond the hardware to the personalities, they circled the wagons to prevent any hint of uncertainty, or even mortality, from marring the image of its stars. Or cutting their Congressional funding.

The stars themselves—the astronauts—were an equally mixed bag: exceptional human beings in most cases, with the curiosity and concern that make you proud that they are our representatives to worlds beyond. Several became and remain my close friends. Many more were harder to know—enclosed in an airspace that only fellow fliers could penetrate. Sally's class contained examples of them all.

Their first order of business was to bond. Following tradition, they selected a class nickname, a contemporary version of Mercury Seven that would define their newly diverse roles at NASA. They settled on Thirty-five New Guys (gender neutral by agreement), or TFNG, illustrated by a merry rendering of thirty-five space-suited upstarts, floating in, out and around the orbiting shuttle like clowns emerging from a circus car. I always thought TFNG sounded like the name of a rock group, perfectly describing the new age music this gang would make. Then I learned that in military parlance, TFNG is how old hands indelicately put down the greenhorns, as in, "those (freaking) new guys." Either way, NASA's newest employees were ready for their tough new jobs. And that meant learning the lingo.

"The hardest part was reading my schedule!" says Anna Fisher, a physician from California accustomed to medical, not aerospace jargon. On her first day at work, she walked into her office on the third floor of Building 4 "and I looked at the schedule and I looked at Dan [Brandenstein, her TFNG officemate] and I said, 'I don't know what any of that means, do you? I can read the times and I know I'm supposed to be doing something and that's about it!'" Fisher was baffled by the acronyms, an alphabet soup addiction so deeply ingrained, they'd been compiled into a thick little book. I snagged a copy soon after I arrived and did a little feature on my favorites. But it wasn't just civilian astronauts and reporters who were clueless.

"I remember a guy who stood up in the front of the class and talked completely in acronyms," recalled another rookie, a test pilot. "Prepositions and verbs were the only words I understood. Even NASA's an acronym."

As were they. Officially, Sally was an astronaut-*candidate*, or AsCan, facing two years of training before being promoted to full-fledged astronaut. That title was held by "the old guys," as the twenty-seven active astronauts from previous selections were affectionately known. Some, like moonwalker John Young, had flown already—in Young's case, on both Gemini and Apollo. Others had been waiting more than twelve years to fly in space and eyed the newbies warily, unwilling to be elbowed out of line by relative youngsters, most of whom didn't even look like them. But most of the "grizzled veterans," another term of relative endearment, welcomed the rookies, grateful for the new brain- and pilot-power to get the shuttle up and running. They would also help instruct the new guys in the ways of NASA, in their new home.

The Johnson Space Center lies some forty-five minutes south of Houston, a 1,600-acre campus of low, boxy buildings identified only by numbers, which author Norman Mailer described as "a number of white cartons set out at occasional right angles on a warehouse floor." Rocket engine parts, real and recreated, are laid out like a giant's lawn ornaments. Cattle once grazed on the flat fields here, amidst miserable humidity. Today, rocket scientists and robot engineers create the next generation of space systems in the high-tech industrial park here, amidst miserable humidity. And the cattle are back—a small herd of Longhorns like the originals, providing a bovine link to the past. Outdoors, it's like living in a Laundromat. Indoors, it's like an icebox, thanks to overcompensating air conditioners. You don't go to JSC for the climate, particularly not in July, which is when Sally arrived from California.

"Hot!" was her terse summation.

She didn't need to look further than JSC's name to understand why Texas was the site of what used to be called the Manned Spacecraft Center. Lyndon Johnson had died in 1973, but his fierce support of the US program kept the dollars flowing when it counted. To accommodate the original Mercury astronauts and the influx of engineers and technicians and managers, developers carved instant suburbs from the Texas scrub, a thriving community of single-family houses and garden apartments on quiet, winding streets named Saturn Lane and Gemini Avenue. Tour buses once showed sightseers where the astronauts lived, back when hotshot fliers, according to legend, traded in their Corvettes if the ashtrays overflowed. Now the new guys were moving in. It was even affordable on Sally's new GS-12 salary—$21,883 per year, five times what she'd earned as a grad student moonlighting as a TA. Sight unseen, she'd signed the lease on a two-bedroom unit in the area called Nassau Bay. Unfortunately, it sat directly on top of the building's laundry room, making things even warmer. But she settled in with Bill, the only astronaut live-in with spousal status. And while NASA had no objection to their relationship, Sally said. "My grandmother probably does."

They put a mattress on the floor and topped off the furniture they'd shipped down with a redwood bookcase purchased en route. From

Stanford, Sally and Bill had detoured north to hike amidst the titanic trees in Muir Woods, then picked out the shelves "to take a piece of California with us," Colson recalls. "We were going to a place we didn't know and Sally said something like, we were going to be hanging out with people with crew cuts and flattops. It was very different from being a graduate student."

Her days now started before eight and often ended long after dark, with lectures on scientific subjects (oceanography, material science, geology, among others) and on the structure and systems of the shuttle (avionics, how fuel cells work, how engines work). There were field trips to other space centers and to various contractors to see payloads or parts of the spacecraft in progress. They trained "more than forty hours a week but less than twenty-four hours a day," in the coy explanation from the fellow who put all those acronyms onto the AsCans's weekly schedules, plotted with bright squares of color on a big bulletin board. "Before the candidates arrived, we spent nearly two years developing a new program that touches on everything from what makes the shuttle tick to how they should make public appearances." The object was to level the knowledge field, to bring everyone up to speed in all disciplines. Both mission specialists and pilots attended everything. "We took aerodynamic classes, which [the pilots] slept through," Sally said, "and they took science classes, which we slept through." Or escaped.

One engineer recalls attending a weeklong aerodynamics course on Advanced Stability and Control, to sharpen his understanding of the shuttle's landing profile. "Just before the start of the class," he recalls, "Sally walked in and sat down in the back row. Okay, that's cool; there's an AsCan in the class. Then the class starts and, rather than being 'Advanced' Stability and Control, it's Stability and Control 101, the same course every undergraduate aeronautical engineering student has to take as a freshman. After a couple hours of this, the class was getting pretty restless, but NASA employees have it drilled into them that, if you sign up for a course, you have to attend as long as you are still breathing because NASA paid good money for that course. So we all sat there for the full five days, even though most of us felt we weren't getting anything out of it. Except Sally. Shortly before lunch of the first day, Sally stood up, picked up her books and quietly departed, never to return. Our take-away from that was that (1) It's good to be an astronaut (which we already knew) and (2) Sally Ride doesn't like having her time wasted."

"She was so young when she came to NASA, but she was already stubborn," says Carolyn Huntoon. "She was always very well mannered, although when she didn't want to do something, you weren't going to push her around."

No one took attendance; no one was graded. But every TFNG knew there was only one test: your first flight. And the only grade that counted was getting named to a crew for that flight. Sally downplayed the anxiety some years later, recounting her years of training this way: "I got in line for my turn to fly in space."

FLYING

Suddenly, she was flying, in the sleek jet trainers called T-38s used by astronauts as their taxis. Sally wouldn't be piloting the space shuttle—no mission specialist would—but she was expected to spend fifteen hours a month aloft in the backseat of a T-38, to learn how to coordinate as a flight crew, how to use navigation equipment and communications procedures, and to get conditioned to high-performance flight. Or, as Sally put it, "getting your stomach turned around and your ears jumbled up."

Before, she had flown only in big commercial airliners. Now she was blissfully climbing the ladder into the iPod-white, needle-nosed jets, parachute slung over her shoulder, fastening her helmet, hooking up the oxygen mask and snapping her four seat belts to slide through the skies supersonically. "Only when I pulled the canopy down and heard it click shut did I get a little apprehensive," Sally confided about her first time in a T-38. "I thought, 'My God, I can't get this off,' but then the pilot said, 'All set?' and I said, 'Sure,' and off we went. Since that first flight I've never been scared."

Gut-churning rolls over the Gulf of Mexico and steep-angled approaches to Ellington Air Force Base were catnip to the former Disneyland ace. In a surprisingly short time, she was handling the controls herself.

"She was the best student I ever had," says fellow AsCan Jon McBride, a Navy test pilot who, like many military colleagues, taught Sally and other first-timers to fly. NASA saved millions of dollars by keeping the training in house, rather than sending non-pilots to Air Force school. It also helped pilots maintain their proficiency. Whether it was off to lunch in El Paso, or dinner in San Diego, Sally got a first-class education, zipping along at 300 to 600 miles an hour, 39,000 feet high (higher than she'd ever flown as a passenger), with the joystick under her command. "She amazed me!" McBride tells me, recalling the time he put her "under the bag"—meaning all of her windows were blacked out—and she maintained total instrument control.

Officially, mission specialists weren't allowed to fly the plane below 5,000 feet in those days—too dangerous, with too much to coordinate in the face of too many distractions. But some of the TFNG pilots either didn't know, or ignored the rules. "Sally could land a T-38 from the backseat as well as I could," says her shuttle-mate, Air Force instructor pilot John Fabian. "She had a feel for the plane." Marine pilot Norm Thagard, who also launched with Sally, says, "She just flew a good airplane. I had my hands close by to the stick, but I didn't touch it."

Rick Hauck, who flew combat missions for the Navy and commanded two shuttle flights, so trusted Sally's ability, he stood by on a trip to Seattle as she did a touch-and-go landing (where you bring the plane down and then take off without stopping) of a Boeing 747 prototype that was empty except for the flight crew. "We were all standing in the cockpit," he recalls. And when the Boeing crew found out that Sally wasn't exactly an experienced jet pilot, "the chief test pilot almost fainted. I've always thought it was partly a testimony to the good flying quality of the plane."

Sally got so hooked on flying, she took private pilot lessons and got her license. Then she bought a part-interest in a small Grumman Tiger owned by another astronaut, which she often took up by herself on weekends.

In her steel-toed boots and bright blue flight suit with pockets that zipped to eternity, Sally found the jet version of her hometown joy rides. "It's the same feeling that I used to get driving a car with the windows down on Mulholland Drive in Los Angeles," she told me. "You know, being a little bit above everything, being able to see a lot, having the wind blow in your face."

And she, like the other women, measured up. "We passed the tests," Sally said. "We didn't get sick."

Mission specialists needed to know how to fly in case something happened to the pilot or the plane. Early into her training, Sally copied down an ominous set of instructions called "Non-Pilot M[ission] S[pecialist] Procedure for Incapacitated Pilot." Among the bullet points: how to turn on intercom, how to communicate MAYDAY, how to eject: "If possible, select an area and aircraft course that will allow ejection over a relatively unpopulated land area with later aircraft impact in the water or other unpopulated area."

That terrifying possibility was rehearsed in the shark- and mosquito-infested waters off Miami, Florida. For three days in July, all the non-military AsCans reported to Homestead Air Force Base for Water Survival Training, jumping into the bay from a fifteen-foot tower and being towed through the waves while tethered to a parachute harness, or parasailing from the deck of a landing craft then plunging into the water wearing full survival gear. They also were set adrift on one-person life rafts, with a fishing line. Sally later joked about finding herself bedraggled, her hair dripping, and asking, "If I'm supposed to be smart, what am I doing here?" She actually enjoyed the parasailing, but was less pleased when a photographer focused on her being hoisted by a helicopter and asked for "a happy look." Or when a reporter asked her to cite the high point of her day. "Four hundred feet," she said.

PFC Dale Ride. He never talked about his World War II service with the Seventh Army in France and Germany, but was riveted to the TV show *Combat!*, which he watched regularly with his daughters.

Joyce and Dale Ride, wedding day, January 29, 1949.

Sally, age one, 1952.

Proud papa with Sally (*left*) and baby Bear, probably 1954.

Family portrait: Sally (*left*), Dale, Bear, Joyce, probably 1955.

LEFT: Bear (*left*) and Sally in the Norwegian sweaters of their heritage, probably 1956.

BELOW: Sally (*left*) and Bear in even itchier Norwegian outfits at the church of their English ancestors, 1961.

Sally in junior high school, the same age as the girls her company would later target.

Tsigane, the family collie. Sally kept a similar photo in her wallet for so many years, its edges were frayed.

Sally (*stretched out in foreground*) with the select group of Westlake classmates
privileged to study at UCLA during their senior year.

With high school best friend Sue Okie (*left*)
at Yosemite, 1969.

Sally ("The Thinker") from her Westlake
senior yearbook, 1968.

13

Bear (*left*), Alice Marble, and Sally, at Deauville Country Club in Tarzana, 1961. Even at age ten, Sally kept her distance from the coach she never liked.

14

Swarthmore tennis champ, 1969.

15

The famous match: Dick Peters (*left*), Billie Jean King (fresh from winning Wimbledon), Sally (age twenty-one) and Dennis Van der Meer, at TennisAmerica, Lake Tahoe, 1972. Ball boy at far left is Martin Luther King III.

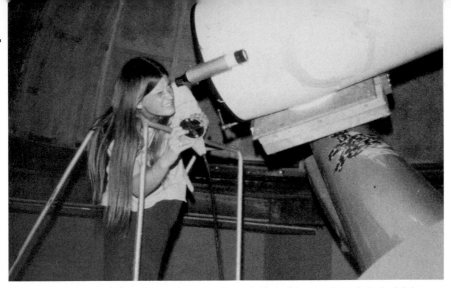

At Stanford, 1970s. As the teaching assistant, Sally had her students help build the mount for the telescope at the Stanford Observatory.

With Molly Tyson (*left*), 1973. "We just wanted to spend time together," Molly says.

Passing by The Dish in the Stanford foothills after her selection as an astronaut candidate, 1978. "They wanted me to go out running," she said of the media, "so I went out and ran."

19

With her parents on graduation day at Stanford: June 1973.

20

21

With Bill Colson, Stanford physics lab, 1978.

Celebrating the announcement in her Stanford office, 1978.

22

Two sisters, two professions, 1978. Bear (*right*) became a minister several months after Sally was accepted by NASA. One of them, joked their mother, would get to heaven.

NASA's first six women selected as astronaut candidates (*left to right*): Sally, Shannon Lucid, Kathy Sullivan, Rhea Seddon, Anna Fisher, Judy Resnik, during a break from water survival training, Homestead Air Force Base, Florida, 1978.

LEFT: After Sally's turn at the end of a tow line in the Florida waters in 1978, she joked, "If I'm supposed to be smart, what am I doing here?"

BELOW: Sally's parachute being towed through the air by a pickup truck during training at Vance Air Force Base, Oklahoma, 1978.

Logging her flying time on a T-38—fifteen hours a month—
Ellington Air Force Base, Houston, 1982.

Poised for takeoff in the back seat of a T-38 (Bob Crippen was up front)
departing from Houston for Florida, June 16, 1983.

The Solar Eclipse team (*left to right*): Hoot Gibson, Dick Scobee, Pinky Nelson, Steve Hawley, Sally, Mike Coats, Malmstrom Air Force Base, Great Falls, Montana, February 1979. At the time, Sally was dating Hoot.

Somewhere over Montana in the shadow of the eclipse, 1979.

With her husband, Steve Hawley, at Kennedy Space Center, Florida, August 26, 1984, four days before Steve's first flight (STS-41D).

31   Rehearsing for her stint as CapCom for STS-2 at Mission Control, Houston.
     Astronaut James Buchli is to Sally's right, July 1981.

32

My interview with Sally before her first flight, Johnson Space Center, Houston, May
1983. "I do feel that there's some pressure for me not to mess up," she told me.

Mission patch for STS-7. Notice the 7, a preview of the real thing. And the biological symbol for woman, another NASA first.

Crew walkout with John Fabian and Norm Thagard, just after 5 a.m., June 18, 1983. George Abbey, who accompanied every crew to the pad, is directly behind them.

Liftoff, STS-7, 7:33 a.m., June 18, 1983. "That was definitely an E ticket," Sally told ground controllers in Houston.

ABOVE: Another perspective from astronaut John Young in the Shuttle Training Aircraft. Florida's Atlantic coastline is visible in the background. Eight minutes later, the crew would be in orbit.

LEFT: Dale Ride, watching his firstborn leave Earth and enter the history books.

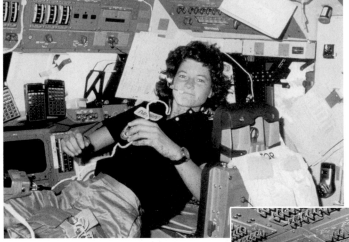

On *Challenger's* flight deck, hovering over the cockpit seats, June 25, 1983. "My favorite thing about space was being weightless," Sally said.

Communicating with ground controllers, flight day four, June 21, 1983.

Self-portrait of the largest shuttle crew to date (*left to right*): Norm Thagard, Bob Crippen, Rick Hauck, Sally, John Fabian, June 21, 1983. Crip said approvingly that they were known as "Sally Ride and the others."

41 The world's first view of the shuttle while orbiting, June 22, 1983. Sally and John
Fabian worked hard to configure the arm for this iconic image of *Challenger* from
the SPAS satellite.

42 *Challenger* lands at Edwards Air Force Base, June 24, 1983. In a phone call to the crew,
President Reagan told Sally, "Somebody said that 'sometimes the best man for a job
was a woman.' . . . You were there because you were the best person for the job."

With two of her heroes: Billie Jean King (*left*) and Gloria Steinem at a postflight reception in New York hosted by Girls Club of America, August 1983.

With Grundgetta of *Sesame Street* after Sally taped an appearance on the TV show in New York, January 1984. "A," Sally tells young viewers. "Astronaut."

Sally (*left*) signing her autograph at the secret meeting with Svetlana Savitskaya (*second from right*). Tamas Gombosi, translator and arranger, is at far right. Hungarian cosmonaut Bertalan Farkas sits next to Sally at his apartment in Budapest, October 1983.

Kathy Sullivan (*left*) and Sally became the first two women to fly in space together, during STS-41G in October 1984. The floating springs, clips, clamps and bungee cord belong to one of the shuttle's sleeping restraints.

Inauguration, Astronaut Hall of Fame, Kennedy Space Center, June 2003. Sally joins NASA legends (*left to right*) John Glenn, Gordon Cooper, Jim Lovell, Buzz Aldrin, Walt Cunningham and Bob Crippen (*at podium*).

Examining a cross section of the solid rocket booster material with Secretary of State William P. Rogers, chairman of the presidential commission investigating the space shuttle *Challenger* accident, at hearings in Washington, DC, February 11, 1986.

Behind the scenes at the Columbia Accident Investigation Board (CAIB), March 2003, with NASA liaison officer Frank Buzzard (*left*) and CAIB chair Hal Gehman. "Sally wanted something from NASA and Frank and I were working out how to satisfy her inquiry," Gehman recalls. "And Sally was leaning over my shoulder to make sure I got it right." An image of the lost crew hangs on the wall.

Meeting the emir of Bahrain at a White House State Dinner with President and Mrs. Reagan, July 19, 1983. Sally and Crip brought the president some of his jelly beans that had flown with them on the shuttle.

Greeting President Obama at the White House, prior to launch of the "Educate to Innovate" Campaign for Excellence in Science, Technology, Engineering & Math, November 23, 2009. Craig Barrett stands to Sally's left, along with former Sesame Workshop CEO Gary Knell.

CEO, Sally Ride Science, La Jolla, 2010.

Surrounded by fans at an
SRS Festival, 2006.

Delivering the SRS Festival keynote at NASA's Ames Research Center in California's Silicon Valley, September 2007.

On July 22, 2003, during a twenty-fifth anniversary celebration of Sally's first flight, at Goddard Space Flight Center in Maryland, third grader Grace Powers read her book report on Sally to rousing cheers.

Tam O'Shaughnessy answering questions at the Smithsonian National Air and Space Museum, May 17, 2013, during a panel preceding the national tribute to Sally in Washington, DC. "She really cared," she told the audience, "about taking care of our air, our oceans, our world."

The astronauts found the press particularly pesky that week; the appeal of six women getting soaked to the skin brought out the worst in them. One television reporter yelled "Hey, Miss," to Rhea Seddon, who glared back and retorted, "It's 'Doctor.'"

THE WOMEN

The crowd-pleasing novelty of female astronauts was reflected in a headline from the *Los Angeles Times*:

> SIX WOMEN ASTRONAUTS BEGIN TRAINING
> NEW GROUP INCLUDES BLACKS, ORIENTAL.

Putting aside the ethnic reference to Ellison Onizuka, a US Air Force captain of Japanese descent from Hawaii (it was 1978), the headline managed to erase twenty-five astronauts from the program. Which is precisely how the press treated them, starting the day they were first announced back in January. "I could have mooned the press corps and I would not have been noticed," writes Mike Mullane. "The white TFNG males were invisible."

AsCan Kathy Sullivan articulated the moment that many remember as producing "ten interesting people and twenty-five standard white guys." After the press conference introducing them, "the twenty-five standard white guys were done [in] about 4.3 seconds," she says, "and had the whole rest of the day free. . . . The other ten of us, we were there . . . way late." Being interviewed. Being photographed. Being asked—women only—about their goals, their beaux, their bodies.

For women in the rest of America, it was a heady time. The republic had survived a number of feminist incursions into its institutions: the integration of Harvard, Yale and Princeton (1969), the first female elected governor without succeeding her spouse (Ella Grasso, Connecticut, 1974), the first woman to drive in the Indianapolis 500 (Janet

Guthrie, 1977), whose pre-Indy breakthrough had inspired the race announcer to declare, "Janet and Gentlemen, start your engines!" That same year, Joanie Caucus of the *Doonesbury* comic strip got her fictional law degree, as did growing numbers of real women. And at the National Women's Conference in Houston, with only three states needed to ratify the Equal Rights Amendment, Liz Carpenter, who had also served as press secretary to Lady Bird Johnson, declared, "If I die, don't send flowers. Just send three more states."

As barriers fell, Americans of both genders grew more comfortable with what the *Washington Post* once called, "the ultra-radical notion that women are human beings." To many in the media, however, a female astronaut remained in that special category reserved by Samuel Johnson for a female minister in the eighteenth century. A woman preaching, he said, is like a dog walking on its hind legs. One is not surprised that it is done well, but that it is "done at all."

Rhapsodic stories depicting six smart women navigating "a man's world" ran in publications from *Paris Match* to *My Weekly Reader*. They were an exceptionally talented group, but each of the six was quickly codified into a caricature that would follow her through her career:

Anna Fisher, twenty-nine, the petite, porcelain-skinned surgeon who wanted to be an astronaut since she was twelve; known as the "skinny brain" in high school; beat out her husband to get the job. *Redbook* magazine would put her on their cover and feature her in several additional articles.

Shannon Lucid, thirty-five, the oldest and tallest (5'11") of the women, and the only one with children (three boys, aged two to nine), whose husband had followed her to Houston; born in Shanghai to missionary parents, educated (biochemistry) and residing in Oklahoma, passionate about planes and spaceflight since childhood.

Judy Resnik, twenty-nine, electrical engineer from Akron, Ohio, invariably described as a raven-haired beauty with a quick tongue; "I was not one of the 'in crowd,'" she said of her high school years. "I was one of the smart ones. It was hard to be both."

Margaret "Rhea" [pronounced Ray] Seddon, thirty, self-described "girly girl" from Murfreesboro, Tennessee, "a tomboy who could crochet," with a blonde, shoulder-length halo and a silver Corvette. As the only female surgical intern at a Memphis hospital, she was denied entry in the doctors' lounge, so relaxed between operations on a chair in the nurses' restroom instead.

Kathy Sullivan, twenty-six, geologist and oceanographer from California (who discovered that she and Sally had attended grammar school together one year), gravitated towards Earth science because "those folks were outdoors all the time and had much cooler adventures"; sturdy athlete at 5'6"; got addicted to flying from her father.

Like Sally, who would forever be shorthanded as the tennis-playing astrophysicist, each of the six had carved out a nontraditional career in a world of often limited expectations. They were, in the words of one of the interviewing psychiatrists, "their own persons, people who have decided for themselves what they wanted to do and have listened less to what others might think."

But in a world still hung up on 1950s notions of femininity, blocking out the static was suddenly less of an option.

"Everyone was watching them," says Carolyn Huntoon, referring not only to the public, but to the scrutiny of the bosses and the worker bees at NASA. "And they all knew that." Huntoon, a biochemist in middle management, was asked to step in as the unofficial den mother for the six women, responsible for everything from hairdryers in the gym to wise and reliable counsel for the sociological venture that no one could have been prepared for. "She made our lives much, much easier," Sally said. "[S]he's one of the very few people that I think I owe my career to."

Huntoon banished bigotry with finesse. "One astronaut told me that he didn't have any problem with the women in the class, but his wife did," she tells me. "I turned to him and said, 'That's *your* problem, not NASA's problem.' " Another time, one of the male engineers (they were almost all male) said "one of the women astronauts had talked to him, questioning what he'd said, and he said, 'I've never heard anything like that before!' And I said, 'Oh yeah? How about the guys, the astronauts, don't they talk to you that way?' Initially, it was hard for them to deal with women who were smart, who had the courage to speak out, to ask difficult questions."

Sally told a reporter, "None of these men had ever been to a meeting where there was a woman who did something other than take notes." It was, she said, understandable. "Out of roughly four thousand technical employees at the Johnson Space Center," she said, "I think there were only four women. So that gives you a sense of how male the culture was. When we arrived, we more than doubled the number of women with PhDs at the center."

At early conferences, someone invariably complained, "There's no one from the Astronaut Office here," looking right through the female AsCan in the room. Kathy Sullivan recalls the curt dismissal she felt at Mojave Airport in California, after a day of flying in T-38s. When they landed on the desert strip and started walking out on the ramp, her colleague, one of the male astronaut pilots, spotted legendary airman Chuck Yeager and shouted out, "Hello! I want to introduce you to Kathy Sullivan. She's flying chase." Sullivan tells me what happened next. "Yeager paused midstride, looked back over his shoulder with quite a sneering look on his face and said, 'Riding, maybe. Ain't flying.' And stalked off!"

Carolyn Huntoon understood the problem. "As soon as the more mature individuals began to depart, things got better." Some at NASA learned on the job. Alan Bean, who walked on the Moon in 1969 and then oversaw the TFNG's early training, dropped his distrust when he heard one of the women lecture on the shuttle's protective tile system. "She knows more about heat shields than I do," he acknowledged. "It's not a male thing."

But the key may have been the women themselves. "There was a real nervousness about having them there," says historian Margaret Weitekamp. To combat it, "I believe those women in the 1978 class came in with the explicit attitude that there's not a problem unless we say there's a problem, and we're not going to say there's a problem. A lot of these astronauts made things work for themselves because they were the people who were invested in making it work."

That was certainly true of Sally, whose ingrained optimism led her to believe—pretty accurately, as it turns out—that she could succeed wherever she chose. And if she couldn't, she moved on to the next square. Now she had five colleagues to help hurdle any obstacles, safety in numbers, thanks to NASA's wisdom in selecting more than one woman for that first class.

Not that they made a pact or shared deep secrets. In fact, the six original female astronauts had little in common beyond their passion to fly, their will to succeed and their distrust of the press. They were friends, not bosom buddies; allies, not blood sisters. But they came together unhesitatingly on issues of common concern, from big questions of policy supervised by Huntoon, to smaller, trivial ones they could solve themselves. Early on, Sally and Anna Fisher slipped off to the mall to buy some khakis and plaid shirts, "the kind the guys wore around the office," Fisher tells me. "We wanted to blend in with everybody and have our technical expertise speak for itself." I ask if they also bought short sleeve shirts and pocket protectors. "Oh no! We didn't want to blend in that much!"

It was a rivalry—a friendly rivalry. Only by working as a team would they fly the shuttle successfully. But once the shuttle started flying, only one crew would go at a time—two to five people at most. Of the six women, only one would be first. The problem was, no one had a clue how to be that person.

"There had been the first man on the Moon, the first man in space, the first man to orbit the Earth—there's going to be a first American woman in space," Bill Colson remembers thinking, "and that person is going to be in the same ballpark. And that's a big deal. Everybody knew that from day one." I ask if Sally was drooling for it. "No. Inside she might have been. But it wasn't something I could see." He says they did discuss other candidates. "There were people who would fall asleep in meetings and we'd check that box and say, 'Okay, that person is not going to go.' And Sally would tell me about little things at the office, like, 'This person will be better in public than someone else.' It was very apparent that NASA was realizing their budget hinged a surprising amount on the success of the astronauts and how they presented to the world and to the United States. So they were really paying attention to that."

Bill and Sally narrowed the field—in their own minds—to three: Sally, Anna and Judy. Which is pretty much how everyone else I spoke to saw it. "And she never said anything nasty about anyone, we just talked about it. And she was doing well, so we could kind of say that she possibly had a really famous future."

They weren't alone.

"We would all get caught up in it now and then and worry and obsess about it," recalls Kathy Sullivan. "There clearly was some kind of a horse race or beauty contest." She came up with her own shorthand guide to how the female typecasting in the media and elsewhere might factor into the minds of those picking the woman to fly first: "blonde surgeon" (Rhea), "flirtatious single gal" (Judy), "Photogenic . . . married gal" (Anna), "slender" (Sally), "taller, stockier . . . married" (Shannon), "not a cover girl type" (herself).

"The agency," Sullivan said, "was eventually going to have to pick one of us."

The "agency," in the minds of many of the astronauts, was a euphemism for George Abbey, the sphinxlike director of Flight Operations (later, director of Flight Crew Operations) who chaired the committee that chose the Thirty-five New Guys (and four subsequent classes) in the first place. He was also known to control crew selection, although John Young claimed that responsibility, too. "I guess you could say, John felt he picked them and I felt that I picked them," Abbey tells me, sharing the Astroturf for the record. Technically, Young's office was the origin of such decisions, and he was certainly included in all discussions, but most of the astronauts understood that the real power belonged to the man they usually called Mr. Abbey. Sally did a fine impression of him. She'd lower her eyelids, mumble "rrrrrr" deep and low, then ask for a beer. She didn't try to mimic his silver buzz cut or sturdy torso. "We had absolutely no idea what his thought process was," she would later confess. "And the more time you spent trying to figure that out, the less you really understood it." A veteran of an earlier class says, admiringly, that Abbey was "the epitome of eccentricity and inscrutability. There were astronauts chosen because they were very good second basemen, or because they could play a wicked trombone. I am not making this up." Another astronaut calls him "more like a chess player than a checkers player. He thinks many moves, and years, ahead."

Abbey was the guy who emphasized the need for team players at NASA, including the one playing softball on Monday nights. I saw astronauts break every date they had when Abbey summoned them to the softball field. Or to the annual Flight Operations Directorate Chili Cook-off he organized. "There was a lot of jockeying for position," a member of a later class tells me, "trying to figure out how they decide. Some people were better at sucking up to George than at being an astronaut. If he didn't like you, you were marginalized." Abbey's mythic status as the man responsible for astronaut careers was whimsically acknowledged during the fifth space shuttle mission, when a photograph of the powerful one was carried into orbit and taped to the middeck lockers. A NASA camera recorded the tribute for the world.

The enigma of crew selection would also provide a rare moment of humor during the somber hearings investigating the 1986 *Challenger* explosion. Henry Hartsfield, a widely respected pilot of one shuttle flight and commander of two, was asked, "How is the decision made as to which astronaut should fly on a particular launch?" His answer set off knowing laughter: "A lot of us wish we knew that."

George Abbey, a graduate of the Naval Academy who became an Air Force pilot (and whose own application to be an astronaut was blocked by the Air Force selection board because he hadn't gone to test pilot school), seemed to populate the early shuttle flights with more Navy than Air Force guys. That wouldn't help Sally. But she shared the view of a colleague who says of Abbey, "I'm very proud of his work. Out of all the flights, the incidents where astronauts screwed up was minuscule."

Sally kept her head down and worked hard, well aware that brains and dedication had distinguished more previous astronauts than double plays at home plate. Just in case, she kept her baseball glove oiled.

FLYING THE ARM

Sally's first real project was a plum. She was assigned to the shuttle's Canadian-built, robot "arm"—the $100 million flying crane called the Remote Manipulator System (RMS) that would be used to lift satellites into orbit and retrieve them from the sky. And any number of other tasks. Along with the astronaut team already in place, she helped verify that the simulators in Houston accurately modeled the real arm, regularly traveling to the original simulator in Toronto to help develop procedures for using the arm in orbit. With its articulated joints at the "shoulder," "elbow" and "wrist," and almost as much dexterity as a human arm, the 50-foot-long, 900-pound artificial limb was a critical part of the shuttle's future. But, Sally understood, "until you actually start using something, it's very difficult to make predictions on how well it's going to work . . . How do you know exactly that you're lifting a satellite cleanly out of the payload bay and not bumping it into the structure? . . . What limits should be put on the use of the arm to make sure that it's kept well within its design constraints?" With tiny, neat printing on graph paper in green marbleized composition books, Sally recorded page after page of notes, most impossible to understand without an engineering degree, like "an op amp failure in the demodulator" and an "OSOP review mtg," just for example. Within a year, Sally would run the RMS office.

"She would do the simulation over and over again," explains Jim Middleton, the chief engineer on the Canadarm program who worked with Sally during her trips to Toronto for nearly five years. "We'd say, 'Sally, do you want to take a rest?' And she'd say, 'No, I will continue to do this until I get it done.'" From eight thirty in the morning until nine at night, Sally stayed at the controls, communicating with Middleton by headphone as she worked the problem, throwing switches and maneuvering two hand controllers—rotating one while moving the other up or down, left or right, in or out—to put the arm through its paces. I tried it myself recently—the simulator version in Houston—and discovered the fine coordination needed to monitor all the movements through a series of screens and two sets of windows—one at eye level, one overhead—as well as some instruments. As astronaut Bob Crippen, who also trained on the arm, put it, "You have to integrate all that in your head to maneuver the arm correctly." They call it "flying the arm," because you make it move the way you pilot a plane. "It's a skill that you wouldn't find normally," Middleton says, "the ability to do the same thing over and over again and repeat it exactly—like a race car driver doing laps, hold the exact time within hundredths of a second. Sally loved perfection. She wanted things to be right."

Astronaut John Fabian, who worked on the arm with Sally, likened it to a video game. He says her experience as a tennis player clearly made a difference. "She had excellent reflexes, and was used to being in a high pressure dynamic situation. I think she devoured every moment of it."

"I remember her coming home from practicing with the robot arm," Bill Colson says. "And she observed with fascination that she was really good at it." He says she liked that "she was now 'competing' with pilots who are known for their hand-eye coordination, and she was actually doing better than those guys, and it was kind of surprising."

Sally's work with the arm would play an important role in her NASA career. But it was only part of the picture.

To simulate weightlessness, she trained underwater, in scuba gear. Only NASA could turn a swimming pool into an acronym—the Water Environment Training Facility, or WETF (pronounced WET-eff).

For a more realistic experience, Sally and the TFNGs flew in the

KC-135 cargo plane known by everyone as "the Vomit Comet," for its stomach-dropping, parabolic loops. She learned, in the plane's thirty-second falls, how not to maneuver. "Your first instinct is to try to swim, but you can't!" Sally said. "You just hang there and flail." Far better, she learned, was to push off the sides. "She'd come home exhausted," Bill Colson remembers, "but she didn't get airsick. She thought being weightless was nice."

Back on Earth, she dove into training manuals, familiarized herself with the 1,800 switches and circuit breakers on the orbiter's control panel, traveled to colleges and other educational centers to wave the flag for NASA. The new dresses in Sally's closet reflected the number of speeches she had to make. And despite her good intentions to keep up with her astrophysics studies, she found herself writing fewer and fewer papers. "I haven't been doing as much research as I would like to, because I'm so fascinated by the astronaut program!" she said. The intensity was incessant. Rhea Seddon said it was "like a year of drinking through a fire hose."

It was also their idea of fun.

HAPPY HOURS, HAPPY DAYS

Friday nights meant Happy Hour at the Outpost Bar. Some of the married astronauts hosted regular parties at home, with a keg of beer bought from retired astronaut Alan Shepard's Coors' distributorship. When Sally found out that Joseph Coors had opposed the Equal Rights Amendment, she stopped drinking the beer. But she went to the parties. Sally and Bill had couples over from time to time, but saw them more often on the volleyball court, where Bill had brought his impressive skill to form an astronauts' team. Sally was also running about twenty to thirty miles a week, mostly out the back gate of the space center, then winding along its northern perimeter. And some nights, just for fun, she would join the other flight-crazed astronauts driving their cars along a quiet road in perfect T-38 flight formation.

They were redefining the macho moxie for a new age. Sally already had the unruffled manner, the steely poise. The Ride restraint meshed perfectly with the stoic NASA ethic, and the little girl who loved to ride the Matterhorn at Disneyland belonged on a rocket. Acquiring the finishing touches seemed to come naturally. Facts were data points, ideas were bullet points, paragraphs were checklists, words were minimal, feelings unmentioned. Molly Tyson, with whom Sally had resurrected a friendship—just a friendship, for a few more years—and who was working on a project in Houston, says, Sally "knew what to do to fit in. She understood how to read an environment, understood what it took to be first." Her appearance had changed, Tyson says. Her old friend was suddenly wearing aviator shades and a leather jacket, classic symbols of laconic bravery.

Sally had also learned that danger was never acknowledged by astronauts. For outsiders like me, it was a tricky concept, and sometimes I forgot the rules. Like the time I was on the air with moonwalker Gene Cernan during one of our ABC News broadcasts. As we counted down to the potentially dodgy first nighttime shuttle launch, I slipped and uttered the word *fear*. Cernan was only half teasing when he corrected me, saying, "Astronauts are never frightened, Lynn. A little apprehensive at times, but never frightened."

The sentiment was usually masked with a favorite NASA word— "interesting," as in "That landing was interesting" (when they'd nearly crashed), or "That was an interesting day" (after their spacecraft was stuck by lightning thirty-six seconds after liftoff). "Interesting" also functioned as an all-purpose descriptive. I teased Sally—apparently more effectively than I'd realized—about picking up the *patois*. In an audio diary that she recorded after her flight, she described a bizarre (and very formal) meeting about peaceful uses of Space in Belgrade, in the former Yugoslavia (which had no space program) with some very uptight Iron Curtain comrades, as "a very, very [pause, chuckle] *interesting* meeting." She then added, with another laugh, "As Lynn says, I use that word when I don't know how to describe something!" Listening in nearly thirty years later, I was amused that my point had been taken.

But the language merely reflected their mind-set.

"We all picked it up," explains Marsha Ivins, who worked with NASA for many years before joining the third group of shuttle astronauts in 1984. "It helps you deal with stuff when it *is* a big deal. You just sort of say, 'We're not going to get excited about anything,' and there are plenty of times when you're well served by it. When things start coming apart, you have to be cool. That's just an operations mode." Ellen Baker, a flight surgeon who also became a member of the astronaut class of 1984, says, "It's an important personal quality, to be able to maintain rational, logical thought in the face of off-nominal, potential dangerous situations or environments. You don't want to be distracted by fear and anxiety when you have a job to do. You have to be able to be a clear thinker and compartmentalize well enough to do your job without being scared."

For Sally, compartmentalizing was second nature. Cool was how she had learned to function on the tennis court. Some of the other qualities that had served her since childhood simply needed honing. Susan Okie calls it the "detached control" that got her through high stress situations, "the characteristic psychic camouflage that has always made her an elusive character."

It may also have been a reaction to the prying eyes of the press. In the code of the corps, questions about attitudes and ideas were not welcome; you never knew how the information might be used. Just as doctors might find a medical condition that kept you from flying, so could journalists print an off-the-cuff comment that sent you to the bottom of the list.

"NASA believes that the organization—and especially the astronauts—must always appear in a positive light to the American public and to Congress," writes Dr. Patricia Santy, a psychiatrist who served as a NASA flight surgeon for Sally and other women from 1984 to 1991. Management, she says, believes "that openness about any problems—particularly emotional or behavioral ones—will erode their public support. Anything considered to be potentially 'damaging' to the agency must be carefully controlled or minimized to circumvent the possibility that funding might be cut."

Taken to its extreme, it meant no one besides an astronaut was to be trusted.

And since the public saw astronauts as "walking wonders," according to another consulting psychiatrist, they did their best to comply. There is a story that rocket engineer Wernher von Braun, who led the creation and production of Germany's deadly V-2 during World War II and then, transferring his allegiance, spearheaded development of the rocket that got US astronauts to the Moon, once was asked to describe how he felt during the countdowns for NASA's earliest launches, the robotic ones that failed so often. "Before the blastoff," he is reported to have said, "you chew your fingers. After the blastoff you talk briefly with newsmen and say, 'There was never any doubt.' "

As the veteran of five shuttle flights tells me, "We just were all dedicated to the idea that we wanted to take this thing that's really hard and make it look really easy. You know," he says, winking ostentatiously and putting two thumbs up. "Being around other people like that tends to reinforce it."

But if you weren't like that, it wasn't easy.

"I didn't really fit in," says Bill Colson, who found his physics research a sorry match for conversations about T-38 aerobatics. "I had nothing to offer. Sally talked about the other astronauts as if they were gods, and I was willing to take a supportive role, but I wasn't good at being a fan. I felt out of place more and more."

Bill also felt awkward about his knowledge of Sally's romance with Molly at a notoriously homophobic agency. Long before "Don't ask, don't tell" gave the US military permission to stick its head in the sand, NASA sent out vibes that sounded more like, "Don't be." Around that time, one gay NASA couple (not astronauts) reportedly purchased separate houses on different streets that backed up to each other, rather than risk being found out at the office. Whether Sally or any of her colleagues knew about such subterfuge is unknown. But as usual, her close friends protected her, entirely unasked.

"I didn't talk about her past when we were at Stanford, and I wasn't going to talk about it then," Bill says. "She never told me, Don't tell anybody about her and Molly. But I might have been a pretty serious hazard." Molly Tyson also worried "that my past relationship with her is a huge liability given the astronauts' concerns about appearances." But as damaging as the information might have been to Sally's career, she didn't seem to care. Her past was past, and never mentioned. If she was anxious then that NASA might discover her gay history, she didn't utter a word to either Molly or Bill.

She did, however, tell Bill that she wanted to live alone. In January 1979, he moved out. It had been a long relationship with many shared intimacies, and they would remain friends and intermittent academic partners, writing a number of physics papers together. But as Colson admits, echoing the thoughts of John Tompkins before him, "Neither of us knew how to talk about feelings. That probably was a fatal thing."

Sally wasn't alone for long.

She briefly dated fellow AsCan Robert "Hoot" Gibson, a thirty-two-year-old Navy test pilot with a rakish blond moustache and an insatiable passion for airplanes. "Sally was just as sweet as she could be," he says fondly. "Really fun to be with, really fun to fly with, tolerated all of our coarse boy jokes, and all of that stuff. But I never heard Sally tell a sleazy joke." He also admired her athleticism. "She was probably one of the best natural athletes NASA ever had. If you went running with Sally, you'd better be ready for a good run. We could go fly together in a T-38 and run around the country. It was pretty cool."

And never so cool as that February, when Gibson convinced the bosses to let him lead a group of pilots and mission specialists to observe the total eclipse of the sun over Montana. It was a glorious boondoggle, disguised as a scientific mission. With Sally in his backseat, along with two other crews, they flew their T-38s north on their grand excursion and parked in the local Air Force base. The next day, they took off, got up to 39,000 feet and raced along as the Moon started to pass in front of the Sun. Traveling at nine-tenths the speed of sound, they got an unparalleled, aerial view of the totality—when the Sun is completely blacked out—for four minutes and ten seconds, nearly two minutes longer than anyone on the ground. The photographs were fabulous; the view out the canopy, even better. Then they flew home past Mount Rushmore.

Sally was exactly where she wanted to be: flying a slick jet, sharing the sky with a new best (boy)friend, looking straight into a solar eclipse, wearing a made-for-swaggering flight suit and hip bomber jacket as she breathed rare air in the company of five colleagues with The Perfect Stuff, at least for that moment in her life. "Sally came into the program fairly casually," Gibson says, "but jumped into it heart and soul. It became a passion and an obsession with her. And she obviously totally embraced it and she lived and breathed space shuttles and the space program."

Sally never found the words to express her adoration for what she was doing. "I just love my job," was the best she could say.

In August 1979, just a year after she'd come to Houston, she was called to a meeting with the other TFNGs. They'd all done so well, they were told, their two-year training period had been cut in half and they no long needed to append "candidate" to their title. Officially, they were now astronauts, proud owners of the silver pin with the shining star atop three trajectories, encircled by the ellipse of orbit. More practically, it meant that thirty-five men and women were now eligible to be assigned to a crew.

STEVE

Steve Hawley, a lanky, redheaded astronomer from Kansas, became one of the TFNGs while doing a postdoc at an observatory in Chile. When he got to NASA, he thought Sally was cute, his term, and that they had a lot in common. He especially remembered reading an interview she'd done: "And it struck me that she'd been asked the same question I'd been asked, and answered the same way: 'Why would you do this? Give up a promising career?' And her answer was word for word what I'd said, 'Because it's your basic once-in-a-lifetime opportunity.' " Hey, Steve thought, she sounds like someone I'd like to know.

But Sally was living with Bill at the time, and when they split up, she started dating Hoot. "So it didn't seem like Bill leaving town was helping that much," Steve tells me. He is very droll.

Sally and Steve became friends. And when she stopped seeing Hoot, they got together. A group of TFNGs were going tubing on the nearby Guadalupe River for the weekend. "I had decided that I wasn't going to go," Steve says. "And the day before everyone was to leave, I was talking to her and she said, 'Why don't you come along?' And I decided I would. So I did. And I think that may have been before we were officially a couple, but the first time I thought maybe there's a chance."

"Steve was probably my best friend in that group of thirty-five, long before we started dating," Sally said much later. "We had a lot in common in our backgrounds: science, astronomy, a love of the stars, a love of the planets, a love of the space program." And a colossal interest in watching any version of *Star Trek* and any game with a ball on TV. In Steve, Sally found a sports fan of equal caliber. They were also both devoted to practical jokes and quick witticisms. Like Steve's comment when he first met his classmates and found himself intimidated by the constant round of military macho as they introduced themselves— "attack pilot in the Navy," "attack pilot in the Air Force." When Steve's turn came, he stood up and identified himself as an "attack astronomer." That became "A-squared," his office nickname, which is how Sally would always refer to him in her notes.

Their friendship grew. They ran together, they worked out at the gym together (in their NASA-supplied blue shorts and tees with the meandering space agency logo that everyone called "the worm"), they discussed their assignments together. And they were equally at home in the land of reserved emotions. "We both have the same general personality, although she was a bit more extreme in terms of being secretive," Steve tells me. "I've never really talked about my personal life, but I can speak volumes compared to her." Steve zeroes in on their lack of communication. "She was a lot like I am in the sense that, when she was worried or upset, she would just be quiet. And that's what I do. So there were lots of time when we wouldn't talk about stuff." By the time they moved in together, in the summer of 1981, they had expressed their mutual love, in the muted manner that then represented Sally's best effort: "I might say that I'm in love with you," is how Steve recalls she said it. He told her the same. They considered themselves engaged. And continued to guard their privacy.

Steve remembers telling Hoot Gibson about their new living arrangement while they were jogging one day in July. "I had cleverly chosen the date of Charles and Diana's wedding to do it," he tells me, "so that no one would notice." The marriage of the British royals that summer was certainly the biggest news of the day. That's where I was on assignment when Sally and Steve set up housekeeping in Houston, which is my excuse for missing the scoop.

But another celebrity event, earlier that year, may have triggered a more significant reaction in Sally. In May 1981, Billie Jean King—Sally's old friend and role model from tennis camp, and the biggest female tennis star in the world—held a press conference to announce that she was being sued for palimony by her former secretary, Marilyn Barnett. "I was outed," King tells me, still angry at being forced to announce her sexuality publicly, before she had come to terms with it personally. And while she was still married. At a time of widespread homophobia, she also saw her endorsements and sponsorships disappear in a flash. "I lost all my money overnight, started my life over at thirty-eight," she says.

Today, King thinks that the fallout from her outing "probably scared the hell out of Sally. That probably put her more into her shell." But Sally never discussed it with her—not then, not later. And she never brought up the subject in any form with Steve. They were a couple now, like any other couple, with the often independent orbits of two very focused astronauts. Many mornings, they set off in opposite directions on their individual assignments, Sally for long weeks to Canada to work on the robot arm and Steve to Florida to work at the Cape. Both had the same goal: to get on a crew and fly. Which meant getting George Abbey to select them. They went about their work with renewed determination.

"One of the things Sally and I did was figure out pretty early on, that it was going to be a lot more important to spend time learning shuttle software than it was solving problems in astrophysics. And I don't recall him ever saying anything, but I believe that was one of George's tests— who are the people who are going to come in and be committed to the program?"

The good news was, there was finally a program.

BACK IN SPACE

On December 29, 1980, *Columbia* was rolled out to the pad at the Kennedy Space Center in Florida. The gleaming white spaceship, mated to its matching fuel tank and sleek solid rocket boosters, would launch the first American astronaut in six years. The entire space community seemed to shift into a faster pace to prepare for this largely experimental bundle of aeronautical wizardry. Most of the hardware had never been tested as an entity, real-time. The orbiter had never flown into space, either with or without a human. No one had ever launched on solid rocket motors, which, once ignited, could not be turned off.

When I visited Houston in March 1981, NASA was abuzz. And a nation that had lost interest in space travel was revving up for the journey. Ronald Reagan had just been swept into the White House and took full advantage of the shuttle program he inherited, yoking his optimism and support to the promise of a new adventure. That's when I first met and first interviewed Sally, by then sporting layers of dark brown permed curls. I asked what she expected to see in space. "A view of the universe out in front of you," she said. Astrophysics, beyond the lab. Three years in training had certainly improved the essay she'd written as an applicant.

I also had my first encounter with John Young and Bob Crippen, the older-school astronauts who would be flying STS-1 (for Space Transportation System-first flight) in April. Young, the "astronaut's astronaut," a veteran space traveler, was also head of the Astronaut Office, but his economical way with words and his reticent manner at the Monday morning meetings (always looking down at his papers), spawned a favorite TFNG joke: "Does anyone know the color of John's eyes?" When Mike Coats, who ascended to become director of JSC after three shuttle flights, tells me this, he adds, laughing, "I still don't!"

Young's pilot, known to all as "Crip," was a strikingly handsome Navy captain and test pilot who'd been waiting more than a dozen years for his first flight in space. Unwaveringly modest and exceptionally competent, Crip disavowed any possibility that flying the first shuttle would make him a hero. "What if it does?" I asked. "I don't know," he said, smiling, with no intention of speculating. "What if it does?"

One month later, on April 12, 1981, from my camera position three miles away, I watched them shoot to the sky with an ear-splitting thrust of power and light that not only dazzled my eyes but pounded on my chest, with waves of energy emanating from the pad. "Go, baby, go!" urged Gene Cernan on ABC News, as the most complicated vehicle in human history rose slowly from the pad, then streaked into orbit to put NASA back in business. Two days later, I helped anchor the coverage as *Columbia* dropped out of the sky with a double sonic boom and glided to a safe landing in the California desert. Young and Crippen were the nation's new heroes.

Sally had seen the launch from the backseat of a T-38. *Columbia*'s success brought her one launch closer to her own. But when?

CAPCOM

That summer, she edged even closer. After nearly three years at NASA, having moved from the classroom to the simulator, from a parachute drop in Oklahoma to "flying" the robot arm in Toronto, Sally Ride was named a CapCom (Capsule Communicator, a relic of the lunar age when spacecraft were little capsules holding human cargo) for the second shuttle mission, scheduled for that fall. It was, Sally said, "a really good assignment, probably the best job in the astronaut office next to flying." Along with a round-the-clock team of other astronauts, she would serve as the interface between the crew—commander Joe Engle and pilot Dick Truly—and the flight director in Mission Control. By ancient decree, astronauts in space speak only with other astronauts on the ground. It was a prestigious job in prime time, often the fast track to a crew assignment, and Sally was chosen, in large part, because of her expertise with the robot arm, which would be flown for the first time on STS-2. "I needed a CapCom who was the right person, because that was a big test," pilot Dick Truly tells me. She would need to know every pitch and yaw of the unwieldy crane, to talk the crew through any anomalies and direct them to solutions.

Sally trained for the next three months, in hundreds of full-blown simulations with the crew and the entire flight team. "I'm very serious about what I'm doing," she told me later. "If I'm given a job or assignment, I feel like I need to do the best job I can. And part of that is probably just pride. I have a lot of pride in what I do, and I don't like to appear stupid. So I work very hard to avoid appearing stupid."

When *Columbia* reached orbit on November 12, 1981, she talked Engle and Truly through every maneuver, as familiar with the camera on the elbow of the robot arm as with the tendons of her own wrist. For the first time, a female voice was the legendary "Houston" of space travel. For the first time, a female astronaut sat at the console in the glassed-in room with its terraced rows of monitors and king-sized, wall-mounted patches commemorating the fabled flights to the Moon and around Earth, all controlled from that room. Sally was smooth and steady and spoke the native language. "After the RMS PRCS test, we need you to auto maneuver back to minus ZLV per the CAP, and I think that's per page 4-42 of the CAP," she said, casually. When an onboard system malfunctioned, meaning the mission had to be cut short, it was Sally who delivered the news, calmly and precisely, to the disappointed crew. Her poise softened the blow, and her good humor punctuated the rest of the trip. As Truly and commander Joe Engle tumbled around in weightlessness like porpoises, beaming down eye-popping images of Earth and the robot arm as it flexed its electromechanical bicep, Sally radioed back, "Super! When do I get my turn?" *Carpe diem.* Thirty-four astronauts must have wished that they, too, could put in their bids through a nationally televised microphone.

Four months later, Sally served as a CapCom for the third shuttle mission. Once again, hers was a calm and very knowledgeable voice, the kind you'd want with you on a risky mission.

In an interview several years earlier, she had bubbled over with enthusiasm about her training, recognizing that once *Columbia* landed safely from its maiden voyage, and once NASA felt comfortable with the shuttle's operations, the floodgates would open. Now that it had launched and landed three times, with no major setbacks, the crews for future flights would start to be named. The reporter teased her with the possibility of flying—and fame.

"I can't wait to get up," she told him. "We're all eager for the first flight to get up and get off the ground. And eager to each get up ourselves. As far as being the first American woman goes, that doesn't mean all that much to me."

"But you wouldn't mind making history that way, would you?"

"I wouldn't mind."

FIRST

APRIL 1982–JUNE 1983

RIDE, SALLY RIDE! AND YOU GUYS CAN TAG ALONG, TOO!

Roadside sign, Cocoa Beach, Florida, June 18, 1983.

Lynn Sherr: *Do you feel under any pressure as America's first female astronaut?*
Sally Ride: *I do feel that there's some pressure for me not to mess up.*

—Preflight interview, 1983

GET READY . . .

In early 1982, with three shuttle missions completed and another three crews in training—all comprised of astronauts who'd been with NASA since the 1960s—George Abbey and Chief Astronaut John Young were eager to get the Thirty-five New Guys into space. After four years, they weren't so new anymore; another class had joined in 1980, adding two more women and two minority men to the growing rainbow coalition. It was time to start showing off NASA's fresh faces.

They began at the top, naming Bob Crippen, the STS-1 pilot, to command the seventh shuttle mission, and Dick Truly, just back from STS-2, to command the eighth. Two seasoned and respected career pilots were being entrusted with the TFNG's rookie flights. Truly, who would later become the first astronaut to serve as NASA Administrator, recalls a meeting with Abbey and Chris Kraft, where "they told us that NASA wanted to fly a woman on seven and an African American on eight. So we started this conversation on how to round out the crews. And they had some ideas, but they took our input too." Truly says that when it came to the women, "it very quickly became a conversation about Sally and Judy [Resnik]. Everybody just thought that they were the top of the heap. None of this was negative about the other women. It was just about who was best."

Crippen says the idea of having a woman on the crew was Abbey's, and that he agreed wholeheartedly. And while "all six females in that group were outstanding, both George and I thought Sally ought to be the first one. I had significant input." He says there were many reasons Sally appealed to him: "Technically, that we'd be using the [robot] arm a lot, and she was one of the experts. And a great deal of it was Sally's personality: she really did work very well with everybody I saw her come in contact with. When you're putting together a crew, you want to have a group that is compatible." Crippen points out that compatibility is critical in a mission that lasts for a week. "You're working very closely together, and if anybody gets on anybody else's nerves, it's not efficient. Also, you're training together for a year, just constantly together, much more than you are with your family. And if there are things that rub people wrong, it kind of festers and grows, and you don't want that in a space flight crew."

Crippen was also taken with Sally's performance as CapCom. "You like people who stay calm under duress. And Sally can do that. She hit all the squares."

George Abbey says John Young, as head of the Astronaut Office, "was part of all this too. John and I talked over all the candidates for the STS-7 flight that would be well suited for the mission, both men and women." Abbey came up with the names. "Sally was on my list," he recalls, meaning she was his first choice among the women from the beginning. "She clearly was the best RMS [remote arm] operator we had." When I first interviewed Abbey back in 1983, right after Sally was chosen, he also told me, grinning at his own political correctness, "She fits the mold that we're looking for as far as crewman . . . or crewpersons . . . are concerned."

Abbey prided himself on tracking the candidates closely. "I felt I had a good idea who were the best qualified," he says. "I said who the STS-7 crew ought to be, and what did he think of it? And in the end John [Young] and I were in agreement on the crew selected."

When Abbey took the list to JSC director Chris Kraft, Abbey says Kraft wanted to discuss all the female candidates, and wondered why Abbey hadn't selected Anna Fisher to fly first. "He thought Anna was pretty well qualified and could do the job," Abbey tells me. "So I had to defend Sally." Abbey says he regularly had to defend all the crew members, and that Kraft "didn't necessarily agree with me all the time, but as long as I could make a good case and argue it, I usually won." With Sally, he says, "I went over her record and what she'd done and how other people rated her and her proficiency and her ability to work well with others. So we discussed it and he finally agreed."

Kraft, who declined several times, without explanation, to be interviewed for this book, took the list to Headquarters, in DC, and "they went with our judgment," Abbey says. "I think they were pleased that we had selected a woman."

The woman in question got the electrifying news early Monday morning, April 19, 1982. Usually, the entire crew was summoned to Abbey's office—the big corner suite on the eighth floor, with huge windows overlooking the campus—and told together. Receiving the mysterious phone call and bumping into others as you walked over to Building 1 was a stomach-churning ritual. That morning, it was a solo act. A secretary called Sally just before the weekly astronauts' meeting, saying that Abbey wanted to see her. Sally speculated—hoped—she knew why. She'd been wondering about the possibility all weekend, having been told, without explanation, to report back to Houston from a brief vacation at Disneyland with Steve. Now she prepared for a guessing game with (her term) the "man of few words."

"He basically said, 'Um, how do you like the job you've got now?' I said, 'Well, what is my job?' He said, 'We thought that maybe you enjoyed what you were doing so much that maybe you wouldn't want to fly on a crew.' "

"George wanted to tell me first," she later said, "to tell me that this was kind of a big deal because I was going to be the first woman to go up, the first woman assigned to a crew. He wanted to make sure that I was comfortable with that. There was no doubt in my mind that I wanted to do that.

"After I met with him, he took me up to Dr. Kraft's office [on the ninth floor], and Dr. Kraft talked with me about the implications of being the first woman. He reminded me that I would get a lot of press attention and asked if I was ready for that. His message was just, 'Let us know when you need help; we're here to support you in any way and can offer whatever help you need.' It was a very reassuring message, coming from the head of the space center."

Both Kraft and Abbey had seen the consequences of celebrity. After the "determinedly modest" Neil Armstrong became the first of our species on the Moon, the enormity of his accomplishment both expanded and constricted his life, making it impossible to walk down the street like any other American. They wanted, Abbey tells me, "to make sure Sally understood what she was getting into." She said she thought she did, which was either a bold expression of confidence or an innocent misreading of the possibilities. How could she possibly have understood the magnitude, the impact, the craziness? The First was the name everyone would know. The First would get the headlines, the speaking fees, the history books. The expectations. How can you grasp what it all means ahead of time? And even if you do, how do you say no to the brass ring?

Back in Abbey's office, the rest of the crew was notified. Other than Crippen, STS-7 was the first mission comprised entirely of Sally's classmates. The pilot was Frederick (Rick) Hauck, a third-generation Naval officer and Vietnam vet, who had warmed my heart during an early interview by articulating his love of flying: "I like the freedom. If you want to make the world turn upside down, you just push the stick." John Fabian, a tall, former aeronautics professor at the US Air Force Academy, an Air Force colonel, and at forty-three the oldest of the New Guys, would serve as mission specialist, like Sally. He was also an expert on the robot arm. A third mission specialist, physician and US Marine and naval aviator Norm Thagard, would be added later, to help deal with the growing problem of space adaptation syndrome, or SAS, NASA's euphemism for the often debilitating bouts of space sickness. They were, George Abbey said, "a group of people who could take on the mission and complement each other."

And they were, as Crip noticed approvingly, widely known as " 'Sally Ride and the others,' which was just right for us!" For a bunch of reserved military guys, it was perfect.

Sally was elated. She had not only beaten out more than eight thousand applicants to get to NASA in the first place, she had now floated to the top of an elite group of six. But she was forced to sit on the news for several hours until the public, and the astronaut corps, were clued in. NASA buried the lede by announcing crews for three new shuttle missions—STS-7, with Sally; STS-8, with Guion (Guy) Bluford, the first African American; and STS-9, a joint mission with the European Space Agency. Newspaper headlines predictably singled out Sally and Guy: a woman and a black were going into space! Bluford generated far less excitement. His gender trumped his ethnicity—the world was used to male astronauts—and besides, he tells me, "I had an extensive flying background in high performance jet aircraft and lots of aerospace engineering experience." The unknown was the female factor: how to support a woman "in a male-dominated cramped spaceflight environment. And no one knew how well a female was going to perform on orbit." In short, Bluford recalls, "The press was more interested in the unique difference of male versus female in space than in black versus white on orbit."

To say the least.

Some five hundred reporters immediately requested private interviews with Sally, all of which were declined. NASA followed standard procedure with a full-crew press conference just over a week later, where Sally, looking younger than her thirty-one years and deceptively demure in a blue blouse with puffy sleeves, with two delicate gold chains ringing her neck, smiled charitably when Crippen introduced her as "undoubtedly the prettiest member of the crew." Then she described two experiments the flight would be carrying and responded patiently to questions from a reasonably polite press corps. (I say that with full objectivity. I was in California covering Jerry Brown's unsuccessful US Senate campaign and saved my formal questions for another time.)

No, she had never thought about being an astronaut as a child. No, she didn't yet have any advice for other would-be female astronauts. Yes, she was honored to be offered "the experience of a lifetime." This from a reporter who wondered how it felt to become "a footnote in history, and a trivia question forever." "Gosh, that's quite an honor!" Sally quipped, laughing amiably at the attempt to rile her. When another tried the oblique approach—"I'm sure you've been asked, many times, how it feels to be the first woman astronaut. How does it feel to be asked that question?"—she parried, good-naturedly, "I've also been asked, many times, how it feels to be asked that question! I think I'm going to get real tired of being asked that question, but probably not as tired as these three [her crewmates] are about being asked how it feels to fly with me!"

The rules of the game were obvious: the media needed a headline and tried valiantly to provoke a juicy response; Sally, determined to be seen as just another dedicated astronaut in the buttoned-down bureaucracy, kept her answers brief, technocentric and unquotable.

Someone brought up the "personal hygiene" issue—"How do you work around that, do you become one of the guys?"—which Sally, laughing, deftly tossed to her commander. "There's no doubt about it," Crippen agreed, flashing his own got-it-covered grin, "the orbiter is not that big of a vehicle and there's not that much privacy. But I'm sure we'll work it out to everybody's satisfaction." He noted that the shuttle had been designed to accommodate both men and women, and that only one modification—"the commode"—had been required. Still, "We're going to become very familiar with one another over the next year or so!"

The bodily waste issue was more than timely. Sally was following closely the campaign to pass the Equal Rights Amendment, which would go down to defeat two months later thanks, in part, to the fuss kicked up by Phyllis Schlafly over the specter of unisex restrooms. You know, like the ones in airplanes. Or in your home. A political cartoon published after Sally's appointment to STS-7 showed Schlafly button-holing a NASA engineer and demanding, "But will there be separate bathrooms?!"

The same themes would chase Sally over the next fourteen months as the press and the public tried to penetrate the not very accessible mind of this most accomplished, most private person in this most unique situation: how did it *feel* to be a woman with all those men? How did being a *woman* change the dynamic of the all-male crew? What was it like to be a *female* astronaut? How many ways could the same query be posed? NASA largely protected her with an airtight training schedule that left little room for idle chatter. And Crippen gave her all the cover she needed, running interference and taking the heat for banning unwelcome interviews. At the press conference, he cut off debate over Sally's capabilities with a definitive pronouncement: "Sally's on this crew because she's well qualified to be here." John Fabian, who had been Sally's classmate for four years and worked with her on the robot arm—some of that time under her supervision—finessed the guy who wondered whether Sally's presence would require deference from her crewmates. "I don't think that Dr. Ride needs anybody to defer to her," he said. "Her capabilities take care of themselves and she'll stand high in any group. I don't think it's an issue at all."

If NASA managers didn't high-five each other after the news conference, they should have. In her first major exposure to the media, Sally won, game, set and match. And her crew closed ranks around her without being patronizing. America's first woman in space could handle herself just fine and the country was falling in love.

Her colleagues' reaction was more complicated, at least momentarily. Whenever a new crew was named—and there were three that day in April 1982—the people who weren't on it were jealous. Some took longer to get over it than others.

"There were a bunch of whiners," recalls Hoot Gibson. "One said, 'Boy you work like a slave and do you get recognized for it? Hell no!'" Gibson took a more genial approach, grabbing his good friend Steve Hawley and dragging him over to George Abbey at the happy hour celebration the evening of the announcement. "And Stevie didn't know what I was going to say . . ." (actually, Hawley recalls, "I said to myself, Oh, crap!") and then Gibson said, "Hey George, Stevie and I wanted to tell you that you really screwed up today." Pause for effect. "You didn't pick us!" Gibson laughs at the memory. "Yeah, I was disappointed. You couldn't help but be disappointed, because they were given their trip to Disneyland. And you weren't. But doggone it, bury those feelings, don't let them show, and be happy for them, and that's what we did."

Gibson and Hawley, like every one of the thirty-five, would later get their own flights; some, many remarkable times. But on that day when the first of their peers were named, it was touchy. Especially for the other women.

"Not getting the nod was a little bit of a wound," admits Kathy Sullivan. "I would have loved to go first, for the vote of confidence it represented and endorsements and everything else . . ."

"I think all of us probably were just a little disappointed that our name wasn't on the list," agrees Rhea Seddon, who by then was married to Hoot Gibson and newly pregnant, and thus able to take the broader perspective. "I sort of figured, God has a different plan for me. And I was not all disturbed to take things a little slower."

Carolyn Huntoon was thrilled for Sally but had five other female astronauts to protect. "Somebody had to be first," she acknowledged, "and everyone was adult enough to understand that, but everyone was an overachiever, and they were used to being first. There was a dip in this office—I felt it." Huntoon called Sally and went into full den-mother mode.

"You got it!"

"Yeah."

"Now, be nice."

"Yes, ma'am."

... GET SET ...

Training for a shuttle mission took a solid year, and the crew would need every second to prepare. Sally and her crewmates moved into a large office on the third floor of Building 4, where they papered the walls with orbital maps and began molding themselves into a team fully alert to each other's needs. By the time of the launch, Sally would say, "we felt like a family of five."

With the usual family hang-ups. Early on, the crew was sent to Building 9, the cavernous home of the orbiter mockup, to go through some drills. They were told to change into flight gear, which meant stripping down to their underwear in the room where their NASA suits were laid out. The entire crew, together. Norm Thagard headed for the men's room. "I'm from the South and I couldn't do it," he says. There were no further assaults on his modesty.

Crippen gave out their assignments. He and Hauck would fly the shuttle. Fabian and Sally would use the robot arm to launch two satellites. Sally would also serve as flight engineer, sitting directly behind Crippen and Hauck during the critical liftoff and landing, following every blink on every monitor, every tick of every gauge, to catch any problems instantly. Anomalies, in NASA-speak. She had to know every contingency procedure, to help run the pilots through precisely ordered checklists if something went wrong. Crippen called her his "third pair of eyeballs." I ask why he chose Sally for the backup job. " 'Cause she's so darned smart!" he says. "Sally learned the orbiter systems very well and she was very good at working in a nice cool, calm, relaxed manner when there was a semi-crisis going on, so she seemed the perfect one to do that for me."

It was like a Broadway opening with rehearsals almost every day. They practiced the flight plan over and over in shuttle-sized simulators that replicated everything from the rumbling of the engines to the turbulence of liftoff. Sally stood for hours in the green glow of computer monitors, punching buttons and nudging joysticks to make the robot arm—visible only as a computer animation—obey. Or to perfect the sequence to launch a satellite, which was also conjured up on a screen representing the deep black void of space. It was like Angry Birds without the birds (or the color, or the gorgeous graphics), with blazing red LED numbers and orange targets brightening the battleship gray of the mockup's console. Sally showed up in blue jeans, but her concentration was as formal as it was on the tennis court, as it would be in space. During one intense session that coincided with the World Series, she ignored the periodic game updates delivered by a sympathetic engineer. Then again, the Brewers and the Cardinals were not the Dodgers.

"She was just all business," recalls Susan Okie, who enjoyed exclusive access to Sally's pre-flight activities. Sally had invited her old friend, then a respected medical reporter for the *Washington Post*, to chronicle her training and write her profile before she flew, a handpicked Boswell for her historic journey. Okie's weeklong series, which Sally hoped would satisfy the requirement for public confessionals, provides an invaluable record of activities the rest of us did not witness. Even today, Okie remembers the serious scientist totally focused on her mission. "She was at her station, and there was a lot of NASA acronym code going back and forth. And she was very geeky, very matter-of-fact and always knowing what to do, not cracking jokes."

For ascent and entry rehearsals in the motion-based simulator, a full-sized cockpit on stilts that tilted you onto your back the way you'd be on a real liftoff, Sally took her seat behind the commander and pilot, sometimes wearing full flight gear, as they moved through the complex timeline that would get the shuttle off Earth and back again. The sessions could last four hours, or thirty-six for a long-duration "integrated sim," in which everyone in mission control was also looped in to get them used to working together.

"It was exciting," explains pilot Rick Hauck. "It was sort of, you pinch yourself and you're that one step closer to doing this amazing thing. And you wind up practicing emergency procedures so much that if anything like that can become routine, it became routine. That was the objective."

At which point, one of the technicians—the diabolical Simulation Supervisor, or SimSup (pronounced "SimSoup," as in chicken noodle)— would drop a virtual sandbag onto their stage, injecting glitch after glitch to test their responses in an emergency. "They were trying to teach us the nuances, to point out maybe a weakness in the procedures or the hardware," Hauck says. "The objective was to build your confidence so that you could cope with anything." If you couldn't, the commander would step in.

"One of the most stressful times for me," Hauck recalls, "was when Crip and Sally and I were doing an ascent simulation, and on several runs I screwed up and killed us." That is, the shuttle "crashed" in simulation. "I was as down as ever, I was a mess," Hauck goes on, "and then Crip said, 'Well, it was a bad day. Don't worry about it. Just focus on getting it better the next time.'"

Hauck, who would command two shuttle missions of his own with distinction, did it better every time. Crippen's advice would also inform Sally's later management style, dovetailing with her own mantra: don't get hung up on the past; move on, focus forward.

Or just laugh it off. During one ascent simulation, when she was still a rookie ripe for some lighthearted hazing, the team of instructors played a trick. They bought a lifelike rubber rat and tied it to some nylon string, then rolled it up onto the glare shield above the cockpit instruments. Sally climbed into her seat and strapped in for the "launch." As the lights went out and the machine was elevated, then rotated backwards, the toy rat tumbled off its perch towards Sally's face. In the dim light of the cockpit instruments, Sally saw it and screamed. "It was a good scream," recalls former NASA flight trainer Frank Hughes, "so good they tried to record it. She thought it was alive." Moments later, Sally was laughing with the rest of them. She took the fake rodent into space with her on the shuttle. When she returned, she presented it to the team of instructors, on a plaque with the title, "The Rat Stuff."

Outside the simulators, they met with technicians at JSC or with off-site contractors to review the tiniest bolt on the flight deck or the button that rehydrated dried food packs. Sally's life was organized into stacks of cue cards—ring-bound sets of instructions that would fit into her zippered pants-leg pocket—and mountain-sized briefing books. When I dropped in to Houston to report on other flights during her training, I could occasionally persuade her to take time off for a game of racquetball or a quick beer. But mostly she studied the contingencies, jogged to stay fit, or strapped into a T-38 to fulfill her flying time. The astronauts lived in their own virtual cockpit, often oblivious to the civilian world. During one T-38 trip out west piloted by Rick Hauck, the plane broke down in Tucson, forcing Sally and Hauck to fly back commercial. As they boarded the jet wearing their flight suits—the only clothing they had brought—and carrying their gear, the captain looked at their parachutes and said, "Is there something about our service you're worried about?"

Sally was happily obsessed. And still an expert at compartmentalizing. When asked whether she was a workaholic, she answered truthfully, "No, I'm pretty good at going home and lying in front of the television and turning off the rest of the world."

TIME OUT

Under a warm July sun on a Saturday afternoon in 1982—not a training day—Sally Ride and Steve Hawley got married in the backyard of Steve's parents' home in Salina, Kansas. The bride wore white—white jeans, just like the groom. Her shirt was striped, his red. Two family ministers—his father, Bernard, pastor of the local Presbyterian Church, and her sister, Bear—officiated, ending with the Jewish tradition of breaking a glass and shouts of "Mazel Tov!" Bear takes credit for that touch. "There wasn't too much religious imagery and I thought we needed to do something to celebrate life," she says. "It was odd."

Only family attended—both sets of parents, his and her siblings—and the baker was sworn to secrecy when they ordered the cake. Sally "didn't want to do something large and involved," Steve recalls. "Keeping it secret was an important part of the plan, which was easier to do if we just got married at my parents' place." Steve arrived ahead of time to get the marriage license, facilitated by a lawyer friend of his father's. Sally flew herself up from Houston in the Grumman Tiger. The wedding photos capture a casual ceremony, with the couple's arms encircling each other's waists, after which they cut the clandestine cake. Both grinned broadly as Sally fed the first slice to Steve—an unlikely gulp of tradition for two nonconformists. At the end of the weekend, the newlyweds climbed back into the Tiger to fly themselves home to Houston, both having exchanged their formal jeans for shorts and TFNG tee-shirts. There was no honeymoon. When they left Salina, the Tiger got diverted into Waco because of thunderstorms. "So," recalls Steve, "we spent our first married night together in a hotel there and continued to Houston on Monday."

He says the timing was Sally's, as well as the stealth wedding. "It was all about minimizing the publicity about her. Sally was afraid of people getting too close." And while they'd never discussed specifics when they moved in together a year earlier, marriage was always on the horizon. Quietly. During dinners in Houston that Sally and I enjoyed several weeks beforehand, she hadn't uttered a word. Much closer friends were equally unaware until the news broke a few weeks later. "We didn't want to make a big deal of it," Sally was quoted as saying in the *Los Angeles Times*. A small paper in Ohio wrote that they had "tied the 'astroknot.'" And Steve still chuckles over the clip his father described from his hometown paper, the Salina *Journal*, which said that the marriage "had been consummated in my parents' backyard. I presume they meant consecrated." In *The New York Times*, the bride was called, inaccurately, "Mrs. Hawley."

Sally never took Steve's name, but she was not above borrowing it in an emergency. Back in April, when she'd been summoned back to Houston from Los Angeles for the big announcement, the two of them—who were planning to return separately on different commercial planes—simply exchanged tickets so she could get home first. In those innocent days before photo IDs and body scans (and before they were married), Sally flew home as S. Hawley. Steve later returned as S. Ride. She didn't offer to return the favor on the shuttle.

Bear was surprised that Sally married Steve. "I was surprised that she got married, period. I saw her as an individual." While I was researching this book, several retired astronauts repeated the rumor that NASA pushed Sally to get married because the agency didn't want a female astronaut who was, in the picturesque phrase of the 1980s, living out of wedlock. Sally told Susan Okie that "she felt less protective of her personal life now that she and Steve were married. That she didn't mind talking about the fact that they'd been living together beforehand, which was the main thing that she'd tried to keep a secret." Why she might have wanted to hide that remains a mystery: NASA hadn't blinked when she arrived in Houston living with Bill Colson, and no one seems to have cared about her living arrangement with Steve. Her bosses denied to me that they pressured her to get married, and Steve said the rumor was news to him. Nor does Steve think that theirs was a marriage of convenience. "I believe that Sally did love me when we got married," he says, "and that she entered the marriage in good faith."

In Steve, Sally again had a soul mate she could trust, a new best buddy with whom she could laugh and swap stories about the simulator. "We really both enjoyed that part of the training," Steve says. "And one of the things we enjoyed talking about were some of the 'sim' cases— you know, 'Here's what they did, and that's really interesting, and here's what I did, and did you think about this?' I just thought that was kind of fun." Sally liked the simulator so much, she once told a reporter, "I still feel like I ought to put a quarter in." Steve is only slightly embarrassed to add, "Our idea of a good time was to sit down after dinner and go through the ascent checklist! People don't think that's very normal."

The Hawley-Ride homestead—a beige-brick contemporary on a quiet, leafy street with a small pool in back and a large fish tank inside— is probably best described as late-century Space Modern. A framed print of the artwork that became the TFNG tee-shirt decorated one wall; photos of the shuttle and T-38s, another. An image of the Moon landing hung in their bedroom. Later, pictures from STS-7 would be added, along with the original drawings for some of Garry Trudeau's *Doonesbury* strips, poking fun at the misadventures of Utah Senator Jake Garn as an astronaut when he finagled his own shuttle ride.

With its shuttle décor and their new Apple III computer—on which they played endless hours of the fantasy game Zork—the house also reflected the updated status of NASA marriages. Like Sally's classmates Rhea Seddon and Hoot Gibson, who had married several months earlier, and Anna Fisher, whose husband Bill Fisher was in the 1980 class, the new generation of marriages brought two equal fliers under one roof, a far cry from the way wives were pigeonholed and kept from the Cape back in the early days. Getting to space so consumed their lives,

Steve joked that Sally's response to, "When's dinner going to be ready?" was usually, "Half an hour. What are we having?"

Theirs was, Steve acknowledges, "a bit of an odd relationship. I don't know that anybody would have said we behaved much like a traditional husband and wife, but of course she wasn't a traditional wife personality. I kind of recognized that it went with the territory."

I ask Steve what he means by "traditional."

"If I was going to Florida for the week, coming back on Friday night, I'd call her up and she'd say, 'I'm going to California for the weekend, see you next week!' Not like, 'Oh, you've been gone all week, looking forward to having you home.' She pretty much did her own thing."

Still, at least at first, they seemed to understand each other, secure in their own verbal shorthand, finishing each other's sentences and communicating with nods and gestures. "By the time we were married and had been living with each other," Sally said, "we got so that we didn't have to talk." Adds Steve, "I knew what she wanted and she knew what I wanted. We didn't talk about where we wanted to be ten years from now."

Nor did they discuss that other topic central to many young marrieds.

One of Sally's early jobs had been babysitting. At lunchtime one day, she made the kids peanut butter and jelly sandwiches. But the kids wouldn't eat them because they said the peanut butter was on the wrong side of the bread. Sally tossed the sandwiches, started over and never babysat again. At seventeen, she told her parents that she didn't want children. Her parents joked that when Sally's nephew, Whit (Bear's son), was christened, Sally was more nervous holding the baby after "the ceremony than she probably will be for the shuttle launch."

Several years later, in the only interview Sally and Steve did together—with NBC's Jane Pauley, who had become a friend of Steve's during the shuttle coverage—the *Today* show cohost tried valiantly to drill down. "Maybe I have no business asking," she said, but "do you think about children?" Sally laughed, more of a nervous pause, and said, abruptly, "Think about it sometimes, but you're right, you have no business asking. We've elected not to answer personal things." Pauley acknowledged defeat and jumped to her next, less intrusive, question.

The wall around their innermost views was, Steve reminds me, jointly constructed. But hers was unquestionably higher. "Talking is contrary to her personality," Steve would tell a reporter some years later. "She's more from Mars than from Venus." Later, Steve would gain many insights into the woman he'd married. Later, he'd question much of their relationship and wonder about her behavior. But when he married her on July 24, 1982, he understood and happily accepted that with her flight on STS-7 less than a year away, the only thing that mattered was her mission. "She was very focused on what she needed to do in her role and I wasn't a priority," he says. "I understood that and accepted it." Steve also understood the bigger picture. "To actually be prime crew and to get to attempt launch was the goal that we all joined NASA for. She didn't really care that much about being first. She cared about being good. And she really worked hard at being good. If she'd been a bozo, that would probably have set women astronauts back decades. None of the six were bozos. But she was just clearly very qualified and very competent. She was the best choice."

As Sally's biggest booster, Steve handled the inevitable comments with aplomb, shaking off every reference to himself as "the husband of . . ." When Salina, Kansas, decided to erect a historical marker for its famous astronaut son, Steve joked that that the sign would read, "Hometown-in-law of Sally Ride." No one in the family was immune. In 1986, when Steve's father was invited by fellow Kansan senator Bob Dole to deliver the invocation for the US Senate (on the first day TV cameras were allowed in the chamber), the guest chaplain was introduced by Republican Strom Thurmond as Sally Ride's father. Reverend Hawley politely ignored the error.

Just before Sally flew, Steve got named to his own crew. "His flight assignment," Sally said, "did wonders for our marriage."

ANATOMY LESSONS

> *Q: Dr. Ride, apart from the obvious differences, how do you assess the*
>   *differences in men and women astronauts?*
> *A: Aside from the obvious differences, I don't think there are any.*
> —Prime crew press conference, April 29, 1982

The double-x chromosome did not affect the way astronauts flipped switches, and NASA made no major changes in its flying equipment to accommodate the eight women now in the astronaut corps (six pioneers, two 1980 additions: Mary Cleave and Bonnie Dunbar). But there were some minor (and critical) adjustments in facilities and outlook. The gym included a women's locker room, with the hair dryers and bigger towels that Carolyn Huntoon had mandated, plus posters of Tom Selleck (courtesy of Judy Resnik). The shuttle's onboard toilet (or Waste Collection System, WCS), a sturdy improvement over the urine-catching condoms ("roll-on cuffs," in prim NASAspeak) and plastic bags (for solid waste) of the Apollo era, had a curtain to give users of either gender some privacy. In addition, the funnel-like device attached to the flexible hose, to suction waste away from the body, came in several wider versions for the women. Rhea Seddon remembers flying in the KC-135, with its thirty-second arcs of weightlessness, to test the urine collection devices. The pressure was, literally, on them. "We would try to go up with a full bladder," she says. But the brief opportunities meant "it wasn't entirely satisfactory."

Sally would be the first female to use the WCS in space. She would also be the first to test the DACT—Disposable Absorption Collection Trunk—a form-fitting and highly absorbent diaper with a super-absorbent silica gel (just like that in babies' diapers) that they wore under their flight suits for launch and landing, when there's no chance to head for the head. And with the seats for the commander and pilot now adjustable, to accommodate the wider range of human sizes flying the shuttle, the shorter legs and arms of future female fliers would fit in fine.

On the social front, George Abbey's office wall sported a hot pink bumper sticker reading "A Woman's Place Is in the Cockpit" and Bob Crippen, the very model of a fighter pilot, learned from Sally Ride never to use the term "manned space flight." In time, Rhea Seddon would prove that flying in T-38s was safe for pregnant women in their first trimester; Anna Fisher would become the first mother to fly in space; and flight surgeons with gynecological experience would replace the unenlightened fellow who tried to get a Pap smear from a female astronaut with an upside down sample stick.

Even the graphics had grown up. The official STS-7 shuttle patch included the biological symbol for Woman.

Ground controllers took their own time. For many months after Sally was named to her flight, every female voice radioed from a T-38 would be met by the hopeful question, "Sally, is that you?" The other women aloft learned to say, "Yes."

Sally also understood that some decisions about her upcoming flight were better made as a group. "Sally was now the prime female," Rhea Seddon says. "But she was very inclusive about, 'Let's all get together and answer this question.' And we had to answer some dumb engineering questions. Like, 'What if all the mucous that women put out will stop up the toilet?' And we're all sitting there looking at this highly placed engineer who'd been there forever, and we're saying, 'What mucous?' And then he blushes." Seddon, an accomplished surgeon, breaks into laughter. "They're engineers! What do they know about women's physiology?!"

Kathy Sullivan got involved during the "bench check" for STS-7, when they reviewed Sally's personal gear. Everything that flew had to be vetted, for, among other things, off-gassing. This was the first time it was considered through a gender lens, and Sally was the guinea pig. "She patrolled the hallways to grab one of us and be sure there was a second view," Sullivan says. "I . . . was around, so I went over with her." The issue was Sally's Personal Preference Kit (PPK), the traveling toiletries case that every astronaut took into space. The women had already lobbied to replace the British Sterling deodorant, the men's hair tonic and the Old Spice shaving cream with more female-friendly lotions and potions. They had also included an item that only NASA could obscure as Female Hair Restraints. We call them rubber bands. A brief flap over how much make-up to include led to a pick-your-own decision. Sally didn't take any.

But the new female PPK had something else.

"Sally opens it up and looks in, and looks up at me with this rolling of the eyes that I had come to know as her 'you have got to be kidding me' look," Kathy Sullivan says. "She reaches in and picks up this edge of this band of pink plastic, and now I can see tampon, tampon, tampon, tampon. Then she reaches the bottom of the string and pulls again, and it was like a bad stage act. There just seemed to be this endless unfurling of Lord only knows how many tampons." They were all strung together like sausages, so they wouldn't float off in the weightlessness of space. A scissors was included in the kit to cut the little tubes apart. "We're both starting to laugh, and mathematics is flashing through my mind. There are some things we know about this. This is a simple physiological process."

Menstruation has long befuddled the brains of those unable to experience it. It has also been blamed for all manner of infirmity. Dr. Randy Lovelace's team concluded that the women who performed so well with the grueling 1959 Mercury astronaut tests were complicated by "monthly physiologic changes . . . [that made them] inattentive and accident-prone." Just over a decade later, a Democratic party activist named Ed Berman (who happened to be a physician) told a female congresswoman (Patsy Mink of Hawaii) that the reason women shouldn't aspire to high office in this country was because of women's once-a-month "raging hormonal influences." Rhea Seddon understood the folklore that threatened the women of her generation: "I'm sure they'll be watching to see if women go bananas because it's just about time for their period to begin," she said as a trainee. "It's foolish, but we have to prove it's foolish. They didn't think that Alan Shepard would be able to swallow or urinate in weightlessness, and he proved that was ridiculous. And I think women will have to prove certain things about their abilities that might seem equally ridiculous."

Until then, the Johnson Space Center was there to help. "I remember the engineers trying to decide how many tampons should fly on a one-week flight," Sally Ride said. "They asked, 'Is one hundred the right number?' "

"No," Sally said. "That would not be the right number."

"Well, we want to be safe."

"Well, you can cut that in half with no problem at all," Sally told them. She was laughing when she recounted the story. So was Kathy Sullivan.

"I think I just fell on the floor . . . That was pretty funny. 'Not quite so many, guys. It's just a bit overkill.' "

Sally wouldn't need any of it. Jogging twenty-five miles a week stopped her periods. The engineers didn't need to know that.

(Much later, the first American woman to actually use tampons in space—a distinction she prefers to keep unpublished—discovered that the capillary action meant she needed a pad as well. NASA wound up letting the women pack their own supplies.)

It was, at least, gender light-years from Sally's first encounter with NASA swag. Back in 1978, when she was invited to Edwards Air Force Base to see another test landing of *Enterprise*, every visiting astronaut—including the women—received souvenirs of the occasion: gold-plated shuttle tie-clips and cuff-links.

Meanwhile, on the other side of the globe, another woman went into space. Svetlana Savitskaya, an experienced, thirty-four-year-old Soviet test pilot, launched aboard a Soyuz 7 on August 19, 1982, on a mission with two male cosmonauts that lasted nearly eight days and included a rendezvous with the space station. Tass, the official Soviet news agency, reported that "no substantial differences in the reactions of the female and male organisms to the influence of space flight factors were found." American officials huffed that the timing of the trip of the second female in space looked suspiciously like propaganda to undercut Sally's upcoming flight. But being number three didn't bother Sally at all.

THE PRESS, THE PRESSURE

The closer it got to liftoff, the more tightly Sally stayed sealed in the protective NASA bubble. When the barrier was breached—when a reporter or tourist trespassed her privacy zone—she could, in her terms, "flip the switch marked 'Oblivious.'" Or, as she said to the guy who asked, again, her reaction to all the buzz about her, "I am so excited to get a chance to fly that I'm able to ignore all you people." She couldn't avoid every interview—and fully understood her new role as a NASA spokesperson—but with twenty or so daily requests in the weeks just before her flight (a "paralyzing" volume comparable to that of the Neil Armstrong days, according to NASA), she had to draw the line somewhere. Ironically, one of the publications that never got an audience was *Life* magazine, onetime benefactor and lionizer of the first generation of astronauts. I have no idea if Sally contributed to that decision, but correspondence between *Life*'s top editor and NASA's top managers makes it clear that the space agency would have liked her to comply. She did not.

On May 24, 1983, NASA held the traditional preflight crew press conference, the last chance for the media at large to understand the mission and to get some good quotes. Sally had grown ever more confident in the year since she and her crew had first met the press, and the gold chains around her neck were now joined by the slim wedding band on her left hand. She nonchalantly drummed her fingers on the desk—a lifelong trait that must have dug trenches onto public lecterns, corporate tables and the frame of innumerable T-38s awaiting takeoff—as she batted back questions from a press corps starved for news. The quality of the inquisition thirty years ago uncovered no Pulitzer contenders; Sally's answers, however, were keepers:

Q: When you're not on duty, what are you looking forward to doing?

A: When I'm not on duty? [Turning to Commander Crippen.] Are you letting me off duty, Crip? [Laughter.]

Q: Has it taken a little bit of getting used to working with four men . . . and do they tend to defer to you?

A: It really hasn't taken any getting used to. I was a graduate student in physics and I was used to working with men. . . . I haven't felt like I've been deferred to in any way. In fact, Crip won't even open doors for me anymore.

Q: Do you have any plans to be the first mother who has traveled to space?

A: You'll notice that I'm not answering the . . . question. [Here, a chortle.]

There were some queries that Sally treated seriously. Did she think the coverage of her was disproportionate? "I think maybe it's too bad that our society isn't further along and this is such a big deal," she said. "But if the American public thinks it's a big deal, then it's probably good that it's getting the coverage that it's getting. I think it's time . . . that people realize that women in this country can do any job they want to do."

As for her promotion to a symbol for womankind, "I've come to realize that I will be a role model," she said at the preflight press conference. "That's something that I didn't come to NASA intending to be. I joined the program to get a chance to fly. . . . What I intend to do is do as good a job as I can, do what I was trained to do while I'm up there, and hope that that provides a good role model."

Sally stopped talking when she was done with her responses—didn't stumble on, looking to clarify or qualify. That is very hard to do. But the would-be Dodgers shortstop fielded every ball with finesse. Even the one that I'd nominate as the dumbest question to anyone of all time. The reporter was from *Time* magazine. And he started by saying he had "a couple of quick questions here, sir, or ma'am." Sally shook the confusion off, laughing. He remained clueless, warming up slowly. "What are you going to do after the end of this flight . . . do you sense you'll become a footnote in history or will you go on the shelf?" The NASA public relations man muttered, *sotto voce,* "Cancel your subscription to *Time*?" Sally took the high road, answering that she'd "get back in line for another flight." The reporter, foolishly, went on. He was wondering, he said, about her training. When there was a glitch, or a problem, "How did you respond? How do you take it as a human being? Do you weep?" Now Sally closed her eyes, smiling and shaking her head as if to say, "Is he for real?" Then she laughed out loud, gestured to pilot Rick Hauck sitting to her right and said, "Why doesn't anybody ask Rick these questions!" The crew, as usual, closed the circle, with Crippen interjecting, "The commander weeps!"

Aviation Week & Space Technology, the industry's poker-faced technical bible, editorialized about the "patronizing drivel" being thrown at Sally during the entire run-up to her flight. They hadn't even heard this one, lobbed after the press conference:

Q: Did you ever wish you were a boy?
A: No, I never thought about that.

No question was too invasive, but no answer generated the headline being sought. Joyce Ride, who'd confessed that her scariest nightmare was to see "Sally on the cover of the *National Enquirer*" had nothing to worry about. And if the question wasn't asked, someone made it up. No one, Sally said, ever asked her, "Will you wear a bra in space?" Still, it persisted in the Sally Ride folklore, complete with a made-up response.

Adhering to NASA procedure, the May press conference was followed by brief, one-on-one interviews for major media, which gave me a personal take for our ABC News coverage. Sally was more relaxed and a bit more forthcoming. "I don't mind people asking me," she told me, "whether I'm going to be doing any of the cooking on orbit, unless it's asked by someone who expects the only reason I'm flying is because Crip needs somebody to serve him coffee." Her flight was important, she said, "because it's something that a woman hasn't done before. And it's more evidence that women can do everything." I asked her—partly in whimsy—"Do you think that you're as good as any male astronaut here?" Sally didn't hesitate. "Yeah," she said instantly, flashing me a look that said she knew I agreed.

Sally's father saw a positive effect to the interrogations. "Sally's answers have been waking a few people up," Dale Ride said. "I think what she's doing, as much as anything, is using these questions to help destroy the stereotypes that men respond one way to a situation and women respond in another." The man who helped raise his daughter without gender limitations had clearly done his job. "It points out the stupidity of believing in the inadequacy of women in handling traditionally male roles," he said.

Sally herself later wrote that the attention made her "aware of what our culture would expect of a woman's reactions and capabilities," aware of the scrutiny "to see if I would crumble or falter. I felt it was important to react with composure and strength." She said she understood how Billie Jean King had felt nearly a decade earlier, when the hopes of so many women rested on her victory over Bobby Riggs. "As a woman, as well as a tennis player, I would have been terribly disappointed if Billie Jean had lost that day, but she didn't. Now I was faced with a similar situation. I didn't want to let other women down."

Launch was set for June 18, 1983—two months later than originally planned, which, in Sally's ever positive outlook, gave her two more months to train. Johnny Carson joked on *The Tonight Show* that the shuttle would be delayed so that Sally could find a purse to match her shoes. America's favorite late-night host would work Sally into his monologue half a dozen more times, but the other frat house gags about her deodorant, her pantyhose and—yup—her brassiere, met mostly with boos or embarrassed silence from the studio audience. In just over a year, NASA's selection and Sally's conduct had transformed female astronauts from a punch line to a matter of national pride.

On June 1, the four men and one woman of STS-7 had lunch with President Reagan at the White House, the first shuttle astronauts to do so before flying. It nearly didn't happen. That morning, Sally and Crippen were at NASA Headquarters for some meetings. As they headed out for 1600 Pennsylvania Avenue with just half an hour to get there, the NASA elevator got stuck between floors. The commander looked at the upcoming first American woman in space and started laughing, then picked up the elevator phone and said, "You're not going to believe this . . ." Someone rescued them and they made it in time to the White House, where Sally sat next to the president.

The new female face of the shuttle beamed out from the covers of major magazines, from *Ms.* to *Newsweek* to *People*. *Time* miniaturized her on the tiny fake foldover flap (twice). Supreme Court Justice Sandra Day O'Connor, who had become the first woman appointed to the High Court two years earlier, and Kathrine Switzer, who had liberated the Boston Marathon for women, were among many who sent telegrams of good luck. *Sesame Street*'s Miss Piggy wired, "BON VOYAGE," asking Sally to test the best eye shadow and lip gloss for space travel in anticipation of Piggy's own turn with the stars. "MOI WANTS TO LOOK LIKE GANG-BUSTERS. KISSY KISSY."

The telegram from a less vain and more experienced fan, Miss Baker—one of the first female monkeys in space—predicted, "I know you will have the ride of a lifetime," and extended an invitation to the rocket museum in Huntsville, Alabama, where she lived in retirement, and where "we'll have a meeting of the great sorority of space."

KSC

Three days before liftoff—L-minus-three in NASA terminology—the crew arrived at the Kennedy Space Center (KSC) in Florida in their matching T-38s. I joined a small scrum of reporters who watched the sleek jets taxi down the runway in formation, waiting and filming as the five crew members disembarked and walked across the tarmac to a waiting microphone. Sally, in her royal blue flight suit with the American flag on the left sleeve, toed the line. "Sure thank you all for coming out," she said blandly. I had never seen her so subdued.

She was putting one foot in front of the other, trying not to get caught up in the magnitude of the moment. And she grounded herself in nostalgia, calling old friends, watching old movies. She had earlier taken the time to handwrite invitations to her guests, for whom each astronaut had reserved seats in the VIP bleachers, plus access to a bus and car passes. The invites were Sally casual: "Dear Bill," she wrote Bill Colson on NASA/JSC stationery, "Want to come to a launch? I just happen to have access to some tickets . . ." Besides her family (now grown to include Bear's husband and toddler son), her list reviewed her life from Westlake to Stanford, from tennis to volleyball physics, with all past and future romances. Molly, who was now out and openly gay, brought her partner. Tam, still just a friend, was there too. Sally's sentimental side extended to her shuttle baggage. Among the items she was carrying onboard: banners for Westlake, Stanford, the state of California; gold rings for Steve and herself; a charm for Carolyn Huntoon; a feather for Molly; silver medallions for her family and each of her five female classmates. Sally's only regret was that she could not share the moment with Elizabeth Mommaerts, her science teacher.

While Sally settled into the crew quarters, her friends and relatives explored the twenty-mile stretch of scrub and marshland from which every American rocket carrying a human has ever launched. The flat strip of the Kennedy Space Center—on an island by the Atlantic Ocean, and across the Banana River from the Cape Canaveral Air

Force Station—is both a preserve for glorious nature and a monument to sophisticated technology. Manatees, egrets and alligators share real estate with a spaceport. Towering above all, the mammoth white Vehicle Assembly Building, or VAB, where the shuttle—like the immense Saturn rockets before it—was mated with its components before its slow parade to the pad. You have no idea how immense the VAB is until you stand beside it, and the numbers barely tell the story: 525 feet tall, 716 feet wide, 518 feet deep. NASA points out that each stripe on the flag painted on the exterior is the size of a tour bus. When you go inside, you feel like an ant. When you look up, you often see clouds inside—and rain. The VAB is big enough to generate its own weather system, a cathedral of technology with a built-in heaven.

To acclimatize her body for space, Sally took some precautions recommended by other astronauts—aerobatics in the T-38, sleeping with her feet elevated. But when she found herself feeling good ("no queasiness, no twinges") she dropped the preps. She seemed calm and collected. When she called me that Friday before launch, L-minus-one, and swung by the press site for her see-but-don't-breathe-on-me wave, she was her mischievous self.

"I remember asking her, 'Tell me why I shouldn't be scared to death,'" Bear says. "And she said, 'Because I'm not. I have complete trust in them, and you may not understand that, but you know me.' We had a conversation about faith. It's informed trust, and she said, 'I know enough about this stuff that it's worth trusting my life to.'" Molly Tyson had earlier asked her the same question, which Sally dismissed, asking, "What about falling into a time warp? Being swallowed by a black hole? What about an attack by the Klingons?"

But later that day, Molly heard something very different. George Abbey had noticed that Sally was "pacing," and summoned Molly to spend some time with her. "You always want the crew to be as relaxed and rested as much as possible before their flight," Abbey explains, especially "first-time flyers. I thought it would be a good idea for Sally to be with a close friend for a bit." Because of the medical quarantine, Molly had to pass a quick physical to gain entrance to the "beach house," on an isolated part of the property. The visit was a surprise to Sally, and the two friends chatted for a time. Molly saw Sally's excitement, "like an athlete waiting to play on Center Court at Wimbledon." Then, as Molly departed, Sally stopped her and said, "I'm aware that this is not without risks. I realize I could die." Molly was stunned. "It struck me as the most vulnerable thing she'd ever said to me," Molly says now. "I had her on such a high, unreal pedestal that I was surprised by even this hint that she was afraid." She thinks Sally was reaching out, looking for some connection to their old relationship, but Molly was too shocked to respond. And Sally didn't follow up. They never spoke of it again.

Sally's candor is rare, but not the sensation. After she returned, she would often gloss over her own feelings by quoting Chief Astronaut John Young's statement about liftoff: "If you show me a person who's not a little nervous before a launch, I'll show you a person I wouldn't want to get in the same room with."

That night Sally had her final pre-flight physical exam, rejecting the anti–motion sickness pills but agreeing to the enema (probably just for convenience) and taking a sleeping pill to guarantee a solid eight hours before launch. She went to bed at 7:00 p.m.

As she dropped into a deep sleep, *Challenger* stood at attention on Pad 39A, the same one from which Neil Armstrong was shot to the Moon. Banks of xenon lights bathed the stack in a brilliant glow against the pitch black sky. Overnight, half a million gallons of liquid oxygen and liquid hydrogen filled the giant external tank.

Seated in the darkened cockpit—keeping watch—was astronaut Anna Fisher, one month away from delivering her first baby. For this flight, she was the lead of the "Cape Crusaders," the team of astronauts who served as the link between the crew and their activities at the Cape. Once the switches in the cockpit were set, a Cape Crusader maintained guard duty to be sure no one accidentally (or otherwise) changed the configuration. "It was fun, and great training," Fisher tells me of her night, lying on her back, all alone, in the darkened vehicle—a pregnant woman in the cockpit, securing the site for the crew with the first American woman about to launch. A scene for the history books.

On the other hand, that same afternoon, Fisher had been at the crew quarters, her belly bump unconcealed by the blue flight suit that all astronauts wore during the countdown. The NASA administrator, passing her in the hallway, took a quick look and said, "Safe flight, Sally."

GO!

In the orange glow of the Florida dawn, Sally lay on her back, strapped into the hard metal seat in *Challenger*'s cockpit, breathing oxygen through the hose connected to her helmet. Four checklists lay open, with tabs to contingency plans, just in case. Straight ahead were screens that would display the pulse points of their path to space, vital information she would monitor for just over eight crucial minutes until they were safely in orbit. When she stretched upward to her left, she could see the launch tower through the window beyond commander Bob Crippen; to the right, outside pilot Rick Hauck's window, the cloudless sky was turning blue. With minutes to go she took her own pulse. 56. Very mellow.

Since awakening that morning at 3:13 a.m.—just over four hours before launch—Sally had been struggling to keep control of her emotions, to concentrate on her job. She had washed and dried her hair, then proceeded to the traditional crew breakfast, where she ate cereal, three pieces of toast and orange juice ("more than usual") "trying to look like nothing unusual was about to happen," as TV cameras recorded her every move.

More cameras greeted the "walkout," flashbulbs popping in those pre–cell phone days, as the crew headed into their Astrovan for the quick drive to the launch complex. Approaching the pad, Sally thought the colossal machine sounded like an animal, gurgling and hissing as if it were alive. Riding up the 195-foot-long elevator to reach the shuttle's entry hatch, she tried not to look down. Before she entered the White Room, where her helmet and hose would be fitted, she used the restroom—"last toilet on Earth," according to one NASA manager.

Now it was time.

"T minus 35 seconds, we're just a few seconds away from switching command to the onboard computers," announced Hugh Harris, the voice of Launch Control.

With less than a minute to go, launch managers handed off to *Challenger*, putting the spacecraft's computers in charge. Instantly, Sally realized, "I felt totally helpless. Totally overwhelmed by what was happening. It was just very, very clear that for the next several seconds we had absolutely no control over our fates. I had a sense of being overwhelmed—maybe the first time in my entire life that I truly felt that way."

The countdown sequence is meticulously calibrated, a precise order of events that every astronaut can repeat by rote. But once the computers take over, the seconds tick by too quickly to follow. Sally just had to feel it.

"T minus 5, 4, 3 . . ."

Challenger's massive main engines roared to life, producing billows of white smoke that enveloped the launch pad and a gentle rumble that rippled through Sally's body. The dark visor on her helmet was down. She held onto her pencil. Three seconds later, the solid rockets ignited, twin crackling sticks of power breaking the force of gravity and heaving the 4.5-million-pound stack upwards. At 7:33 a.m. on June 18, 1983, her world changed.

"And liftoff, liftoff of STS-7 and America's first woman astronaut. And the shuttle has cleared the tower."

"All of a sudden," Sally said, "we were going someplace."

Challenger rotated counterclockwise as it streaked through the skies, a ballerina pirouetting to stardom.

"Roll program," radioed Crippen from the flight deck, his voice straining above the thunder.

Sally, too, fought the turbulence to follow her script and call out, "LVLH," a reminder to Crip and Hauck that the cockpit switches should now reflect the Local Vertical Local Horizontal position of the spaceship. When she pronounced the next milestone—"forty seconds"—they were nearly three miles high and supersonic. The ride was noisy and rough, shaking their seats and rattling their heads in their helmets, but, Sally observed, "We all seemed to be clipping along pretty well, and really very confident, a little bit buoyant." Two minutes in, they left Earth's atmosphere, and the rockets split away with a whitish-orange flash, the brightness startling Sally. Now the ride smoothed out, solid and steady on the mighty engines. And quiet enough so she could lift her visor. She checked the instruments and displays to confirm that all was in order, so invigorated that she barely noticed the buildup of 3G forces pushing her body into her seat as she bent her head to turn the pages of her checklist.

"Roger, MECO [Main Engine Cut Off]," confirmed ground control.

Right on schedule, the main engines shut down and *Challenger* hung free, nearly 68 miles high. It had taken eight and a half minutes.

Sally did the standard astronaut trick of setting her checklist in front of her and watching it float. "I wanted to try out all the different things I could do," she said. Next to her, John Fabian emitted whoops of joy. A little over two minutes later, Crippen fired *Challenger*'s smaller engines to boost them into their proper orbit; a second firing would come half an hour later. From some 184 miles high, traveling 17,500 miles an hour, Sally reminded the world of her California childhood.

"Houston, *Challenger*. Have you ever been to Disneyland?"

"Affirmative."

"That was definitely an E ticket."

"Roger that, Sally."

It was only years later, when she'd had time to assess her experience through the lens of time and disaster, that she could describe "the psychological and emotional feeling that come along with the actual launch . . . fueled by the realization that you're . . . sitting on top of tons of rocket fuel and it's basically exploding underneath you. It's an emotionally and psychologically overwhelming experience. Very exhilarating. Exhilarating, terrifying, and overwhelming all at the same time."

Her parents felt it without leaving the ground.

As Dale Ride watched his firstborn climb into space atop a white-hot column of power, he dropped his jaw in pure amazement. Or just relief. Tears ran down his grinning face. His wife, Joyce, looked stunned, and held the waiting press at bay with a broad smile, a cup of water in her cocked arm, and a mock threat: "The first one who asks how I feel gets it." Then she upheld the family's reputation for quick wit when asked her advice to future space travelers. "Think about your mother!" she urged. Finally, she added this benediction to a day that had turned out, well, heavenly: "How about, God bless Gloria Steinem!"

The prominent feminist, who had watched the launch a few feet away from the Rides, predicted, "Millions of little girls are going to sit by their television sets and see they can be astronauts, heroes, explorers and scientists." Antifeminist activist Phyllis Schlafly, who had also been invited by NASA, thought it was fine that Sally, not she, had flown: "I have no desire to be an astronaut," she said. "My eighteen-year-old daughter doesn't want to be an astronaut either." No mention of sanitary facilities.

My seventy-nine-year-old mother also didn't want to be an astronaut but was thrilled that I'd brought her to Florida to experience the moment. "I've seen the horse and buggy," Shirley Sherr told me afterwards. "I've seen the car and the train and the airplane. And now this." That a woman was aboard was, she said, "Perfect."

An estimated half million people cheered the launch from cars, trucks, boats and tents lining KSC's waterways and highways that morning. Some wore Sally Ride tee-shirts; others drank a rum cocktail called Sally's First Ride, as Sallymania swept the Space Coast. A ten-year-old salesgirl peddled shuttle pencil sharpeners ("You pull out the exhaust to sharpen your pencil"). Wilson Pickett's 1966 rock anthem, "Mustang

Sally," the one Sally said she had "been running from since I was fifteen," blared over countless American radios: "Ride, Sally, Ride." A restaurant marquee in Cocoa Beach made the lyrics more inclusive: "Ride, Sally Ride! And you guys can tag along, too!"

Every day for a week, there were stories about the mission—and its star mission specialist—in print and on the airwaves. Everywhere but the Soviet Union, where the government-controlled press instead ran two stories on her predecessor by twenty years, Valentina Tereshkova.

After anchoring the liftoff and preparing a piece for that evening's newscast, I signed off with an "attaboy!" to the folks in charge, however belatedly. "Technologically, NASA is pushing towards the twenty-first century," I said. "But in human terms, it has finally entered the twentieth."

SALLY'S RIDE

NASA makes spaceflight look easy. You burst through the atmosphere, unbuckle the straps, then float like a leaf in the unrestrained universe of weightlessness. In fact, Sally felt "not disoriented, not strange, but mentally I was unused to not being able to control my body. I really flailed around." Her audio reflections, recorded several months later, reveal a slightly longer adjustment to the alien environment that she'd inhabit for seven days. When she drifted down to the middeck area, retrieving something from her clothing locker was nothing like opening a dresser drawer at home: "I'd pull out a locker and I'd find myself unable to look at the contents, because I'd be stretched out holding the handle, with my feet out straight behind me. And things would come floating out. It took a long time to figure out how to grab onto something without you floating off faster than it does. How to contain all the things that really want to be floating around."

Stowing her kneeboard (the tablet strapped to her thigh) in the locker required five full minutes; removing the harness she wore during liftoff and stuffing it into the storage bag "took me a lot longer than it should have, and a lot longer than it would have even a day later. . . . Anything I had to do that . . . required manipulating equipment or body . . . I didn't know how to do it." Sally remembered from her KC-135 flights that breaststroking, without the density of water, wouldn't work. To swim through space, she had to push off something solid to get traction. She felt like a "baby deer" on a "frozen lake," in a scene from a "slapstick comedy."

She also felt tired, "a sudden and overwhelming urge to close my eyes. And it took all the strength I had to keep them open." Assisting John Fabian in the launch of the first satellite "was a struggle," she admitted, "getting the cameras set up—powered, selected, the right switches uncovered." She stuck with the checklist and the Canadian communications satellite made it safely to orbit. Halfway through the sequence, she was alert again. She then took the lead on a similar set of commands—flipping switches, coordinating computer inputs—to deploy a communications satellite for the government of Indonesia. Several hours into the flight, *Challenger* had earned nearly $20 million for NASA.

When ground controllers later wished them a good night, after saying it had been a good day, Sally radioed back, "You think it was a good day for you? You should have been up here!"

Sally was thrilled that she never got ill, never needed medication for space adaptation syndrome, but, she said to her tape recorder, "I was aware that my stomach was there." When the orbiter was positioned upside down, so that looking out the window meant looking down at Earth, she felt strange, "uncomfortable at first. . . . I liked being right side up." That's how she stayed for the first few hours. When she went below, she avoided floating down the ladder head first. When she ate her first meal, she couldn't relax. "I couldn't anchor myself without tightening muscles somewhere—generally stomach or back muscles, and that was uncomfortable for eating."

But she did manage part of the turkey sandwich she'd packed into her pocket, then three hearty meals a day for the rest of the trip, from scrambled eggs (dehydrated, in a pouch, heated on electric coils in a small aluminum suitcase-like contraption) to an apple-grapefruit drink that she especially liked. Within a day or two, she was feeling not only fine, but superb.

Later that week, Sally and John Fabian floated up to the flight deck to take turns using the robot arm to lift yet another satellite out of *Challenger*'s cargo bay—the West German platform called SPAS-01 (*Shuttle Pallet Satellite*), a 15-foot-long flying Tinker Toy full of experiments. Fabian took the first shift, skillfully manipulating the hand controllers to stretch out the arm, grapple the SPAS and pluck it from the bay. The object was to drop it into space—in the same orbit as *Challenger* itself—so that Crippen and Hauck could fire some jets for a rendezvous, the first tests of the shuttle's ability to maneuver in close proximity to another object. This would be critical for future missions, including docking with the still-unbuilt space station. Fabian's turn went flawlessly.

So did Sally's, a celestial game of toss and catch that would have made Sandy Koufax proud. The release, she said, felt just like the simulation. "But the act of going up and capturing a satellite was a little more scary." In the simulators, "if you miss, it's just a virtual arm going through a virtual payload, and no harm's done. . . . I remember thinking, 'Oh, my gosh. This is real metal that will hit real metal if I miss. What if we don't capture this satellite?' "

In the midst of the maneuvers, with the SPAS orbiting on its own, they went off script—with Crippen's permission—to give Mission Control a surprise. Sally and Fabian had quietly worked out a procedure to manipulate the arm into the number 7—for this, the seventh mission. He worked the controls and she sent the signal to the satellite that activated its onboard camera, the timing carefully arranged, according to Fabian, "so that we could catch the space shuttle against that black sky with the horizon down below." That was the picture they wanted, the first ever taken of the shuttle in orbit, a self-portrait with a pedigree.

"We spent a lot of time taking that picture," Sally said, "so that everybody would know it was STS-7 that took it."

Sally, have a ball!

—Steve Hawley's advice to Sally before she launched

Whenever she could, Sally headed for *Challenger*'s windows and stared outside. The views she later described often combined what she'd seen from this and her subsequent flight. "I got to look at coral reefs off the coast of Australia," she said of the view that has awed every astronaut. "I could see glaciers in the Himalayas, I could see deforestation in the Amazon." She also saw smog over Los Angeles. When they passed over Florida, she could see all the way up the coast to New York.

In orbit, racing along at five miles per second, the space shuttle circles the Earth once every 90 minutes. I found that at this speed, unless I kept my nose pressed to the window, it was almost impossible to keep track of where we were at any given moment—the world simply changes too fast . . . it's embarrassing to float up to a window, glance outside, and then have to ask a crewmate, "What continent is this?"

Traveling in space, she said, was a lesson in geopolitics:

I also became an instant believer in plate tectonics; India really *is* crashing into Asia, and Saudi Arabia and Egypt really *are* pulling apart, making the Red Sea wider . . . The Great Wall of China is *not* the only manmade object visible from space. [She saw] spiral eddies [in the oceans], wakes of large ships . . . The lights of cities sparkle . . . On one nighttime pass from Cuba to Nova Scotia the entire East Coast of the

United States appeared in twinkling outline. Lightning . . . day to night and back again during a single orbit—hurtling into darkness, then bursting into daylight . . . Part of the fascination with space travel is the element of the unknown—the conviction that it's different from Earth-bound experiences. And it is.

Years later, when Sally was walking down a New York sidewalk with Andrew Chaikin, a friend and fellow space buff, Chaikin pointed up to the blue sky, dotted that day with clouds. "I had decided in my head that that's the way it might have looked when you looked at Earth from space," he tells me. "And I turned to Sally and said, 'What do you think? Is that what it looks like?' " Chaikin laughs at his own presumption. "She shook her head and said, 'It's so spectacularly different!' "

But the spectacle that most captured Sally's attention was one that would shape the rest of her life's work, the one she would mention every chance she got.

> I remember the first time that I looked towards the horizon. I saw the blackness of space, and then the bright blue Earth. And then I noticed right along the horizon it looked as if someone had taken a royal blue crayon and just traced along Earth's horizon. And then I realized that that blue line, that really thin royal blue line, was Earth's atmosphere, and that was all there was of it. And it's so clear from that perspective how fragile our existence is. It makes you appreciate how important it is to take care of that atmosphere.

She would occasionally change the metaphor: the atmosphere was Earth's spacesuit; or it was "about as thick as the fuzz on a tennis ball." So narrow, "a strong gust of interplanetary wind could blow it all away" . . . "it's everything that separates us from the vacuum of space. If we didn't have that atmosphere, we wouldn't be here, and if we do anything to destroy that atmosphere, we won't be here. So it really puts the planet in perspective."

In time, that view would become her incentive, but for now, Sally was literally on a high. With the rest of her crew she helped grab President Reagan's jellybeans out of the air; she tumbled around like a fish in a pond, usually wearing shorts and a TFNG tee-shirt, in stocking feet, in the shuttle's pressurized environment. She strapped herself on to the treadmill and ran around the world, an exercise to stave off muscle loss. And she did it all to the sound of the Beatles and the Beach Boys, whose music she'd transferred to sixty-minute audio cassettes that she played on her Sony Walkman. Her tapes also included the Lovin' Spoonful, the Jefferson Airplane, Lou Christie, the Eagles, Kenny Loggins, Janis Joplin and Jim Croce. Sally later lamented that with NASA's three-cassette rule, she had only three hours of music. Digital players were more than a decade away.

Sally confirmed that the toilet's new funnel system for women functioned smoothly. "It was a lot like sitting on a vacuum cleaner," she later said. Unfortunately, the WCS mechanics broke down on the fifth day, so they all ended up using the toilet without suction, which was a primitive, but acceptable alternative. During liftoff, Sally also determined that the DACT, the women's diaper, worked fine.

At night, she hooked her blue sleeping bag onto the middeck lockers, crawled in and slept comfortably, her arms floating up in front of her face, like a puppy on its hind legs. Sometimes she'd awaken after a few hours, and glide to a window, with music in her ears. There'd be plenty of time to sleep when she got home, she thought. The ebony sky stretched endlessly, with, she wrote, "Earth as a nightlight."

HOMEWARD BOUND

The press maintained its love affair with Sally, breathlessly reporting every sighting from NASA's cameras. And the agency passed another milestone when astronaut Mary Cleave served as CapCom. For the first time, a woman in space communicated with a woman on Earth. The moment was more memorable than their exchange.

Mary Cleave: It was nice workin' with you last night.

SKR: See ya, Mary.

MC: Bye bye, Sally.

"To me that was a big deal, and to Sally, too," Cleave tells me. "But we didn't talk about it. We were probably the generation that just tried to fit in, not stick out."

Challenger was supposed to return to KSC on Friday, June 24, the first of what NASA hoped would be regular landings in Florida. Valuable time (to prepare the next launch) and money could be saved by not having to ferry the spaceplane cross-country from California. So Joyce and Dale Ride, along with Bear and her family, had stayed put for the week, following the progress of the flight with increasing confidence. One day, while their daughter was in orbit some 200 miles high, they went to the beach and flew a kite. It was, says Bear, "a good description of how they raised us."

But bad weather at the Cape forced *Challenger* to land at Edwards Air Force Base in California. The Rides joked that they could have stayed home since Encino was only about one hundred miles away. Instead, I offered them the chance to watch the landing from the privacy of the ABC News trailer, and asked if we might videotape their reactions. As a result, when the shuttle dropped out of the sky and Crippen steered it down the middle of the runway on the dry lake bed, we captured the exuberance: Dale pumping his fist in the air as his celebrated daughter came back to Earth, Joyce screaming and punching two fists, after which both Rides slid their hands across the sofa and held each other tight. "Hot dog!" Joyce finally exclaimed, tossing her hat in the air. "Do Presbyterians light candles? I'll go light a candle."

Sally emerged from *Challenger* in her light blue flight suit with a vivacious smile. As the crew walked the tarmac inspecting the shuttle, she and Fabian slid their arms around each other in the pure pleasure of the moment, and the 6'1" Air Force pilot hugged the 5'5½" astrophysicist with such energy, her feet left the ground. "When I see that videotape I smile to myself," Fabian tells me. "Because I kind of half lifted her and that is not like me to do that! I think we were just so overjoyed at being back on the ground and having succeeded in what we were doing. And the machine looked so great, it really did. You always worry about damage to the machine and getting it ready to fly again. I think it is the sheer joy of mission completion."

For Sally, it was simply sheer joy.

"The thing that I'll remember most about the flight is that it was fun," she said from the landing strip. "In fact, I'm sure it was the most fun I'll ever have in my life."

She'd done it. She'd done it without messing up. She'd done it so well, there was no room for doubt that any woman could do anything in space. But Sally would soon appreciate the insight from another astronaut after an even more momentous space flight fourteen years earlier. As Neil Armstrong, Buzz Aldrin and Mike Collins headed back to Earth from the Moon, astronaut Jim Lovell radioed up to them from Houston, "I just want to remind you that the most difficult part of your mission is going to be after recovery."

6

·····························

REENTRY

JUNE 1983–JUNE 1985

Welcomed home by Mickey, Kennedy Space Center, July 1983.

Two weeks before he set foot on the Moon, Neil Armstrong was asked whether he thought the magnitude of his mission, and the celebrity of being first, would affect his carefully guarded privacy. Armstrong did not. "I think a private life is possible within the context of such an achievement," he said.

—July 5, 1969

WELCOME HOME!

Slicing through the atmosphere amidst an inferno of bright-hot molecules was the easy part. Sally's return to Earth on June 24, 1983, had
been cocooned by the shuttle and its heat-dissipating tiles, making the
passage from space perilous but predictable. The only thing weighing
Sally down now was gravity, as her body readjusted to the terrestrial
environment. It felt like a dead weight. When she turned her head, the
room spun; when she walked, she bumped into things. But less than an
hour later, she was prancing along the tarmac with her usual bounce.

Re-entering civilization was something else again.

"The moment we landed, that protective shield was gone," Sally later
explained in an oral history for NASA. "The transition from being inside
this insulating bubble just before flight, then being in orbit—which is
quite far removed from people and from the media and from just kind
of the day-to-day world for a week—and then coming back down and
almost being thrown to the wolves . . ." Translation: the wolves were the
press. Sally's year of training had screened out most of the ruckus before she flew. She had gently but firmly deflected invasions into her very
private self with carefully calibrated or mission-specific responses, then
escaped back to the simulator. She never saw the box of clippings that
her mother collected; didn't watch her own interviews on TV; declined
to frame the magazine covers bearing her picture. Most would remain
piled in cartons in her closet for decades, untouched, alongside the
heaps of awards. But now she was center stage, NASA's newest offering
to a world hungry for heroes, coming face-to-face with the sort of public
inquiry she had managed to avoid for thirty-two years. "[J]ust the sheer
volume of it was something that was completely different for me," she
said, "and people reacted much differently to me after my flight than
they did before my flight. Everybody wanted a piece of me."

Ellen Baker watched it begin at Ellington Air Force Base in Houston, where the crew was flown later that afternoon—still jaunty in their
light blue flight suits—to reunite with families and friends. When Sally

stepped off the plane, she and Steve hugged as warmly and excitedly as two kids at a prom. Baker also got a big hug. Normally, that would have been the end of it, because normally, just a few people showed up. No ropes, no ceremony. But Sally's name had attracted a swarm of reporters and photographers, with headlines and deadlines to meet. "And you could see the look in Sally's eyes at that instant. It was, 'Oh my god, everything's changed now.' It was a really striking moment that I recognized and I think she recognized. It's like, you're not Sally anymore, you're something else now."

Something, or someone, whose every act was analyzed.

When limousines transported them to the nearby Johnson Space Center for a reception, a NASA protocol officer handed Sally (and no one else on the crew) a bouquet of flowers. She took them. But en route to the makeshift stage on the steps of Building 1, Sally, who rarely carried anything, even a purse, gave them back and lined up with her crewmates. All the spouses were there, too, and each of the four wives held a red rose. Steve Hawley, Sally's husband, recalls that he'd declined his flower, which left the couple free to link their arms around each other as Sally beamed and waved during the ten-minute ceremony. The crowd (mostly JSC colleagues) cheered. The crew cheered them back: this was the team that had helped make it happen. At the end of the festivities, the NASA guy, no doubt under orders, tried one more time to unload the flowers, but Sally politely gestured "no," quickly engaging in conversation with Steve and George Abbey.

The next day, Sally got slapped with Bouquet-gate. "No White Roses for a Crew Lady," blared the headline in newspapers across the country. The first American woman in space, said the article, had "spurned a large bouquet of flowers after returning from her historic voyage.... [She] shook her head and turned her back [on the NASA man], leaving him standing with an armful of flowers. She had said before the six-day mission that she wanted to be treated no differently than her crewmates."

The alleged perpetrator was stunned.

"That one little action—giving back the flowers—probably touched off more mail to me than anything I ever did or said as an astronaut," Sally later wrote. "I received hundreds of letters, almost evenly divided in what they said. Half of those who wrote were incensed. 'How could you be so rude and ungracious as to give back the flowers? That's just like you feminists.' The other half were thrilled. 'Good for you! You let them know women don't just want flowers.' The truth was, I hadn't been making a big statement one way or another. I just wanted my hands free."

Nothing was simple anymore.

Eager to avoid a media stakeout at their house, Steve had booked a room at a local hotel. But as he checked in at the front desk (with Sally safely stowed in the car), he saw a reporter he knew and realized the press would be staying at the same hotel ("I mean, getting a reservation right outside the front gate probably wasn't the smartest thing to do," he admits). So he phoned fellow astronaut Dan Brandenstein, who lived nearby, and asked if they could spend the night. The Brandensteins happily took them in. Then, Steve recalls, "we got blasted in the media for not showing up at the house so that they could film us!"

It wasn't just the media.

When *Challenger* was diverted from Florida to California, NASA decided to placate the VIPs stuck at the Kennedy Space Center—each of whom anticipated an introduction to America's newest superstar—with another female astronaut from the Johnson Space Center. "Someone went through Building 4 and it wound up being me," Kathy Sullivan says. She had smarted when Sally got the nod, but sportingly agreed to fill in that day. When she arrived at the Cape and faced several thousand people eager to bask in astronaut glory, she instantly understood that Sally's precious experience was about to be hijacked. "And I was just really glad that she had a few hours to absorb it and make it her own, to just let it soak in with her crewmates. And I also thought, if this is what you get for going first, she can have it!"

ON THE ROAD

For the next few months of her official NASA tour—a rite of flight required by every astronaut since Alan Shepard—Sally carried the NASA
flag across nearly as many borders as she'd overflown in the shuttle.
At the Kennedy Space Center in Florida, a Plexiglas-helmeted Mickey
Mouse gave her a kiss. In Sacramento, she was the star of Sally Ride Day,
a home-state toast led by Governor George Deukmejian that attracted
more crowds and security than had turned out for Queen Elizabeth II.
In Las Vegas, when asked if she'd received any good commercial offers,
she responded, "I wouldn't trade this job for one million dollars."

Sally was hailed as a hero, a heroine, a Genuine American, the first
Valley Girl in space (true) and the first Presbyterian in space (not true,
and anyway, only a hereditary possibility).

In New York, the crew received the keys to the city from Mayor Ed
Koch, a perfectly legitimate event that I'd helped arrange through my
friend the deputy mayor. It was the only way I could snag Sally and Steve
for a low-key, weekend escape at our Long Island house, where she hung
out in shorts and bare feet and enjoyed fresh clams and a James Bond
movie. And where I had the distinct pleasure, over cocktails, of introducing her to Betty Friedan, whose pioneering push for women's rights
had helped make Sally's ride possible. "Thank you," the astronaut said to
the feminist. Back in the city, Sally quickly dismissed the police officer
assigned to protect her, and with Steve back in Houston, relied on my
husband to body-block the crowds at a few events in her honor.

She fully understood her assignment and carried out most of it
without complaint. "A show of public support is critical for NASA to
maintain its budget," she later explained.

In Washington, DC, home of the votes, she briefed members of the
Congressional Space Caucus on the success of the robot arm (where
Steve was introduced as "Mr. Sally Ride"), spoke at a National Press
Club luncheon (where her male colleagues were "available to answer
questions"), and got a tee-shirt from Oregon senator Robert Packwood

that read, "A Woman's Place Is Now in Space." Most of her activities included the other STS-7 astronauts, because whenever possible, she extended every invitation to them, too—in part to share the spotlight, in part to deflect it. "I tell people that Sally Ride made me famous," John Fabian says, not ungratefully. Norm Thagard had reason to see it differently. During their tour of the Rayburn Office Building, a TV crew, eager to get a shot of Sally with the photogenic Crippen, and the others, shoved Thagard aside and mashed him against a wall, unaware (or, worse, unimpressed) that he, too, was a member of the crew. It wasn't an isolated oversight. In Sally's presence, everyone else disappeared. "She was a huge target," Fabian says. "[I]n today's political and terrorist environment, I think we would have reason to really be concerned about it. But fortunately, at the time all we had to worry about was Norm getting knocked into the wall."

At a reception for five hundred gushing admirers at the Air and Space Museum, Sally donated "something that was very close to me during the flight: my flight suit." Then she and the crew showed their home movies. Sally's charm and Crippen's charisma captivated the local pols. At one table, Lynn Cheney, wife of then-Representative Dick Cheney, conferred with Republican lobbyist Nancy Reynolds, and told a reporter, "We're just trying to decide which would make the better candidate, Crippen or Ride."

Sally and her crewmates attended a White House State Dinner, at which she was seated between President Reagan and the guest of honor, the emir of Bahrain. She discussed weightlessness with the latter (who wore a golden dagger in his waistband) and found him "very well informed on the subject." She also told him she'd seen his island country clearly from the shuttle. Sally later said the president, with whom she had already dined once and spoken to on the telephone when he called to congratulate the crew at the landing, was "a very charming person."

She was very diplomatic. Her politics stood at least 180 degrees from those of Ronald Reagan, and she bristled at what she saw as an unusual level of White House interest in her appearances—too many command performances for someone who disliked being commanded to perform. Steve Hawley says Sally felt "used. She felt like she was being forced to do things that she didn't believe in, and were for the benefit of causes and individuals she did not support. Because somebody at the White House wanted it, because somebody in the Reagan administration wanted it, or somebody at NASA Headquarters, or in Legislative Affairs, or because Senator so-and-so wanted it."

She was also disturbed by the politicization of her flight, as illustrated by the kerfuffle over Jane Fonda. The movie star and her husband, Tom Hayden (who represented the district where Dale Ride taught, in the California Assembly), were among those invited to the STS-7 launch, and Fonda, like other famous women in attendance, was quoted prominently in the press. The next day, NASA Administrator James Beggs got a call from White House Deputy Chief of Staff Michael Deaver. "What the hell was Jane Fonda doing there?" Deaver asked. "Nancy Reagan is mad and I am mad and everybody is mad." The controversy cost the NASA public information officer his job; he was reassigned to another, less glamorous, agency. Fonda responded to the flap by calling Sally "a true role model . . . able to rekindle the kind of spirit and enthusiasm that the space program had twenty years ago." As for the objection to her presence by an administration not celebrated for its feminist policies, "Just because the White House has a 'gender gap,' " Fonda said, "is no reason for NASA to have one too."

Sally made no comment. At the end of the White House dinner that July, she and Crippen presented the president with a small package of the favorite candy he'd given them—now enhanced by having flown on STS-7. "Far-out jelly beans," Crippen explained to the tickled leader of the free world. Reagan replied that he'd "save them for the museum."

The silliness was part of the package. Among the mountain of requests Sally turned down—including parades, conventions, fundraisers, endorsements and endless requests from politicians either for themselves or their constituents—was the chance to sit for a portrait of herself in jellybeans. She also eschewed opportunities to dedicate a school in Fairbanks, Alaska, to have her cat photographed for a cat food calendar (she didn't have a cat), and to give one man's son a pep talk "to help him get motivated." At its height, NASA tracked the calls for her appearances at twenty-three an hour.

"Interest in space flight ebbs and flows, so you try to capitalize on it while it's still fresh," NASA spokesman John Lawrence said. But he added an important caveat: "We believe we should use the astronaut to promote an understanding of the space program, not an understanding of the individual astronaut." It didn't always work out that way.

Sally had perfected the art of the interview to keep reporters focused on the mission, not herself. She had learned to repeat the question as part of her answer to maintain her concentration after the hundredth or so repetition. "Did you think at that moment, 'Wow, I am making history'?" asked one interviewer. "You know," Sally answered, "I thought at that moment, 'Wow, I get to *do* this.'" *Et cetera.*

And she had polished her speech to a fine shine, knowing when to pause for laughter or gasps or applause. Every telling sounded spontaneous. But she was only half kidding when, speaking to two thousand members of the American Bar Association in Atlanta, she told a questioner who asked if she was afraid to fly, "I was a lot more scared getting up to give this speech." It was a familiar complaint. In 1962, Mercury 13 pilot Jerrie Cobb had admitted as much before testifying to that congressional subcommittee about letting women become astronauts. "I'm scared to death," Cobb confessed to the chairman before the panel began. A representative from Illinois who overheard the conversation asked her, during the hearings, "How do you reconcile this emotional statement with the fact that an astronaut must be fearless and courageous and emotionally stable?" Cobb answered honestly, to appreciative laughter, "Going up into space couldn't be near as frightening as sitting here." More than twenty years later, Sally could confirm Cobb's concern.

Worse, the second the subject turned to herself, she grew anxious. The cocktail parties, the meet-and-greets, the autographs. And the creepy.

"I remember going to a talk and some guy got up and said, 'I'd like to make love to you!'" recalls a Westlake classmate. "What could she say? She was a NASA representative. How could she say, 'Go to hell?'" At another event many years later, a woman walked up to Sally after a speech and said, arms outspread, "I collect hugs. Can I have a hug?" Sally stopped her short and said, politely, "Uh, no." There were also stalkers, several, persistent and threatening enough to keep both JSC Security and the FBI on alert. At least one would later be escorted off campus by the University of San Diego police; another would fill her voice mail with shrill messages. The stalkers freaked Sally out. In time, she would stop answering her phone, guard her home address and wind up living in a house with a gate.

"I think she was kind of traumatized by all of the public attention she had to go through," Susan Okie tells me. Sally was "enough of an introvert that she had to force herself to do that day after day. That's really the price that she had to pay."

It had happened to her predecessors, too: Charles Lindbergh, Neil Armstrong, and all the rest, whose noble deeds were trivialized by endless repetition and frivolous requests for quotes. The media can be very trying. Handling it was part of her job, and some of it made sense. But for a severely private person like Sally—who had to psych herself for every public appearance—the consequences were dire.

At the height of her fame, she was losing her sense of herself. And the joy of her trip: "wanted to describe, but to friends," she noted in a typically brief summary of events. "[S]poiled it (demystified, devalued, depersonalized) describing it to press."

Tam O'Shaughnessy says Sally talked about losing her equilibrium, about getting really shaky from the constant torrent. "I felt anxious and unsettled," she told Tam. "I knew I needed help." At some point, she consulted a psychologist. "And the person"—she never said who— "helped me figure out what to do." The specifics of her therapy remain unknown, but in a lineup of bullet points on the pages of one slim memo book, Sally seems to have jotted down the lessons. She called the effort ("emotional, psychological") required for all the public relations "draining," and referred to her "Jekyll/Hyde" contrast: the "hermit side" of her character, eager to "avoid grps, avoid mtg people," fighting the fact that she was "always watched." She also indicated that like so many others seeking release, she felt better in New York City. Walking there, she observed, was "therapeutic"—the "freedom, exercise, anonymity, in the midst of crowds."

Unfortunately, that's all she wrote.

NASA, which wasn't unsympathetic to Sally's distress, asked Carolyn Huntoon to help filter out some of the less important requests and travel with her to some of the others. The two women had made a joke of Sally's fame, and Huntoon jokingly addressed Sally as "AFWIS"—America's First Woman In Space. That's how Sally signed her notes back. "You'll always be that," Huntoon reassured her, "nothing will take it away."

Huntoon saw Sally's anxiety firsthand when she had to convince her to attend the ceremony at a Texas school newly named in her honor. "I think she was embarrassed," Huntoon recalls, "so she wasn't going to go. But the center director got a call from a muckety-muck somewhere and called me. I called her."

"What can I do to get you to go?" Huntoon asked.

"If you'll take me, I'll go," Sally responded.

They made the trip. And as they walked up to the school, they heard a chorus of little voices singing the new school song:

We are proud of our school, Sally K. Ride . . .
We will always take a challenge and always do our best,
We love to take that challenge at anything we choose,
At Sally K. Ride, we'd rather win than lose.

Sally turned red, then pulled herself together and said, "Okay, I can do this." She was, Huntoon says, doing her duty. "I remember her telling me later that having me with her really made a difference. I hope so. But if she really didn't want to do something, she wouldn't do it."

Case in point: *The Bob Hope Show.*

THANKS FOR THE MEMORIES

NBC-TV was inviting viewers to "Blast Off with Bob" for his tribute to NASA: *25 Years of Reaching for the Stars*. Alan Shepard had agreed to be a guest, along with Neil Armstrong, Bob Crippen and Guy Bluford. Shortly after she returned from her flight, NASA asked Sally to join the cast. Never a fan of Hope's politics or his use of showgirls as props, she declined. NASA tried again. She still said no; she didn't want to do stupid skits. The folks at Headquarters in Washington asked Gerry Griffin, director of JSC in Houston, to intercede. "He's promised to talk about her achievements," they said of Hope. "Nothing funny where she's involved. It will be a serious thing."

Griffin remembers sitting down with Sally at a beer bust one night and relaying the request. "And I could see her stiffen a little bit. And she looked at me and said, 'No, I'm not going to do that.' And I said, 'Really? Why not?' And she said, 'Because I don't like the way he exploits women.' And I said, 'Okay, but he is kind of a national icon and he wants to tell the story about you correctly.' And she continued to look at me and said, 'No, I'm not going to do that.' She had a look on her face unlike anything I'd seen before, and I knew it was final. I knew I was at the end of my rope. I couldn't order her to do it."

Sally's protectors at JSC weren't surprised. "She wasn't going to be with Bob Hope, because he wanted good-looking babes hanging over him," one comments. "The blondes with not a lot of clothes."

Bob Crippen remembers, with amusement, that Sally then disappeared. "We couldn't find her. She got out of town. She was AWOL."

Steve didn't know where she was either. On the one hand, he saw her side of things. "I supported her decision on the Bob Hope show. I think she'd had enough of what she could stand of having NASA tell her what she needed to do," he says. "And I think she felt she was being used politically for things that were inconsistent with her politics."

On the other hand, he was annoyed. "I thought that her reaction was a little inappropriate—going AWOL and not telling anyone, in particular not telling me, and not taking responsibility for her decision," he tells me. "Particularly given that she accepted the assignment with the knowledge—although probably not in detail—that this was going to happen. And it was almost like, now that she's had her good deal, she doesn't want to go through with her part of the bargain. That's a little harsh, but some version of that. It was some time before she told me where she was. She'd gone to California."

Specifically, to Menlo Park, where a small house on a quiet street became her occasional refuge from the blare of publicity. Molly Tyson lived there, with her partner, and Sally felt safe with them. She'd come to lie low, she told them, because NASA had indicated that turning down Bob Hope was like refusing the Pope. And she joined in whatever the activity: softball practice, a margarita party, charades, or a twelve-mile run alongside Molly's partner, who was training for a marathon. Sally completed the run without any practice. Bill Colson, her old beau, stopped by to grill a big salmon. When the party got too crowded, Sally would slip off to escape the fuss. Friends, she noted bluntly but briefly in her notebook, take "photos/show you off." Sally "welcome[d] hiding vs. too many activities." But overall, it was a comfort zone. Sally called it her "hideout."

America's new favorite astronaut, whose picture was pinned on an incalculable number of teenage bulletin boards and whose achievement now inspired so many big dreams, felt most authentic, not on national TV clowning about her flight with a comedian, but hanging out with her friends, gay and straight, where no one asked for her autograph. In trying to tame the double-edged sword of fame, Sally was coming to grips with her own needs. Ambivalent about her celebrity, she was considering her options.

"I think that Sally did want fame and success," Bill Colson tells me, "but did not want to have to explain what she had accomplished to get there. She enjoys the attention she is getting, as long as she can keep observers at a distance. She has this kind of need to be in the background and the foreground both. She'd like everybody out there to know about Sally Ride, but not have to deal with them every day."

There might have been a glimmer of that when she visited with us in New York earlier that summer. One night, when her picture was on the cover of every magazine at every newsstand and we were valiantly protecting her from unwanted attention, Sally came to dinner with us, along with Billie Jean King and a few others. At the end of the meal, the waiter came by our table with a pen and asked King to sign the menu. My husband, who adored Sally, teased that he saw a flash of green jealousy in her bright blue eyes.

None of which would have changed her mind about Bob Hope's show. The incident didn't surprise anyone, least of all Gerry Griffin. "She was a person of principle, stuck to her guns," he tells me with admiration. "A strong personality who knew what she wanted to do, and how to do it. It's the same characteristic that led her to do such a fantastic job with the robot arm and all of that. If she didn't understand something, she'd ask. If someone told her something she didn't believe, she said so. Sally didn't suffer fools very well."

Or the US State Department.

INTRIGUE IN BUDAPEST

In September 1983, Sally took her postflight, praise-the-shuttle tour to Europe, three weeks, eight capital cities. Her moral support this time was pilot Rick Hauck, and together they convinced the brass that it would be healthy to bring their spouses. Then, says Hauck, he and Sally put their heads together and decided, "we've got to establish some ground rules with this. For example, no appointment would last more than fifty minutes. We must have a bathroom break every two to three hours. If we're face-to-face with the public for four hours, we have to have a fifteen-minute downtime where we're secluded, or away from the public. After six days we need a full day off." NASA bought it all. It would be a "fascinating and educational but exhausting trip," Hauck tells me. In London, at the Royal Society, Sally saw the Charter book with Isaac Newton's signature. At a reception there, a leader of the European Space Agency mentioned that he'd ridden on Space Mountain at Disney World, and asked her how it compared to the real thing. Space Mountain, Sally told him, was much scarier. They dined with the Russian ballet star Natalia Makarova, a space enthusiast. Sally and Steve jogged through Belgrade, then she and Hauck showed their film. They were greeted by Queen Beatrix and Prince Claus in The Hague, and by the King of Norway in the ancestral home of both. "Dolly [Hauck's wife at the time] and I kind of basked in the radiance of Sally's celebrity," he says. "All four of us had fun together."

But nothing compared to Sally's escapade in Budapest.

They'd been invited to a meeting of the International Astronautical Federation, a chance to promote the US shuttle program to more than 650 space scientists and engineers from some 32 nations, including the Soviet Union, which had just been branded the "Evil Empire" by President Reagan. There was only one caveat: one month earlier, a Korean Air Lines passenger jet en route to New York from Seoul had been shot down by a Soviet military plane, killing all aboard, including a US congressman. The charges of murder and espionage flew back and forth, a tense escalation of the Cold War leading to strict instructions for Sally, Rick and Steve: no mingling with the Soviet cosmonauts. No vodka toasts with the other side. Above all, no photos of our heroes snuggling up to East-West space cooperation. In other words, "show our film, give press conferences, high profile on the one hand," Sally said, perplexed by the challenge, "but low profile on the other. We didn't really know how we were going to handle that."

The Americans obeyed at first, avoiding the Russians while striking up an acceptable friendship with the Hungarian cosmonaut, Bertalan Farkas. Then, during one reception, Sally felt a tap on her elbow. "And I turned around and there was Svetlana [Savitskaya, the second Soviet woman who had beaten Sally into orbit], who I recognized immediately. And she said, 'Sally.' And I said something like, 'Hello.' And she said, 'Congratulations on your flight.' And I said, 'Thank you very much, congratulations to you.' And all the time I was kind of looking over my shoulder, wondering where the cameras were and how I was going to get out of this." If Hollywood had been orchestrating the scene, the music would have been ominous. Sally was more than keen to speak with her counterpart—they were two of the only three women who had ever flown in space—but feared the questions from reporters that would turn their meeting into an international incident. "We were trying to avoid a story: 'Female Astronaut Meets Female Astronaut and What Do They Think?' I didn't know what to say next, and she didn't either, so we exchanged smiles and both turned away."

Sally never mentioned this incident publicly. But she recorded the intrigue on her cassette player when she returned from Budapest in 1983, an audio account that vibrantly recalls the complexity of Cold War politics.

Sally spent the next fifteen minutes reassessing. She worried that she'd been rude, continued to feel uncomfortable, reminded herself that she was there representing the State Department. But longed for more conversation.

Meanwhile, she and Hauck did their jobs: signed autographs, gave interviews, listened to speeches, showed their film, went through receiving lines. But the situation nagged at Sally for another day. It was an uncommon opportunity, and Sally never let a good opportunity pass her by. The next morning, at an event at the Institute for Physics—Hungary's equivalent of our National Science Foundation—Sally made her move. She approached the Hungarian translator she'd gotten to know, Tamas Gombosi, and said quietly, "You know, I'd really like to get a chance to talk to Svetlana. Do whatever you want with that information." Gombosi picked right up on it. "Maybe we can arrange that," he said. "I'll talk to you tonight at the ambassador's reception."

Now it became a full-blown cloak-and-dagger operation. "I didn't know what I'd gotten myself into," Sally said. "I didn't mention it to either Rick or Steve, just thought I'd wait and see what Tamas came up with. I had the distinct impression that Svetlana wanted to do it."

That night, at the embassy reception, Gombosi discreetly informed

Sally that she and Steve were invited to Farkas's apartment, "and there will be other people. Are you interested?" Sally said, "Yes," and that she'd check with Steve. Gombosi told her to meet him in the hotel lobby at 9:00 p.m.

When Sally and Steve got back to their room, they discussed the invitation "as much as we thought we could," Sally said, unsure whether they were being bugged. Steve felt uncomfortable about going, and Sally felt uncomfortable going without him. She went up to Rick Hauck's room to fill him in, as the senior member of the crew. "Sounds like a great opportunity," said the man who had piloted *Challenger*. "You need to go do that." Sally drifted down to the hotel coffee shop. "And I started to get myself psyched up to meet Tamas in the lobby at nine."

By this time, the scene was worthy of Hitchcock. As rain drenched Budapest and darkness veiled their journey, Sally was whisked away in a chauffeured car to an old building that reeked of faded elegance. They walked around back to enter and climbed a set of stairs. Would the secret police be waiting? Or worse yet, a photographer? Would Sally's little caper send the US to war?

Not even close. Farkas's apartment, Sally discovered, was large and comfortable with thick carpets on the floor and . . . Yes! Rocket pictures on the wall! "Just like us!" Sally said, delighted. "First thing you see was the picture of their launch!" She started to relax.

When Svetlana arrived a few minutes later, with a male cosmonaut, both women were initially wary. "I tried to put on my friendliest smile," Sally said, "and they made some joke like, 'No press!' We were both obviously a little bit tense and yet very much at ease at the same time. Svetlana came over and sat down in the armchair next to mine."

And that was that. The two women immediately connected, chattering away—with Svetlana's pretty-good English, Tamas's translations and a smattering of sign language—about everything from their relationships with their crewmates (equally good) to the aerodynamics of their landing ("they didn't understand 'no engines' "), to the experiments done on Sally's body ("None"). The latter surprised them. Soviet scientists monitored their cosmonauts' bodies throughout the flight. But Sally made a "they didn't get their hands on me" gesture, which led to good-natured mutual agreement on their fear of flight surgeons. They'd all had the same experience sleeping in space (giggling as each demonstrated the way their arms floated up), and neither woman had suffered from space sickness. "Just like us!" was the phrase they all repeated, over and over.

"There was sort of a code between the two women," Tamas Gombosi, the coconspirator, tells me. "It was obvious that they understood each other. From the first minute they just showed so much affection for each other." And wanted to share their stories. Svetlana presented Sally with Russian books, dolls and a scarf—so many presents, Sally felt "outgifted." They signed autographs for each other, mostly on Soviet first day covers that the cosmonauts had taken into space. Sally pulled out an STS-7 charm that Svetlana could wear as a necklace, and promised her the TFNG shirt she'd worn on the flight—the one she was wearing that evening underneath her blouse. Sally would deliver it to Gombosi the next day.

At one point, cameras came out, but, sensitive to Sally's position, they asked if photos were okay. By the end of the evening, she and Svetlana had their arms around each other, and everyone was posing together, the only visual record of a forbidden summit. "We felt a real kinship, a real affinity for each other," Sally said. "I felt closer to her than I'd felt to anyone in a very long time. Partly because I understood a lot of what she'd been through, and she understood a lot of what I'd been through, and we felt camaraderie. We were sort of the only two people in the world that were in the situation that we're in, and we seem to be very similar types of people." When she got home, Sally told Carolyn Huntoon that Svetlana "probably would have made it through our selection process, and I think she probably would have beaten me out. I got the impression that we're very much alike."

Sally stayed at the apartment for six hours, "and the time just flew past. We were all just having a super time." When the final toasts were over—she and Svetlana drank juice while the men drank vodka—Sally rode back to the hotel in the same car as the Russian cosmonauts. It was 3:00 a.m. The streets of Budapest were deserted. And the secret mission was back under wraps. "Don't get into a wreck!" they all told the driver, jovially. "An accident," Sally later observed, "would wipe out both space programs at once."

Svetlana made it clear that they shouldn't enter the lobby together. So they dropped off Sally, and then headed for the garage entrance. The two women hugged. "When I left there, I thought I had a friend for life," Sally said.

She never told her USIA sponsors about the evening. Never made an official report about it. And except for some written communications vetted by the government, never spoke to Savitskaya again. She did, however, record in her brief journal that in Europe, she especially enjoyed "getting away from lawyers, decisions, commitments. Just carrying out [the] program—with some amount of freedom . . . as in NYC."

Also, she ate goose liver, a Hungarian delicacy that "really tasted good: Like tender Wienerschnitzel!" Sally hadn't changed much in twenty-two years.

If Budapest opened Sally's heart to the opportunities of international cooperation, Oslo reminded her of the battles still to be waged. Not Oslo itself, nor its country—she enjoyed being back in the land of her ancestors, buying a Norwegian sweater to show off her heritage and some postage stamps for her still growing collection.

What alienated her (and Hauck) was their meeting with the US ambassador, Mark Austad, a former radio and TV commentator (known as Mark Evans) who invited them to his home for a luncheon. While giving them a tour of the house before the meal, he noted that it was their last stop on a grueling tour. "I'm sure it's been a tiring journey," he said. "I guess it's like rape. If it's inevitable, you might as well lie back and enjoy it." Hauck says he and Sally looked at each other in shock. "Our jaws dropped. We were speechless. You could see the color drain from the ambassador's face as he realized he's just made a very big mistake."

Somehow, they made it through the buffet, after which the ambassador got up to attend the opening of the Norwegian parliament.

"Sally, to her credit, said, 'Mr. Ambassador, before you leave I have a word of advice for you.'

"He said, 'Yes. What is that?'

"She said, 'Back in the United States, rape jokes aren't funny anymore.'"

INSPIRATION

"A," Sally says, standing in her flight suit with a winning smile. Then, "Astronaut," completing the *Sesame Street* equation, at which point, through the magic of television, she levitates up and off the screen thanks to a personal rocket at her feet. The look on her face is pure bliss.

That's the part Sally enjoyed. That's what made the mission, and the publicity, finally, gratifying.

"I saw in the eyes of the girls and the women and the grandmothers that I met, what it meant to them," she told me in 2008 during a twenty-fifth anniversary celebration of her flight. "And I knew it was important, but I didn't realize the emotional impact it had on so many women, just realizing this was something a woman could do that no one thought she could do. And I think it changed a lot of attitudes, it changed a lot of aspirations. For young women in college it made them think about their careers differently."

Sally had invited me to the party at the Goddard Space Flight Center in Maryland, and I found her unusually reflective. Her flight, she said, "was a moment in history when women in the United States saw that they could do something that they hadn't thought of before. That women were viewed in a different way, and it didn't have to be me, but there had to be a first woman for that perception to be realized."

"But we're glad it was you," I said, unnecessarily.

"I'm glad it was me!" she agreed.

Individual moments drove it home for her. The female translator

in the former Yugoslavia who "started crying when she met me because I was someone who had broken barriers that she had never even
dreamed of. That was very emotional for her, and it really made an
impact on me." The eight-year-old girl in the audience who "raises her
hand to ask me what she needs to do to become an astronaut. I like that.
It's neat! Why? Because now there really is a way. Now it's possible!"

As columnist Ellen Goodman wrote, Sally was not just an astronaut,
she was a First Woman, a status that carried "a load of other women's
frustrations and hopes. . . . First Women bear a special responsibility to
those who didn't come before them and those who may—or may not—
come later. . . . Being a full-fledged First Woman means taking every
step for womankind."

Sally's friend Barbara Barrett, with whom she would later connect
over their shared love of aviation and science, connects it to the perceptions of 1980s America: The way people thought then, she says, "If a
man does something badly or well, it's the man. If a woman doesn't do
it well, it's the gender."

Sally had seen it with the flowers on her return. People were "watching me carefully and measuring what I did. I felt a huge responsibility
to do the right thing, to be a strong role model for women. Not that
I had planned to do anything crazy or irresponsible after my flight, but
more than ever, I was conscious of all those people out there—especially
young girls—looking to me as the model I'd never had myself, of what
they might become." She hadn't understood fully "how much it would
mean to so many women, to see a woman become an astronaut. I think
until we see a woman like ourselves accomplish something, it's hard
to form the pictures in our head that allow us to imagine doing such a
thing ourselves."

Sally said it all came together a year later, when New York congresswoman Geraldine Ferraro was chosen as Walter Mondale's running
mate on the Democratic ticket in the 1984 presidential election. The
two women had met briefly beforehand, when Ferraro's name was being
mentioned as a serious candidate for the job. That June, Sally visited

Ferraro's congressional office and posed for photos with her staff. "None of them have ever asked for my autograph or to have their picture taken with me," Ferraro joked, possibly truthfully. Sally gave her a tee-shirt bearing the vice-presidential insignia, and the photo of the two women holding the aspirational clothing made papers around the country.

At the time, the notion of a female vice presidential candidate was as audacious as that of a woman flying into space had once been. But the lobbying was fierce and the time was right. And the straight-talking congresswoman from Queens was a natural new ally for Sally—her extrovert twin, almost a generation older but equal in her commitment to women's rights.

As the only reporter to cover both full-time, I saw the connection firsthand; felt the electric charge from two women whose elevation to cultural icons filled a centuries-old void. Ferraro, like Sally, tapped into a deep yearning, one that crossed political lines. When she was nominated at the Democratic convention in San Francisco, her acceptance speech acknowledged the moment:

> Change is in the air, just as surely as when John Kennedy beckoned America to a new frontier; when Sally Ride rocketed into space . . .
>
> By choosing a woman to run for our nation's second highest office, you sent a powerful signal to all Americans. There are no doors we cannot unlock. We will place no limits on achievement.
>
> If we can do this, we can do anything.

"I was as moved by that as many women had been by my flight into space," Sally said. "For the first time, I understood why it was such an emotional experience for so many people, to see me accomplish what I had, as a woman."

On Ferraro's campaign trail, thousands of Republican and Democratic women alike, and plenty of men, too, felt the same way, showing up at rallies with their daughters, the tiniest of whom they boosted above the crowd so they could see what a female candidate at the top of the ticket looked like. Most wouldn't vote for her—elections were about politics not gender—but the possibility she represented was intoxicating.

In a 1984 poll of college-educated women asking them to name their favorite role model, Ferraro came in first, with Sally and Supreme Court Justice Sandra Day O'Connor tied for second. At a private lunch, Sally told the vice presidential candidate, "I don't mind being second to you." Earlier Sally had said, "There always has to be a first. And once that happens, society changes."

BACK TO WORK

On August 30, 1984, STS-41D launched, carrying a crew of six, including Steve Hawley. It was the fourth try for *Discovery*, which had been delayed for more than two months. Sally watched with her in-laws at the Kennedy Space Center. "A launch is always a spectacular experience," she said afterwards. "It's obviously a special feeling, though, when your husband is going up." Also on board was Judy Resnik, about whom Sally said, "I'll be glad when there are two of us, so she can take some of the publicity." Judy shared Sally's belief that her personal life was none of the public's business, and Sally had often wandered into Judy's office and collapsed on a chair to bemoan the latest demands on her time.

The mission started off smoothly, but five days later, when a buildup of ice outside one of *Discovery's* waste ports threatened to come loose and smash into the tail on entry, Sally was in the simulator trying to help other astronauts figure out how to position the robot arm to knock it off. She worked through the night, plotting a complex procedure to reach the arm around to a blind spot and dislodge the chunk. The plan was radioed up to the crew; it worked. Steve was spared a spacewalk, and *Discovery* came home safely.

Sally's de-icing scheme had interrupted her own training. A year earlier, in the midst of her publicity tour, NASA had assigned her to another mission, designated STS-41G, bringing Sally back into the system and giving her acceptable cover to turn down anything she didn't like.

It was more than just cover. Once again, Bob Crippen was assigned to be her commander, but he was in the midst of training for yet another flight that would launch earlier. "They wanted to see how fast we could turn crews around," Crippen explains. "So I told George [Abbey], 'The only way I could do that is if Sally is on my crew.' I said, 'Put Sally on [41G] again as my flight engineer and she can sit in for me. She knows how I like to do business.'" So for six months, as Crip's "pseudo-commander," she sat in the left-hand seat during ascent and entry simulations, taking the rookies through the paces. For Dave Leestma, a Navy test pilot serving as a mission specialist, Sally was a perfect surrogate. "She knew how Crip would react to situations," he tells me. Once during an ascent simulation, Leestma was changing some settings on a caution warning system, "and I was reconfiguring as fast as I could, and Sally said, 'Slow down, you'll make a mistake. You don't have to go that fast, just make sure you're right.' Sure enough, we get on orbit, there are two pints of adrenaline in my system, and I'm doing the same thing. And Crip leans over and says, 'Slow down, Dave!' "

The pilot was Jon McBride, the Navy aviator who'd helped teach Sally to fly a T-38. Another mission specialist was Kathy Sullivan. STS-41G would be the first flight carrying two women, and they joined forces to take advantage of the frequent (and thoughtless) mix-ups by some reporters, often introducing themselves as "the other one." But sharing the shuttle with Sally, who was still a boldfaced name, slightly dimmed the spotlight, even before they launched. Sullivan got back by wearing a name tag reading, "Sally" with a bar over it—in other words, "NOT Sally." "I recall rather a scowl on her face, but I thought it was fun," Sullivan says.

Sullivan would also do an Extra Vehicular Activity (EVA), or spacewalk, but lost the title of first female in the world to do so when Svetlana Savitskaya, Sally's new pal, flew again and did a spacewalk in July. Svetlana also deprived Sally of becoming the first woman to fly in space twice. The battle over titles was irrelevant to the astronauts. For Kathy, being the first *American* female spacewalker was just fine—in fact, "for me, *my* first spacewalk (*any* spacewalk, for that matter) was just fine," Sullivan tells me.

On launch day, October 5, 1984, it was Sally who pushed Sullivan to the front of the line and in full view of photographers as the crew exited the building to head toward the pad.

The flight lasted nine days with a crew of seven, the largest yet. Experience, it turned out, counted. When they reached orbit, Sally "got graceful very fast," according to Leestma, who felt the initial clumsiness of a rookie. And when a number of mechanical glitches threatened various tasks, Sally's on-the-job savvy helped save the day. First, the solar panels on an Earth-observing satellite failed to extend properly, despite attempts from both the shuttle and ground controllers. Sally and Leestma, frustrated by the lack of response to the checklist, turned to their own ingenuity. Here is how high-tech problems get solved in outer space:

"Let's shake it," Leestma suggested to Sally. She turned to the commander. "Crip, do you mind if we try?" When he said, "I trust you, Sally, just don't break it!" they got to work. With the satellite, a cumbersome albeit weightless boxcar, dangling from the end of the robot arm, Leestma configured the computer as Sally maneuvered the joystick and the dials, at much higher rates than they'd ever trained for. Some combination of aerodynamic pressure, the heat of the sun and chutzpah made it work—by chance, as they were flying over California. Problem solved.

Sally also repaired a broken antenna after pulling out all the lockers on the middeck area and threading her way through a jungle of wires. The inflight mechanic had again earned her keep.

Afterward, it was more of the same.

"It's like you're not even in the room when you're around her," Leestma says, of postflight crew events. "Everyone is just focused on her! You could just see the stars in people's eyes—especially college age and younger women—people actually had a hero they could look up to, for things other than sports or politics or whatever. Somebody who had accomplished something because of her education and her competence."

Like everyone else, the crew protected her. "People would say, 'Are you Sally Ride?' And we'd say, 'Nope. Looks like her, but isn't.'"

One day Sally wanted to buy a new car, something sporty and fun. Leestma, a car buff, took her to buy a bright red Pontiac Fiero, a low, boxy wedge. When she wrote out the check the salesman said, "Are you . . . ?" Sometimes, she couldn't hide.

With two successful flights, Sally got back in line. Sort of. Her celebrity meant she would never be one of the gang, and some of her colleagues found her behavior "distant." Despite repeated public statements of loyalty—"I'm intending to stay with NASA as long as they'll let me stay"—her thoughts were starting to wander.

Still, she was there for NASA when they needed her. And true to her principles. In April 1985, yet another on-orbit repair session required astronaut Rhea Seddon to help gin up a device to try to reach a balky switch on a satellite in the payload bay. With advice from Mission Control, Seddon dug up a needle and thread and stitched the plastic cover of a briefing book to a long handle to make what became known as the fly-swatter. CapCom Dave Hilmers radioed up his congratulations. "Those two look super," he said, adding, "tribute to a fine seamstress." Later, when Sally arrived at Mission Control, she radioed up to Seddon that she'd corrected Hilmers's intended compliment "and told him, 'That was a surgeon.'" All in good fun, but it was working. When Seddon thanked a different CapCom for a clutch of teleprinter messages he'd sent up to *Discovery*, he responded, "Just think of it as a daily run by the mailman, excuse me, mailperson, mailperson."

In June 1985, Shannon Lucid launched on STS-51G. All six of the original women had now flown. That same day, NASA announced that Sally would be a member of her third mission, scheduled to fly in July 1986.

Later that month, Sally went to Atlanta to help open the convention of the National Women's Political Caucus, an activist group of progressive women from both parties (to whom Sally had once written a $75 check). Gerry Ferraro, who had gotten shellacked, along with Walter Mondale, in the '84 election, was greeted with a thunderous ovation from the nearly two thousand feminists of both parties attending the meeting. Their feisty resolve was evident in one of the most popular buttons on sale: "We Haven't Come That Far and Don't Call Me Baby." Ferraro pointed out that with only two female governors and two women in the US Senate, "The battle is far from won." Sally told the audience that science was doing no better than government. Girls, she said, were discouraged from studying science and math in school, and young women faced barriers entering careers in the field. "That's something we have to work hard to overcome."

If you listened closely, you could hear the rustle of wings being unfurled.

EXPLOSIONS

SPRING/SUMMER 1985–SUMMER 1986

Tam, Atlanta, 1985.

Everyone has three lives: a public life, a private life and a secret life.

—Gabriel García Márquez

TAM

"I was in shock that I was in love with Sally, and that Sally was in love with me. I couldn't believe it. It was just like, What?"

Tam O'Shaughnessy had first met Sally on the junior tennis circuit, when they were both preteens in the close-knit community of gifted kids and ambitious, carpooling parents. Tam's mom and Sally's dad became pals while toting their kids to the tournaments; Tam and Sally melded with a group of Southern California regulars whose friendship endures today. And while Sally was nearly a year older, Tam—a "tall, elegant pixie," according to one friend, with "beautiful, wide open eyes," a turned-up nose and high cheekbones, crowned by short brown hair— was by far the bigger star.

"Sally was good, but not the best in the pack," Tam says, matter-of-factly. "We only played one time. I won." Tam had grown up hitting with, among others, Stan Smith, who would be ranked number one in the world in 1972. Her childhood coach was Billie Jean King, whose brother, Randy Moffitt, was later Tam's first serious beau as a teen. Tam and her doubles partner, Ann Lebedeff (now professor and Head Women's Tennis coach at Pomona-Pitzer Colleges), were among the top-ranked junior teams in the country; in 1969 they were ranked number 3 in women's doubles nationally (Billie Jean King and Rosie Casals were number 1). As the game got tougher and she joined the fledgling Women's Tennis Association (WTA) pro tour, founded by King, Tam was ranked as high as number 52 in women's singles in the world. She played Wimbledon once and the US Open twice.

She was a serious contender despite the "pressure to not be jocks" that Tam saw applied to all the junior girls. One evening in 1970, at dinner with two of the top male players, the men encouraged her (she was eighteen) to quit the game. "They told me that my calf muscles were pretty large and muscular," Tam tells me, "and that continuing to compete in tennis, and work out, would only make them larger. They said that I was such a nice and attractive girl, they would hate to see me change."

Tam stuck with tennis for four more years, leaving the circuit at twenty-two to work with Billie Jean and Larry King at their company, King Enterprises, in San Mateo, where she was founding publisher of the first *WTA Newsletter* among other publications. By then she knew she was gay. She reconnected with Sally at nearby Stanford—while Sally was getting her master's and doctoral degrees and working at *Sports-woman*, a small rival to the Kings' *womenSports*—where they competed in platform tennis tournaments together and covered some tennis events for their respective publications. On one trip to a WTA tournament in Palm Springs, Tam and Sally wound up playing a spur-of-the-moment set against commentator Bud Collins and sportswriter Barry Lorge. "It was a disaster," Tam recalls. "Bud played barefoot and Barry stood at the net. Sally and I played like ducks out of water. We hadn't played tennis for many months and we couldn't get a ball in the court." The guys ("mediocre club players," Tam says dismissively) "beat us!" Collins, recounting the incident in his own imaginative style, calls his team "a couple of hacks" and takes tongue-in-cheek credit for driving Sally away from tennis and launching her astronaut career.

Off the court, Tam and Sally occasionally met for dinner, including one evening when Tam served steak and wine in her apartment overlooking San Francisco Bay. Sally would later tell Tam that her feelings for her old friend started to change that night, but at the time they were just pals, with the kind of long history Sally cherished. Tam was among the girlhood tennis buddies cheering on Sally's STS-7 launch in Florida.

In 1985, Tam was living in Atlanta, teaching eighth-grade biology. About six months earlier, she had broken up with another woman after a long, serious romance. One day Sally—who had seen Tam nearly half a dozen times on some post-STS-7 speaking trips to Atlanta over the past year or so—called to say she'd be back in town on business. They went out to dinner, then back to Tam's place to talk.

"Sally and I talked about this many times," Tam tells me, reaching for the details, "and we couldn't remember exactly what happened. I think it's sort of typical when people start feeling something romantic for each other. There's one moment when you realize that you feel different than you thought you did. And I remember we were sitting on the couch, and I leaned over to pet my dog, Annie, when out of the blue, Sally put her hand on my back. And I just felt different. And Sally did too."

"We are in trouble," Tam told her.

"We don't have to do this," Sally said.

But they did. "I saw the look in her eyes," Tam says now. "She was in love with me, and I realized in that instant that I was in love with her, too. It was amazing. And we were absolutely stunned."

How, Tam thought, could she have those feelings for Sally, who'd been her friend since she was a kid?

Tam's family—two "wonderful but wacky parents"—shared the same middle-class values and beliefs as Sally's mom and dad, minus the constancy of Dale Ride. Her father was "a free spirit who should not have had children." When he split, leaving behind Tam, thirteen, and her two sisters, her mom was the "hardworking, responsible, loving single parent. I was the one in the family who took care of everyone." The despair she saw in her mother, plus her sorrow over her father's departure, left Tam overwhelmed. She withdrew from the world, didn't graduate from high school because of her grade in one course. But she bounced back quickly, and after her tennis career and publishing success, made up the credits and earned her BS in biology, the field of her dreams, at thirty-one—the year Sally first flew.

Tennis saved Tam at first ("I loved whacking the ball"), along with the more stable households of families like the Moffitts (Billie Jean and Randy's parents). Hanging out with the other kids on the circuit gave her some of the grounding she'd missed. Years later, Sally supplied a similar solid base. "She gave me the stability I longed for but never had growing up," Tam says. What Sally got from her, Tam says, was "the emotional outlet she yearned for but never learned how to express. Sally couldn't verbalize her emotions, couldn't talk about why she felt the way she felt. We completed each other."

"Sally saw in Tam someone who could be incredibly nurturing and kind and loving," says Kay Loveland, another former tennis pal who was then practicing psychology in Atlanta. She was one of the few who spent time with them as a couple almost immediately after they got together. "When Tam loves, there are no holds barred. And I bet that felt so good to Sally."

But the contrasts that brought them together also threatened their new relationship.

"Sally was worried that I was too into talking about all the emotional stuff, that I was too fiery," Tam recalls. "And I was worried about all the opposite things: that she couldn't give enough and that she couldn't get emotional. Will she be able to tell me everything about herself and how she feels? So we had a few months of just trying to figure out how serious it was. It took us a little while to decide that it was a relationship we both wanted to keep." Tam elaborates: "I'm very private too, but Sally is really hard to know in the deeper recesses. I wanted someone I could get to know in a way that I could talk about everything. I wasn't sure Sally was capable of that." Still, Tam says, "We were both just madly in love with each other—we hardly ate. When we saw each other, we just wanted to be together. Really, we both lost a lot of weight."

They were both pretty trim to begin with.

Over the next few months, Sally traveled to Atlanta regularly. "It was just impossible for us not to be together," Tam says. Kay Loveland saw a playful, passionate pair. "You could just tell there was this bloom of love," she tells me. "They would hold hands, or touch shoulders. They were so comfortable just being together. They didn't need a whole lot of other people around them." Loveland says that during a period of real estate transition, when she and her husband, Joe, invited Tam to stay with them for a few weeks, Sally moved in, too, perfectly relaxed about sharing Tam's bedroom in their home. "They were both quite open around me and my husband," Loveland says, "and neither Sally nor Tam ever asked me to keep their relationship a secret."

But their involvement was not more widely known, certainly not by Sally's husband.

"She was famous, she was married," Tam says. "I knew that NASA was very conservative, and Sally was still an astronaut. And on some level I just don't think we thought about it. We loved being together, and we were very discreet. She certainly didn't want to hurt Steve."

Steve Hawley was deep into training for his next mission. He knew that Sally and Tam were close friends, and while it did seem that Sally was absent more than usual, he never put the two together. That she was unfaithful to their marriage never crossed his mind; there were lots of things they never talked about. And plenty more that kept Sally busy, apart from her compelling new romance.

VICTORY LAPS

She served two more missions as CapCom, including one in November 1985, during which she had to relay the news of a power disruption at the ground tracking station in Dakar, Senegal. An alien had invaded the computer works, leading to a momentary outbreak of giggles in Mission Control. "The cause of the fluctuation was found to be an eighteen-inch monitor-type lizard," Sally told the astronauts orbiting Earth, reading from the printout. "The lizard was dislodged with a screwdriver and scampered away." As the crew aloft and her colleagues in Mission Control guffawed, Sally barely made it through the message, laughing as she concluded, "The lizard was last seen moving at a rapid pace across the plains of Senegal."

In October, she became one of the first two members of the Women's Hall of Fame established by the National Women's Forum in Washington, DC. The other inductee was Supreme Court Justice Sandra Day O'Connor, also a Stanford alumna. Later that month, Sally visited the National Women's Hall of Fame in Seneca Falls, New York, birthplace of the American women's movement, where she returned a white silk scarf worn by pioneering aviator Amelia Earhart that she had carried into space on her second mission. Earhart had disappeared during her round-the-world flight in 1937, a loss noted by Gloria Steinem in a handwritten thank-you to Sally for appearing on her interview show. "Before you, we had Amelia Earhart—but it's great to have one who came back." In 1988, Sally would be inducted into that Hall as well.

She threw out the first ball at a World Series game in Kansas City;

then, from their seats behind the dugout along the first base line, she and Steve cheered the victory of his hometown Royals. In November, Sally became the seventeenth person to receive the Order of Magellan at the Circumnavigators Club. Others included General Douglas MacArthur, Neil Armstrong and Norwegian explorer Thor Heyerdahl, whose raft Sally had seen in Oslo. In December, the 1985 Associated Press survey of 1,700 editors and reporters from newspapers across the country listed Sally second among the twenty-five most influential women who "have the strongest effect on both public policy and public opinion." Heading the list was *Washington Post* publisher Katharine Graham.

A year and a half after her first flight, Sally remained an American hero, with no public hints of the personal fissures below the surface. Steve Hawley, however, was beginning to feel the cracks. On January 12, 1986, he flew into space aboard *Columbia* on STS-61C, his second flight. Sally, he says, "did execute her responsibilities as a crew spouse"—which meant being there—"but she pretty much made it clear that she wasn't enjoying it." Her postflight publicity demands, he tells me, had been stressful both on her and on their marriage. "I tried to understand what she was going through and be supportive, but I still wasn't a priority for her." Steve recognized at the time that among the many things they had in common were "our personalities, which inhibited having long conversations about our relationship." Today, having reconsidered, he reminds me that he did not know Tam was more than a friend. "I guess if I was clueless about that, I could have been clueless about other things."

But the Hawley-Ride marital troubles, and Sally's love affair with Tam, would shortly be overshadowed.

At the beginning of 1986, with twenty-four successful shuttle missions, NASA eagerly toted up its accomplishments. In five years, all thirty-five members of Sally's class had flown; they had walked in space, launched and landed both at night and in Florida, placed twenty-one commercial satellites successfully in orbit, and performed a number of scientific experiments. NASA was promoting its four orbiters (*Columbia, Challenger, Discovery, Atlantis*) as a fancy fleet of trucks ready to deliver the world's satellites. The Kennedy Space Center, they boasted, was starting to look like a space port. Management had declared the program "operational," saying the shuttle finally offered regular access to space. Fifteen launches were scheduled for the rest of the year—nowhere near the twice-a-month schedule NASA had promised, but still pretty ambitious for an agency that had barely flown nine the year before. The word they were using for the performance of the most complex space machine ever built was *routine*. Unfortunately, "routine" wasn't news, and the broadcast networks were losing interest. Whether that reflected or drove public apathy, the result was the same: NASA needed support from all fronts to maintain its funding and, thus, its momentum.

That's partly why NASA finally agreed to send a reporter on the shuttle, a gesture that certainly got my attention. After four years of transcribing most astronauts' descriptions of what it was like up there— "neat" being their version of an expressive adjective—I had been among those lobbying NASA to let a professional explainer fly, to let one of us explain what space travel was actually like. When the Journalist-In-Space competition was announced, Sally volunteered to write me a recommendation. She believed then that civilians from other professions could gain "a different perspective on the experience," and might help broaden public interest in the program. I also think she saw my recommendation as the kind of favor you do for a next-door neighbor's kid. Fully aware that I would read what she wrote—and no doubt convinced that she could arrange never to fly with a greenhorn like me (me, the Greek major who had avoided physics because botany seemed a more useful college science)—she typed out an essay that made me sound like Brenda Starr with wings:

As someone who has talked to Lynn across a microphone several times, I consider myself well-qualified to evaluate at least some of her journalistic talents. Each time she interviewed me, or reported a story I was familiar with, she did so with professionalism and integrity; her stories reflect an understanding of the (often technical) subject matter and a sensitivity for the (often reluctant) subject.

. . . Lynn has a talent for translating complex technical concepts into images that a non-technical audience can understand. . . . I experienced the thrill of a launch, the magnificence of orbital flight, and the rush of re-entry, but I have been frustrated to find that I don't have the talent to communicate those experiences. I think Lynn does. She is the journalist I would choose to report on the emotions, sensations and thoughts that are part of an adventure that I have experienced, but can't describe.

On the line marked "relationship to applicant," Sally wrote, "Interviewee/Friend." She signed it on January 7, 1986. I thanked her profusely and started packing.

Journalists, however, would have to wait their turn. Along with downplaying the risk of space travel, NASA was promoting the shuttle as a platform for education. The first civilian chosen to fly would be a schoolteacher.

CHALLENGER

"I don't think any teacher has been more ready to have two lessons," Christa McAuliffe told reporters at the Kennedy Space Center. "I just hope everybody tunes in." At age thirty-five, McAuliffe, a social studies teacher from Concord, New Hampshire, had won NASA's first civilian-in-space competition, a public relations gambit to involve school kids in the shuttle and energize the program. She was assigned to the mission called STS-51L, on *Challenger*, with commander Richard Scobee, a rugged-looking Air Force test pilot who had flown combat missions in Vietnam; pilot Mike Smith, a Navy test pilot and Vietnam veteran as well; mission specialist Ron McNair, a saxophone-playing physicist (with a PhD from MIT) who'd been the second African American to fly; mission specialist Ellison Onizuka, an engineer from the Air Force Test Pilot School; and payload specialist Greg Jarvis, an engineer with Hughes Aircraft. The flight engineer was mission specialist Judy Resnik.

By late January, the flight had been either scrubbed or rescheduled four times. On Tuesday, January 28, 1986, it was cleared for liftoff. Icicles fringed the tower, and onlookers could see their breath in the unusually frigid Florida temperatures, as NASA started the final count-down to an 11:38 a.m. launch. Around the country, millions of students, teachers and principals were tuned in to see one of their own fly into space.

I wasn't there. Like most members of the regular space media, I'd been sent to California, to cover the robotic mission of the Voyager 2 spacecraft during its close encounter with the planet Uranus, nearly two billion miles away. The first-ever images of the mysterious, gaseous planet were magnificent: yard-wide ice boulders forming Uranus's nine rings; ten new moons orbiting the cold, dark planet, tiny stones in the mosaic of the universe that scientists would study for clues to our own existence. That, rather than the schoolteacher, was deemed the signifi-cant space story of the week.

So I wasn't among those shivering at the Cape and staring into the clear blue sky when, seventy-three seconds after liftoff, the pillar of fire pushing *Challenger* skyward split grotesquely into plumes of smoke going nowhere, as chunks of the shuttle careened crazily off course. The rockets veered one way, the tank another; the crew compartment shot up, then down, to rest, finally, at the bottom of the Atlantic Ocean. Seven lives lost, the vehicle destroyed, the space program crushed. The *Challenger* explosion was the worst space disaster in the world.

Sally Ride didn't see it, either. She'd been in Atlanta for a long week-end, celebrating Tam's thirty-fourth birthday. When the shuttle blew up, Sally was on a commercial airliner, headed back to Houston. The pilot, unaware of his famous passenger, announced the awful news through the PA system. "My heart sank," Sally later recalled. "I didn't know what to think. I wanted information and I wanted it now." She pulled out her NASA badge and made her way to the cockpit. "They let me put on an extra pair of headsets to monitor the radio traffic to find out what had happened. We were only about a half hour outside of Houston; when we landed, I headed straight back to JSC."

The loss shrouded the Astronaut Office. Four of their classmates from the Thirty-five New Guys were dead: Dick Scobee, El Onizuka, Judy Resnik, Ron McNair. Scobee and Resnik had been Sally's seatmates at the 1978 press conference when they were introduced to the public. "These were people that I had known for eight years," she said. "I'd worked with them every day, I'd gone to dinner at their houses, I knew their families. So they were very, very close, close friends." And, she said, they "were killed in a way that we could experience and could understand. Steve had been on the flight before the accident. It could have been him. I was scheduled to go up a couple flights after the accident. It could have been me." Sally couldn't get her mind off the place she'd sat during her liftoffs, right behind the commander and pilot. Right where Judy Resnik sat as well. "When I visualized what's going on in the cockpit during that accident, Judy's seat is where I picture what must have happened and what they must have been going through."

Challenger, which had twice carried her to space and back, was now shredded; the robot arm, which she'd used so successfully and helped form into the iconic 7 in happier times, had been ripped from its moorings and drowned in the sea. All shuttle flights were suspended indefinitely.

Like everyone else in the tightly tethered community that lived and worked together, Sally put her grief on hold as she helped with logistics for the families and the funerals. When I saw her two days later, her face was still ashen. I'd covered the story from California, then flown to Houston for the nationally televised memorial at which President Reagan would speak. My husband, Larry, who'd also been in California, joined me the night before the event. We had dinner with Sally, Steve, and Steve's father, Reverend Bernard Hawley, who'd been invited by

George Abbey to deliver the opening prayer. I asked what his message would be. "We have to give people permission to cry," Reverend Hawley told me. It was, I thought, a tough task when your audience includes a corps of stiff-upper-lip astronauts. But he did and they did. The entire nation wept.

The next day, Larry and I were at Sally and Steve's house when the phone rang. The NASA administrator was calling, asking Sally to be on the presidential commission to investigate the accident. It would become known by the name of its chairman, former Secretary of State William P. Rogers. Among the other distinguished members from industry and aerospace: rocket scientist Albert "Bud" Wheelon, who helped develop the CIA's network of spy satellites; moonwalker Neil Armstrong; Nobel Prize–winning physicist Richard Feynman. Sally was the only shuttle astronaut, in fact, the only current NASA employee named to the blue-ribbon panel, a vital link to the space agency with an intimate grasp of how things worked, and a space traveler's compulsion to pin down the problem that could have killed her, too. It was a dismal but critical job, another one of those moments to seize. "I need to do this," she said quietly, as she hung up the phone.

Much later she elaborated: "It was very difficult, but on the other hand, every one of the astronauts wanted to be doing something, contributing in some way to getting NASA back on its feet, and investigating what went wrong." The destruction of *Challenger*, she said, "wasn't something that I could walk away from, no matter how painful it was. If nothing else, I needed closure. I needed to know what the answer was and that NASA was going to do something to fix it."

THE ROGERS COMMISSION

A grieving nation had grown increasingly angry, demanding answers. The twelve men and one woman charged with finding them had 120 days to submit their report. They would interview more than 160 individuals in more than 35 formal sessions—some closed, many open to the public and the press. The latter was mandated by the chairman, who understood the role of the media surrounding an issue that had long been part of the national spirit. Americans believed that flying in space helped define them; the obliteration of *Challenger*, its crew and the future of exploration threatened the national spirit.

In a short time, the physical cause of the explosion became clear: the seal made by two O-rings (twelve-foot-diameter rubber gaskets shaped like an *O*) on the right-hand solid rocket booster—made up of circular sections stacked and clamped together—had failed, allowing hot gas to escape. The gap was no thicker than a human hair, but that was enough. Within a minute after liftoff, the super-hot temperatures and immense pressure fed a vicious flame that licked out through the joint and dissolved the strut connecting the rocket to the orbiter. As the suddenly freed booster pivoted free, it smashed into the wing of the orbiter, then into the thin aluminum skin of the external fuel tank, igniting the fireball that tore *Challenger* apart. The astronauts never had a chance. There was no escape system.

NASA's launch tower cameras had provided the first clue: a two-second series of puffs of black smoke emerging from the rocket joint at liftoff. *Why* it happened took a bit longer. No one correlated the O-rings to the cold temperatures at first.

Sally, it turns out, delivered some of the earliest evidence.

Someone—I still don't know who—slipped her a report, three columns of print on one sheet of paper, measuring the resilience of the O-rings in cold temperatures versus warm. The results were unmistakable: launching in sub-freezing temperatures could be lethal, and management knew it. And yet they went ahead and did it. Sally understood the implications; she also knew that if the report were traced back through her, it could get the source fired. So on the evening of Friday, February 7, after a meeting—they had just been sworn in a few days earlier—she was walking down the basement corridor of the Old Executive Office Building with another commission member. Don Kutyna, a two-star Air Force general responsible for all its launch vehicles, had distinguished himself investigating an earlier Titan rocket crash. Sally described him in her notes as a "boyish, avid worker" who kept chocolate in his briefcase. Her kind of guy. Silently, Kutyna tells me, Sally "reached into her notebook and gave me the sheet of paper, enclosed in plastic."

Kutyna took a look and realized that he, too, had to get the information out without leaving a trail to the original leaker. So he figured out a way to plant the concept—rubber O-rings, cold weather—into the mind of Feynman, the maverick Nobelist with whom he'd struck up a friendship. Feynman never knew the source, but he got the connection. And he knew how to illustrate the problem. At the commission's next public meeting, he tightly compressed a sample of the rubber O-rings used in the shuttle's solid rocket motors with a small clamp, then dunked it into glass of ice water. When he pulled it out and released the clamp, he discovered that the rubber didn't stretch fully back into shape for several seconds. The ice water had significantly reduced resiliency—a critical factor for a material needed to seal the gap in the contracting and expanding joints of the shuttle's rockets.

"I believe that has some significance for our problem," he announced.

Feynman's show-and-tell made the evening news that night and made clear what had happened to *Challenger*. "I thought it was pretty cool," Sally told me. "It was a good illustration for the public." She never connected his demonstration to her information, never let me in on the secret. Only after her death did General Kutyna reveal the story.

But testimony uncovered a problem within NASA, even deeper than that of the O-rings: a culture drowning in flawed decision making and an unrealistic launch schedule that put pressure on everyone to sign off on equipment before it was ready to go. Management, Sally wrote in her notebook, had been "stretched to the limit" during Steve's last launch just two weeks before *Challenger*.

Sally dove in with her usual intensity and energy. She often worked eighteen-hour days, analyzing data, interviewing her own sources, digging up information, parsing the testimony for inconsistencies. She spoke regularly with Crippen, with Steve (still "A²" in her notes), and with a host of other astronaut friends, each of whom had been assigned some area to help. And she constantly checked in with the investigators hired for the commission. During the hearings, she and Neil Armstrong sat in the front row, flanking the chairman, occasionally exchanging glances of disbelief as they heard from people at the Marshall Space Flight Center associated with the solid rockets. As Sally listened to witnesses, she took meticulous notes on lined paper in a spiral-bound notebook on whose cover she had pasted the patch of the doomed mission, the names of the seven crewmembers clearly visible every second of every day. In fine black pen, she drew neat bullet points outlining her questions about the revelations. There were no doodles in her notebook, no unnecessary sounds or words in her inquiries. And as the truth came out, she got tougher, and angrier. When one manager rationalized the dispute over the temperatures by saying that every new flight "has had to break frontiers," Sally, agitated, said, "The time you go through frontiers is during testing, not during the flights. That's the way it's supposed to work!" When another testified about damaged O-rings in an earlier flight (there would turn out to be fifteen such examples) an aerospace reporter in the audience, whose mouth had dropped open in shock, happened to catch Sally's eye. "She looked at me across twenty-five meters," he said, "and just rolled her eyes to heaven like, 'Oh my Lord.'"

I am not ready to fly again now. I think there are very few astronauts who are ready to fly again now.

—Sally Ride, March 1986

Sally was deeply moved by the testimony of two engineer-managers for Morton Thiokol, the maker of the solid rockets. At a closed session at the Kennedy Space Center, Roger Boisjoly said that in the prelaunch meeting, managers (from Thiokol and from NASA) had acted exactly opposite to the approved standard. "We normally have to absolutely prove beyond a shadow of a doubt that we have the ability to fly," he said. But Boisjoly said he and others were having to prove why "we *couldn't* [emphasis added] fly at this time, instead of the reverse." It was a reckless violation of NASA's own rules, and Boisjoly had risked his career to speak out against his company.

In her notebook, Sally wrote, "CRIP: 'prove to me you're ready to fly' is normal NASA philosophy." She added that John Young, head of the astronaut office, had said, "if the risk is unassessable, don't take it . . . 'don't know, don't go.' "

Another Thiokol engineer, Allan J. McDonald, dropped his own bombshell. He said he spoke out at the launch decision meeting about the effect of cold on the O-rings, but that no one would listen to him. "And I still didn't understand how NASA could accept a recommendation to fly below forty degrees. . . . I made the statement that if we're wrong and something goes wrong on this flight, I wouldn't want to have to be the person to stand up in front of board of inquiry."

When asked whether he felt "unusual pressure from NASA officials, to go ahead with the launch," McDonald answered, "That is an accurate inference, yes." McDonald also said that he refused to sign off on the decision, a highly unusual action.

The statements riveted the commission. "When I got done, I could hardly contain myself," McDonald tells me today. "I had tears coming down both sides of my eyes. It didn't have to happen. And Sally Ride could see that, and that was kind of at the end of the meeting. And she got up out of her chair, came over and gave me a hug and said, 'God, I'm glad somebody finally told us what really happened. That took a lot of guts.' And then Roger [Boisjoly] got up, and she walked up and hugged him too."

No reporter witnessed the exchange—it was a closed session—and when I mention to McDonald that the hugs sound out of character for Sally, he agrees. "It surprised me as well." Sally never spoke of it.

• ◆ •

All along, I'd been asking her for an exclusive interview, something to get behind the scenes. She'd declined at first, immersed in her homework, too busy or too tired to consider it. She looked pale and drawn, and I didn't push. Finally, she agreed.

We were in Florida that week, at the Kennedy Space Center, where the hearings were being held. At 7:30 on the morning of March 6, evading the rest of the press, she came to my motel room at Cocoa Beach, sat down, slipped off her shoes, and for the only time during the life of the commission, had her say. She wouldn't discuss the investigation itself but conceded that the revelations about the flawed decision-making process and the lack of rocket testing had affected her deeply.

> Lynn Sherr: Were you angry?
>
> Sally K. Ride: I was disturbed, I think is a good way to put it.
>
> LS: The shuttle management has said that the program is fully operational. Do you agree?
>
> SKR: If you mean, did I believe that we could launch every three weeks? That was really stretching the system, I think. Just from the point of view of putting a lot of stress on a lot of very competent engineers and possibly spreading the people and the resources a little bit too thin.
>
> LS: What about private citizens on the shuttle? Like Christa McAuliffe. [I did not have to say, "Like me, the one you wrote the recommendation for." We were both thinking it.]
>
> SKR: I think that we may have been misleading people into thinking that this is a routine operation, that it's just like getting on an airliner and going across the country and that it's safe. And it's not. Now, maybe they did understand the risks, maybe they didn't, and I think that that's NASA's responsibility and I'm not sure that NASA had carried out that responsibility.

Her final comment is the one that grabbed the headlines.

LS: You've flown on the shuttle twice. Knowing what you know now,
    would you fly again?

SKR: I am not ready to fly again now. I think there are very few astro-
    nauts who are ready to fly again now.

By the time the final report was presented to President Reagan in
June 1986, five months after the accident, the indictment of NASA was
complete: the O-rings were flawed, the signs of danger had been ignored, the risks minimized. Moreover, the flight rate was unacceptable
to guarantee crew safety. In a separate appendix to the commission's
findings, Richard Feynman compared launch decisions at NASA to Russian roulette. He concluded, "For a successful technology, reality must
take precedence over public relations, for nature cannot be fooled."

The shuttle program was shut down for more than two years while
the rockets were redesigned and management reconfigured. Plans were
abandoned to fly private citizens, meaning the end of the Journalist-in-
Space competition. Of the 1,703 applicants, I had made it to the last cut,
one of forty semifinalists. But neither I nor Walter Cronkite nor any of
the others on that list would become the first reporter in space. As Rick
Hauck told me in 1988, just before he commanded the first return-to-
flight mission on *Discovery*, "I think maybe we were beginning to think
we were infallible."

The findings were profoundly disturbing to Sally, the experience
even more so. As one of her colleagues put it, "The giants we thought
would make the right decisions were not giants at all." And Sally had to
censure those giants, some of the same ones who got her into space in
the first place. "It was a very, very difficult time for me," Sally later confessed, "for all the reasons you might expect. It was very hard on all of
us. You could see it in our faces . . . I looked tired and just kind of gray in
the face." At one point, during a break in the testimony, she had slipped
away with Tam to a cottage in La Jolla, California, to walk on the beach
and watch the sun set over the Pacific, a few days of soothing reassur-
ance in the face of death. A chance to mourn quietly.

• • •

The *Challenger* explosion and its aftermath would likely have been a turning point under any circumstances; given Sally's personal situation, even more so. But she was buoyed by her colleagues in Houston. "Just seeing how the accident hurt them," she would later say, "how much effort they put into the investigation and how important it was to them to understand what had happened, sort of restored my confidence. I really saw NASA responding the way I always assumed that NASA would respond." As usual, she did not dwell on catastrophe. In a spiral-bound notebook like those in which she'd recorded the proceedings of the hearings, Sally jotted down her observations of her fellow Commissioners, with her familiar entertaining and unvarnished take on a special group of individuals coming together at a unique time.

Neil Armstrong had been her hero from the time she watched him land on the Moon, but she couldn't resist noting that he struck her as "a little paunchy . . . wearing a slightly baggy, slightly 'hick' suit—color of bale of hay and alfalfa." And that he stumbled coming down the steps into the conference room. And lit a cigarette. For all that, she felt a special kinship with him and described a scene that surely would have made headlines, had any of the press been quick enough to notice: After their first meeting during a cold, snowy day in the Old Executive Office Building in Washington, DC, she and Armstrong wanted to evade the media out front. So they ducked out a side entrance and decided to walk to the hotel, about half a block away. Armstrong had come straight from the airport, with luggage, and "I offered to carry his brief case," Sally wrote. Then they turned a corner, and found themselves walking "down the street behind [the] press—unnoticed—me carrying one of Neil's bags."

Richard Feynman, she said, was "eager to investigate on his own . . . chomping at the bit," wearing "sick green shirts, non-descript slacks." But, she noted, the physicist had "2 new 3-piece suits (and a haircut) for [the] White House ceremony." Sally was impatient with his ego, noting that he used NASA offices "at [a] time when [Chairman] Rogers wanted to establish independence" from the space agency. And that he talked to himself and "beat drums on [his] desk"—holding imaginary drumsticks over the surface.

One commissioner was "puffy," with a "red face/red-nose." Another, "a little 'stilted' . . . in an old-fashioned way . . . called me 'Dr. Ride' even in informal situations."

Sally was sensitive to how she was addressed. Several of the witnesses, most of whom she'd never met, had called her "Sally." Then, "it looked as though someone put out a memo that said, 'don't do that,' because soon even people I knew well were using 'Dr. Ride' in the hearings."

Sally particularly liked her co-commissioner Dave Acheson, a "tall, well-built" lawyer in "crisp, fashionable shirts [and] Washingtonian suits," who "looked like [he] enjoyed tennis, boating, etc." He also "looked like he should have a pocket watch." Sally called him "invaluable toward the end—long hours, steadying influence, mode of equanimity, very thorough editor." He had, she noted, been given the job of "containing" the irrepressible Feynman.

The best surprise was Art Walker, her Stanford thesis advisor, with whom she had fun reliving the "student/prof relationship." Walker told her, "I guess I won't win all of our arguments." She also noted, without comment, that her distinguished African American mentor "was taken for a waiter/maître'd at an early function," either by a member of the commission or a NASA official.

The one member about whom she had nothing nice to say was Chuck Yeager, the sound-barrier-busting test pilot who had given both the Mercury astronauts and Kathy Sullivan such a hard time. "[I] never met him," Sally wrote. "Saw him for about 1 hr. at one of our early closed-door sessions in DC . . . he left early. That was his only appearance (asked no questions, looked bored)." Yeager did not participate further. "Showed some class by not coming to final ceremonies," Sally wrote, adding, "would have shown more by resigning from Commission."

Sally's final jibes pricked some of the more ludicrous moments of a group whose camaraderie and leadership otherwise impressed her. Among her observations:

One technical writer tried to sell a very early draft of the report to CBS. He was fired.

A note from the chairman answered the question, "How do you address a problem?" this way: "Dear problem."

And then there was the day when they were meeting in a windowless room at the Pentagon to discuss—no kidding—the color of the leather-bound cover of the report. When it came down to a choice between maroon and blue, Bob Hotz, an otherwise highly respected aviation writer and editor in chief of *Aviation Week & Space Technology*, made the politically unforgivable mistake of suggesting, as Sally noted, "that as the female I could be our color coordinator . . . I deferred." The sexist *faux pas* horrified Don Kutyna, whose Air Force training had sensitized him to the virtues of gender neutrality in all situations. "After a painful pause, during which all could see Sally's jaws tighten and eyes pierce, she replied slowly, firmly, 'Why me?' " Kutyna recalls. "Deathly silence." A vote was taken and maroon won—that was Sally's choice, too. But Hotz, she wrote, "had apparently already given go-ahead for blue . . . when report showed up . . . it had a blue cover . . . and I was accused."

Sally's copy of the (blue) leather-bound report, her name stamped in gold on the front, contains signatures of some of the commissioners, just like her high school yearbook. From Bud Wheelon, "Your calm company made this long journey wonderful." From Dave Acheson, "I enjoyed making a new friend." From Richard Feynman, "Great to get to know you—and share an office." Sally said they never shared an office.

SPLIT

One Sunday that year—no one remembers the exact date—Sally went home to Houston and talked to Steve.

"You're going to hate me for this," she said.

"What?" he asked.

"I think I don't want to be married anymore."

Steve took a breath and said, "Remember when we got engaged? I told you that what I wanted for you in life was to be happy, and if that's what you want to be happy, then okay."

And that, Steve tells me, was basically that. He was more than upset, his life torn apart. "But you know, it didn't come as a big shock to me. In some sense it came as a relief." He had, he says, "questioned her sexuality for quite a while, since we spent a lot of our marriage more as roommates than husband and wife. I had concluded by then that I didn't really want a roommate. And I had begun to contemplate, 'How the hell am I going to get out of this?'" The last year or so had been difficult. "She was gone all the time, partly with the *Challenger* investigation. And even before that she was gone a lot—kind of doing her own thing. It doesn't sound very charitable to say, but I always felt that her priority in our relationship was her and never me or us. Because I loved her, I tolerated that for as long as I could. But my sense was that she was beginning to sort of chart out what she was going to do next, and it didn't look necessarily as if I'd be part of that."

I ask Steve if he thought at the time it had anything to do with *Challenger*.

"Yeah, I did. She was clearly unhappy at NASA, and with NASA. And I thought part of it was she just had to get away from NASA, and if that meant getting away from me, that was what it was going to have to take. 'Cause I wasn't going to leave NASA. She didn't ask me, but I'm sure she assumed that."

Sally *was* on her way out of NASA, but not yet. And breaking up her marriage was difficult and painful. She had loved Steve and would remain friends with him for the rest of her life. But just as she had never told him about Molly, she would never tell him about Tam.

8

NEW TERRITORY

AUGUST 1986–AUGUST 1987

The Ride Report.

- *Mail rent check*
- *Start phone service*
- *Rent furniture?*
- *Call Crip*
- *Need: Secretary/staff*
- *Tickets and advance: HOU-DCA*

—To Do list from Sally Ride's notebook, August 1986

NASA HEADQUARTERS

Washington, DC, in mid-August is no day at the beach. On the other hand, it's not Houston. And Sally was very glad to be out of Houston. After eight years, she still found its climate—both meteorological and political—oppressive. And with the shuttle fleet grounded, the prospect of waiting at least two years for another flight held no appeal. So when her work with the Rogers Commission was done in June 1986, she made herself available to the new NASA administrator, James Fletcher.

"I had been planning to leave NASA after my third flight," she later said. "From the day I entered the astronaut corps, I had planned to return to research in a university environment. I reevaluated that thinking in light of the accident. I decided to stay at NASA for an extra year, simply because it was a bad time to leave. I wanted to stay a while to help the recovery process."

Unaware of her exit strategy (as usual, Sally told no one, although her lack of engagement had fueled speculation in the astronaut corps), Fletcher hitched NASA's biggest challenge to its brightest star, appointing her Special Assistant to the Administrator for Strategic Planning. In other words, Whither NASA? It was, Sally explained to me, a chance to "step back and look at the big picture, to help determine NASA's goals beyond the space station." She acknowledged with a laugh that the agency was being examined under a massive, unsolicited microscope. "We've been getting a lot of help from outside groups who say that NASA has no vision, no focus. And I think it's fair to say that . . . we've definitely lost sight of what our goals are."

It was also a chance to figure out, Whither Sally? Having left Steve, she moved to Washington by herself (Tam was now teaching college biology in Atlanta) for what would be a full year. She rented an apartment in a two-story building on Capitol Hill—walking distance from the office—and furnished it from the Ikea store near Dulles airport. After spreading all the pieces on the floor and assembling her new shelves and chairs, she started to construct answers to the problem at NASA.

In Houston, Carolyn Huntoon, whose concern for her female

charges extended beyond the Johnson Space Center, figured that Sally might need someone at Headquarters to show her the ropes, "to take care of things that were not her top priority—getting an office, doing the paperwork, finding the resources, figuring out budgets. That's not what she was brought there to do," explains Alan Ladwig, a savvy program manager who had worked with Huntoon on some educational projects. Ladwig, an outspoken admirer of Sally's who definitely needed a new job, was nonetheless wary. Several times, he'd been told, Sally had refused to allow the student experiments that Ladwig oversaw on her flights. And he still carried a grudge. So at their introductory meeting, he put it to her: "What did you have against student experiments?" Sally looked at him quizzically and said, "What are you talking about?" When Ladwig repeated the story, she said it wasn't true, "This is the first I'm ever hearing about this." Ladwig realized what had happened: "It's just the way some people down at JSC will act if it's something *they* don't want to do. They'll put the burden on an astronaut. Because Lord forbid anybody argue with an astronaut!"

He also asked how her long-range planning report would be any different from all the ones already sitting on the shelves.

Ladwig's candor—along with his irreverence for bureaucracy and his sharp wit—matched Sally's own, and she made him her trusted assistant. Their friendship and collaboration would last a quarter century, in the partnership she preferred. "I became her sidekick: Tonto to her Lone Ranger; Louise to her Thelma; Rhoda to her Mary," Ladwig says good-naturedly. "Sally and I were opposite in many ways," he says. "She was introverted and didn't like giving presentations; I was mouthy, could talk all the time. But we got on the same page instantly."

Part of his job, he says, "was to help keep people away from her who were enchanted by the celebrity of Sally Ride. I was the gatekeeper. Everyone wanted to brief her, to hear what she had to say about the future of NASA. I had to be the filter of who was legitimate and who would waste her time. And Sally didn't tolerate wasting time. I always thought she was driven to accomplish something every day."

Sally had been briefed by the administrator on the immense scope

and delicate subtexts of her task: she would have to include the thinking of top management from each of the NASA centers; she would be
dealing with disparate, disjointed groups, each of which had its own
concept of where it fit in; she would have to reconcile what each group
thought *its* role was with their view of the *agency's* goals; she would have
to anticipate questions from the public, from Congress, from the Reagan administration; and she would have to take into account the needs
and plans of everyone from the US Air Force Space Command to the
contractors for commercial satellites. She would, in effect, be rocketing
beyond the space shuttle, even as its program was being restructured.

Next to each of the sectors, Sally started to fill in names she might
call on. In the same precise handwriting that had documented her post-
STS-7 trip to Europe and her findings in the *Challenger* investigation, she
listed the astronauts she most relied on (Crippen, Hauck, Fabian, and
Steve Hawley), the NASA managers she still respected (Huntoon, Abbey)
and some of her new pals from the Rogers Commission (Kutyna, Wheelon). One earned a separate line: "Neil—in Washington? Get advice/
perspective." (Some things never change. She spelled it "advise.")

Her early bullet points indicated the direction she was headed.

- Agency doesn't need another study—need an understanding and
  coalescing of current goals.
- Space Shuttle is not a goal, but means to achieving several goals.
- "Bold New Initiatives"

Sally tapped NASA's smartest brains to help formulate the most
promising objectives. Previous studies were scrutinized and ranked for
their application to the problem. Advocates had to defend their projects.
And "when she didn't understand something, she would ask very direct,
open questions," says John Niehoff, who was the lead scientist on the
Mars proposal. "She wasn't shy about her ignorance in certain subjects."

Early on, the possibilities were distilled to four likely options: send
humans to Mars, build a human base on the Moon, study Earth from

space, send robots to the outer planets. Sally remained neutral about which she preferred, a stance she may have had to defend. Mars was the well-known favorite of NASA administrator Fletcher, who—according to one scientist—walked into Sally's office and told her to drop almost everything else. "And she just flat-out ignored him," he says. Fletcher's wasn't the only partisan voice. "I think a lot of people wanted Mars to be *the* answer," says Alan Ladwig. "The Apollo old guard wanted another hurrah, another major national goal, like the Moon, and they assumed that money would follow, that NASA would be the lead agency again."

Each sector clamored for its own pet project: "Pick Mars!" "Go to the Moon!" "Planet Earth!" "Robots!" Sally listened to them all, balancing the points of view. "She had a way of creating an environment where everyone had a voice," says Al Diaz, who worked as a program manager in space science. Another NASA scientist calls her a classic leader: "She just exuded a quiet confidence. She'd provide encouragement. And yet she'd also push back and tell you when you were barking up the wrong tree. So she'd say, 'Okay, getting people to Mars. Fine. But how do you start the process?'"

Sally had learned well from the inclusive and transparent command of Bob Crippen on the space shuttle. "I spent a lot of time watching the way he worked, the way he learned things, and the way he worked with other people." But she added her own unique touch. For instance: "She took a look at all the people assigned to various initiatives," Ladwig recalls, "and she saw a bunch of old white men. And she thought, we need to get young people involved. So she asked Fletcher to put out a call for each center to nominate a young, up-and-coming engineer or scientist or whatever. She called it the 1A Task Group. What the hell that stood for, I don't remember. But these were ten or eleven young people that she worked directly with. Up to that point, nobody really gave a damn about what young people thought."

The young people thought their trip through the skunk works was heaven.

"Oh my god, it was beyond delightful!" recalls James Garvin, a self-described "career science geek" who joined the team as a thirty-year-old. "To be able to work with someone as heady as Sally, who really challenged us to think out of the box and to give her a framework, it was great! She took our little team, paraded us in front of the administrator. I mean, I was briefing the administrator, having been at NASA just three years. Sally gave us the ball to run with, whether it was crazy or not, and that was thrilling. And it really gave us a chance to see how the leadership of the agency worked."

Garvin, who would become Chief Scientist at NASA's Goddard Space Flight Center (its flagship science center and a hub for the engineering of science in space), compares Sally's mandate to the fantasy element "unobtanium"—a nonexistent substance with impossibly perfect properties. "If the vision's great but not realizable, then it's really no good," he says, recalling her directive. "It has to have enough legs to be sustainable. It was kind of like a graduate seminar in the future of space leadership—in my case, representing the science pull; for others, the engineering push, and even the communications aspect." Communications was no small issue in 1986. Information was exchanged with face-to-face meetings, phone calls, and a baffling internal telemail system. There was no email, few computers, and status was defined by the quality of your typewriter. "If you had an IBM Selectric 3 with two elements," recalls Alan Ladwig of the Cadillac of machines, "you were really something!"

For Brian Muirhead, then a young engineer at NASA's Jet Propulsion Laboratory (JPL, headquarters for robotic deep space ventures), being part of the 1A Team occasioned his first visit to Goddard, where he joined the group seated in a real conference room—"long wooden table, fancy chairs and big windows." But unlike the "graybeards," he says, who did the previous studies that were watered down by the strategic planning process, "we were not to be held to a particular political standard. We were going to be the free agents, and Sally was going to be the Top Cover—like the military guys above you who cover for you while you go and do things you're not meant to do."

It was a daring ploy in an agency whose risks tended to be taken beyond Earth's atmosphere, not within the gravity of Washington's boardrooms, but Sally wanted to bring some fresh air into an ailing system. It gave Muirhead, now chief engineer at JPL, "a pretty good dose of reality. It wasn't quite a loss of innocence, but it was certainly a recognition that the nature of business in Washington is always a Faustian deal. The best ideas, the best intentions, the best strategies are rarely the ones that get picked, because there are forces that drive you in some suboptimum way. But I'm still an idealist—that's true of all of our team—we were all idealists that Sally fostered and encouraged. And it was part of her nature as well."

Flying a desk had never been Sally's dream, but in the post-*Challenger* downtime for the shuttle, it was a perfect transition. Crusader Rabbit was back on the job, this time saving the space agency.

All adventures—especially into new territory—are scary...
—Sally Ride, *To Space and Back*, 1986

In October 1986, Sally's first book was published, *To Space and Back*, an account of her flights written specifically for children. Her coauthor, Susan Okie, says that partnering on the manuscript was almost as much fun as the preliminary conversations. "Meeting with publishers was hilarious, because they all showed up thinking that they were bidding on her autobiography, *The Sally Ride Story*, and we had to disabuse them of that notion." Instead, the book, which was Sally's idea, answers basic questions about being weightless, sleeping in space, and yes, using the toilet. And "it explains exactly how I felt going into space," she told a reporter. "The combination of pictures and words does it so much better than I could when I was standing up on a stage." Sally included photographs of missions besides her own, to show other astronauts on the job. Publishers, she said, wanted to know " 'What was it like being the first woman in space?' But I thought we could make the point that there are men and women astronauts very subtly, just by showing pictures of men and women working together in the space shuttle."

Under Okie's prodding, Sally worked hard to make the experience of being launched understandable to her young audience. They dedicated the book to the memory of Elizabeth Mommaerts, the high school physiology teacher who had opened their teenaged minds. But just before it was ready to be printed, *Challenger* exploded, leading Sally and her publisher to reconsider the appropriateness of a book with smiling astronauts tumbling in weightlessness. "We both felt it was perfectly valid," Sally said at publication. "Kids bounce back easily. When I go out to give a speech these days, kids don't ask about the accident at all. They ask about future-oriented things . . . It's the *adults* who ask about the accident and my reaction to it." A second dedication was added, to the memory of the seven dead astronauts.

While it may not have damaged American children, *Challenger* had blown up her relationship with her coauthor. After the accident (when the book was at the printer), Okie—who did not normally cover NASA—was pressed into service by her editors at the Washington *Post* to help report the story, and she contacted a number of the people she'd met while interviewing Sally for her pre–STS-7 series of articles. That's what journalists do, especially in a crisis. But, Okie says, "Sally called me in a cold fury, just icy cold fury on the phone. And I don't remember what she said but it was like, 'Why are you calling my friends? You have no right to do that. Stop calling my friends.' I mean, she was really, really furious. To her, it was a major betrayal. And I couldn't even speak, I felt completely unable to fight back. I felt terrible, but I said, 'Don't you understand, this is my job? You asked me to come down as a reporter. What do you expect me to do in this situation?' She wouldn't speak to me for a long while after that."

More than half a year later, Okie came to Sally's office at NASA Headquarters to sign books together for some friends. The first thing she noticed was how Sally had adapted to the system. "She was on and off the phone the whole time. And I remember hearing her organize the schedule for a meeting so that it would happen when some key person would be out of town and not able to attend. And I remember thinking, Wow, she's turned into a bureaucrat, she knows how to work the Washington system here."

More troubling to Okie was the way her old friend dismissed her. She arrived with her children, still in a stroller, so Sally could see them. "And she completely ignored them," Okie says, "and there was no sort of hashing out what had happened, there was never any really full conversation about why she'd been so mad. It was just like ice water, just chilly."

The hostility Okie witnessed was rare. Perhaps she noticed because she was better attuned to the woman she knew so well; perhaps it felt so harsh because she had violated Sally's tacit No Trespassing rule at the agency she felt bound to protect. Other friends complain that without any obvious provocation, they might not hear from Sally for weeks, or months, or even years. That she'd ignore their calls and emails for long periods of time. And then she'd be back, friendly as ever. That happened to me, too. In time, Susan and Sally would also reestablish their relationship—although not quite, Okie says, to the level it once was. They would write no more books together.

People who didn't know Sally nearly as well never felt her wrath. She either avoided them or made up a story. In a series of interviews to promote her book in October 1986, Sally was the consummate NASA team player, declaring, in response to questions about her earlier bombshell to me, that with the agency's new rules and with shuttle training about to resume, she now had "no qualms" about going up, that she was certainly willing to fly. But she must have had her fingers crossed behind her back when she told an audience of California college students that after her Washington assignment she would return to the astronaut corps. By then, she knew she was leaving. Make that the fingers of both hands when she was asked by a reporter, yet again, if she wanted to have children. "That's something my husband and I keep to ourselves," she said, with divorce proceedings already under way.

DCA-ATL-DCA

Weekends were for Tam. In the language of airport abbreviations, Sally was flying from Washington to Atlanta and back; or Tam came to visit her in the Capital, where they walked and ran around the Mall, visiting their favorite works by Degas, Calder and Rodin in the Hirschhorn Museum. They were especially partial to the sinuous bronzes by Henry Moore, inside and around the Sculpture Garden. At night, they'd walk to the pizza place for a pie with extra cheese, then stop at Bob's Famous Homemade Ice Cream shop for two pints of Jamocha Almond Fudge to take home. While Sally worked on the future of NASA, Tam worked on her master's degree in biology.

At thirty-four, Sally had come to terms with the fact that she was in love with another woman. "She was fully committed, utterly with me in every respect," Tam says. "There was no, 'Oh, should I do this?' She was there, physically, emotionally, mentally. I was surprised by how open Sally was, being a same-sex couple." Tam describes the passion of their intimate life, showing me a small sculpture of two women embracing, that Sally commissioned as a present for her. "Sally was very affectionate, very loving," Tam says.

Privately, Sally was embarking on a partnership for life. Publicly, she was still the loyal astronaut.

THE RIDE REPORT

Over the course of the yearlong study, Sally pushed her team for the best possible scenarios, editing and rewriting various drafts through many review processes. "She would call at the very tail end of the workday, when I'd already been at it for fourteen hours," says Terri Niehoff, a technical writer based in Chicago who was the report's official editor. "And she'd say, 'I know you're going to be mad, but I want to fit one more paragraph in.' And I'd say, 'Sally, we're at the end of the page. If I add a paragraph we're going to have to take one out.' And she'd say, 'Okay,' and would work on it. She would not say, 'You figure it out, I'm outta here.' She would stay and work late, and it was later for her than for me." Sally, she says, was aiming for precision. "She would argue with me between using an 'a' versus a 'the,' the singular versus the all-inclusive. She didn't want to give an impression that she didn't want to give. And because a lot of the input was coming from other people, she had to filter that, and put her own voice on it."

In the end, she listed "four bold initiatives," fulfilling her original vision, options to "restore the United States to a position of leadership." That was the theme and the title: *Leadership and America's Future in Space*. Everyone called it the "Ride Report."

Here, in unusually direct language, is the evolutionary approach she laid out for NASA:

Send Humans to Mars: "Settling Mars should be our eventual goal," Sally wrote, "but it should not be our next goal." The Report outlined an orderly, unrushed expedition to establish a Martian base—not a "one-shot foray or a political stunt." Sally cautioned against a "race to Mars" which would invariably lead to timetables. "Schedule pressures, as the Rogers Commission noted, can have a very real, adverse effect."

Build an outpost on the Moon: Return to the site of humankind's greatest space adventure to construct a lunar station, to explore the resources of our nearest cosmic neighbor. This to counter the "considerable sentiment that Apollo was a dead-end venture, and we have little to show for it."

Explore the Solar System robotically: Sally was distressed by the slowdown in US planetary launches and particularly noted the growing presence of uncrewed Soviet spacecraft on Mars. Although it lacks "the excitement of human exploration, it is fundamental science that challenges our technology, extends our presence, and gives us a glimpse of other worlds."

Launch a Mission to Planet Earth: "Virtually everyone exposed to this initiative recognized its fundamental importance," she wrote, "and agreed that 'whatever we do, we have to do this...' " When's the last time you saw language like that in an official government document? The report urged NASA to launch a series of satellites that would observe and record global change, and it emphasized the shared aspects of the project. Only by enlisting international cooperation—led by the US—could the planet be monitored, and secure.

> NASA should embrace Mission to Planet Earth. This initiative is responsive, time-critical, and shows a recognition of our responsibility to our home planet. Do we dare apply our capabilities to explore the mysteries of other worlds, and not also apply those capabilities to explore and understand the mysteries of our own world—mysteries which may have important implications for our future on this planet?

Neither the concept nor the name was original: a group of NASA scientists had been promoting rigorous studies of the home planet for more than a decade, first sounding the alarm based on evidence from the hole in the ozone layer. To little avail. "NASA was an organization driven to explore, and Earth science wasn't recognized as exploration," explains Al Diaz. In most of the NASA hierarchy, observing microchanges in Earth's atmosphere was like watching paint dry; planetary missions were the sexy quests. And few wanted anything to derail the primacy of the astronauts. "To be in Earth science at NASA is to be treated as a stepchild," says Dixon Butler, who was the lead advocate for the Mission Planet Earth initiative. "Our only job is to observe Earth from space, but that one essential mission... is a direct threat to everything else the agency does, because you can always say this is more important than human spaceflight, so you have to take a pause in human spaceflight."

Sally understood the implications. "She wanted to articulate it in a way that NASA could appreciate," Al Diaz tells me. "And that was the 'mission' determination. Before that, Earth Science was seen as a kind of long-term operation that dealt with remote sensing and applications.

But Sally became the Earth Science equivalent of Carl Sagan. She popularized it, made it something more tangible that people could relate to."

And she elevated Earth from our boring backyard to an exotic planet, a shrewd enticement for an agency that wanted to explore planets. Sometime later, Sally met with Senator Al Gore (who chaired the Space Science Subcommittee of the Commerce Committee) and Senator Barbara Mikulski (who was on the Senate Appropriations Committee) to review the report. They asked her what NASA could do most effectively. "Mission to Planet Earth," Sally replied, invoking the mystery of an extraterrestrial adventure. The two senators asked why. "There is a deep suspicion in the scientific community," Sally told them, "that there is intelligent life there."

NASA wasn't thrilled with Sally's report. " 'It's not exactly getting a warm embrace,' one NASA manager said. . . . [S]enior officials initially debated whether the report should be released at all." It was too blunt, too even-handed. And Sally had made Mission to Planet Earth seem more urgent than Mars, the administrator's baby. Finally, NASA decided to print two thousand copies, a relatively small run for a yearlong job that had involved hundreds of employees.

A week before the release, Sally invited *Aviation Week*'s Craig Covault in for an exclusive briefing—knowing he'd stick to the facts and not try to sneak in any personal questions. At the end of his backgrounder, Covault, who felt that administrator Fletcher was not rising to the challenge of the beleaguered NASA, asked Sally if she thought he should be fired. "She was still an active astronaut," Covault says, pointing out the delicacy of the question about her boss. "So she hung her head down—I don't think she wanted to make eye contact—and she said, 'Yes.' Just barely out of her mouth."

At 6:00 a.m. on an August morning, Terri Niehoff flew from Chicago to Washington with the first printing: fifty 63-page reports in a big, heavy box. When she got to Sally's office, the two women hijacked a dolly and wheeled the cargo up to the Administrator's office on the seventh floor of the old NASA building on Maryland Avenue. Sally went in alone. When she reappeared wearing a radiant smile, she signed Niehoff's copy. "A success! . . . I promise to stop making changes now . . . special thanks for eliminating 90% of my semicolons!"

DONE

Sally didn't want a news conference, didn't do any more interviews. The report, she said, could speak for itself. The press reviews were glowing, applauding a commonsense, budget-conscious, clear-eyed plan of action. It presented, editorialized the *Los Angeles Times*, "a galaxy of space projects . . . [that could] restore the agency to its earlier professionalism." Some noted the comments she slipped in at the end, calling for an increased emphasis on education in a broad range of science and technology. "This means capturing the imaginations and interests of young people at an early age in their educational careers," she wrote, "and encouraging them to pursue studies that will prepare them to actively participate in the space program."

Her last assignment at Headquarters was brief—two months as acting Administrator of the Office of Exploration, a newly created position (recommended by her study) to help set up a coordinated, "serious focus" for everything related to human spaceflight.

In August 1987, Sally Ride retired from NASA. She had announced her departure plans three months earlier, on her thirty-sixth birthday, the same month her divorce from Steve became final. NASA had to contend not only with the public surprise over her resignation, but with the consequences of her privacy. When the news of her divorce leaked out, a Houston reporter sent NASA a scathing letter, noting that the agency hadn't mentioned it. And that, he said, was typical of how "astronaut biographies are often short of information." NASA wrote back with an apology: they had just learned of the divorce themselves. Sally did no interviews on either subject.

In the decade since she saw the article about NASA's search for female astronauts, Sally Ride had flown to fame, flown again, helped investigate the space agency's greatest disaster, and made bold suggestions for its future. To say that she was grateful for, and a proud former employee of, NASA would shortchange her passion for the job, the experience, the debt, and the concern she felt. NASA had put her not only into space, but on the nation's front pages and in its history texts. Her flight would forever open doors and replenish her bank account. She was fiercely loyal to NASA, and it would always be part of her past, present and future; she was so eager to promote and protect the space agency, she might well have hidden her private life to help preserve its image. And perhaps even retired to spare them any embarrassment. "I think she knew," Tam says, "that our relationship would be difficult if she stayed at NASA."

No experience could ever equal the rush of riding a rocket or floating weightless. But having reached the literal—if not professional—high point of her career four years earlier, at the very young age of thirty-two, Sally was ready to move on. Some of her TFNG classmates would stay for many more flights; Steve Hawley flew for the fifth and final time at age forty-seven, only retiring from NASA after thirty years.

Not Sally. She packed up her apartment and headed to California, back to Stanford, the first step in her transition out of NASA. Having gone up into space and seen the future, she now turned her gaze downwards, towards Earth—just like all the other stars.

DOWN TO EARTH

SEPTEMBER 1987–SEPTEMBER 2000

Earth view, English Channel, from STS 41-G, *Challenger*, October 1984.

Gone from NASA, Sally embarked on the search for her next mission with renewed focus, redirecting every question about the ethereal toward the more substantive:

> TV Interviewer: *Was it spiritual as you kissed the heavens?*
> Sally Ride: *You know, what was absolutely amazing to me was the feeling I had looking back at Earth . . . it's remarkable how beautiful our planet is, and how fragile it looks.*

ARMS AND THE WOMAN

Nowhere was the crusade to protect Earth taken more seriously than at Stanford's Center for International Security and Arms Control (CISAC, now the Center for International Security and Cooperation), the influential think tank where, in September 1987, Sally joined those trying to keep the world from blowing itself up.

And nowhere did she feel more grounded than in an academic setting. "I love the university environment," she said. "I love research, I love teaching. It's what I planned to do before my career took a little bit of a turn with the astronaut corps. So going back to a university environment was a natural for me."

It was exactly the mood realignment she craved to contemplate her second act: a quiet sanctuary with open offices and hallway conversation where she could flex her brain, focus on something significant, and avoid having to talk about herself. More than one hundred requests for meetings or interviews languished in the Stanford publicity department. "We're not NASA, and she's no longer an astronaut," explained a university spokesman. "She wants to be private."

Physicist and arms control expert Sid Drell, codirector of the center, had offered her the prestigious two-year science fellowship after being introduced by Sally's Westlake classmate Brooke Shearer and her husband, Strobe Talbott, of *Time* magazine. "She was very serious, asked sharp questions and indicated that she had an interest in thinking about space and arms control," Drell says. "She wanted a new challenge."

With the Cold War smoldering and the Berlin Wall still dividing East from West, the chance to study international security issues and help reduce the threat of nuclear weapons attracted some of the best minds in academia. Condoleezza Rice, then a Soviet specialist and an assistant professor at Stanford, was one of the first of her new colleagues Sally met, although Rice laughs about her clumsy initial encounter with the famous astronaut. "I thought to myself, 'What am I going to say when I meet her?' " she tells me, recalling her nervousness. "And then I blurted out, 'What's it like to go into space?' " The two women hit it off instantly, sharing laughs over the chauvinistic measure of armament buildups ("mine's bigger than yours" was the basic missile standard) and cheering on the Stanford (or any other) football team together. Their mutual passion for sports often found them watching games on TV—usually in Rice's apartment at the low-rise Pearce-Mitchell Condo complex, because her TV set was larger. And while their politics would diverge, the woman who would become Secretary of State under President George W. Bush says that CISAC was "pretty moderate. We didn't argue."

Sally's research focused on verification of nuclear warheads: how to count and confirm the other side's arsenal. Her degree in physics and her hundreds of hours in orbit were the perfect credentials to study rates of emissions and calculate radioactivity in outer space. Her experience dealing with real systems, like the shuttle, was even more valuable when she teamed up with two other physicist fellows to disprove the popular notion that nuclear warheads on sea-launched cruise missiles could not be monitored. They needed to understand the logistics, and the magic of Sally's name opened up some usually impenetrable ports. "We went down inside the launcher on a destroyer, and we visited a factory where they assembled the cruise missiles," recalls George Lewis, one of her co-researchers. The third partner, John Townsend, accompanied Sally "on a battleship that carried sea-launch cruise missiles, and then on two different attack submarines, where the commanders gave us a tour of the torpedo rooms where the missiles were deployed." The paper they produced validated their premise, and they hoped it would influence US policy during negotiations with the Russians. But events overtook their ambitions. "The Berlin Wall came down, and the Soviet Union became less of an issue," Townsend says. The missile inspection issue faded without their contribution.

Sally opposed any militarization of space. In 1985 she had told an audience at Mount Holyoke College, "I happen to be one of the people who think that space is not a good place for any weapons." She was talking about President Reagan's proposed Strategic Defense Initiative (aka "Star Wars") with its space-based system to intercept enemy missiles.

When an administration official came to CISAC to brief the fellows in 1987, one of Sally's colleagues watched with awe as she courteously "destroyed the speaker's credibility with a couple of simple questions about the scale of the drawings and the imagined payload capacity of the rocket needed to put the various materials into space." US rockets, she knew, had no such heavy lift capability.

Some years later, delivering the Drell Lecture at Stanford, Sally included anti-satellite weapons in her list of no-no's. They would, she said, be "disastrous," in part because of the potentially deadly consequences of a piece of errant space debris hitting a functioning satellite. "What if anti-satellite testing proceeds and we start testing rockets that clobber satellites and explode them in space?" she asked in 2002. "What if enough of that goes on that there's the equivalent to a test range up in low-Earth orbit?" Sound familiar? That is essentially the plotline of *Gravity*, the 2013 3D thriller where the characters played by Sandra Bullock and George Clooney (along with their crew and shuttle) are clobbered by lethal chunks of orbiting satellite shrapnel and stranded in space. The white-knuckle sequences are relentless. But *Gravity* is fiction, more splash than science, digital magic from a movie studio. The real thing had put Sally and her crew at genuine risk three decades earlier, when a small pit appeared on one of *Challenger*'s windows during STS-7. "We didn't know what it was. An awful lot of analysis was done while we were in orbit to make sure that the strength of the window would sustain reentry. It did. We were all fine." Tests afterward identified the culprit as a small fleck of paint—from heaven-knows-what abandoned object—whipping around the planet so fast, it gouged a small dent in the window. "Well," Sally explained, "a fleck of paint is not the same as a small piece of metal traveling at that same speed. So, as soon as you start increasing the amount of junk in a low-Earth orbit, you have an unintended byproduct that starts putting some of your own quite valuable satellites at possible risk."

Protecting Earth, she believed, also meant keeping an eye on the Russians after Glasnost. Her understanding of Soviet space capabilities had grown enormously since the night she'd swapped stories with Svetlana Savitskaya during their clandestine rendezvous in Budapest. Russian space officials had become more candid, and the newly available files indicated major progress in their cosmonaut program. In a 1989 article she coauthored for *Scientific American*, Sally weighed the impressive status and robust potential of the Soviet space program against the *angst* over US space policy. It was a barely disguised jab at the US to get its space act together. "Can the US manage its own, more sophisticated space technology well enough to mount an equally powerful program? Certainly it can, but not without the ingredients that characterize the Soviet program: long-range political and financial commitments that nurture long-range goals." Imagine the thrill: the magazine that had so engrossed Sally as a youngster and provided her with puzzles to tease her brain, now bore her byline. Sally was starting to appreciate the upside of her celebrity. Which continued to be formidable.

John Townsend, who made the cruise missile field trips with Sally, calls her "easily the most famous person I've ever worked with. In science, it wouldn't be uncommon, when you were seated in a room, to have a bunch of Nobel laureates scattered around. No big deal. But when Sally was involved, it was different. At one meeting, when she wasn't there, everyone was asking, 'What's Sally going to do? Where's she going to get a job?'"

Sally wondered the same thing. At the end of her two-year fellowship, Drell tried to get one of the Stanford departments to name her a professor. But no department would accept her. Stanford, her beloved alma mater, turned her down.

"The stupidities and parochialism of what goes on in departmental faculty meetings—it's as amazing as it is legendary," Drell says. He resigned from CISAC in protest. "In the department's view, she didn't have the kind of published scientific literature which they said meant she'd be a great scientist. Stanford blinked." Drell was furious. But Sally, he said, was "calm and cool. And other universities looked to Stanford and said, 'You must be crazy.'"

ASTRONAUT RIDE TO PURSUE

DUAL INTERESTS AT UCSD

—*Los Angeles Times*, June, 1989

UNIVERSITY OF CALIFORNIA, SAN DIEGO

Nearly five hundred miles down the coast, the University of California, San Diego (UCSD) knew that getting Sally Ride was a coup, which they secured with a dual appointment: professor of physics (with tenure) and director of the California Space Institute (CalSpace), the statewide coordinator for space-related research throughout the UC system. "The package of these two was very attractive," Sally said. "This will allow me to pursue my interest in physics and in the space program." She hoped to expand satellite coverage of Earth to permit more remote sensing of environmental problems. And, she said, "I'd like to have an impact on [space] policy." Earth was not just her scientific priority; it was where she was planting her feet for the next phase of her career.

And while the Stanford rejection was a situation ripe for resentment, Sally never uttered a word of regret. "I was furious," Tam O'Shaughnessy tells me. "But she took it in and then just spun it around. She said, 'Okay, they don't want me, just move on.' So instead of dwelling on the failure, she just wiped it out of her brain and replaced it with UCSD, who valued everything she'd done." Sally never held a grudge. "She still loved Stanford. She just thought about it the way she wished to. She was a genius at doing this, to maintain her positive attitude, her confidence, and move along."

This from the woman who'd told a reporter before STS-7, in 1983, "I haven't had any major disappointments or any major failings."

It was just like the photo of her victorious tennis match on the shelf; like the letter home from Swarthmore about making the hockey team; like getting an A (first semester) in Melvin Schwartz's Electricity and Magnetism class. "Sally would always turn things around so that it was her decision," Tam says. "She learned very young to turn things in her favor, to always maintain her self-confidence. Anything that was negative, she'd turn her own way. So I imagine there might have been some negative things out there, but she wouldn't see them, she wouldn't hear them, would not respect the professor who tried to exclude her."

Tam knew Sally better than anyone. Their relationship had solidified over four years and tens of thousands of miles, as they crisscrossed the country regularly to be together. When Sally was at Stanford, with a reasonably flexible schedule, she spent many weekends in Atlanta, where Tam was finishing her master's program at Georgia State and about to embark on her doctorate in ecology at the University of Georgia. "We were always talking about science," Tam says, "because I was hungry to learn about physics and chemistry, and I loved to talk about biology—living things—and the connections among life, lands, oceans and air." During both summers, Tam packed up Annie, her three-legged cocker spaniel, and moved into Sally's condo, half a block from campus. At the Stanford Arts Festival one year, the women bought matching gold rings, Tam's distinguished by a turquoise stone. Sally's is visible in many photographs, on the fourth finger of her left hand. One day, at a bookstore, Tam picked up Isaac Asimov's *Is There Life on Other Planets?*, a new book for young readers, and showed it to Sally. Asimov's ability to make complicated concepts clear made them realize that there might be a way to get children interested in the fields that had hooked them both. The germ of an idea was born.

Each time Tam returned to Atlanta, Sally felt unsettled. The long-distance relationship was taxing. For the second and last time of her life she consulted a therapist, who, she told Tam, said that unlike some people, who needed only "partial relationships," Sally needed "a full relationship"—intimacy, living together, being in the same place at the same time. So when her future after CISAC looked uncertain, she interviewed at Clemson, Georgia Tech, and other schools near Atlanta, because that's where Tam was based. The offer from UCSD ended that. Sally prepared herself for more planes and travel, and headed to San Diego.

Then, in September 1989, another ball Sally couldn't control. Dale Ride entered the hospital in Los Angeles for routine prostate surgery and had a sudden, massive heart attack. At a very premature sixty-seven, Sally's father was dead. The man she had trailed as a youngster, the doting dad who had taken her to tennis matches and pushed her ever higher and bequeathed her his ready smile and affable outlook, the proud papa who would brook no bias when it came to his daughters, was gone. Sally was distraught. She called Steve and asked for the phone number of his father, the minister. "I think she just needed somebody to talk to about this," Steve says.

She also called Tam. "She said she needed me in California. So I went out for the memorial service and stayed a week or so. And then she got extremely shaky. She said, 'I can't take the long distance anymore.' So I left my PhD program and moved to California."

Sally bought a large townhouse on a bluff in La Jolla, the seaside community just north of San Diego. Tam got a job teaching biology at nearby San Diego Mesa College There would also be a house in Atlanta for a few years. They moved in together permanently, partners for life, despite Sally's aversion to making long-range personal plans. Setting goals for NASA, it turns out, was infinitely easier than doing it for herself. When it became clear that the relationship was serious, Tam asked Sally, "So tell me how you're thinking about us. Is this forever for you? What do you feel?"

Sally answered without emotion. "You know I can't think more than five years ahead."

"And I said, 'What? Excuse me? You're supposed to say, "Yes, it's forever! You're the love of my life!"' You know? '"This is it." You've got to be joking, you can only look five years ahead?'

"And she was dead serious. She said, 'That's how I've always been about everything, I can't look that far ahead.'

"So it just became this thing with us. Five years went by and I'd say, 'Okay, are you going to sign up again? Are we renewing?' And then another ten years went by."

And so on.

They would live, work and love together for another twenty-three years, hiking and running along the trails and cliffs at nearby Torrey Pines State Reserve; playing catch in the back yard or ping-pong in the garage; reading *War of the Worlds* or *The Invisible Man* to each other; toning their bodies with yoga or Jane Fonda's exercise tapes; two strong women, one's yin to the other's yang. When they sat together in the living room, their legs were usually in contact. When they traveled together on airplanes, Tam says, "our little hands would be touching under the blanket." They would stroll beneath the night sky, looking for constellations or watching the Perseid and Leonid meteor showers. And where once they had boogied together as a group of girlhood tennis players, they now slow-danced to Linda Ronstadt and Madonna and Emmylou Harris. Their language was the romance of the ordinary: "Goose, I'm home!" Sally would call out as she entered through the garage at day's end, colliding into Tam's arms. "I love you," they said to each other as they dropped off to sleep. "Behind closed doors," Tam says, "she was just a loving little puppy dog."

It would surely enrich the narrative to add Sally's own distinctive voice to all this, to see it through her eyes. But almost nothing exists, on paper or in pixels, about her private time with Tam. Her lively letters describing her day-to-day adventures had stopped after college—no doubt she was too busy being an astronaut; then, her celebrity and the distress over various stalkers, made her wary of committing anything personal to print. The only journals she kept as an adult focused on her work, not her personal life. And unlike her days at NASA, when reporters occasionally pierced the protective tiles and secured a comment about, or an image of Sally and Steve together, Sally and Tam's years together were lived, by choice, out of the public spotlight. Sally never reached out to friends or family members to discuss any of it. That simply wasn't her way.

Tam shows me the few existing brief mementoes she kept, tantalizing glimpses of their life together: A computer printout of a reservation

Sally made at the Four Seasons Hotel for a surprise weekend in Boston; a hastily scribbled note left on Tam's pillow when Sally had to leave early one morning, reading, "Sleep well!" And a jocular greeting card Sally once sent her. "You're not fair!!" says the critter on the front. Inside: "You're excellent." Sally signed it with her initials: "Love, SKR." Once, on a sticky note attached to her solution to a trigonometry problem, Sally wrote to Tam, "Isn't physics wonderful! (you sure are). Love, The 'mad physicist.'"

The recollections of insiders are equally engaging and terse. When one friend commented, "You two are great!" Sally said, contentedly, "Yeah, I'll keep her."

Even the modest group of snapshots of just Sally and Tam together— hiking with friends, or cuddling one of their dogs, or speaking on the same stage—lack the mugging-and-hugging quality common to so many couples in today's image-obsessed generation. They were, Tam says, just too busy with their work to sit down and pose for formal photographs.

Slim pickings for the historical record, but their mutual devotion over more than a quarter century paints an adoring picture. Billie Jean King, who, along with her partner, Ilana Kloss, spent time with them, talks about an affection that went beyond the physical: "You could tell by their tone of voice, the way they looked at each other, spoke to each other. I could see it, I could feel it." Grenn Nemhauser, a former WTA executive, and her partner, Lindsey Beaven, a onetime top-ten British player, spent many weekends with them, hiking and playing the occasional friendly game of tennis. "They were just easy to be with," Nemhauser tells me. "And fun. We just laughed the whole time."

Kay Loveland, Tam's psychologist friend in Atlanta, says it was about looks and actions, not words. "I never heard Sally say, 'I love you,' to Tam. But you could tell they were in love by the way they would touch each other when they'd go by." She watched them joke together and tease each other, remembering the "wry Sally smile." Loveland also was taken by Sally's tenderness with Tam's pets, Massie the cat and Annie the dog. "I would see this soft side of Sally with the animals. She was just gentle and sweet with Annie when she took her for a walk," she tells me.

And it could harden to stone if anything threatened the animals. Once, on an airplane stuck on a hot tarmac, Sally uncharacteristically used her famous name to get results. With Maggie and Gypsy, their two bichon frises, confined to the hold, she approached a crew member and got the dogs out of the belly of the plane and into the first class cabin with her. Sometime later, Gypsy, at seventeen, was so weakened by cancer and chemo, she could barely walk. Sally would put Gypsy in the passenger seat of her black Porsche Boxster, drive to the nearby soccer field, and set her softly into the grass for fresh air and a feeble attempt at exercise. One day, Tam went along. "And this young guy came over to Sally and said, 'I hope when I get old that somebody takes as good care of me as you're taking care of that little dog!'"

Remembering the scene, Tam tells me, "That's why I actually think she would have been a wonderful parent. She had that gentle, soft, caring side of her." Tam says she loves children herself, and earlier in her life foresaw having her own, "when I felt like I had my act together and could be a really good parent." She also remembers talking to Sally about it, "and I told her she'd be a remarkable parent. And she said she just really didn't think she wanted kids. She was just dead certain about it, the way she could be about some things. Zero interest." The subject went away.

Sally and Tam traveled—to Santa Fe and Taos, where they developed an appreciation for Native American artwork; to Hawaii, where they hiked Diamondhead and where each had her first massage and spa experience; and to Australia for twelve days, where Sally delivered a series of talks. It was, Tam says, "the longest vacation we ever took together."

They also worked through each other's family issues, with Tam pushing against Sally's natural reticence to express her emotions. She helped Sally think through ways to get Joyce, her mom, through some health problems. Sally helped Tam figure out how to help get her mom, Judy, resettled in a supportive community when Judy retired. When Tam was afraid to go on an interview for a PhD program in biology at the University of California, Riverside, near where she grew up, Sally packed up the dog, got on the plane and accompanied her to the university. Years later, that's where Tam would earn her doctorate in school psychology. "Sally helped me get over some of the hard memories of when I was a kid," Tam says. "She helped me blossom into who I really was. Sally liked to fix things, make them better."

Sometimes, though, Tam found that frustrating. Because "on an emotional level, sometimes there isn't a fix, and what you have to do is just talk about things and get to the depth of things. Sally and I were able to talk about everything, but it doesn't mean I always got the answers," she adds with a laugh. "She did open up more and more over the years, and I think I helped Sally at least reach into her emotional side. But a conversation about how Sally felt about something or someone lasted about five minutes while I could have discussed it for much, much longer."

They were two independent women with a shared life in a shared home, where they had separate phone lines, separate bank accounts. And for a long time, separate careers. When Tam started as a professor at San Diego State—doing research and writing while training school psychologists—Sally was evolving her own teaching style, motivated by the same perfectionism for her classrooms that had driven her to success at NASA. And the same challenge. Before her flight on STS-7 she'd said, "There are a few people waiting to see how I do. There are people within NASA who need convincing . . . [It's important that] I don't do anything dumb." That's exactly what she found when she first got to UCSD in 1989.

PROFESSOR

Inevitably, there were skeptics. "She came as a full professor in the physics department, but she didn't look and smell to many people like a full professor," explains Richard Somerville, a climatologist whose office was directly above Sally's CalSpace digs at the Scripps Institution of Oceanography in La Jolla. "She hadn't published a large number of research papers, and not everyone was enthusiastic. Some people felt that she'd been hired as a celebrity and imposed on us. So she arrived under a bit of a cloud."

A very famous cloud. That fall, Billy Joel released "We Didn't Start the Fire," ticking off the names of fifty-six historic figures or moments over the past forty years. "Sally Ride" came between "*Wheel of Fortune*" and "heavy metal suicide." As the song shot to the top of *Billboard*'s Hot 100, Sally heard it on the car radio. So did Billie Jean King, who would turn up the volume to catch Sally's name every time it played.

At UCSD, about one hundred requests poured in each week: "Could Sally autograph my child's report?" "Could my child interview her for a report?" "Could she send a photo?" Sally stopped answering her listed phone and got back to work.

She hunkered down, preparing for her classes by spending countless hours researching, writing, and even sketching the concepts she wanted to convey on pages of binders that filled several shelves. No detail was too tiny. For Plasma Physics, a rigorous, upper-level course, she made notes to herself about what to write on the front board and what to write on the side board. She flagged which theorems to spell out, which to circle, planning everything, never just winging it. And just like the examples that had so captivated her during Elizabeth Mommaerts's physiology class at Westlake, her analogies came from real life. A very exotic real life.

To explain the refraction of waves traveling through media of different densities, she used the space shuttle, showing how communicating with Earth meant using different wavelengths to travel through the ionosphere—which is, after all, plasma. Landing the shuttle gave her another easy-to-grasp explanation: as the orbiter reenters the atmosphere from the ionosphere and glides down to Earth, losing altitude, the air gets denser, so the shuttle goes slower. "The plasma changes, it puts drag on the shuttle, and that's how the shuttle lands," explains Karen Flammer, her colleague in the physics department and close friend, who would fill in when Sally had to miss class. "The shuttle doesn't need to put on the brakes, it's just natural plasma physics! It's an example that all students can not only grasp, but would be excited enough to remember and to understand the physical concepts." Flammer says it was a very unusual approach. "When I took the course as an undergraduate, the professor wrote the final equation on the board and never took the time to explain it. Sally really tried to simplify it, step by step."

She illustrated her lectures with graphs, tables, charts and pictures, some of which she drew by hand on transparencies for projection. "Sally liked to model science," Flammer tells me. "She just became this Excel freak, got really excited when she tried to graph something." Her creativity was especially evident in a course she conceived for first year physics majors called Exploring the Solar System (Physics 163). To compare the environment on Earth to that on planets at different distances from the Sun, she invented an astronaut visiting San Diego and an astronaut visiting Mars. And she described the kind of space suit an astronaut would need to visit both locations, which explains how the temperature and atmosphere are different. "Who else would think of that, wearing an astronaut suit?" Flammer asks.

Sally's examples spanned the solar system. She asked her students to compute the trajectory for a spacecraft mission to Venus, to consider why there might be no ozone layer on Mars, and to estimate the kinetic energy an asteroid of a certain size, speed and density would have when it crashes into Earth. Sometimes she brought the examples closer to home. "It was not just learning how to solve an equation about why a raindrop is in a spherical shape, the physics of it," recalls Lauren Martin, who taught science for ten years after taking one of Sally's classes in 1991. "It was more, when the raindrop falls, how are you going to know where it's going to pool, and where it's going to puddle? Now this you can apply it in your real life, almost the engineering of it. Because the way I'd always experienced physics majors, they think it is the be-all and end-all of the world—everything stems from physics. And that's true. But if you don't understand how it fits into the real world, you don't understand it or see it that way. And she brought it to life and made it applicable."

Sally's teaching skill was evident to her sister years earlier. "When she came back from Swarthmore and was living at home for a while, I was struggling with Algebra 3 or whatever it was," Bear says. "And I didn't get it. And she just sat down and taught it to me patiently, and with kindness, and I thought, whoa! She was a fabulous teacher."

That was also the opinion of most of her UCSD students, who gave Sally nearly perfect grades in the uncensored listings by CAPE (Course and Professional Evaluations), the student-run organization that collects feedback on the faculty. Although a small number found her "presentations listless" in Electricity and Magnetism, she clearly had learned something from her Stanford Professor Schwartz, with quizzes that "taxed them severely." Mostly, her courses, in the Zagat-like CAPE syntax, were "enthralling," "top-notch," offering a "unique perspective," and Professor Ride "charmed students" with "mesmerizing lectures" and "lucid explanations" of "stimulating material." One class was "tremendously engaging" with midterms that were "a breeze." Sally, wrote a student exuberantly, "undressed extraterrestrial physics until it stood there buck naked for everyone to comprehend." That, like most of her raves, was for Physics 6 (Physics of Space Science and Exploration, or Physics for Non-Physics Majors) which Sally called "Physics for Poets," a nickname she lifted from the Stanford catalogue. Even I might have understood the concepts with exam questions like this:

Design a scale model of the solar system. Let UCSD's Main Library [a decidedly angular structure] represent the Sun (assume that the library is a sphere(!), 50 meters in diameter). Now, to create the "solar system": (1) pick objects of roughly the right size (compared to the library) to represent the planets, then (2) put your "planets" the proper distance away from the "sun."

What objects would you choose for the planets, and roughly where (in terms of reasonably familiar locations like WLH [Warren Lecture Hall], downtown San Diego, etc.) would you put them?

"She could articulate and explain things in laymen's terms that just made sense," says Joanna Rice, a public relations executive who says her work with health care products has been informed by the science she learned from Sally in one of the big lecture halls back in 1993. "It was almost a logic class. And she made it clear that no question is a stupid question. She wouldn't roll her eyes and look at you and say, 'What part of this aren't you getting?' "

There were, she says, things you couldn't get away with. "If someone came in late, she'd give them this cold look, and she'd stop and wait for them to get situated. And she'd be looking at them the whole time, like, 'Why are you late to my class?' And then she'd say, 'Okay, are you ready?' And you couldn't b.s. her about not getting your assignments in. She wasn't cool about that. But she was cool about, 'I can teach you physics.' "

Mike Baine was so inspired by Sally as an undergraduate, he changed his major from electrical engineering to physics. "This," he explains, joking, "is part of what her students later referred to as the Sally Ride Distortion Field. She would be able to instill a level of confidence in her students to do things that they would not attempt on their own." Sally, he says, "made it look so easy. She empowered a level of responsibility within her students that was well outside the norm. It was successful because there was no way that we were going to disappoint her. And when we did figure things out that she was particularly proud of, you could really hear it in her voice. You could hear the pride and the ownership, that what we produced did work." Baine says her enthusiasm "was contagious. It was hard to leave a meeting with her without feeling wide-eyed optimism for the future."

Baine's comments were repeated to me over and over by Sally's students and friends alike: they didn't want to disappoint her, to let her down, to land beneath her own high bar. And it wasn't just science.

Sally became Baine's doctoral advisor (one of only a handful of grad students she took on), spending hours in her sparely furnished physics office on the top floor of Mayer Hall going through draft after draft of his thesis. She was as tough on his grammar as his physics, wielding a red marker like a surgeon. "She really cared about all aspects of her students' work," Baine says. "And took the time to make sure that we were producing the best work that we could. And that it should meet a basic standard before we submitted it to the world." In other words, that it should meet the expectations she set for herself.

Once again, Sally was exactly where she belonged. Or back where she belonged. Baine, who became a chief engineer at NASA, saw it firsthand. "She was a scientist first," he tells me. "A scientist who took a detour through space."

INSIDE THE BELTWAY

And a scientist who wanted to help.

Sally testified numerous times before congressional panels, with the aplomb first noticed by Brian Muirhead, who had accompanied her to Capitol Hill in 1987 when she briefed members on the upcoming Ride Report. "Here we are in a big congressional meeting room, with a small army of the press putting their giant lenses about four inches from her face," Muirhead recalls. "And she just didn't blink. I could see the astronaut in her." Muirhead also noticed that "she was probably very glad to be done with it!"

She was often invited to explain Mission to Planet Earth. Before one hearing with the Senate Committee on Commerce, Science and Transportation, its powerful chairman, Senator Ernest Hollings of South Carolina, announced that he wanted assurances it would provide more than just "a better weather report." After Sally's appearance, Hollings called the program "the most challenging and exciting concept that this committee has seen in quite some time."

Legislators on both sides of the aisle regularly contacted her for input into their pet bills. "Please call and let's get together next time you're in town," scrawled Senator Barbara Mikulski at the bottom of one official letter. "I need your help and advice." It was the influence Sally had hoped for. But if she enjoyed her role as a political advisor—and the occasional accompanying ego trip—she detested the bureaucracy. She saw it more as her civic responsibility—giving back to the government that had gotten her into space.

In 1992, when a presidential commission was convened to clarify the role of women in the nation's armed forces (women had served in some combat roles but without official sanction), Sally was also asked to testify. Although she could not be there in person, she sent a supportive statement that was read into the record by her friend and STS-7 crewmate, Rick Hauck, who was also testifying. Her experience in "the predominantly male Astronaut Corps," she wrote, having "twice been part of a close, primarily male team, confined in close quarters in a life-threatening situation," was relevant to the military situation. As was the camaraderie that the crew developed. "Space shuttle crews provide ample evidence that this camaraderie can be achieved and maintained as easily on mixed crews as on all-male crews . . . The fact that we were a mixed crew caused no problems and had no adverse effect on our routine or on our performance."

Her voice was the stamp of authority; her name, the magnet that could fill a meeting room. Or better. More than one political operative drooled at the prospect of the first American woman in space becoming a candidate for office. During the 1984 presidential primary, when a crush of candidates flooded the Democratic field (including astronaut-turned-senator John Glenn), a political cartoon considered the possibility. "And in the latest presidential straw poll," announces the TV anchorman in the caption, "Cranston, Hollings, Mondale, Hart, Glenn and Askew were stunned by Sally Ride who captured 89 percent of the vote." In 1992, when third-party presidential candidate Ross Perot was looking for a vice president, a bemused colleague left a phone message slip on Sally's desk telling her that a UPI reporter had called "re: rumor that Ross Perot has asked you to be his running mate!!(??)"

Don't, as they say, hold your breath. Sally had no interest in opening her life to public scrutiny or conforming to the ponderous ways of

Washington. What she did enjoy was using her analytical skills at very high levels, as with the Technology Assessment Advisory Council to the Office of Technology Assessment, on classified and less secret studies relating to national security. In October 1992, she joined a prominent group of scientists and engineers endorsing the Clinton-Gore presidential ticket. When the Democrats were elected, Sally led their science and technology transition team, which meant analyzing the status of the Federal Communications Commission, the National Institutes of Health, the National Science Foundation, the Office of Science and Technology Policy, the National Space Council (a modified version of the group LBJ had chaired thirty years earlier, when he alleged he was powerless to help put women in space) and NASA. It was an immense responsibility for a new administration, whose party had been out of power for a dozen years. What were the issues? Who were the key personnel? Sally, whose year at NASA Headquarters had left her unimpressed with the egocentric culture of the capital, was nonetheless excited about the challenge. From her office on Vermont Avenue, she issued a report dealing with everything from cultural diversity to the availability of travel vouchers, and recommended, among other things, a strong emphasis on education to prepare "the cadre of scientists and engineers needed for America's future."

Her December 1992 memo on NASA was more specific. The shuttle program had moved ahead since *Challenger*, with the successful return to space in September 1988 on *Discovery*. New astronauts had been named, including the first two female test pilots. And a new orbiter, *Endeavour*, had joined the fleet to replace the one that was lost. Still, Sally reported, NASA faced a number of urgent problems, from "confused" planning to "a shortage of women and minorities in its senior management positions" to money woes. President George H. W. Bush had announced the goal of sending humans to Mars, but Congress had provided no funding. Mission to Planet Earth required "rapid increases in budget." The entire space agency was underfunded and "in turmoil . . . The appointment of an Administrator is critical."

If you didn't know Sally, you'd have thought she was lobbying for the job. The word on the street was that she was practically sworn in. She was not. According to a member of the transition team who prefers to remain anonymous, both President-elect Clinton and Vice President-elect Gore telephoned her several times to request her to be the new NASA Administrator. Each time, she said no. Al Gore doesn't remember the specifics, but Alan Ladwig, Sally's executive assistant on the transition team, recalls a conversation with her one day: "What's the latest: are you going to be the administrator?"

"No, I turned it down."

"I thought that when the president asks, you can't turn down the job."

"Well, at seven-thirty this morning I turned down the job."

Richard Somerville, her colleague in La Jolla, found himself answering phone queries from the press when they couldn't find Sally, asking what her demands were. "And I said to her, 'What do I tell them?' And she said, 'I'm not interested in that position. There are no demands. No means no.' And I'd paraphrase that for the reporters."

With the rumors flying, Carolyn Huntoon once asked Sally what it would take to get her to accept the big job. "If they'd move it to California," she deadpanned.

"I remember thinking at the time, it was too bad," says the transition team member who told me about the offers, "because she's one of the toughest, most single-minded people." But she wasn't waffling, he says. "She never wanted to come into the system. Her service on the team was good citizenship that she donated."

"Sally was so committed to the public good that she never put herself ahead of the mission," says John Holdren, who served as a science advisor to the Clinton-Gore administration. "It was always about what she could do with her talents to make a better world. So we found ways to exploit her in a part-time capacity." She did agree to become one of eighteen members of the President's Council of Advisors on Science and Technology (PCAST), a group of private-sector individuals from business, education and research organizations. Over a period of five years, she flew to Washington every few months or so for presentations and studies of national issues, sometimes with the president or vice president at the table. Early on, with the fall of the USSR and worldwide concern over the safeguarding of nuclear weapons and fissile materials, and partly because of her experience with CISAC at Stanford, the president named Sally to a special PCAST panel chaired by Holdren to review the risk that such materials could be stolen from inadequately protected facilities in Russia and end up in the hands of rogue states or terrorists. The subject matter was critical for U.S. security, and Sally had the required clearances for the intelligence materials. The report that resulted was classified: only an overview was presented in open hearings to a Senate subcommittee, and one member of the full PCAST recalls having to get special clearance for a briefing in a White House basement room. The findings led President Clinton and Russian President Boris Yeltsin to agree on measures that sharply reduced the danger; in the words of one report, "to make the world a safer place."

EARTHKAM

There was another way to protect the planet.

What if kids could see Earth the way it looks from space? What if they could not only see Earth, but home in on it as if they were aliens exploring a new planet? And what if they could take pictures of Earth—close-ups of any spot on the globe—from their own desks, the way astronauts did while in orbit? Seeing the big picture was a first step to solving its problems.

"We came up with the idea of putting a camera onboard the space shuttle, aimed at Earth, that could be controlled by middle-school kids from their classrooms," Sally explained about the 1995 project. "It combined just the 'gee whiz' of the space program with the actual hands-on involvement for the kids." She described it as "giving kids a piece of the space program."

They called it KidSat, then EarthKAM (the precursor of Moon-KAM), for *K*nowledge *A*cquired by *M*iddle School Students. NASA spent close to $1 million per year to fly it on five shuttle missions, then moved it to the permanent platform of the new International Space Station, which started operations in 2000. It's Mission to Planet Earth, youth version. In class, students learn the orbital track of the Space Station and determine what regions or features they want to capture in the available path. Close-ups of the destruction wrought by hurricane Katrina? Evidence of melting glaciers? A bird's-eye view of their hometown? Then they find the proper longitude and latitude, calculate when the Station will be in range, and key in the coordinates on the Earth-KAM website, checking the weather to be sure no clouds will block the shot. At Mission Control in San Diego—a specially constructed chamber at the Science Engineering Research Facility (SERF), with three rows of consoles that Sally modeled after the real thing in Houston—the information is processed by UCSD students who get course credit and real-time experience dealing with NASA engineers. They process the requests and send them to the Johnson Space Center, where the officer at the Space Station EarthKAM desk relays them up to the Space Station, circling the planet some 250 miles high.

There, a dedicated high-resolution digital camera, facing out a window of super-optical quality glass, is connected to a laptop computer. When the commands reach the computer, the camera shutter is snapped. Then the recorded bits of data flow back down the chain so that finished images can be posted on the internet, ready for a serious Earth science report. It is efficient, it is cutting edge, and it is empowering children.

"You mean, the real shuttle? In space?" asks a fifth-grader about to try it for the first time.

"Any time a teacher can make something real for the kids, real and exciting," says Diane Bowen, who used the program in her Brunswick, Maine, classes, "then they say, 'Well, I can do this.' It's about giving them the experience." One of her students is now getting her master's in science education; another is a math teacher.

Karen Flammer, the UCSD space physicist who helped Sally develop the program and now runs it, says the college students were equally energized. "They developed all the code, did all the work, all the supervision. And I saw that it was a better experience for them than anything they've ever done in the classroom." Sally's presence, she says, made the difference. "I saw what she would elicit out of people. You get the sense of what she expected out of herself, and somehow it seeps out of her to everybody." Even to Flammer, a third-generation physicist. "I stopped doing my research and I just said, I want to do educational outreach for the rest of my life."

Sally saw it as the first step to fix the problems she had seen from the shuttle.

"The next generation, the kids in school today, know a lot about climate change," she said. "They're concerned about it, they're interested in it. They want information about it, and they see it as a challenge to them, to help develop those solutions, and help understand the science, develop the new technologies." The kids, she said, "are so committed to this that it's making science and engineering cool again."

Kids were moving further and further to the forefront of Sally's concern. She was a frequent visitor to Space Camp in Huntsville, Alabama, where the enrollment of girls shot up from 8 percent to 30 percent when her first flight was announced. One 1993 camper, Chelsea Clinton, the thirteen-year-old daughter of the U.S. president, was so "awestruck" by Sally's presence during her keynote address, she heard nothing she said, a valuable lesson to Clinton to rein in her enthusiasm until after the speech is over.

By then Sally had cofounded a series of summer workshops on climate change for graduate students and master teachers (that would reverberate back to the classroom) at Caltech, "to bring scientific understanding to a national conversation on climate change that was already spinning toward a political battle," according to planetary scientist and now JPL's (Jet Propulsion Laboratory) chief scientist Dan McCleese. "Her first flight in space changed her enormously," he tells me. "She had this strong desire to be more than a witness, wanting to contribute knowledge as well as perspective."

The irony is worth noting. Sally, who never wanted her own children, was making them the focus of the rest of her life. Was she remembering the happy, intellectually privileged times of her own childhood? Paying forward the treasure of her own success? Or simply caught up in the excitement of awakening young minds, and, professionally, planning for the future? Again, no explanation from Sally about her *feelings* towards her audience. But now, it was all for them. The royalties from her first children's book in 1987 (an impressive $12,400, that she was not permitted to keep as a NASA employee) had been donated to a charity, the Children's Defense Fund.

She would write the rest of her children's books with Tam—six lively scientific adventures about Earth and space: *Voyager* (1992), *Third Planet* (1994), *Mystery of Mars* (1999)—with an artist's conception of a female astronaut on the Martian surface; *Exploring Our Solar System* (2003); *Mission Planet Earth* and *Mission Save the Planet* (2009). The lightbulb that had gone off in their brains with the discovery of the Asimov book at Stanford grew into their own version of science for kids, a literary partnership to illuminate the field for youngsters. "Sally always said that she was the better editor, and I was the better writer," Tam says, describing their collaboration with matching laptops, stretched out on the living room carpet, surrounded by photographs and story boards and colored pens. "We would brainstorm an outline, then we would divvy up the essays to write." Sally did the physics and space science, Tam the biology and chemistry. Both worked on geology and Earth science. They would each write separately, then read their drafts aloud, a "fun and scary ritual over a cup of tea." During months of back-and-forth reading, writing and editing, they'd craft the whole book, choosing photographs and sketching out illustrations to educate young readers while grabbing their attention. The results are as informative as they are charming.

For *Voyager*, Tam came up with the idea of telling the story through the eyes of the two spindly spacecraft. For *Mission Planet Earth*, they explained the effect of water and carbon dioxide by having kids follow a single atom or molecule on its journey around the planet:

> Let's follow a carbon atom as it travels around the planet. We'll pick one that's part of a carbon dioxide molecule just entering the air—maybe exhaled by a sleeping dog. It would ride the winds for about ten years and travel around the world several times. During this time, it would make its tiny contribution to Earth's greenhouse effect. Then one spring day, it might float into a minuscule hole in a leaf hanging on a tree. It would be carried in a watery stream inside the leaf's veins into a green chloroplast—the part of a cell where photosynthesis takes place. Wham! The carbon dioxide molecule is attacked from all sides by other molecules. First, the oxygen atoms are stripped away from our carbon atom. Then, hydrogen, other carbon atoms, and new oxygen atoms are stuck on. Now our carbon atom is part of a sugar molecule inside the leaf.
>
> A hungry mouse might eat the leaf . . .
>
> —*Mission Planet Earth*

Sally's excitement about the books was evident in every signed copy. She sent me *The Third Planet: Exploring the Earth from Space*—an engaging and literate early look at Earth as a system—and playfully apologized for not including something close to my home where she'd visited: "Sorry, no pictures of Long Island . . ." She also tucked in a copy of the research paper she'd just coauthored, "Nonlinear Thomson Scattering of Intense Laser Pulses from Beams and Plasmas." Her note advised, "Read whichever you prefer!" My choice was apparently the same as that of the American Institute of Physics, which honored *Third Planet* with its prestigious Science Award in 1995.

THE SPEECH

Sally didn't need to do any more research papers. Her credentials as a professor were secure, and her passion for science education and its advocacy was becoming more than a sideline. All this as her voice was sought on an increasing variety of platforms. For big bucks.

UCSD's Richard Somerville teased Sally about her work outside the ivory tower. "I told her that playing around with NASA toys and Space Camp was not going to get her academic advancement. And she looked at me as if I were mentally handicapped and she said, 'Richard, if I need money, I give a talk!' She had figured out that she didn't have to conform to every academic norm, that her celebrity had insulated her against some of the pressures." And that being a famous astronaut did, indeed, have its benefits.

Over her lifetime, she would make hundreds, maybe thousands, of speeches, from Hartford, Connecticut, to Fullerton, California; for L'Oréal and Nestlé, Raytheon and Northrup Grumman, the Girl Scouts and *Glamour* magazine, ultimately earning up to $25,000 per lecture. Her talks would evolve as her career expanded, from her venture on the shuttle to the demands of equity for women; from the lessons of *Challenger* to corporate risk management; from the value of sports to the necessity of science education. But most still began or ended with the perennial crowd pleaser. "Not to worry," she emailed an upcoming host who was concerned that her speech might not touch on the obvious. "I ALWAYS show my slides and talk about space! We could use the title, 'Reach for the Stars,' which allows me to talk about . . . anything."

The slides were travel snaps from on high, her shuttle's eye view of planet Earth, a constant jaw-dropper for the audience and an endless source of ribbing between Sally and me. "Have you seen my slides?" she'd ask innocently, telling me about her latest conquest of a sold-out auditorium. Um, yes, Sally, more than a few times. The thing is, they never got old.

But for all her skill and experience, it never got easy, never became rote.

"I would see her nervous, and I would see her sweating it," says Karen Flammer. "And I would be on the plane flying back east, and I would see her going over her notes, putting her earbuds in, or her Bose earphones to tune everything out, and I would think to myself, 'Now, Sally, you've given that talk like fifty thousand times.' I think she took great pride in what she did and in doing it well. But no, I don't think it ever came easy."

Unlike so many of us who give speeches all the time, Sally did not have a template of her presentation sitting on her hard drive, ready to freshen up and print out for a new venue at a moment's notice. Instead, she handwrote her outline each time—often the evening before, beneath letterheads from the Waldorf-Astoria, the Arizona Biltmore, the Ritz-Carlton at Buckhead, or whatever she found on the hotel nightstand. She'd jot down bullet points of the trailblazing flight whose timeline was etched in her brain; she'd note the same reliable family anecdotes ("Dad didn't know what an astrophysicist did!" "Mom said one of us would get to heaven!"); and she'd painstakingly sculpt a set of data points to connect with whatever audience she was facing. Once on stage she was fine, safe with familiar words and thoughts, where no one could get to her. "Sally said the only time she felt like she was alone was when she was standing in front of a podium, about to give a speech," Susan Okie tells me. "Isn't that weird?" Yes. And to get to that refuge, before every performance, this innate introvert who had seen Earth from outer space—a planet holding seven billion humans—needed to steel herself, to quell her constant anxieties about appearing before a crowd of several thousand. Deep breath, relax the shoulders, calm the nerves.

"It took a lot out of her," Tam says. "I said, 'Why don't you stop doing this?' But she couldn't help her middle-class upbringing. She always thought the speeches would dry up." Of course, they never did.

Money had never been Sally's priority, which worked out well with her earliest years as a wage earner. As a graduate student with TA gigs, she was lucky to get peanut butter money; at NASA, her government salary topped out at $59,212. At UCSD, her twin appointments finally lifted her to the low six figures. With the books and the speeches and her election to a number of corporate boards, she was starting to see her income shoot up. "Now that I am out of the government, and becoming more of a capitalist . . ." she wrote to one of her editors, she was willing to consider more book signing appearances. And more outside ventures. Sally liked watching her bank account grow as she assembled the pieces of the big project in her mind. It was almost ready. Meanwhile, what else was out there?

SPACE.COM

It sounded like a great idea.

Lou Dobbs was on the phone telling Sally about his new start-up, Space.com, a website to aggregate news and background about space and science; one that would bring outer space to cyberspace. "I was enthralled by the possibilities," she told a reporter at the time. "This is a great opportunity. I've enjoyed communicating to the public, and the internet is the medium of the next millennium."

Sally did her homework, calling me and others in the media for information on Dobbs, who had just left CNN and was tapping into deep pockets in the financial community. And although, as she told me, she got less than rave reviews about her potential new boss as an office mate, she was impressed with his contacts and vision. And she signed on as president of the new venture. It was September 1999, and anything online had a golden aura. "Never underestimate the value of stock options," she said, only half-joking, to writer Andy Chaikin, as they shared a limo to the airport after work one day.

"It was the dot-com era," explains Alan Ladwig, who set up a Space .com office in Washington. "Lou raised all this money, had a genuine interest in space. It was exciting to be part of that, part of the ground floor." That was figurative. The new start-up occupied fancy offices on the thirty-fifth floor of a building at Times Square—with, according to one employee, a great view of the ball dropping on New Year's Eve.

Sally's job, he said, was "to be the name, to legitimize Lou Dobbs's plans."

Which were?

"That would be the problem," Ladwig goes on. "He wanted to be all things in the space media content. And that ended up to be the hard thing to figure out. What was that? And how to make money out of it? He never quite figured it out."

Dobbs, who did not respond to numerous requests to be interviewed for this book, was described by a number of Space.com employees as a smart risk-taker and a demanding boss who could also terrify employees in what several called "a toxic environment." Figuratively and literally. With antismoking laws firmly in place, Dobbs regularly lit up in his own office, according to eyewitnesses. And what some call his verbally abusive manner—especially insulting and humiliating to women, they say—sent more than one to the ladies' room in tears.

Never Sally, although she did wind up putting out some of the stress fires.

"She was the voice of reason, and she really took good care of us," says Emily Sachar, Space.com's editor-in-chief, who found Sally "extraordinarily present, in the weeds with us. She was not a figurehead president, she was very much there." One of her first innovations was an adjunct education website called SpaceKids. Another was to ban the use of the word *manned* from the domain.

Mitchell Cannold, the company's chief operating officer, says, "Lou may not have realized that he was getting more than Sally Ride the astronaut. She was central to building the strategic partnerships"—with NASA or the aerospace industry—"and understood how to make it a teaching tool for a younger audience."

Sally relished her new position and for most of 1999–2000, threw herself into the work, commuting several days a week from Atlanta (she'd taken a leave from UCSD), where Tam was doing research and teaching graduate students. Early on, my apartment in New York was her hotel, and I saw the first inklings of corporate longings in my friend. She told me about the site's "pages" and "unique visitors" and prospects for future growth, at a time when such concepts about the internet were just entering the language. She was also refining her management style, with healthy doses of both encouragement and humor. When journalist Todd Halvorson was hired to open the Space.com bureau at Cape Canaveral, he hung a sign on the new office—a construction trailer in the Kennedy Space Center Press Site parking lot—reading "Sally K. Ride Executive Office Building." Sally sent him an autographed picture reading, "Get back to work!"

So what went wrong? It may have been Sally's disillusionment with the way the business was being run. Or her inability to get certain initiatives going. Or, according to one colleague, because "she found herself doing too much damage control, so it wasn't as much fun as she thought she needed it to be."

Or maybe it was the day she held a meeting in her glassed-in office. Dobbs was there, along with some other executives, as well as Karen Flammer, Sally's friend and UCSD colleague, whom she'd hired as a consultant to validate the science articles posted on the site. Flammer doesn't recall the topic that day but says Sally was frustrated with Dobbs, with the organization, with how things were done, even before the meeting began. Her jaws were tight, her teeth clenched. "And you could just tell. But she didn't say anything." Flammer also knew Sally as a levelheaded listener who never interrupted while someone else spoke. That day, it was different.

"They're talking," she says, "and it's going back and forth, and all of a sudden, Sally picks up her notebook and slams it down and shouts, 'Everybody, right now, get out of my office!' "

It was, Flammer says, very dramatic. And very loud. She had never seen Sally get angry before. She had never heard Sally raise her voice. No one had. The room cleared. "And I sat there and said, in a very small voice, 'Do you mean me too?' " Sally said no, that Flammer should stay. But she never said another word about the flare-up. Never discussed it. "She just needed time to cool off," Flammer tells me. "That is the only time in seventeen years I ever saw her like that."

Sally's flare-up was more than rare. She had been icy to her friend Susan Okie when Okie's journalistic responsibilities had, Sally thought, compromised their friendship; she had occasionally frozen out other friends or colleagues for a variety of reasons; she would, from time to time, clam up with her closest friends. But a full blown rant, even a brief one, was unknown. Much later, when reminded about it by Flammer, Sally would acknowledge that it happened. But she never explained why.

Not too long after the incident, in July 2000, Sally resigned from Space.com. It was widely viewed as a loss to the company, which, several days later, was restructured. Some 20 percent of the staff was laid off. The venture, in the words of one employee, "was extravagantly funded but intrinsically flawed." Dobbs went back on television.

Sally went back to Atlanta, and soon after, she and Tam moved permanently back to La Jolla. There would be no stock options, no fortune. But she still had her speeches and her teaching job and her boards. She also, she thought, had a better idea for a business.

10

SALLY RIDE SCIENCE

JANUARY 2001–MARCH 2011

Sally Ride Science Festival, Atlanta, 2002.

Her hair fell into a short, sleek pageboy now, and her suit was a smart tweed, more corporate than astronaut. So when Sally Ride checked into a hotel one evening, the clerk didn't recognize her. When he saw how she'd signed the register, he looked up, astonished, and asked, "What's it like to have the same name as a famous person?"

CEO

Sally had refused countless opportunities to link the fame of her name to a commercial product. Not just the biographies and the movies-of-the-week, but the posters and the authorized tee-shirts. There were no Sally Ride dolls, no candy bars. She wasn't a purist—she had endorsed a study skills game and made all those speeches—but her instinct was always to decline. On her way to turning fifty, Sally found a way to make her celebrity meaningful.

"Sally called me late one night," says Karen Flammer, "and she said to me, 'Karen, I want to start a company, are you in?' And before I said, 'What are we going to do?' I said, 'Of course I'm in.'"

So were Terry McEntee, Sally's longtime executive assistant; Alann Lopes, a computer programmer, and Tam. Sally and Tam had been discussing the idea for some time, how to turn their passion for connecting girls with science, into a business.

This is what Sally had been building up to. Being first was fine, but she didn't want be the only one. She wanted to awaken young female minds to the wonder of science that had captivated her; she wanted to inspire and insure the next generation of America's mathematicians and engineers and physicists and astronauts. She wanted to teach them, as she'd been taught, that if you're a girl, you can do anything. She wanted them to see, as she had, beyond the stereotypes. And she wanted to make it a business, a business that would make money, because that would attract the talent to make it work.

The plan was ambitious: provide science events, programs and products "to support and sustain," as the mission statement reads, "girls' natural interests in science and technology, and to catalyze a change in cultural perceptions of girls and women in these endeavors." Writer K. C. Cole gave Sally credit for "making sure that girls get to share in the adventure that is science."

The company, incorporated in 2001, was called Sally Ride Science (SRS), but it was briefly known as Imaginary Lines, for the invented lattice of longitude and latitude that gives the globe its parameters. Imaginary Lines also suggests the illusory barriers between the genders that divide society, and between the nations of the world. Sally, like all astronauts, knew that looking down on Earth from space, there are no borders separating countries or anything else.

She also understood the dire warning from a bipartisan commission, that a "steady decline in science achievement" had engulfed the US in a "rising tide of mediocrity," making us "A Nation at Risk." A later panel would find that the erosion of America's technical and scientific strength threatened our economic and strategic security. The science-first urgency of the post-Sputnik years—the impetus that Sally always credited for her own smooth passage through physics to NASA—had evaporated over half a century. By the end of the decade, with four out of five jobs about to require science and math skills just to get living wages, she said, Americans were not prepared.

Sally liked to point out that all the hydrogen in our water, like all the helium in our balloons, and everywhere else, has been here since the Big Bang, dust from exploding stars, ready to combine into more complicated elements that make our lives possible. Similarly, her concept for science education, if not its form, had percolated for decades. The girl who loved the balance of math and the clarity of physics, the young woman who skyrocketed to the stars and to stardom on the power of a fine education and a social movement, would, as an adult, apply the same logic, along with the same encouragement and opportunity, to the next generation. "Maybe I had just lived long enough," she said. "I thought that this was something that was really worth using my name and using the visibility that I could bring to it. It felt worthwhile."

As the only founder with business experience (after her year at Space.com), Sally became CEO and went in search of initial funding. Asking for money required a new set of skills, and she overcame her anxiety with the expediency of a flight engineer. She tapped into her Rolodex for advice from high-powered friends, created a list of potential investors, then contacted them. If someone turned her down, she moved on to the next. At first, according to former Harvard Business School professor Myra Hart, who informally advised Sally when she drafted her business plan, "It wasn't about the money, but the money was important in order to deliver the mission."

Sally's pitch would anchor the company's *raison d'être* for the next decade plus. It was a simple equation that persists: While the numbers have increased, women are still underrepresented in many scientific fields—notably engineering, mathematics and computer sciences, and physical and Earth sciences—a lopsided gender ratio that increases from graduate school to the workplace. And it isn't for lack of early interest. Little boys and little girls love science and math equally. But girls drift away in droves during the middle school years—grades five through eight—when the cultural taboos and gender assumptions kick in.

"A girl who says she wants to be a rocket scientist might get a different reaction from her friends and her teacher than a boy who says he wants to be a rocket scientist," Sally pointed out, perhaps remembering her high school friend's mom who scoffed when Sally said she wanted to be an astrophysicist. "It might not be cool for a girl to be the best one in the math class." Was she thinking about the teacher who made her cry by saying scientists weren't creative?

"When you turn on the TV," Sally said, "any engineers you see are apt to be male, not female. When you open the newspaper, you read about male engineers, not female engineers. As a result, twelve-year-old girls don't really think of those areas as possible careers." She nailed it with a simple illustration. Ask a kid to draw a scientist, she said, "she's likely to draw a geeky guy with a pocket protector. That's just not an image an eleven-year-old girl aspires to."

The buzz term is STEM education—science, technology, engineering, mathematics—an awkward acronym that has crept from the garden to the classroom. Sally, whose years with NASA made her sensitive to arcane allusions, generally avoided it when addressing nontechnical audiences. She had a better way to put it.

"We need to make science cool."

• ◆ •

The timing was tricky. The nation was focused on terrorism, not technology, after the attacks on September 11, 2001. Sally had spent that long day at the house she and Tam owned in Atlanta, watching the horrid news on television and checking in with her own sources in Washington. She was one of the first people I called from our ABC News studios in New York, and long before we knew the details of United Airlines flight 93—the one that crashed into the field in Pennsylvania—she had imagined the scenario. "That's the story I want to know," she told me. "What went on with those passengers?"

A few weeks later, she tried to calculate the fallout for her own project. In her SRS notebook she jotted down, "effect of terrorism: investors? Sponsors? Publicity?"

Not everyone signed on. "[A] lot of people," Sally recalled some years later, "said, 'This is not a business. There aren't any girls interested in math and science . . . There aren't very many women in engineering, so there can't be many girls who are interested in math.' " Sally answered with facts, citing the 1972 legislation barring sex discrimination in education, including athletics, that did not exist until she was halfway through Stanford. "Before Title IX, you could have concluded that girls didn't want to be doctors, that girls didn't want to be lawyers, that they didn't like to play sports. And you would have been just reflecting the expectation of the time. What was different about me was, I didn't run into that one person, that counselor or teacher or parent, who said, you should be doing something different, this is not for you."

And if she did run into that person—like the professor at Stanford who had never seen "a girl physics major"—she simply ignored him and moved on.

Sally's reputation for integrity, and the clarity of her goal, got SRS off the ground quickly. "At that time it was not clear what type of business it would become, but I so believed in its purpose and in Sally that it did not matter," says Silicon Valley businesswoman Judith Estrin, one of the angel investors. "I was struck by how open and authentic she was, and

I invested because I believed in the cause. There was a thoughtfulness about how the company was trying to shift the culture, to shift awareness." Board member Jane Swift, the former lieutenant governor and briefly acting governor of Massachusetts, calls it "double bottom line investing: funds invested for a return and also to do good."

MAKING SCIENCE FUN

And to have a good time. Sally's exuberance over her flight on STS-7— "the most fun I'll ever have in my life"—was not just back-to-Earth hyperbole. In 1970, before she abandoned her tennis dreams, she took a break from a tournament to visit the Seattle Science Center, where she was dazzled by, among other things, the math exhibit in which kids learned about numbers and shapes by using brainteasers that were solved by putting pegs into holes. On stationery with a Snoopy cartoon that read, "Dogs accept people for what they are," she wrote to her boyfriend, John Tompkins, that the museum "introduced advanced subjects in a very understandable way (even for me!) [with] . . . incredible displays, demonstrations . . . of the 'Random Walk' theory, perspective, cycloids: soap bubbles . . . orbits." She was especially thrilled by a section with gyroscopes and optical illusions entitled " 'science can be fun,' which did a pretty good job of amazing me."

Three decades later, that same spirit infused the Sally Ride Science Club, the website she and her partners created where girls could learn and play. Next came Sally Ride Science Festivals—one-day events on college campuses where youngsters could listen to a speech by a scientist or astronaut, participate in science workshops and enjoy a high-tech street fair to launch marshmallow rockets, construct toothbrush robots, play science bingo, learn about the DNA of strawberries, hear the heartbeat of a golden retriever and choose among environments from the tundra to the jungle to "Design Your Own Alien." Or just get their faces painted and eat space ice cream.

The first festival was at the University of San Diego in October 2001. A year later, at the one cosponsored by the Massachusetts Institute of Technology (MIT) in Cambridge, Massachusetts, kids also learned why the blood vessels of giraffes might provide valuable lessons for future astronauts. That's part of the talk I gave when Sally persuaded me to share my own little scientific expertise with an audience of eight hundred enthralled youngsters. It was one of her smaller crowds. From California to Maryland, Texas to Kansas City, each Sally Ride Science Festival attracted up to fourteen hundred preteens and their parents, with a cadre of aerospace engineers, advanced mathematicians, other female astronauts and whoever was needed to help steer them into everything from analyzing meteorites to finding a cure for cancer. Sally's sister, Bear, joined the team, along with Terry McEntee, to organize and run them for more than a decade. Role models were everywhere; inner-city kids met their first scientists; private school girls wired their first circuit boards.

Boys were invited, too—no discrimination in Sally's world. "And the boys would talk about how interesting it was to be in this room full of girls," says Maria Zuber. "So we'd say, 'Hey, now you know how girls feel!' "

Zuber was also at the Sally Ride Science Festival in Cambridge, her home turf as professor of geophysics—now vice president for research—at MIT. "You could tell when you walked around and watched the kids at these events that she had really found a formula that worked. Being a scientist or engineer is very mysterious to a lot of kids. Girls tend to be social and like to work in groups, but they have a picture of someone in a white jacket locked up in a lab who never sees the light of day or speaks to other people. So a lot of what I'd do is talk about how wonderful it is to work in teams. And I'd wear khakis and a blouse, or blue jeans. We wanted kids to see scientists as regular people. And one student said, 'If I become a scientist when I grow up, do I get to wear blue jeans to work?' "

Sally, whose wardrobe would grow to include the occasional thousand-dollar St. John's jacket with open-toed little heels (showing red-polished nails), often donned her blue flight suit for the kids, the one with the NASA patches promising adventures you could only dream of. After describing her flights, and showing home movies or slides, she answered the kids' questions, speaking to them as if they were grown-ups without equivocating: "Is there life in space?" (No, not so far.) "Where do rockets go when they burn out?" (Into the ocean.) "How did you shower?" (With a water gun.) "How gross was the food?" (Not. We had peanut butter.) "Do you have any pets?" (Yes.) And always, the one about the bathroom. Sometimes she told them what happened when she spilled a bottle of water in space. "The water would come oozing out, and just sit there in the middle of the room. The good news is, if you spill something, it doesn't fall to the ground. But the bad news is, you have to chase it around the room." Then, with long lines of youngsters and their parents waiting, she patiently autographed their books and programs, with the signature she had streamlined so many years earlier.

"Girls can do science," said one California girl, wearing a necklace made of electronic components that glowed like a star. "It's not only for boys."

"If she can do it, so can I," said another.

A fifth-grader moving up the queue for Sally's autograph was asked if she'd rather be a famous, gorgeous rock star or an astronaut. After a long pause she said, "An astronaut. It would be cool to see something no one else has."

To these kids, Sally was the rock star.

Mike Coats, Sally's TFNG classmate and veteran of four spaceflights who became director of the Johnson Space Center, saw her clout with thousands of youngsters, including his own daughter. "You can't grasp the effect when a woman stands up in a flight suit at the head of a class," he tells me. "The kids are just mesmerized. How important that is for young girls to see a woman in a position of authority in their business!"

HEADWINDS

Sally's feminism, which had forever expanded the definition of NASA's manned spaceflight program, formed the critical core of everything she undertook. Girls needed examples like her and her science peers early in their lives, she believed, to combat what she called "a built-in headwind that women face."

There was the woman she met who "was the best biology student in high school and had the highest exam scores. At the end of the semester, a teacher told her: 'I'm sorry, but I'm going to have to give the award in biology to a boy, because it's more important to him.' "

And the mom who told Sally proudly that her mathematician daughter had just won the state math competition, but then added, "And I don't know where she gets it! I was never any good at math, and I don't know any women who are!" Sally pointed out the subtle dissuasion. "This mother didn't realize that the message that she was *completely* unconsciously sending her daughter was, 'You're not normal. You're not like every woman I know.' And what's the most important thing when you're twelve? It's to be normal." As a result, that little girl might "start internalizing these messages and think, well, she's also good in French literature, and maybe that is something that maybe her mother thinks is more normal for a girl, or a woman to study."

No wonder, she said, little girls and grown-up women had such low expectations for themselves: "You see high school boys get C's in math and say, 'I'm going to be an engineer.' And high school girls who get A's in math and say, 'I'm not good enough.' " It was a disconnect Sally would try to repair all of her working life, often giving women that extra push when they didn't recognize it themselves.

She took every loss personally.

"One time we were sitting outside and she said, 'A lot of people just don't understand how the whole structure has been so unfair for women,' " recalls Shirley Malcom, who runs Education and Human Resources at the American Association for the Advancement of Science (AAAS). "And she talked about the fact that she was a world-class tennis player and went to Stanford, and the guys could get a scholarship, but the women were not offered scholarships for sports. And you don't realize that not only does that send a signal about your relative importance, but it has monetary and financial consequence."

As the director of CalSpace for seven years, Sally had sponsored the work of female scientists and tried to get one woman promoted from assistant to full researcher long before the woman herself had asked. "I wasn't thinking I deserved advanced promotion," says Lucy McFadden, who wound up with a career at NASA's Goddard Space Flight Center. "And in my position now I fully believe that most talented scientists, and women especially, need continued cultivation."

In 1995, Sally had headed up a short-lived Girls & Women in Science initiative at UCSD, with a small conference funded by philanthropist Frances Lear to explore the status of female scientists and learn why young girls disengaged from the field. Lear also offered Sally a $30 million grant for a center focusing on women and science. Sally turned it down, and later told Tam, "Darn, I should have taken the thirty million."

In 2005, Sally was asked to comment when Harvard president Larry Summers, in a speech, questioned whether the lack of women in science was due to "issues of intrinsic aptitude." The implication, echoing Sigmund Freud's tiresome, "Anatomy is destiny" and widely viewed as sexist, detonated a national debate. Sally, in an interview with *USA Today*, turned metaphorical. "Suppose you came across a woman lying on the street with an elephant sitting on her chest," she said. "You notice she is short of breath. Shortness of breath can be a symptom of heart problems. In her case, the much more likely cause is the elephant on her chest. For a long time, society put obstacles in the way of women who wanted to enter the sciences. That is the elephant."

When I spoke to her later that week, she was less creative but equally exasperated: "What," she said shaking her head, "was he thinking?"

Later that year, Sally's commitment to women's rights was recognized by the megaprofessional services firm Deloitte, who hired her to chair its pioneering Women's Initiative, an external advisory board to support and promote its female employees. She set the tone early at a meeting with Deloitte CEO Jim Quigley. He spoke with passion about the company's desire for gender balance, and the goal to increase the number of female partners, principals and directors to 35 percent.

"Jim," Sally asked across the table, "what's the ratio of the people you're recruiting?"

"Well, of course it's fifty percent," he answered.

"Why isn't your goal for partners, principals and directors fifty percent?"

Quigley got the message. "And she holds my feet to the fire, and I respect and appreciate that very much," he said, smiling.

Over a period of seven years, at a series of meetings with Deloitte employees and with the council (where she sat in the middle, not at the head, of the conference table), Sally drilled down through Deloitte's employment data and examined patterns of advancement to help expand women's opportunities. What everyone who worked with her mentioned over and over was Sally's style—quiet but commanding, more suggestive than demanding, collegial rather than controlling. Nobody—here it comes again—wanted to disappoint her. Shelly Lazarus, head of Ogilvy & Mather, the advertising and marketing agency, sat on the Deloitte board for five years with its first chair, former Republican representative and Secretary of Labor, Lynn Martin. "Lynn would cajole, harass, insist, just drive people to do what she wanted them to do," she says. "Sally patiently and calmly got people to the same place, more by her sense of principle. When Sally said, 'This is what we have to accomplish,' you couldn't look away."

Martin said having different personalities was important, because you never want to have two leaders the same. "I'm from Chicago. I believe you do kick a person when they're down!" she tells me, laughing. "But Sally knew how to ask the right questions—not like a congressional 'I'm gonna get you.' More like, 'Hey, wait a minute, how does this work over seven years?' She knew how to make sure the question wasn't loaded to get someone, but was loaded to get a response. She understood the corporate mind-set."

Just as she did at her own company.

THE COMPANY

Sally had become commander of her own Earthbound spacecraft. Management was a constantly developing skill, further expanding what she'd learned from her shuttle commander, Bob Crippen, and practiced only briefly at NASA Headquarters and at Space.com. She was a quick study and had Crip's ability to do everything. Eager to get started— but economically—she emailed Terry McEntee to find "the cheapest/ easiest (i.e., doesn't take much of our time) ways to get things like business cards, furniture, quotes for services, etc." She met with potential funders, attended conferences of math and science teachers, assimilated the vernacular of education—procurement dates for products, state by state, grade by grade—and could turn on a dime. When an opportunity arose for a deal with McGraw-Hill, a major player, in New York, she flew in with a team that made a detailed pitch. Lawyers were standing by to write the contracts.

She practiced everything with her colleagues, treated every conference like a first-time encounter. The meetings with her shareholders made her particularly anxious. She would rehearse with her cofounders and board members, reviewing their—and her own—remarks during repeated dry runs.

Sally Ride Science, built on the sponsorship model, got more investors and more corporate sponsors. Under Tam's supervision (she had retired from San Diego State University to work fulltime at SRS, where she would become its chief operating officer), they developed *Cool Careers in Science*, a series of books on everything from microbiology to veterinary medicine, geology to engineering, green chemistry to Earth science. Each of the dozen books features kid-friendly profiles of scientists made human, with dogs and cats and hobbies like skiing. Most of the scientists are women. "We're putting a female face on every one of these careers," Sally said. Another set of books breathes life into the physical, earth and life sciences. The library is more than eighty-strong.

And because national studies also revealed that most science teachers in kindergarten through eighth grade had little or no formal science schooling, they set up a series of weeklong summer teacher training academies to infuse selected educators with the strategies and enthusiasm to train others back home, who would then teach kids. In one activity, educators were given a box with the top glued shut and asked to figure out what was inside. They could shake it, slide it, gauge the weight and the shape—any kind of scientific method. But they were never told the answer. The point: to arouse their curiosity as a way of stimulating them to arouse their kids' curiosity in science class. Science as fun, science as logic, from the top down.

Sally convinced ExxonMobil to fund each Sally Ride Science Academy for $1 million a year, which Ken Cohen, ExxonMobil's vice president of public and government affairs, described as his own company's self-interest. "I asked to meet with her in connection with the work we were doing in STEM," he says. "We wanted to start having an impact with young women and girls in that field. We employ scientists and engineers and we want a diverse group of people, we wanted to encourage more young girls and women to go into that field," he tells me. "It's important for the country. And as you know, it's an area where Sally was a rarity. She was very clear what she wanted to accomplish in putting these academies together. And she truly had a passion to see other youngsters follow her path. She tried to understand what our goals were and we tried to understand hers—trying to find the sweet spot between what we both were trying to accomplish. It was easy to partner with Sally."

Not so easy, perhaps, for an environmentally proactive company like Sally Ride Science, run by folks who wanted to save our "fragile planet," to link up with an oil behemoth. Tam calls it "one of those compromises you do in business. But these people really care about STEM education, and they put their money behind this." Sally usually acknowledged the unlikely alliance during her keynote address at the Academies. She would make a wry comment about "oil spills" or "oily money," with a grin and a glance towards the ExxonMobil rep in the room. And then, just as she'd always done, she'd move on.

Sally also got Hasbro, the toy company, to sponsor an annual toy design competition, called TOYchallenge, involving several thousand kids from around the country, a playful way to teach the engineering process. A documentary by filmmaker Dori Berinstein, *Some Assembly Required*, captures the excitement in 2006 as teams of middle schoolers brainstorm and then build their entries: a punching bag with flashing electronic lights; a wacky baseball game for the swimming pool; a boogie board with a built-in face mask. They learn as much about teamwork and cooperation as they do about electronic circuits. As one youngster from a Harlem team says after they win the prize for team spirit, not for their treasure hunt game, "We didn't get all of heaven, but we got a piece."

Sally's new mission generated its own missionary zeal, fairly oozing out of the La Jolla office during my visit in October 2012. Technically, it's in the basement—one flight below the main floor in a medium-high-rise building in a mini industrial center. But the budget digs have plenty of floor-to-ceiling windows to bring in the California light, with mobiles of seahorses, dolphins and other playful creatures giving it a middle-school atmosphere populated by instructors who grew up learning about Sally in their history texts.

Leesa Hubbard, who left her teaching job in Tennessee to work with SRS (and who has the circular NASA logo known as "the meatball" tattooed on her hip), says simply, "It feels good to work here. I feel like I get to be Santa Claus for teachers." Sandy Antalis, who served as director of professional development, went to the company because of Sally. "The first time I heard her, she spoke so passionately about the next generation of children," she says. "If you weren't on board before that, you were signing in blood afterwards. I had tears in my eyes." Brenda Wilson, who served as vice president of content, says it started at the top. "Normally you get a job and see that the emperor has no clothes," she says. "With Sally it was the opposite: she got better, she grew in stature."

The hagiography is discomfiting, except that I hear it over and over.

Meredith Manning, the company's former vice president of marketing, says the kids were the reward. "The fact that Sally could have done anything, and that she chose to put her name on, and all of her credentials behind, STEM education, that is very, very powerful. And you go to the festivals, and you hear from a girl who has never been on a college campus, or never met a scientist, and the light that shines in her face. Wow. That's why I do this!"

That's what drove Sally too, and it was clear from the decorations in her corner office. Her only visible souvenir of STS-7 was a framed Disneyland E ticket, like the one she'd memorialized during her launch. But on the credenza was the children's book about the solar system that she wrote with Tam; on the wall, a framed membership card for the first Sally Ride Science Club. "There were just so many times where we'd be dealing with kids," Maria Zuber tells me, laughing, "and she'd look at me and say, 'They totally get it!' And they did."

MOONKAM

That enthusiasm is also what inspired Zuber when she invited Sally to brainstorm on a new project she was proposing to NASA: a robotic mission to the Moon, with twin satellites to study lunar gravity. There was room, she said, for something else, "something amazing, off the charts, creative." Sally immediately thought of EarthKAM—for the Moon. "She said, 'How about putting a camera on the spacecraft?' Her company would put together classroom exercises that students could use in the classroom to study images to learn about the Moon." They actually proposed two cameras—with four camera heads for different viewing angles on each satellite—and put together a slick video with the irresistible faces of children contemplating the Moon. NASA, famously tough on pitches, with a rigorous review process, bought it—wowed by the children and by the presence of the first American woman in space. "Everybody treated the cameras like they were just as important as everything else," Zuber says. "Because people on the team, they all have kids!" At the end of the day, "half the board got up and went to meet Sally." And agreed to give Zuber and Sally $1 million to fund it.

MoonKAM launched on the GRAIL (Gravity Recovery and Interior

Laboratory) mission in March 2012, the two spacecraft smartly named *Ebb* and *Flow* by fourth-graders in Montana. That's what fires the imagination of the fifth graders I meet in New Jersey, whose teacher, Marilyn Ortiz, had given up teaching high school when she realized that these elementary school kids didn't have basic skills in science. Their enthusiasm over the lunar images was shared by students from all fifty states, who swapped the pictures like baseball cards over the course of nine months; they talked about craters and lunar seas as they walked down the halls; and when they got home, they bragged about what they'd done. Julie Miller, a science teacher-coach in Olathe, Kansas, says parents would ask her, "What is this technology that let my kid bring home a picture of the Moon that she says she took?"

For SRS board member Jane Swift, the fact that Sally built a company and a set of projects throbbing with such sentiment is a key to understanding her. "When you did one-on-one interactions with Sally, her passion didn't emanate from her persona," she tells me. "But when you went to the things she created, it was very intense and wonderful and celebratory—all the words you might not use to describe Sally herself."

The company was her new excitement, the goal she was seeking after the bank shot of her famous flight. It allowed her, finally, to combine her most deeply held principles: equity for girls and women, the elegance of science and the magic of space. "Stimulate a creative mind, and then anything is possible," Sally said. She called it "a business imperative, a global imperative." A high school friend thought Sally saw it as "a moral imperative, striving for something higher, to bring the next generation along."

For Sally, her own role was inescapable. "There have been many women in space, but I'm the one that people remember," she told a reporter in 2010. "That gives me a major responsibility to talk to girls, to young women—to help them appreciate that these are careers that are wide open for women."

The goal so enticed her, Sally shed much of her native reserve to promote it. Toni DiMartino-Stebich had first worked with her as the public relations manager at Space.com, constantly begging Sally to do interviews. "As the first American woman in space, Sally was 'the get,' but she didn't exactly want to be gotten," she tells me. At SRS, however, where DiMartino-Stebich also did PR, "for the first couple of years, Sally granted almost every interview request. It was wonderful! It wasn't that she changed overnight, but she was happy to put herself out there for something she believed in so strongly." She noticed "the care Sally took with the girls during the Q&A portion of her speeches . . . how she lit up during the festivals where she spoke with every girl, took pictures and gave autographs. I remember a few reporters challenging me when they learned that Sally did not have children of her own. Some couldn't understand her mission even when I replied that Sally was an educator above all."

Space author Francis French, another member of the SRS team, also saw the "transforming experiences" of the Sally Ride Science Festivals. "It was thousands of girls just having fun. If, a second before, they saw science as a boring, lonely occupation, now they said, 'Wow, this is not what I thought it was!' And I saw that moment so many times." He also observed Sally's ability to turn on the charm when it was needed— whether at a festival or an event for Deloitte or somewhere else—but notes, "it was not something she would do naturally. I saw it afterwards. She'd finish and she'd just be tired, and she'd say, 'Let's get out of here.' And we'd go around the back so we didn't run into anyone else. She found it exhausting." At one videoconference, French recalls, Sally started doodling, "big, underlined, bold letters, DO NOT WANT TO DO THIS. They were notes to herself that I was supposed to see."

Sally's tolerance for public exposure only went so far; with her own company she could finally control it. "It's not so much that I don't like the attention," she told a reporter on the twentieth anniversary of STS-7 in 2003. "It's that I want to have a life. I'm the sort of person who likes to be able to just walk into the supermarket and not be recognized. I can do that most of the time now!"

In 2007, Sally retired from teaching at UCSD to spend all her time with her company. "Science education is my passion," she told an interviewer. "It's going to be that for the foreseeable future."

DUTY CALLS

FEBRUARY 2003–FALL 2010

Columbia Accident Investigation Board, 2003.

Reporter: *Now that you're focusing on education, what will your role be with NASA?*

Sally Ride: *[Space] has been my life for the last twenty years in one way or another . . . It's who I am. Don't expect me to try to divorce myself from the space program, because it's not going to happen, and I don't want it to happen.*

COLUMBIA: ANOTHER HORRIBLE DAY

On the morning of February 1, 2003, Sally was in Orlando for one of her science festivals at the University of Central Florida, less than an hour's drive from the pad where she'd first flown to fame twenty years earlier. And where the space shuttle *Columbia* was due to land a little after 9:00 a.m. Sally was sleeping in, still on California time, when she got a phone call from Bear, a few rooms away. Ground controllers had lost contact with *Columbia* as it reentered the atmosphere. There had been no communication with the crew for more than ten minutes. "Oh, that's not good," Sally said, and clicked on the TV.

She knew where the astronauts *should* have been, strapped into their seats, helmet visors down, screaming through the atmosphere at 17,000 miles an hour and watching out the windows as the orbiter collided with the molecules, turning everything an eerie, glowing pink and orange. It had been compared to flying through a neon tube. But then they should have slowed down, and the crew should have radioed Houston as the spacecraft appeared like a tiny white dot in the clear blue sky to drop safely onto the runway. Instead, Sally watched with the rest of the world as the dreadful news emerged: *Columbia* had broken apart on its way back to Earth, killing the crew of seven. Five men and two women were gone. Pieces of debris were already turning up in a hideous path from Texas to Louisiana. It was, she thought, "another horrible day."

Shock waves like those from the *Challenger* explosion, almost seventeen years to the day earlier, rippled through Sally's body. After eighty-seven successful missions, it had happened again. And it had happened, again, while the public, and the families of the astronauts, were watching. As President Kennedy had said on the day Alan Shepard became the first American in space, "Our failures are going to be publicized . . . and there isn't anything that we can do or should do about it." Sally was rocked but faced her own immediate decision: would youngsters still want to celebrate science and space in the wake of the horror? Should they cancel the next day's Festival?

"But then, the more we thought about it," she later said, "and the more we talked to folks, the more we thought that it would be important for the girls, their parents and their teachers, probably as well as for us, to have an opportunity to get together to ask questions, to get some answers to really try to put this into some context and perspective."

So Sally rewrote her speech, pulled on a pink turtleneck and jeans, summoned up her Right Stuff smile and answered tough questions from kids with ponytails and braces who sounded wise beyond their tears. "Why wasn't there a backup plan?" "How do astronauts feel about going up into space now?" "What good has come out of yesterday's tragedy?" Gradually Sally helped turn the preteen grief session into a rallying cry. "She just affirms for the girls that yes, life carries some risks," said a teacher who drove her students six hours across Florida from Panama City, "but that you don't have to be afraid to do something just because of the risks. She helps girls 'get it.' " In return, their resilience strengthened Sally. "We need kids to look to the stars," she told them, with an unusual catch in her throat. It was, she later said, "not an easy day."

Sally also told the girls, in response to a question, that yes, she had helped investigate the *Challenger* accident, but no, she wouldn't be doing the same for *Columbia*.

One month later, after the Columbia Accident Investigation Board (CAIB) kicked into gear, the newly appointed chairman, retired Navy Admiral Harold Gehman, recognized the need to add some outside experts to the technicians on board, and to get some continuity with the last catastrophe. He called Sally.

"She was reluctant to do it," Gehman tells me. "She was very busy—teaching and her other activities, and could not commit to the seven days a week that she knew the board was working." Gehman assured her that she didn't have to move to Houston, and that with her background and the dedicated support staff, she would only have to put in a few days a week. "It took forty-five minutes to convince her," he recalls, "but with Sally we got a scientist, a veteran of the *Challenger* investigation, and we got an astronaut. She exceeded our expectations."

Sally was the only person to sit on both the *Challenger* and *Columbia* investigation teams. She was also, Gehman says, "the only one of the thirteen people on the board anybody wanted an autograph from!"

Once again Sally found herself putting in sixteen-hour days to understand how astronauts had died. Once again she examined NASA work schedules and interviewed shuttle personnel, penciling her notes in yet another little notebook with the mission patch of a dead crew on the cover (and, on her To Do list, a memo to call A^2—Steve Hawley—to get his thoughts). And while the shuttle had disintegrated during entry, the problem had begun, again, at launch. This time, it wasn't O-rings. A backpack-sized chunk of insulation foam from the external fuel tank (where it was connected to the orbiter) had cracked off and struck the leading edge of *Columbia*'s left wing, punching a hole in the tiles that protected its vulnerable aluminum frame. In space, it didn't matter. But as the orbiter passed through the turbulence of the atmosphere on its way home, the breach was penetrated by superhot gases, compromising the integrity of the craft and ripping it apart. Once again, the crew didn't have a chance.

"Follow the foam," Sally jotted down, looking for new problems. But the similarities to what she'd seen with *Challenger* made her realize that little had changed. There had, it turned out, been previous such foam strikes, essentially ignored, just as with *Challenger*'s O-rings. The old Apollo culture that said, "Prove to me that this will work" had been supplanted by "Prove to me that this is unsafe," just like the decision to launch *Challenger*. And the pressure of trying to launch too many shuttles, too quickly, had once again impacted human life. Sally isolated the problem quickly.

Lisa Reed was a former shuttle training instructor enlisted to help with the investigation. One day, at the CAIB offices across from the Johnson Space Center in Houston, she lined up all her documentation on a twenty-foot-long table and asked Sally to take a look. Reed thought there was evidence that shuttle maintenance and training schedules were becoming very compressed, leaving less time between missions to prepare both the crew and the orbiter. Everyone was feeling the squeeze as the tempo picked up to meet the flight schedule; pressure had built up to a dangerous level. But she didn't divulge her conclusions. Sally, she says, "came in and started at the left end. She grabbed a handful of Goldfish snacks from the bowl in the middle, and with her hand on her chin, popping the Goldfish, made her way from one end of the table to the other. She would ask a few questions, look at the material. And she analyzed the situation so quickly, she found the exact same things I was seeing. She understood."

The chill of history repeating itself crystallized Sally's thinking. At a briefing for the press in Houston's Hilton Hotel ballroom on April 8, 2003, she articulated it for the world: "I'm hearing a little bit of an echo here."

"You could have heard a pin drop in the room," says Gehman. "We were kind of sniffing around this idea that the engineering at JSC had failed again, but we hadn't zeroed in on it. Hadn't made it a priority. We were still looking for widgets and brackets and foam. That single statement significantly reinforced in us the need to change the direction of the investigation. She caused us to reconsider where our priorities were." Specifically: NASA's culture, engineering, management and risk assessment. It wasn't just *what* happened, it was *why*. "It was a giant contribution," Gehman adds, "like changing the course of a ship. Subtle but profound."

Sociologist and author Diane Vaughan, who had analyzed the 1986 *Challenger* explosion and famously coined the phrase "normalization of deviance" to characterize the problem, was also invited to testify before the CAIB and aligned her theories with Sally's "echoes" statement. She believes that "the power of encapsulating it that way—to put it before the public in one simple sentence—was really stunning." Equally impressive, she says, was Sally's demeanor. "She clearly had an investment in terms of her personal, emotional level," Vaughan says. But in meetings with her team, Vaughan found that Sally "wasn't outraged. It was a research task for her. Everyone else was very excited—as if NASA were the enemy and this was the elite team trying to find out what happened. Sally, of course, having been an astronaut and also on the *Challenger* commission, was more deeply affected than anyone but remained truly professional."

And she had learned how to move mountains without leaving fingerprints.

During the *Challenger* investigation, she'd secretly given the information about the O-rings to another commissioner, to keep her name from implicating the NASA source. With *Columbia* she would do her end run around her former bosses by using the press.

The CAIB investigators were concerned about NASA's continued insistence that nothing could have saved the crew. The impact area was not visible to the seven astronauts onboard, but despite requests from some engineers, mission managers never tried to get images—through spy satellite telescopes—to examine the foam damage while *Columbia* was in orbit. There was, they said, no point: a spacewalk would have been fruitless because there was no way to repair it.

The board wasn't convinced and directed NASA to put together a team to test the theory. Their conclusion: if NASA had recognized the fatal damage to the left wing, a rescue mission using another shuttle, and a string of spacewalks, might—might—have been successful. The CAIB folks prepared to announce the results at a briefing the next day but worried that NASA management might get wind of it and try to discredit their findings. So the investigators decided to leak them to a reporter. Sally was the leaker; Todd Halvorson of *Florida Today* (and her former Space.com colleague), the leakee. Sally made the phone call.

"I was in the media newsroom in Houston," he tells me, revealing his source for the first time. "And I remember running outside when I saw who was calling on my cell phone." Halvorson stood there scribbling down notes as Sally gave him the details. His paper ran the story the next day under a provocative headline:

DARING RESCUE MAY HAVE SAVED COLUMBIA CREW

QUICK ATLANTIS MISSION POSSIBLE, STUDY SAYS.

It quoted an unnamed "senior investigator" [Sally] as saying, "It would have been high drama, but there was a realistic chance . . . of returning the crew." The "investigator" added that *Columbia*'s crew could have stayed in orbit for thirty days, plenty of time to get *Atlantis* off the pad and transfer the astronauts with spacewalks that "would have been sporty, but . . . not impossible."

"It was all clearly very distressing to Sally," Halvorson recalls. "And I became *persona non grata* with NASA at first for writing the story." But the rescue scenario was included in the CAIB's final report, along with harsh criticism of the space agency's "[c]ultural traits and organizational practices detrimental to safety . . ." Or, as Sally later told me, shaking her head in sorrow, they knew both the O-rings and the foam had not performed properly on occasion. But "they never stopped to fix the problem, never stopped and understood it."

Her anguish, and her anger, were palpable. In an email to her CAIB colleagues just before publication of the report, she provided, as requested, a summary of the earlier Rogers Commission's findings. It was uncharacteristically late in delivery. "I've been putting this off," Sally wrote, "because it's so irritating to go back and read that report . . . Though the quotes aren't as good as Yogi Berra's, it's definitely Deja Vous [sic] all over again." At the very moment she was celebrating the twentieth anniversary of her historic flight, and being inducted into the Astronaut Hall of Fame, she was finding it harder than ever to support NASA. "There wasn't any of that quality that Mission Control is almost famous for," she told *The New York Times*, "which is grabbing onto the pants legs of a problem and not letting go until it understands what the problem is and what the implications are. And that didn't happen in this case."

The *Columbia* accident and subsequent inquiry didn't tear Sally apart the way *Challenger* had. It did, however, shred her faith in the system. It would, she said, be her last accident investigation.

Her service to the government, however, was far from over.

Sally was the top choice for anything space. People always wanted her involved. And she was there for everything.

—Lori Garver, Deputy Administrator, NASA, 2012

BACK TO THE FUTURE

Sally made it clear that she still wasn't interested in the NASA Administrator job. Lori Garver, then the agency's lead for Barack Obama's 2008 transition team, remembers a conversation where Sally laughed and said, "I was wondering when you'd call!" But, Garver says, "it was really very obvious that she just didn't want it. My takeaway was, 'Please don't have the president ask me.' But she would help out in whatever way she could."

She had endorsed the Obama-Biden ticket during the campaign and would serve as a consultant or on a number of government and private industry boards, including both the National Math and Science Initiative (2007), a program to invigorate K–12 science and math education by training teachers and recruiting college students to become teachers; Educate to Innovate (2009), a national campaign to stimulate science training, largely outside the classroom; and Change the Equation (2010), an industry-driven initiative to improve achievement in the field, especially among females and minorities. At a time when the US ranked twenty-first (out of thirty industrialized nations) in science, and twenty-fifth in math, it called for a more rigorous curriculum, to transform the national dialogue to include science, technology, engineering and math. At the press conference announcing formation of Change the Equation, Sally said, "Literacy is not just being able to read anymore. It's being able to read, to calculate, to analyze."

Earlier, in June 2009, she was asked to serve on yet another panel to determine America's future in space. The Review of United States Human Spaceflight Plans Committee—known as the Augustine Committee, for its chairman, former Lockheed Martin CEO Norman Augustine—would be the initial blueprint for the Obama administration's plans. Sally shoehorned it into her schedule. "Too busy," she emailed me, ". . . just agreed to be on Norm Augustine's committee reviewing the human spaceflight program (which is, by the way, in need of 'review')."

After *Columbia*, the shuttle had again returned to space, with safety-first modifications and rigorous new procedures. But it was scheduled to be retired in a year, and the International Space Station was destined to be deep-sixed in the South Pacific in 2015. Was that the right course? And should the US continue the George W. Bush–approved Constellation program, with new rockets to transport astronauts to orbit and beyond? With government dollars in short supply, the findings of the panel were especially critical.

Sally rolled up her sleeves for another labor-intensive summer, lugging her laptop to meetings and working through the night for four months. Augustine remembers getting her 2:00 a.m. emails about critical issues. He had enlisted her, he tells me, because she possessed "the credibility that comes from experience, the courage to say what needed to be said and the fact that she was not a zealot. Her strongest suit was judgment. To have good judgment you've got to be able to detach yourself from things you may care a lot about. You've got to have the ability to look at the facts, to look at the other side of the argument and to weigh it very fairly." At the final public hearing in Washington, Sally stood at the microphone and presided over a set of slides and statistics for nearly two hours in a deft economic analysis of the existing NASA plan. The way things stood, she pointed out, the new rocket system would not be completed until after the Space Station was planned to be shut down. Or, as her fellow panelist and friend Wanda Austin, CEO of The Aerospace Corporation, tells me, "by the time you build the rocket to get there, the 'there' is gone."

As a result of the committee's report, Constellation was killed, the shuttle extended by a year (Sally had also considered longer options), and the Space Station extended to 2020. (It has since been extended to 2024.) To ferry our astronauts there, the United States agreed to buy space on Russian rockets—our former enemy, now a taxi service—and to actively support commercial ventures. Long-range goals would include Mars, its moons and an asteroid. "Sally really was a major architect of the report," John Holdren, director of the Office of Science and Technology Policy, tells me, "which in turn became a major shaper of President Obama's space policy, and the plan ultimately worked out with the Congress. Sally's fingerprints are all over that."

And it set off a major controversy. Much of NASA, along with some of Sally's closest colleagues—including Bob Crippen—argued vehemently that ending both shuttle and Constellation threatened America's primacy in space. Neil Armstrong coauthored an op-ed with Jim Lovell and Gene Cernan saying the bold leadership of President Kennedy had been betrayed: "We will have no rockets to carry humans to low-Earth orbit and beyond for an indeterminate number of years. . . . John F. Kennedy would have been sorely disappointed."

Space historian John Logsdon says the criticism from NASA's "old guard" was understandable. "It threatened the heritage that they were so much a part of," he tells me. "They underestimated the ability of a reformed NASA to carry out a human spaceflight program differently from the way they had known it." For the Committee, it was all about their mission. "We tried to do what we thought was right for the country," Norm Augustine explains. "It took a lot of courage for Sally to do what she did. Because she was a product of NASA, her name was built with NASA. She was challenging the organization of which she was the offspring."

She was also trying to preserve it. "She had high expectations for NASA," Wanda Austin tells me. "She knew what it could be."

THE SECRET

2001—FEBRUARY 2011

At home with Tam and Gypsy, 1992.

They should let girls be who they want to be, and not pay any attention to the stereotypes.

—Sally Ride, 1986

Her life embodied authenticity, being true to herself and not having to conform to the demands of society or any other authority. That was also the far-reaching goal of Sally Ride Science: to allow children—especially girl children—to follow their hearts and minds into science or any other field, no matter what tradition dictated.

Ironically, and unfortunately, it was not how Sally felt able to live her own personal life.

Publicly, her relationship with Tam—the most significant and by far the longest lasting of her lifetime—yielded to a business decision.

"Corporate America is really nervous about gay women," Tam tells me. "When we started Sally Ride Science, we were just worried that it would affect the growth of the company, the sponsorships. We both lived through Billie Jean's horrors, of being gay and being in the public eye. And we both were afraid it would hurt the business. So we elected to be private about it."

Tam prefers the word *private* to *secret*, and wonders if they might not have lived the same way in the non-business world. Sally had never announced their relationship in her previous careers, either; had never, in psychologist Kay Loveland's terms, "claimed" Tam as her partner in public the way she "claimed" her male relationships. In a society still anxious about same-sex couples, it was a lot easier for a woman to say "my husband" than "my gay mate."

Among their close group of gay and straight friends, Sally and Tam were not closeted, socializing at each other's homes and in restaurants. They were regulars at the WTA Tournament in La Costa and always bought a table at the annual Billie Jean King and Friends fund-raiser held in Pasadena, to which they invited old tennis buddies. They also traveled extensively, staying together in hotels and attending public functions together. In 2010 they went to the Masters Tournament in Augusta at the invitation of Exxon, their SRS partner. And they attended each other's university events, as well as SRS occasions, including annual education conferences and meetings. Tam kept nothing from her best buddies, many of whom became Sally's friends as well. But Sally told no one, not even the insiders.

Billie Jean King had been rejected by a world hostile to homosexuality nearly two decades earlier—before Sally first flew, before she even moved in with Steve. When Sally became a celebrity, she and King had often spoken about careers, about the special responsibility of being in the public eye. "She asked me things like, Why did I do what I did? How did it feel being the leader of a movement?" King tells me. "And you could tell by what she was thinking that she wanted to set the world on fire."

But Sally never asked about the effect on King's career of being gay.

"Never. I thought it was weird," King says. "But she knew what I'd been through. At the time, it was on the news every night at six and eleven." In the years since, society grew more educated and more tolerant, and King's leadership in women's rights was widely celebrated. She also spent time with Sally and Tam as a couple.

"Selfishly, I thought it would be great if Sally came out, and if Tam came out, but I knew they weren't there. I thought it would be great for an example of being gay and being powerful and all the wonderful things, to be yourself and to be authentic. And also, if you see it, you can be it—you know? The more examples you have for children, it just empowers them, gives them hope. But it's easy for me to say, I'm in a different place. When you're not in that place, you're just frightened."

Because of her own experience, King says, "I would never 'out' somebody. I don't believe in pushing. There are certain people who, when you're around them, you know they don't want you to go in a certain place. That's the feeling I always got with Sally and Tam. They just didn't want you to go there. You know, we're friends, let's enjoy each other, we're gay, whoop-de-doo. But that was it."

Tam confirms her friend's observations. "We never publicly said, 'We're gay.' We didn't like labels of any kind, but especially the ones referring to sexuality: queer, lesbian, homosexual."

The social stigma began early.

Tam recalls the time as a teenager on the tennis circuit, in the dark ages of the mid-1960s, when the word spread to "be careful," whatever that meant, around two specific women because "they are lesbians!" The implication—that lesbians might corrupt unsuspecting young girls—was as pervasive as it was absurd, a relic of mostly bygone days. Tam mocks the warning but still shivers at the fear it produced. "And we were indeed cautious around these great players because you just think, 'Oh my gosh, what are they going to do?'" Tam's admiration for the tennis talent of one of the women overrode her anxiety, and she actually had a conversation with her. But the damage to her psyche continues to reverberate.

"The word *lesbian* still brings back those memories," she says. "I don't even want to be called gay. And Sally thought the same way—you know, straight people don't have to say, 'I'm heterosexual.' So why should we have to? It's probably true that if either of us had been with a guy, we would have been open about it and said things like, 'This is my boyfriend,' or 'This is my partner.' But publicly, we never said the words to let people know we were a couple."

Only now does Tam fully understand the insidious nature of what's been called "internalized homophobia," or negative feelings about one's own homosexuality that, in their case, led them both to keep their relationship largely to themselves. "Sally and I were not afraid of being gay," she says. "Sally wanted to be with me. Being with a woman fit her better, for whatever reasons, and that's how she was going to live. But it didn't mean she wasn't afraid and anxious in certain situations." Tam tells me about the time they went to a resort in Arizona for a few days, on vacation. When they walked into the dining room to join the breakfast buffet line, she says, "there was silence, people turning their heads. It made us miserable." The experience was not one they wanted to repeat.

Joyce Ride says she knew that her daughter and Molly were more than just roommates at Stanford but never said anything. "It wasn't a big subject for conversation at the time," she explains. When Sally married Steve, then divorced him, "I took her word that it was because she wanted to leave NASA and Steve didn't." As for Sally and Tam—who attended holiday celebrations at her home together for some twenty years without announcing their relationship—Joyce says she figured them out "a long time ago. But I didn't concentrate a lot on it. I didn't think it was that big a deal. I'm very nonjudgmental. Also, I think because Sally was such a public figure, the less said the better. That was her decision." In the occasional letters she wrote her daughter, Joyce always sent greetings to Tam.

In 1995, Sally's sister, Bear, was divorced. Within a year she came out as a lesbian and formed a permanent couple with Susan Craig, also a Presbyterian minister. Bear took her mother out to lunch to break the news. Joyce "didn't skip a beat," Bear says. "She was not surprised. Unflappability runs in the family, too."

I ask Joyce whether she attaches any significance to the fact that both of her daughters turned out to be gay. "Not that I can think of," she says. "But it would have surprised their father."

How might he have reacted?

"I think he would have accepted it. He was very proud of both of them, so fond of both of them, he would have accepted anything. Even being Democrats."

Joyce's ability to deflect the emotional with a zinger is both exasperating and infectious. I ask which might have concerned Dale Ride more—that his daughters were gay or Democrats?

"Probably that they were Democrats."

Bear doesn't remember Sally's reaction, but does recall that her sister was always very supportive, and that she came to Bear and Susan's commitment ceremony in 2000. Still, while Bear and Susan were open about their life together, and got married in 2008 when California briefly allowed it, and while Tam had told Bear about her relationship with Sally (some ten years after they'd moved in together), Bear and Sally never discussed it with each other.

Bear tries to explain the inexplicable. In their family, she says, you didn't find things out unless you asked. She laughs about the time her mother, over lunch, slipped in the fact that they were related to Robert E. Lee. "I was thirty-five and I didn't know," Bear says. "I asked how this could be. She said, 'You never asked.'" And, Bear tells me, since she didn't see Sally very often, she just never discussed her relationship with Tam or asked about her sexuality.

Susan Okie did—much earlier, before Tam was part of Sally's life. In February 1981, while Sally was at NASA (but more than a year before she was named to her first flight), she invited her high school friend, then at the *Washington Post*, to New York where she was giving a speech. She also offered Okie the extra bed in her hotel room that night. It was, Okie recalls fondly, "kind of like when she used to sleep over" when they were teens. Okie had been surprised when a colleague at the *Post*, a sports reporter, told her that Sally and Molly Tyson had been a couple, and decided to find out for herself. "So I asked her, when we were both lying in our beds. And she said, 'No, Molly wanted that, but I didn't, and that's not true.' "

By that time, Sally had already revealed her romance with Molly to two people. First, Bill Colson, back when he was courting her. Then, in 1976, when she was on the Stanford rugby field, to her tennis pal, Ann Lebedeff. "She told me she'd had an affair with a friend," Lebedeff recalls. "She trusted me." But as a NASA astronaut hoping to get selected as the first American female to fly, the stakes were much higher. Although Sally had never asked either Molly or Bill to keep the secret, perhaps she worried that with Okie, the information might appear in print, which could certainly compromise her career; perhaps she was concerned about the reaction of someone from her pre-Stanford days in a still-homophobic society. Or maybe it was something else entirely. Whichever, the truth was never made clear to Okie. "It haunts me that she was so closed-mouthed, and it hurts," she tells me. "When I asked her about Molly, I wasn't being critical. I just wanted to know. I grew up with her, I felt like we were such good friends, and I'm pretty good at hanging on to my friends. She was like a locked box."

Even more so when it came to Tam.

Around 1995, when Bill Colson and Sally were no longer close friends but still collaborated on some physics papers, he met up with her in La Jolla. "And I have to admit, my interest in Sally has never really wavered all that much," Colson tells me, "so I was exploring." He asked Sally if she was in a relationship. "And she said, 'No. It seems like things only last about a year.' So I figured she was in a series of relationships." By then, Sally and Tam had been a couple for nearly a decade.

Susan Okie ran into a similar response early in 2011, when her friendship with Sally, ruptured after *Challenger*, was back on cordial terms. Okie, no longer a journalist, was in La Jolla, where she and Sally met at a restaurant and discussed the possibility of Okie's writing some school curriculum material. Sally suggested she contact Tam, identifying her as her business partner. Sally also mentioned that she lived nearby, vaguely pointing into the distance. She never mentioned that Tam lived there, too.

I had the same experience when Sally spent some nights at my apartment in New York in 1999, during the Space.com start-up. She giggled over the house gift she'd brought me—a pair of socks embroidered with giraffes, which she knew were my animal addiction—and we spent relaxed dinners and evenings together discussing her new venture and the ways of the world. She had often mentioned Tam as the coauthor of her children's books, and it had occurred to me that they might be, or might have been, together, but I didn't know for sure, and—yes, Bear—I never asked. Sally never volunteered the information.

"I think it's one thing to be private," says psychologist Kay Loveland, who spent so much time with Sally and Tam in Atlanta and La Jolla, "but not to tell a friend that you're in a relationship that is meaningful to you—there's something very sad about that. She wasn't sharing a good part of who she was."

In 2002, just as the new company was getting started, Sally and Tam moved into a spacious and breezy, five-bedroom Spanish-style house with a pool out back and a view across the hills to the Pacific Ocean and the sunset. With its white rugs and clean, spare furnishings, enriched by prints of Navajo artist R. C. Gorman on the wall and a collection of glossy black Santa Clara pottery, it was (and is) a bright and welcoming house. And it served as a refuge for two busy women who preferred quiet time together most weekends and evenings. On occasion, when

Tam suggested opening it to an SRS board meeting, or a Christmas party, Sally declined. "I want," she said, "separation of church and state."

Sally cherished her safe haven. Still an introvert despite years in the public eye, she was able to "just let herself be who she was," Tam says, "a nerd, a jock, an academic homebody . . . with a woman to love for life." Over time, Tam also saw her grow, becoming more open about her feelings with some close friends, letting them into her life.

But her need for self-protection led to some awkward moments with others.

Paula Levin, Sally's UCSD faculty colleague and her (and Tam's) friend as well, was having lunch with them in La Jolla one day, "and it was clear that there were topics off the table. I remember saying, 'What are you guys going to be doing this summer?' And there was this dead silence. One or the other responded personally—'what *I* will be doing.' It just seemed like such a natural question."

Brenda Wilson recalls the day Sally stopped by her office at Sally Ride Science and knelt down to greet her dog, Guido. "He jumped all over her," Wilson says, "I'd never seen him this crazy about anyone! She laughed and laughed and loved it. I asked what kind of dog she had, and she said, 'A bichon frise, they're the best.'" And then, Wilson tells me, "Sally got the weirdest look on her face, like she'd overstepped. Because Tam had a picture of their bichon on her wall, and everyone thought it was just Tam's dog." Wilson also spotted the matching rings Sally and Tam each wore on the fourth finger, left hand.

The truth was widely known but totally unspoken. Karen Flammer, one of the SRS founders who now serves as senior science advisor, says, "You'll hear this from a zillion people. It was like a secret that was never a secret. And I mean to anybody at the company. We all talked about it—and not behind their backs, but without them being present. And nobody cared. But everybody knew."

Flammer says that on the one hand, the respect they showed each other was endearing. "They looked after other and took care of each other at meetings," she tells me. "If Sally sensed that Tam maybe wasn't feeling that she was getting recognition for something, Sally would immediately say, 'Oh, well, Tam is in charge of this and has done that.' And then if Tam sensed that Sally had had enough, Tam would figure out a way to say, 'Okay, let's end this meeting.' It was incredible to watch."

On the other hand, Flammer says, shaking her head, "Tam couldn't even be acknowledged for being her partner. That had to be hard."

Terry McEntee, Sally's executive assistant and another SRS founder, occupied a unique place in Sally's life and saw the couple from a unique vantage point. She began working with Sally in 1995, starting with EarthKAM and then running interference on any number of critical problems. When McEntee moved to San Clemente, about an hour up the coast, Sally asked if she was interested in arranging a flexible schedule to allow her to continue working at UCSD. McEntee knew and respected Sally as a calm presence "with no airs, who wasn't dropping names. I never dreaded going to work." She became a loyal and trusted business confidante, and later, a devoted friend—yet another like those throughout Sally's life who protected her without being asked. "People outside the office would occasionally ask me, 'Is Sally gay?' " McEntee tells me. "And I'd just answer that I had no idea." In fact, Sally never told her that she and Tam were a couple, but McEntee realized the situation when, for instance, she would drop something off for Sally at the house they shared and saw two cars parked in the garage. Without specific instructions, she knew what her job entailed.

McEntee remembers being asked to make a hotel reservation for Sally without realizing that Tam was going to be there, too. "And once Sally doubled back with me and asked me to be sure that Tam could check into the room if she arrived first," McEntee explains, "because, Sally said, 'Tam gets upset if she gets there early and can't get in.' " Clearly, Sally was sensitive to the situation and wanted to be sure Tam was comfortable. "There was this tenderness," McEntee says. After about ten years, Sally seemed more casual about acknowledging Tam's presence, and would tell McEntee that she was traveling to a meeting and "Tam is going to join me." But especially in those earlier days, as she

saw it, "Tam was always in the background—that's what their relationship demanded for Sally. And Tam was willing to go along with it. It
must have been hard on her. And I think it had to have taken some toll
on Sally in terms of guilt."

When I ask Tam whether keeping the secret took a toll on Sally, she
pauses, thinks, and finally responds, "No, because she was an expert at
compartmentalizing, and she was a very happy human being. She liked
who she was in the world, she liked her life." Tam does agree, however,
that secrets take a toll on others. "Molly was a toll long ago, because
Molly wanted to be more open, and Sally didn't know how to do that,
couldn't even think of it. But the real toll is felt in another way by Sally's
close friends—Billie Jean and many others who wish she'd confided in
them about her life, her feelings, her illness."

Tam doesn't count herself in the same category because, she says,
Sally was much more open with her. And because she and Sally lived
equal, independent lives. "I never once felt that she was in charge of my
life or in control. I never once felt resentful. I took full responsibility
for the few compromises I made during our relationship—leaving my
ecology PhD program at the University of Georgia, which I loved; not
having children; not being as open about being gay; not having as open a
home to our friends as I would have had by myself or with a less private
mate."

Tam reminds me of an afternoon in Pasadena, when she, Sally and
I met for tea during a rare moment when our schedules were in sync.
By that time, I was barely in touch with Sally, although I did usually let
her know when I was on the West Coast. I don't recall the specifics of
that day, but Tam does, and she recounts them, in aching detail: "It just
feels uncomfortable," she tells me, putting herself back in the moment.
"It just feels like there's a gorilla sitting at the table and no one's talking
about it. Who am I, and how am I supposed to act? How am I supposed
to look at Sally? So I was uncomfortable a lot, and I think much more so
than Sally, because Sally sometimes is unaware of other people"—this
understatement makes Tam laugh—"she doesn't care, she's herself, she's

this grounded person, and she's there at the table and she's talking to you and she's not thinking, 'What is Lynn thinking?' or 'What about Tam?' She just doesn't think about those things."

It is a moving and candid picture of her uneasiness, but Tam relates her feelings more from analysis than anger. "I think one of Sally's strengths was that she was so in the now, she was so present in everything," she says. "You know, if you're talking to her you're really talking to her, and she doesn't have an agenda, or things she must talk about, or try to convince you of. She's just there talking with you. I don't think she often concerns herself or thinks about the relationship or what other people might be thinking of the actual situation. She was happy to see you, wanted me there, and that's it. There's nothing else going on."

Tam wants me to understand that Sally included her in her life—made sure she was invited to everything she did, just as Tam did with her. But, she adds, "not in the explicit way to say, 'This is my partner' publicly." Tam doesn't blame Sally. But she does wish, for instance, that Sally had been more willing to socialize at home. "I talked to her all the time about having friends over more," she explains. "And she would say, 'Yes, let's do.' She always wanted me to be happy. She would try. I also talked with her about my need to get to know her more deeply especially in the emotional realm," Tam says. "Why didn't she like delving into her emotions? What might happen if she did? I asked her these questions and she said she didn't know why. And then we were working too hard at SRS, and I just felt a little distant from her.

"So I almost left her."

They had been through bumpy times before, rare arguments when Sally's blue eyes would widen, her mouth tighten, and there would be dead calm. She could be very stubborn. Sally "did not like feeling out of control" and would say, "I'm not mad, I'm not upset," while quietly simmering with a taut jaw. One time, Tam asked Sally to join her on a cruise with some of their friends. Sally declined. "She didn't like cruises, had been on one with Steve and hated it." So Tam set off without her, "and Sally turned into a fourth-grader. She was the most jealous brat.

In every phone conversation, she would hardly talk, would not tell me what was going on in the office. She was making me pay. When I got home, I said, 'You made me a little miserable. But I had a good time. What was that about?' And she said, 'I'm sorry, I was awful.' She said she just didn't like it that I was away somewhere without her."

Tam reconsidered the situation. "I thought hard about what I had with Sally and what was missing. I wished she could talk longer and say more about her side of any discussion other than work. But we loved each other passionately. And we had so much together and shared the same values and interests that it was ridiculous for me to even think of leaving her. No one is a perfect mate, but Sally came close enough.

"We didn't talk about it, but she knew that I was thinking of leaving her. And then we're happy as little larks again, and I'm back in the fold."

For more than two decades, Sally had been burning the candle at both ends and in the middle. Besides her day job, her government service and other outside commitments, she had also served, or was serving, on the boards of Caltech, Mitre, Apple (briefly), and The Aerospace Corporation, among others. Her contributions to space travel were recognized with honors named for some of the men whose pioneering efforts had made her own ventures possible: the Lindbergh Eagle (1985), the von Braun award (1995). Her excellence in tennis and her work on behalf of women in all sports earned her the NCAA's Theodore Roosevelt ("Teddy") award (2005). She was inducted into the California Hall of Fame and won the Minerva Award (2006) from her home state. Sally also won the Jefferson Award for public service (1984).

There were some less demanding gigs, too. In 1999, she made a cameo appearance as herself in TV's *Touched by an Angel*, encouraging Sherry Stringfield's character, a hesitant astronaut, with this promise: "First time you look down on Earth, it will change your perspective on everything." A few years later she made a TV commercial for Office Depot, a perky fantasy in which she helps a stumped young student identify the First American Woman in Space (by getting his attention—

"Psst!"—and pointing conspicuously to herself), then turns down a ride home in the kid's mom's car, saying, "I'll take the shuttle!" In 2003, she swung a bottle of champagne across the bow of a new Carnival Lines cruise ship at Port Canaveral, just down the coast from the Kennedy Space Center. She had earlier christened a Goodyear blimp. In 2009, she participated in a high concept film-and-still shoot for Louis Vuitton with Apollo astronauts Jim Lovell and Buzz Aldrin, that took two days during a 30-mile-per-hour windstorm in California's Simi Valley and required getting tied with a rope to the trunk of a car so she wouldn't blow away. "Hope they paid you a fortune—and then some," I emailed her when I saw the photographs by Annie Leibovitz in the magazine ad. She responded a few hours later: "My mortgage is paid for a while. (Ok, quite a while.)" The fee was $200,000. Sally declined the opportunity to appear on TV's *Dancing with the Stars*.

By 2011, most of the outside work was history. As CEO of Sally Ride Science, she was working nonstop and flying high. The company had resulted from a logical, although unplanned, progression: from writing children's science books, to learning the data revealing how society's messages to girls and boys affected their participation in scientific careers, to dreaming up the alphabet video game, to launching and running the company. Sally was part of another team, this one of her own creation.

The accidental astronaut had created her new life—on purpose—and seemed to have the planets aligned. She could draw on her NASA fame when necessary and shop for soy milk without having to sign autographs. She had plenty of money in the bank. Her life with Tam was the one she wanted. In February 2011, Sally Ride Science was looking to expand. The future was as bright as the flames of the rockets that shot her into space.

A VERY PRIVATE THING

MARCH 2011–JULY 2012

Terry McEntee (*left*) and Karen Flammer celebrate Sally's sixtieth birthday, May 26, 2011.

Lynn Sherr: *Did you believe Sally was going to make it?*
Bear Ride: *Yeah, I did. I always believe Sally, and she believed she'd conquer it. When she went up on the shuttle I said I was nervous. She said she wasn't, so I said, "Okay."*

DIAGNOSIS

Sally was exhausted. "I want to rest," she told Tam after a meeting, "I don't feel well." When Tam noticed the yellow tinge to her skin, she got worried.

They were in San Francisco for the National Science Teachers Association conference, a major event where Sally Ride Science took its usual booth at the Moscone Center. They were also announcing a partnership for new educational products—a series of science books with activities to explore phenomena like photosynthesis and respiration. That Thursday evening, March 10, 2011, they showered and dressed, then headed to the launch party at a local restaurant, where Sally delivered her remarks to celebrate the deal. A friend leaned over to Tam and whispered that she thought Sally looked very ill. Now alarmed, Tam urged Sally to make a doctor's appointment for the next day and booked a morning flight back to San Diego. It was the beginning of a sobering new passage for both women that would last more than sixteen months.

Sally's internist performed an ultrasound and saw the bad news immediately: a tumor, nearly as big as a golf ball, in her abdomen. He thought it might be pancreatic cancer. A CT scan at the UCSD hospital confirmed it. Sally and Tam watched the screen as the alien image appeared. "And everything went from there," Tam says.

They hugged, they cried, they reviewed the medical facts, and they tried to wrap their scientific minds around the numbing incongruity of a terrifying diagnosis. How could Sally, a fitness fanatic who, at fifty-nine, was in better shape than most teenagers, have cancer? How could this woman who had transformed her diet from fried steak and hash browns to roasted salmon with green herbs be facing a life-threatening illness in her gut? It was not self-pity, more an attempt to comprehend the monster that had just ambushed their lives.

The location of the tumor at the head of the pancreas, and its involvement with the surrounding blood vessels, made it difficult to remove cleanly. The medical term is "borderline resectable." That meant several months of chemotherapy and radiation, which doctors hoped would shrink the malignancy. It would also give them a chance to observe the behavior of the disease before surgery. Dr. Paul Fanta, who would become Sally's oncologist at UCSD's Moores Cancer Center, says pancreatic cancer is as difficult to understand as it is to treat. "It's so easy on the diagram to show it," he tells me. "Patients say, 'Why can't you just cut it out?'" But its proximity to so many critical organs and nerves complicates matters. Even with treatment, Sally's prognosis was not good. Pancreatic cancer kills 38,000 people a year—out of 45,000 new cases. It is the fourth leading cause of death from cancer, despite being the tenth most commonly diagnosed. The five-year survival percentage for cancer confined to the pancreas is 24 percent; for metastatic disease, it is 2 percent.

Sally decided to seek a second opinion at the renowned M. D. Anderson Cancer Center in Houston. Her friend Amy Mickelson, wife of Phil the golfer, had been successfully treated there for breast cancer and set up an appointment. "Sally and I felt like we were zombies in zombie-land," Tam says. "It's huge. Our little hospital in San Diego is like this little teeny place, very intimate." Registering under a pseudonym for confidentiality—Terry (for Terry McEntee) Tsigane (the collie)—Sally spent two days bouncing from doctor to doctor. When she heard the same diagnosis, and the same recommended treatment, and learned that the surgeon she'd already seen was considered one of the best in the world, she headed home and put herself in the hands of the team at UCSD.

"And once she made the decision," recalls Dr. Andrew Lowy, director of Surgical Oncology, "she said, 'Okay, I've gotten all the opinions. I want you guys to take care of me. Let's do it!' She was as easy a patient as you can get. She was a partner with you, whatever you asked, she was there and ready."

TREATMENT

Sally moved into mission mode. The engineer in her saw a problem to be solved; the scientist, an unknown to be explored. She got out her notebook and made a new set of checklists: "What to expect (1) This week; (2) from chemo; who to call; Dates for blood work." Her bullet points inventoried the known and the unknowable: "Imodium for diarrhea, Numbness/tingles; Neuro effects; Use creams/lotions; Check IV site daily; Alcohol wipes."

Well aware that cancer doesn't lend itself to logical conclusions, but too well trained not to follow protocol, she and Tam researched the situation as thoroughly as they investigated the possibility of water on Mars. After reading studies linking meat and dairy products to increased health risks, they both became strict vegans. Convinced that a positive attitude and environment might help, they stopped watching TV news and banished negative thoughts from their conversation. They took up meditation and acupuncture, while Sally continued her regular regime of stretching, flexing and working her muscles, with weights, on the treadmill and jumping rope.

She would need every bit of strength she could muster. To prepare for her chemo, a port was surgically implanted into a vein in her chest so that toxins could be streamed throughout her body. The first round lasted three months. "It was a pretty tough regimen, the most aggressive chemotherapy we had," explains Dr. Fanta. Then came twenty-eight days of radiation, targeted directly at the tumor. Sally quizzed the radiologist: "Are you sure you got this right? Do you have the physics right?"

She got tired, with the bone-wearying fatigue from the chemical barrage on her system. Her mouth grew sensitive to cold, her legs "a little wobbly," she wrote in her notes. And she lost weight. But she didn't really get sick or lose her hair. Not yet. Sally and Tam made the best of it, taking picnic lunches to the hospital during her infusions. At home, the enormity of the adversary sometimes overwhelmed them. "We both broke down a lot," Tam recalls, a catch in her voice. "We would look at each other and say, 'Okay, how are we going to beat this?' "

The word that counts is *we*. Sally and Tam grew even closer, recognizing that cancer, like so many cataclysmic events, is more easily tolerated with a partner. What was attacking Sally's body was also breaking Tam's heart, and they took every step together. Caregiving creates a level of intimacy beyond romance. They would hardly be apart for the rest of Sally's life.

At first, they kept the bad news to themselves. "We needed time to figure things out," Tam says. "And Sally felt like she had not one ounce more energy to see people or deal with the press, who would get on it. This came first." The medical team didn't need to be warned about confidentiality. "It was—it is—a very private thing," Dr. Fanta tells me.

But they had a company to run, too, so Tam told a key member of the board, then some others, that Sally had major digestive problems. Enzymes. That's all. A few months later, Sally and Tam told the truth to Bear, who immediately came to La Jolla with Susan to help during chemo. Along with Tam's two sisters and her best friend, the only others who were told were SRS cofounders Karen Flammer and Terry McEntee. They were also let in on the secret that they'd always known, that Tam and Sally were a couple. Suddenly the house where few were ever invited became the center of all of their lives. Bear said she and Susan had never been upstairs before, in Sally and Tam's bedroom.

Curiously, the new secret wiped out the old, at least for Tam. "I became much less concerned about being gay," she says. "I was the least homophobic I had ever been my whole life. I would hold Sally's arm if she needed help out of the car, I would kiss her in front of Bear. I would sit next to her on the couch when Karen and Terry came over for [SRS] Founders' lunch each week. I could tell Sally was okay with these public affections except that she couldn't quite relax when I kissed her on the lips in front of Bear."

One afternoon, when Sally and Tam were sitting on the white leather couches in their living room drinking tea, just the two of them, they realized that they wanted to formalize their relationship. "I've been thinking," Sally said, "that it might be a good idea to become official with the state of California." Sally had taken legal steps to insure Tam's right to inheritance when she wrote her will back in 1992, but wanted to be sure about her estate. And more.

"We wanted that connection," Tam says, breaking into tears. "We just wanted to be closer together and stick together any way we could." They'd missed the five-month window for same-sex marriages in

California in 2008, but back then they didn't think they'd needed it. *We know who we are*, they'd reasoned. *We don't need a piece of paper to tell us how we feel and what we are to each other*. And they hated labels. But that was then, back when life seemed limitless. Now, in the summer of 2011, they decided to register as certified domestic partners, a California legal procedure for which you can download the application from the internet. Tam did so, then mailed it in. "We hated the term—'domestic partners,' " Tam says, "but we liked the notion that it was the closest we could get to saying that we were each other's lifelong love." The partnership became official on August 15, and the onionskin certificate arrived in the mail. To celebrate their status as "domestic hens" (their riff on the legalese), Sally went out and bought two brightly colored miniature porcelain hens (maybe one is a rooster) to perch on their shelf.

And when, at the hospital, she had to fill out forms or answer questions from the medical staff about Tam's relationship to her, she said, "We're partners," or "We're domestic partners," just like that. For the first time, Sally could openly say they were a couple.

She also quietly compiled a playlist for her iPhone with the songs that defined their attachment, the songs they had listened to and danced to over the years, *their* songs: "Harvest Moon" by Neil Young; "Light in Your Eyes" by Sheryl Crow; "This Is Us" by Mark Knopfler and Emmylou Harris; "Sometimes You Can't Make It on Your Own" by U2. Sally titled it "TEO" for Tam Elizabeth O'Shaughnessy, who would not discover it until long after Sally could no longer hear it.

SURGERY

By October, the preliminary treatments were completed, and while Sally's tumor had shrunk only slightly, there were no obvious signs that the disease had progressed. "She was somewhat beat up by the treatment," Dr. Lowy tells me. "But she was fully functional, walking a lot, and her nutrition was much better. She was certainly healthy enough to have the operation." Sally had regained some of the weight she lost to the metabolic effect of the cancer cells; she had her hair cut short. She prepared herself for the extensive and exacting surgery known as the Whipple procedure.

On October 27, 2011, Dr. Lowy, a veteran of more than three hundred such operations, removed part of Sally's pancreas, bile duct, stomach, transverse mesocolon, superior mesenteric vein and intestine, as well as her gallbladder. Then he reattached the small intestine to her pancreas, bile duct and stomach. It took six hours as the surgeon peeled back and reconstructed layer after layer of organs. There was no visible disease. That was the good news. The bad news was that the disease was more extensive than they'd believed, involving more blood vessels. "It was disappointing," Dr. Lowy says. "After all that treatment, when you still have disease, it's not good." Still, "our hope was, get her to recover, give her other therapy, and keep her in remission for a prolonged period."

Tam went into the ICU and hugged and kissed Sally. Bear came too. When Karen Flammer saw her, Sally, just recovering from the anesthesia, waved and whispered, "I had the quickest oxygen recovery!" Flammer laughs. "Of course! That's her competitiveness!"

The actual recovery was grueling: ten days in the ICU with constant titration of pain meds. When the nurses seemed confused about the ratios for her dosage, Sally helped them with the math. Going home brought a new set of challenges. Without a section of her pancreas, which provides enzymes for digestion and absorption, she needed special nutritional supplements, streamed into her body from an IV attached to a pole on wheels. Twice a day, she injected herself with blood thinner. Tam became a constant caregiver, flushing the catheter inserted into Sally's arm, then setting up infusions of the prescribed fluids; pricking Sally's finger to test for blood sugar before and after meals. She learned to keep the syringes sterile; to recognize the buildup of fluid in Sally's limbs; and drove her to the ER when something went wrong, invariably, in the middle of the night.

Sally never complained, just tried to make sense of the lethal, aggressive enemy.

"She had extraordinary coping skills," Dr. Fanta says. "And she was so disciplined. She just looked at it as a scientist and tried to understand it." Occasionally she'd ask him, "Why isn't this working?" And he'd have to say, "Don't you understand? We don't have that control."

For most of this period, Sally continued to work—by phone if necessary. In August, before the surgery, Tam accompanied her on a private jet to Houston for a meeting with executives at AT&T, where Sally was being recruited for the board. Sally was excited about the possibility and still wanted to make a difference. Her lean body had become whisper thin, down to a size 2, then 0, from her normal size 4. But the prospect of the board energized her.

DECLINE

By the end of 2011, Sally was showing more effects of both the disease and her ordeal. She was as skinny as a stick, with her salt-and-pepper hair trimmed close to her head. She got a wig. By the time she hung her favorite ornaments onto the Christmas tree—a tiny space shuttle, a moose bearing a tennis racket and the date 1989 (the year she and Tam started living together)—her surgically shrunken stomach prevented her from eating much. Sally abandoned her vegan diet for 1960s comfort food: macaroni and cheese, and Ina Garten's meatloaf. *Barefoot Contessa* on the Food Network was a daily TV ritual. When a CT scan in January showed cancer in her bones, Sally started a new round of chemotherapy. There were blood transfusions, more chemo.

And there were some good days, when Sally actually attended meetings and went out in public. In February, she and Tam traveled to San Francisco, where Sally ran a Women's Initiative meeting for Deloitte. More than one executive didn't realize that she was ill.

In April Sally flew commercially to Salt Lake City, where AT&T formally asked her to join the board. The invitation thrilled her, and she was sure she would be able to accept. In a chipper voicemail to Tam that night, she said she felt good, had eaten some ice cream and was back in her hotel room watching *Chopped* on the Food Network. "See you tomorrow. Bye!" she said merrily into the phone. It was her first venture on her own in more than a year. She weighed one hundred pounds. Lynn Martin, who'd first suggested Sally to the AT&T board, thought she looked anorexic.

Sally's random bursts of energy, combined with her perennial upbeat outlook, likely convinced her that she would make it, that she could be one of the few to beat the odds. It certainly kept her illness off the public radar. I was among the many unaware of her situation. So in April 2012, when I learned I'd be in La Jolla to promote a new book, I emailed her to make a date (and teasingly invited her to come see *my* slides). Sally responded quickly, setting up a time for us to meet for drinks. I was looking forward to a reunion, and so, apparently was she. But that afternoon, as I arrived in town, I got the following email:

> Yikes—woke up this am with a bad case of stomach flu . . . just managed to crawl to the computer. Believe me, you don't want this! I'll have to cnx [cancel]—but on the bright side, it gives you more time to go over your slides. . . .

"She thought she could see you," Tam says, remembering, "and then didn't have the energy. If only we had just invited you over."

It was the last time I heard from Sally.

In mid-May she called the CEO of AT&T to tell him she could not join his board, that she had to take care of her health and was hopeful for a recovery. On May 26, she celebrated her sixty-first birthday.

On June 1, Sally was scheduled to go to Washington, DC, for a MoonKAM conference with kids and teachers, led by Maria Zuber. Instead she delivered a short, cheery statement via Skype. Her appearance startled everyone who knew her. She was just too scrawny, and the wig looked like a wig. Still, no one was told.

A few days later, she took a car service to a board meeting up the coast in El Segundo for The Aerospace Corporation. Sally had told CEO Wanda Austin that she was ailing (not with cancer) and was resigning, but Austin wouldn't hear of it, telling her to get better and do whatever she could. Someone at the meeting said she looked quite ill.

GRACE

By early July, nearly sixteen months after her diagnosis, Sally was failing fast. She had been weakened by a new round of radiation and by the accumulated assault on her once finely tuned body. "Her ability to tolerate additional therapy was just not there," Dr. Fanta says. "And that's when we brought up hospice."

Sally was at the doctor's office in a wheelchair—gaunt, her legs swollen—with Tam at her side. They looked at each other, incredulous. *Hospice?* They'd thought for sure she would get better. That's what had kept them going, as the chemicals dripped into her veins and the waves of radiation bombarded her tumor. Even curled up with pain, Sally had been an optimist. "Always positive," Dr. Fanta agrees, "in the face of such horrific stuff going on and the loss of self-esteem. Because she's losing muscle mass, and she's not used to that; she can't work out. It's just robbing a little of her day by day. And she was just, sort of, 'Can't we slow this down a little?' "

One day she couldn't make it downstairs for morning tea. Then she couldn't make it to the next room. Tam ordered a hospital bed and set it up right next to the one they'd shared in the master bedroom, so she could watch over her, and so Sally could watch the glorious sunsets. On the shuttle she'd seen sixteen sunsets every twenty-four hours, as *Challenger* traversed Earth's time zones. How many did she have left?

Tam's days revolved around keeping Sally comfortable, adjusting the angle of the bed, the position of the covers, the amount of oxygen, washing her hair, rubbing her back. The erosion of Sally's future, Tam says, never compromised her spirit: "She was still this dignified, proud Sally, still had a sense of humor, still had a sparkle in her eyes. That's how she chose to view it. That's about playing the cards you're dealt in the most positive way."

Cancer had also loosened Sally's reserve. She cried every day. "The walls broke down on her emotions," Tam says, disconsolate. "With the tears coming down, her lips would shake. And I'd sit by her and try to soothe her; I'd ask her what she was crying about and she'd say, 'I'm not sure.' I realize that she was going through a ton emotionally, but never knew how to connect it to words. She couldn't verbalize her grief. It made me sad that I couldn't help her more."

In the end, Sally did open up, with precious gifts for Tam.

"You're my rock," Tam said to her. "What am I going to do without you?"

"You're my rock, too," Sally said. "I'm not sure you really know that. You've helped me over the years as much as I've helped you."

Tam catches her breath amidst her own tears, and tells me about another "very sweet moment," in those last few weeks. "I wish I had another twenty-seven years with you," Sally said. The memory evokes a sad smile. "And that was pretty good for her to be able to say that. It wasn't five anymore. We'd moved to a new unit."

Later that day, as she and Tam clung to each other and focused on the inevitable, Tam said she wanted to hold a celebration of Sally's life—not a memorial—for family, close friends and colleagues. Sally liked the idea, and planning the event engaged both women's minds, a welcome respite from their grief. They picked the site, the speakers, the tulips and the open bar. Then Tam went downstairs to do some errands. But the more she thought about it, the more she saw the disconnect: After nearly three decades, how would she identify herself? "I didn't know who I would be publicly," she tells me. "How would I say who I was to the people at the celebration? Who was I to Sally?"

She went back upstairs to share her concerns. Sally listened and then said, "I want you to decide. Whatever you want to say, how much you want to say, is fine with me. It will be all right." A few hours later she added, "I've been thinking things over. Being open about us might be very hard on NASA and the astronaut corps. But I'm okay with that. Whatever you think is right is fine with me."

In the moment that mattered most, Sally came through.

"I thought long and hard," Tam says, numb with the responsibility, "because here we'd been protecting her as a role model to young girls and boys, and to NASA, protecting her legend, her image. And I had to decide." Tam consulted with Bear and with Karen Flammer, both of whom urged her to go for it. Another friend wasn't sure. But Tam was. "I decided that it was time to be open. I'm really proud of being with Sally for twenty-seven years and I'm not going to hide it anymore. I wasn't sure the world was ready, but it felt important to be honest. Sally's integrity was impeccable except for this, so it was time be truthful. So I did what I did and I know I had Sally's blessing on it."

Tam sat down to compose Sally's obituary, eager to frame her life—and Tam's part in it—accurately, and ready to post on the Sally Ride Science website when it was needed.

Sally never saw it. It was time to say good-bye.

At her request, Bear brought her children—Whitney (Sally's thirty-year-old nephew) and Caitlin (her twenty-four-year-old niece)—for tearful last words.

Joyce also arrived, for a mournful farewell that, though brief, nonetheless surpassed any mother-daughter encounter they'd had. They spent no more than fifteen minutes together—Sally was drained, and had to rest up for every sentence—but in the Ride family annals, they were huge. After some teasing exchanges, Sally said to Joyce, "Our Norwegian blood notwithstanding, I wanted you to know that I love you." Joyce's response was as succinct as ever: "And I, you." That was all. It was, says Bear, who was there, the first time Sally had told her mother she loved her. And Joyce nearly got there too. That's what she meant, Bear says. That's how she did it. "It was really rough on Mom," Bear says, "but she's a tough Norwegian."

• • •

With Tam, Sally held nothing back. She told her to sit down, in a chair next to her hospital bed. "I know you know I love you," Sally said, "but I want you to know how much our relationship means to me—the length of it," she smiled—"but also how much we love each other, and all the things we've done together, all the things we've accomplished." Then they embraced.

Earlier, in a conspiratorial voice, Sally had asked Dr. Fanta about the end game.

"You know," she said, "I want to talk to you about things that I can't really talk about, maybe that you can't talk about. When things come to the end, I don't want to suffer."

"Well," he replied, "we take oaths not to expedite things, but believe me, you're not going to suffer." Then, keeping it light, he added, "I thought you were going to tell me about Roswell or Area 51!"

There were no aliens but plenty of morphine. Sally did not suffer. Even as the cancer depleted her body, a smile brightened her face. At Dr. Fanta's last visit, the Beatles were playing in the background; as he left the house, Tam came running out with a signed copy of one of the books she and Sally wrote. "Sally knew my daughter's birthday was coming up," he says, wistfully. Sally also sent him a note saying, "Thanks for the love."

On Saturday, July 21, Dr. Lowy, the surgeon, came by with his nurse and found Sally feeling "very good. She seemed really at peace and content and comfortable. She had so much strength and such an incredible sense of grace about her." He chatted with her about tennis, and about space, and Sally described the moment during her launch when the solid rockets ignited. "She said it was the only time of her life that she remembered feeling that she wasn't in control of something," Dr. Lowy tells me, "and that that was the scariest thing." And then, he says, she motioned her hands towards the bed and the IV drip and her deteriorated condition, "and she said, pointing, 'kind of like this.' "

Tam realized that Sally was getting tired, so she stepped in to remind everyone of the time Sally was giving the keynote speech in an auditorium during one of the Sally Ride Science Festivals. When a little girl asked about weightlessness, Sally said, "Imagine that right now you can float, that gravity isn't holding you down. Everyone in this room would rise out of their seats and keep rising toward the ceiling. And if you wanted, you could push off someone and do somersaults all the way across the room!" It was a magical scene, reliving one of Sally's happiest moments, and one of the last to penetrate her consciousness. That night, she slipped into a coma.

On Monday, July 23, with one of the hospice nurses by Sally's side, Bear played Sally's favorite childhood TV show on her iPhone: *Crusader Rabbit*, with its jaunty theme song. Later that morning, with Sally's breathing getting labored, Tam, Bear and Susan gathered around her bed. Tam kissed her and whispered, "I love you." Bear held her hand. At 10:10 a.m., Sally drew her last breath.

OUT

The news of Sally's death from a brutal cancer startled and saddened the nation. She was still a hero, still the icon, still, at sixty-one, the daring young woman in the flying machine. But for many, the last line of her obituary—the one Tam had written for the company website, the source for every major news report—became the headline: "In addition to Tam O'Shaughnessy, her partner of twenty-seven years, Sally is survived by . . ."

The revelation that she was gay touched off a minor shock wave. From the Twitterverse to the blogs to the op-eds and the letters to the editor, reactions ranged from raised eyebrows to outright hostility; from deep pride to spiteful anger. But the seismic shift in public attitudes over the last decades turned the controversy inside out. The loudest resentment to the news about Sally came, not from bigots who were threatened by her sexual orientation (although some few spewed their venom publicly, and I have no doubt others exist), but from some in the LGBT (Lesbian-Gay-Bisexual-Transgender) community, furious that she had not signed on to promote the cause. How dare Sally not 'fess up and be a gay rights activist! What a loss! It was, according to one advocate who spoke more out of sadness than wrath, "a missed opportunity."

I can't parse this scientifically, and I haven't tallied up the words, but it is my strong sense from reading many such postings and printed articles that the very wide majority of those weighing in felt quite the opposite; that most believed it was Sally's choice to make. "How many ceilings is one human expected to crack at a time?" asked one blogger. "Not everything should be about sex," wrote another. "There really are important accomplishments that people make without needing to bring sex into the picture." Or, as a creative poster put it, "A great woman passed away—it really doesn't matter if she was straight, gay, bi, poly, or polyurethane."

Bear, who says she was forced out of her job in the ministry when she came out in 1996, defended her sister with a genetic explanation for the famous Ride privacy—"We're Norwegians"—and a loving salute: "I hope it makes it easier for kids growing up gay that they know that another one of their heroes was like them."

Some months later, when she and Joyce visited the California Science Center in Los Angeles to see the mothballed space shuttle *Endeavour*, "a couple of lesbians accosted Bear," according to Joyce, "and asked why Sally had never mentioned her sexual orientation. My response was that it probably never occurred to her that it was anybody's business."

I ask Tam if she thinks they both missed the revolution, wondering why they didn't seem to be aware of the enormous social progress that allowed many same-sex couples to enjoy their lives openly. "I think we were working so hard at Sally Ride Science that we didn't quite appreciate how much things had changed in the last five years," she says. "Didn't appreciate that it probably would have been okay to not be so worried about sponsors." Tam is grateful that gay rights advocates are out there advocating but defends Sally's and her own insistence on choosing their own battles. "We were pushing other boundaries in science and math and technology," she tells me. "So in a way that ended up fulfilling what Sally needed in terms of doing good work to provide more opportunities for more people in our country, and for girls in particular, and minorities. Sally stood up for being true to herself as an athlete, a scientist, an astronaut, and an activist for STEM equality. She chose not to stand up for gay rights. She didn't want to be defined by the lesbian/gay label just as she didn't want to be defined by a gender label. We both didn't like categories, didn't want to define ourselves by our sexuality. We wanted to be beyond labels."

The argument makes more sense when you consider the back story, described by an online supporter with a vivid sense of history: "Cut Sally Ride some slack. She made her career in a type-A, patriotic organization with strong ties to the military. Of course it was hyper-macho and homophobic. 27 years ago was 1985 and the closet was pretty damn full . . ."

That's certainly the NASA I knew, and while it's changed today, I think it is a key to Sally's secrecy. When Sally made her deathbed pronouncement to Tam—a dramatic metaphor with the added pathos of truth in this case—she underscored her loyalty to the agency that had launched her career and given her a global platform, an agency that regularly creates miracles, with a wholly deserved reputation for the superhuman. I covered it, I get it, and I agree. NASA is a hero factory with good reason. The scientists and engineers and technicians make "out-of-this-world" an everyday activity. But it is also an agency rooted in military conservatism, where alternative lifestyles were once as welcome as an invasion of the Pod People. "Other" was unacceptable. "Gay" didn't fly. Of more than 530 individuals of all nationalities who have flown in space since 1961 as of this writing, Sally is the first, and remains the only one, now known publicly to be gay.

If one proposed rule had gone through, no one else would have had the chance.

Around 1990, according to Dr. Patricia Santy, the former NASA flight surgeon, management quietly ordered a working group of physicians to list homosexuality as a psychiatrically disqualifying condition for astronauts—even though the medical group pointed out that it was not such a disorder. "The issue was, how do we make sure we don't accidentally accept any homosexuals? How do we disqualify them?" Dr. Santy tells me. "They were, really, good old boys." The ban never materialized. One of her physician colleagues at the time, considering the laws of probability, wondered aloud if management realized it was likely they had already selected homosexual individuals. Management was aghast.

Given the fear of AIDS in that era, and the hostile environment of homophobia, no one I spoke to believes that any known gay person would have been selected as an astronaut; nor, certainly, that Sally would have flown on STS-7—or any shuttle—if NASA had known, or thought, she preferred the company of women.

"Back in 1983 that probably would have been horrible," agrees Hoot Gibson, Sally's onetime beau and a five-trip shuttle veteran. "NASA is just terrified about anything controversial. I did the first Mir docking [the first US shuttle rendezvous with the Russian space station] and they were afraid we'd drink vodka with the Russians."

"It was not very acceptable back then," says Rhea Seddon, Gibson's wife and another of Sally's TFNG classmates, referring to homosexuality, not alcohol. But, she says, it was largely self-imposed. "I think Sally would have felt badly if she had embarrassed NASA, because we all wanted to do the right thing—so that other people could do it, so there wasn't any bad press about stuff that was going on." Image was everything.

"Could NASA have handled gay?" asks Kathy Sullivan, another TFNG. "I doubt it. But 'Could they have handled it?' is only one question. 'Could they even have contemplated it?' is another." Remember, no one ever asked about sex. Sullivan points out the difference in the decades by relating the comment of a friend who dismissed the fuss over

Sally's sexual orientation as irrelevant. "Oh, come on," she said, "Really? That person, that accomplishment, that's the best you can do?"

That's the big picture, and Paula Levin, Sally's faculty colleague, agrees regarding Sally's academic career. "Not UCSD," says Paula Levin. "They're indifferent to sexual orientation. But I think Sally Ride Science would have been a disaster, because she was held up as a role model, encouraging girls to be science-oriented and (as Sally always said) to reach for the stars." Brenda Wilson, the former SRS executive, agrees. "Sally made the right choice. There would have been a whole lot of mothers in the Midwest who wouldn't have let their daughters go to the festivals."

I tell Levin it makes me sorry that Sally had to face that. "Totally," she says, "but Sally was very strategic. And she made the sacrifice. So did Tam."

When I received the phone call from Terry McEntee on the afternoon Sally died, I thought only that I'd lost a friend, that the world had lost a hero. As I learned the truth and watched the debate unfold, my selfish response—Why didn't I know?—was replaced by a more general one: Why did it matter? And then, Oh, Sally, what did it cost you to keep your secret? Her silence, I thought, was less a loss to the gay community than to Sally herself and to those around her.

That Sally had missed her own coming-out party did not surprise me. Being the First American Woman in Space was both an honor and a burden; being the First (known) American Gay in Space might have robbed her of what little privacy she had left. Without Tam's yearning for honesty, Sally may not have revealed a thing. Now that truth, and she, could be put to rest.

STARDUST

Tam and Bear dressed Sally in an old Stanford tee-shirt, a worn pair of sweatpants, a pair of socks Bear had given her, and her favorite beat-up mukluk slippers. Two weeks later, her ashes were buried next to the grave of her father on the tree-shaded lawn of tiny Woodlawn Cemetery in Santa Monica, near the park where she often played tennis tournaments. The remains of her grandparents—the ones whose families came to California from Norway and England, the children of the Mennonites and the Methodists—rest there too. At Tam's request, she'll be there someday as well, sharing Sally's headstone as they shared their life.

Bear, with her usual eloquence and sweet irreverence, led the tiny gathering of family and close friends in a simple ceremony laced with humor:

> We've come here first to remember Sally—
> to remember her times of courage and unrelenting fearlessness;
> her times of humor and fun;
> to remember her as both an untamed spirit
> and a loyal partner, friend and family member;
> to remember who she was as a trailblazer and a role model,
> and who she was in her more vulnerable moments with those she held
> close. . . .
> to mourn the empty place she once filled with her wisdom and
> laughter,
> her commanding presence and her deep sighs of impatience.
> To mourn the true passing of the official Ride Glower.

One family friend reminded everyone, "Physics teaches that nothing can disappear without a trace . . . Sally will never be lost." And Susan Craig placed her with the elements: "Sally came from Stardust, and to Stardust she returns."

As they dropped rose petals on her grave, a recording of Bing Crosby played in the background, singing the song Sally learned as a child and lived as a woman: "Would you like to swing on a star?"

IMPACT

Trajectory of GRAIL spacecraft carrying MoonKAM towards Sally Ride Impact Site on lunar surface, December 17, 2012.

What do you do after you make history? Sally decided to continue to make history.

—Maria Zuber, October 2012

MOONPRINTS

Mission Control fell silent. The commands had been uploaded, the trajectory set, the final rockets burned. In a few seconds, if all went well, two robotic satellites with solar wings—they looked like flying washing machines—would crash onto the Moon, a controlled collision to avoid earlier Earthly debris and to celebrate success. With their fuel nearly spent, the twin spacecraft that had been chasing each other around the Moon for fifteen months, were done. The GRAIL scientific analyses were complete. MoonKAM had snapped its last image and the cameras were shut down. More than 240,000 miles away, at NASA's Jet Propulsion Laboratory (JPL) in Pasadena, California, several dozen folks in shirtsleeves and sweaters held their collective breath and stared at the bleeps crawling across their monitors—mechanical heartbeats dive-bombing the Moon, rising up and over a ridge, then on to their target. As they sped to the surface at a mile per second, a disembodied voice on the speaker counted down, "Impact in three . . . two . . . one . . . zero. We have lost signal."

For this mission, lack of communication was good news. Just before 2:30 p.m. Pacific time on December 17, 2012, *Ebb* and *Flow* smashed into the southern face of a mile-and-a-half-high mountain near a crater named Goldschmidt. Technicians burst into applause and congratulated themselves on their navigational triumph.

Then, the surprise announcement from principal investigator Maria Zuber: To honor the memory of the woman who'd invited kids to share the journey, MoonKAM's final resting place would be named "after our teammate Sally Ride." Zuber had alerted me to the news earlier and fancifully imagined the distant monument as Sally Ride Massif. Her own mountain! I couldn't help musing that apart from the tribute, Sally might have preferred a softer landing on the Moon. Then I caught the irony. They were naming a crash site for her, a *controlled* crash site, the perfect amalgam of her daring and reticence, and a fitting postscript to her *Far Side* humor. Alan Ladwig, visualizing the slippery touchdown, joked that they should call it the Sally Ride Skid Strip. Bear and Joyce, devoted Westerners, were pulling for Sally Ride Gulch. NASA, apparently short of poets that day, settled on the Sally Ride Impact Site, a thud of technocracy leavened only by Bear's delighted message of thanks: "It's really cool," she said, "to know that when you look up, there's this little corner of the Moon that's named after Sally. We hope kids will be inspired by that as well."

Sally's vehicular footprints are located near the Moon's North Pole, some fifteen hundred miles north northwest of the spot where Neil Armstrong became the first of our species to get lunar dust on his boots in 1969. That was the landing Sally had watched as a teenager the night before her tennis tournament, so many rocket burns before. Now the two space pioneers shared cosmic turf, as well as the world's grief. Armstrong had died just one month after Sally.

EARTHWORKS

The dents in the Moon left by the satellites and their cameras are huge—deep impressions that will likely remain forever. But Sally's impact here on Earth is more profound. A child of the Eisenhower years who was inspired by Kennedy, marched against Nixon, flew under Reagan, then advised Clinton and Obama, she captured and challenged the *zeitgeist* on the way to changing our world. Lucky in her timing, she was ready for the moment. During her sixty-one years on the planet—minus 343 hours, 47 minutes, 32 seconds in space—she joined, then helped lead, the boldest steps yet taken to explore and protect the big blue marble that is our home. As the popular image of women progressed from Doris Day to Buffy the Vampire Slayer, and the real boundaries were expanded from the secretarial pool to the ocean of space, she helped prove that The Right Stuff doesn't require the right plumbing; that girls and women can do anything they want. Sally paid a steep price for the fame that came with her adventure, but she finally learned how to use it to return the favor.

"She wanted to show that she wasn't a novelty, not a onetime flash in the pan," her friend, Senator Barbara Mikulski, tells me. "And that being the first, she wasn't going to be the only."

In addition to the approximately 200,000 middle school kids who took more than 100,000 images with MoonKAM, another 300,000 from more than fifty countries have used EarthKAM, its older sibling, for some 50,000 Nikon moments with our own planet. Many of the 600 UCSD undergraduates running Mission Control for both cameras have traded up to jobs at NASA or in related science fields. Today, the Sally Ride EarthKAM—another posthumous naming opportunity— continues to snap away, the longest running public engagement activity on the International Space Station.

By the end of the 2013–2014 school year, Sally Ride Science will have held 100 Science Festivals (attended by some 85,000 youngsters), eight TOYchallenge competitions (entered by some 40,000 students), and published eighty-two books on science and science careers for kids. Its Academies or Institutes along with other programs, will have trained nearly 20,000 teachers, impacting another million-plus students. Taken together, Sally Ride Science is projected to have directly touched the lives of more than two million youngsters in just thirteen years. Even more now, as the company, under a new CEO, expands digitally. But it's not just about numbers. For many of those eight- to twelve-year-olds, Sally's presence, and that of so many other astronauts and chemists and marine biologists that she recruited, provided the eyes-on connection that she believed helps them realize their own possibilities. It was, in her former UCSD colleague Frances Hellman's words, "one more example that it isn't about men in white lab coats."

"Sally was an 'existence proof,'" explained an astrophysicist from JPL. "She proved that it was possible to work in space physics and as a space scientist and be female at the same time . . . that you could make it all the way to the top and accomplish amazing things in these fields— and still have a pair of ovaries."

A biologist who was inspired by her as a little boy wrote, "She smiled at us, and told us that happy people were doing very smart things. She told us that *doing* smart things could make us happy."

Christian Harrison, known as Taz, was the chief technological officer at MoonKAM, a Yul Brynner lookalike with his bald head, handlebar moustache and two earrings. "She had such a commanding presence. I was intimidated at first," he says of his mild-mannered boss.

"And only after you left her presence did you realize that she was really short." It was, he says, "that ability to be bigger than you actually are."

And to live with contradictions. Craig Barrett, the former CEO of Intel and a fellow Stanford graduate, discloses a little-known fact about the famous astronaut, which Barrett discovered when Sally visited his wife, Barbara, and him at their Montana ranch. On an ATV outing one day, as they rode up a steep cliff, Sally stopped, got off her vehicle and huddled against the mountain. "I'm afraid of heights," she confessed. It never kept her down. Craig Barrett worked with Sally on a number of blue-ribbon boards dedicated to expanding the reach of science education. He asks rhetorically, "What could make a life more special?"

Barrett spoke at a national tribute to Sally at the John F. Kennedy Center for the Performing Arts in Washington, DC, a public celebration of her work in May 2013, six days before what would have been her sixty-second birthday.

She was also honored on the floor of the US Senate, in the Congressional Record and on the NASA website, where fans from around the world conveyed their sympathies:

"Condolences from Norway, land of some of her ancestors."

"I hope she will enjoy her new life in outer space."

"I wrote to Sally when I was twelve years old. She sent me a signed photo and letter. This photo has traveled with me through college dorm rooms to my first office working at JSC."

"She was one sharp cookie!"

Tom Hanks Tweeted his condolences from Hollywood ("She aimed for the stars. Let's all do the same"), and astronaut Suni Williams downlinked hers from the International Space Station (Sally "paved the way for all of us"). Svetlana Savitskaya sent her "deepest regrets" from Russia, recalling (without divulging their secret rendezvous) "our warm and sincere communication that allowed us to understand each other without a translator."

Steve Hawley, now professor of physics and astronomy at the University of Kansas, and happily married for nearly a quarter-century to communications executive Eileen Hawley, released a warm and generous statement, noting, "While she never enjoyed being a celebrity, she recognized that it gave her the opportunity to encourage children, particularly young girls, to reach their full potential." Sally, he said, "allowed many young girls across the world to believe they could achieve anything if they studied and worked hard. I think she would be pleased with that legacy."

In South Central Los Angeles, a new elementary school was named in honor of the distinguished alumna of the Los Angeles Unified School District.

In addition, NASA established an internship in her honor, and the Navy is naming a new research vessel after Sally, to ply the waters and search beneath the seas for the same scientific revelations she sought in the stars.

President Obama awarded her the Medal of Freedom, the nation's highest civilian honor, noting her work "to keep America at the forefront of space exploration" and "to inspire young people—especially girls—to become scientifically literate and to pursue careers in science, technology, engineering, and math." The citation called her story "[t]he tale of a quiet hero. . . ." And the president, speaking for all American families, said, "Today, our daughters, including Malia and Sasha, can set their sights a little bit higher because Sally Ride showed them the way."

In October 2012, there was a small, private celebration of Sally's life at the Torrey Pines Lodge in La Jolla—the event that she and Tam had talked about in the weeks before her death, and that Tam had then planned. Bear Ride, drawing on some of the scientific data her sister had shared, compared Sally to a wave. "A wave," she said, "begins with a disturbance in the universe that travels through space and time, bringing along with it a transfer of energy." Quoting from science writer K. C. Cole, Bear continued, "A wave spreads its influence, carrying energy and information away from the original source. . . . For example, when a star bursts in space it sends out ripples into the universe that'll eventually lap up onto the shores of Earth. [A] wave keeps right on going, long after whatever started it has gone by it. Sally was that wave."

In Houston, at the Johnson Space Center, a tree in Sally's honor was planted in the Astronaut Memorial Grove for all fallen astronauts. The live oak bearing a plaque with her name grows between those for Mike Lounge, with whom she'd shared the Grumman Tiger, and Pete Conrad, who had walked on the Moon while Sally joined the moratorium against the Vietnam War during her Swarthmore days. After a brief ceremony attended by her crewmates, some other TFNG friends, and a number of former and present NASA folks, I joined the line to drop a long-stemmed rose atop the freshly dug soil.

How the landscape had changed since the day she saw that article in the *Stanford Daily*. When Sally joined NASA in 1978, her class of six women represented just under 10 percent of the astronaut corps; by June 18, 2013, when NASA announced a new class of eight (including four women), female astronauts in training or assigned to technical duties, plus the new astronaut candidates, represented 28 percent of the corps. Women have lived in space (Shannon Lucid, Sally's TFNG classmate, once held the duration record after 188 days on the Russian space station). And they have died there. In all, 57 women from nine countries have flown in space. Many of the forty-five American female astronauts' careers were either motivated or facilitated by Sally's.

"It never occurred to me to be an astronaut until I saw Sally giving a speech at MIT," says Catherine (Cady) Coleman, who got her BS in chemistry the year Sally first flew. "I'd seen a lot of astronauts on TV, in pictures; none of them looked like me," she explains. "Then I meet Sally Ride and I think, maybe that could be me." Coleman has flown twice in the shuttle and spent more than five months on the International Space Station.

Coleman was one of nearly two dozen female astronauts in Houston during the memorial ceremony for Sally, the first time so many, from so many different classes, had gathered together.

Ellen Ochoa was a graduate student in electrical engineering at Stanford (with a BS in physics) when Sally first flew. "I'd started thinking about being an astronaut," she tells me, "and seeing another woman, who had a physics degree like I did, made me think I wasn't completely crazy to apply." Ochoa became the first Hispanic woman in the world to fly in space, and ultimately completed four shuttle missions. She is currently director of the Johnson Space Center.

See one, be one, as Billie Jean King puts it.

"My parents took me to see *The Right Stuff*, Sally flew in space, and Kathryn Sullivan would do a spacewalk," says Dottie Metcalf-Lindenburger, who became an astronaut in 2004 and flew on one shuttle mission. "I was in third or fourth grade, and it really changed what I thought was possible for me."

"I was in elementary school when I first heard her name," says astronaut Tracy Caldwell Dyson, who has flown on the shuttle, on the International Space Station and done three spacewalks. "And [I] grew up knowing that women could accomplish just about anything that they set their mind to."

Most of the newer astronauts never knew Sally personally, but many sought her out. Kate Rubins was born in 1978, the year Sally and her five female classmates went to NASA. It was the first year a girl could think about space without being regarded as if she'd just landed from Pluto, which, then, was still a planet. In fact, being an astronaut, Rubins says, "was the very first thing I can ever remember saying was what I wanted to do." As a student at Stanford when Sally was on the faculty, Rubins snuck in to audit her Physics 6 class. "My friends were crashing fraternity parties," she tells me laughing, "and I was crashing Sally Ride's physics lectures!" Rubins is awaiting assignment for her first flight to the International Space Station.

Sally's contribution to their careers may have been best articulated by three-time shuttle veteran Pamela Melroy, one of only two women to have commanded a shuttle flight.

"It wasn't until after I became an astronaut that I discovered the most important gift that Sally gave me, which is that she was tremendously competent," she says. Being first, she told the crowd at the Kennedy Center tribute, requires extraordinary performance. "The reputation of everyone who comes after you depends on how well you do. Sally opened those doors and smoothed the path for all women because she was very good at what she did."

So good, that her legacy upended convention. Cady Coleman tells me about the day she took her four-year-old son, Jamey, to a reception at the Johnson Space Center. When they came upon a life-size cutout of an astronaut in a spacesuit, helmet on and visor down, Jamey asked, "Mommy, is that you?" Coleman told him no. "Well, if it's not you," Jamey said, "then whose mommy is it?"

It is a tribute to all the first women, not just Sally, that the question gets asked; it is a mark of society's ability to adapt that the story gets an approving laugh. But it is a reminder of the never-changing times and an echo of Sally's first flight, when every woman's voice from a T-38 was assumed to be hers, that when she died, more than one TV news organization illustrated her life with footage of a female astronaut (presumably, Sally) tumbling around in the KC-135, practicing weightlessness. The aerobat was Anna Fisher.

Fisher, now sixty-five, is the only one of the original six still working at JSC (although not as an active astronaut), and I remind her about a comment she made when I interviewed her after the 1986 *Challenger* explosion and asked her thoughts about the death of Judy Resnik. "I'm really going to miss Judy," she'd told me then. "I'm going to miss getting to have a reunion when we're all eighty years old." Still true, she says, lowering her eyes.

But while the six are now down to four, their spirit is as vital as the drive that got them there in the first place. Rhea Seddon, still blonde and still in the health care business, although no longer a practicing physician at sixty-five, is back in Tennessee. After three successful missions she tells me with gusto, "I love that my AARP card is sitting in my wallet next to my Victoria's Secret card!"

LOST IN SPACE

In many ways, the arc of the shuttle paralleled that of Sally's own professional life. She became known as the program began, and her flights soared as shuttlemania enveloped America. When the program shut down after the loss of *Challenger*, she left. And as the shuttle rose again (then fell, then returned successfully), she was there for the investigations, there as NASA's conscience, always on call. And just as the shuttle always returned to Earth, so did Sally, directing her attention to this planet first. As often as she could, she helped reinvent NASA, putting cameras on its spacecraft and turning kids into virtual astronauts so that they could join in the fun. The last shuttle flight, STS-135, landed on July 21, 2011, just as Sally entered the last year of her own life. Like her, it sent out invaluable ripples from its own wave—not only the Hubble Space Telescope with its matchless lens on the universe, and the International Space Station, for which it delivered modules, but a world of intangibles.

"It taught the American space industry an awful lot of engineering lessons that I believe in the long run will pay dividends," Kathy Sullivan, now acting administrator of the National Oceanographic and Atmospheric Administration, tells me. "We may sneer at all the 'foolish jingoism' of Apollo and that silly competition, but look at Canada, Europe, China, Japan, India, Russia. They rightfully seek to be space-faring nations, bringing a cascade of benefits. Not the least of which is the confidence and pride and appetite for a bold future that it instills in all people. And that is not a small thing."

All that in a machine that was far less sophisticated, by several orders of magnitude, than the smartphone you slip into your pocket; a machine that lasted thirty years.

Today the shuttle fleet has been dispersed to various museums around the country, relics of a different time. *Enterprise*, the prototype that Sally saw practicing test landings back in 1977, before she was chosen to be an astronaut, stopped traffic as it rode a barge up the Hudson River to New York's Intrepid Sea, Air and Space Museum. *Discovery* went to the Steven F. Udvar-Hazy Center in Chantilly, Virginia, *Atlantis* to the Kennedy Space Center in Florida, and *Endeavour*, the fifth and final orbiter built, to Los Angeles. By chance, on the day after Sally's tree-planting while I was at the Johnson Space Center, *Endeavour* made its last pass overhead, a bright white spaceplane bolted to the top of a 747. As hundreds of employees drifted out of their numbered buildings in the morning sun, the pilot circled wide and low, so that all could get a long last look at the vehicle riding piggyback. I saw tears, I saw salutes, I saw the wistful acceptance of decisions made elsewhere. *Hail, Shuttle, and farewell.* One longtime engineer, despondent that *Endeavour* was being flown to retirement in California, not back to Florida for a new launch, told me, "You don't like to see it going West."

Many believe NASA's human spaceflight program has lost its direction on a wider scale, that the grit and guts that got us to the Moon have been dissolved by niggling bureaucracy. That Congress and the White House have abandoned a critical priority. "The amazing thing was, we accomplished it in eight years," said moonwalker Charlie Duke at an event celebrating the last human lunar landing forty years earlier. "Today you wouldn't even be able to write a proposal in eight years!" Apollo 7 veteran Walt Cunningham added, "We have converted ourselves to a risk-aversive society." Gene Cernan calls theirs "the golden age of space," and predicts humans will return to the Moon because "curiosity is the essence of human existence." No doubt, but in a very different way. Soon, women and men with considerably fewer scientific or aeronautic credentials than the pioneers of Mercury, Gemini and Apollo, or than Sally and her TFNG classmates, will pay commercial operators to fly them to the edge of space—tourists who are less fit but perhaps no less driven. Private industry will also help transport our next generations of astronauts, wherever they venture.

NASA had already changed by the time Sally flew, and it continued to evolve as she tried to help set a new course. Or courses. But she never gave up on the inspired minds that gave her the reverberating gift of knowledge. It's what she told audiences in all those speeches across the country, where she inspired them to reach, as she had, for the stars, and beyond.

She did it again on February 7, 2011. Frances Hellman, professor of physics at the University of California, Berkeley, had invited her to deliver the annual Regents Lecture, a prestigious Berkeley tradition. The auditorium was packed with university officials, students, members of the public and an unprecedented number of girls and young women. Sally, psyching herself for the moment, went over her notes ahead of time in the ladies' room, propping her laptop on the sink to review the slides she had shown so many times before.

When Hellman introduced her, Sally bounded to the podium, her short brown hair gleaming, red jacket skimming her slim body over black pants. She delivered the speech with certainty, smoothly matching her comments to the images from the space shuttle, seamlessly pausing for the laughter, the applause, the gasps of wonder that she knew to expect. Her opening always set the tone:

> When astronaut Jim Lovell of Apollo 13 fame was circling the Moon, he looked back at Earth and called our planet "a grand oasis in the great vastness of space." That's extremely unusual eloquence for an astronaut. You're not going to hear any more of that today [Laughter].

Sally moved on to the story of her selection as an astronaut, the drama of launch (where you "go from a standing start to 17,500 miles an hour in eight and a half really fast minutes"), the joy of weightlessness. And with the help of photographs that had every tongue in the hall hanging out, she pointed out the entire north-south protrusion of Florida in one frame, the gradations of turquoise in its surrounding ocean, the "orange smudge" of Philadelphia's lights at night, the royal blue line of the horizon, "where Earth ends and Space begins." Then, after more travel snaps, she transitioned to the message that had shaped her post-NASA career. "Carl Sagan once said, 'It's suicidal to create a society that depends on science and technology in which no one knows anything about science and technology.' And of course he's right." She cited the grim statistics about the current state of education: US students way below their peers overseas in math and science; high school and college graduation rates depressingly down. Middle school kids being taught physical sciences by teachers with no credentials. "Maybe it's not surprising that we've got a problem with science education."

Then she made her pitch:

Our global competitiveness depends on the next generation of scientists and engineers. So it's really important that we inspire the next generation of rocket scientists and environmental engineers. It's also critical to prepare the core of the future skilled work force. That's because in the next decade or so, fully 80 percent of the jobs in this country—and that includes just basic living wage jobs—are going to require some background in science, math or technology. So it's really becoming an equity issue. If the kids in school today don't get a good education in math and science, they're not going to be competitive even for basic living wage jobs when they graduate.

That, she explained, was why she had cofounded Sally Ride Science: to keep girls from losing focus in middle school; to change the image of the Einstein lookalike to someone more like them; to teach kids that scientists don't work alone in basements, but in groups. "Scientists don't memorize the periodic table," she pointed out. "They solve problems, they ask questions, they try to get at the answers, and they devise experiments to try to teach them things. Often they get results that they don't expect, and they learn more when they get an answer that they did expect."

She ended with her trademark plea:

"We need to make science cool again."

OUT AND ABOUT

In May 2013, when Sally would have turned sixty-two, the LGBT employee group at the Johnson Space Center, called Out and Allied, released a nine-minute video called *It Gets Better*, in which gay and straight colleagues (including JSC director Ellen Ochoa) celebrate diversity. The project, part of a national outreach to high school– and college-aged individuals, was in the works long before Sally's posthumous coming out, but Out and Allied chairman Steve Riley thinks her news helped their cause. "I think we've made tremendous strides," he says, understating the transformation. He believes it's only a matter of time before an openly gay astronaut will be at NASA.

Tam O'Shaughnessy is astounded and energized by the outpouring of support that resulted from her brief public confession. "I would give anything for Sally to know what I know," she says, "the respect, the love for her, and for us. Dammit, the world changed, and I wish she could know what it feels like." Tam is especially gratified by the more than two hundred condolence letters she received from public figures such as Bill Clinton and Al Gore, from lifelong tennis pals, from business associates, whose acknowledgment of their relationship marks another step of social acceptance. Senator Barbara Mikulski wrote of "the recent death of your dear partner . . . Sally could have used her fame in many ways, but she chose to use it to teach and inspire girls to study science. I know you played a big role in that." Rick Hauck, the pilot on Sally's history-making flight, said he hoped "that the memories of your shared life's work and love will keep you smiling."

At the Washington, DC, tribute (which Tam conceived and guided, and for which she raised the lion's share of the funding), she stood before some two thousand people in the audience when she was announced as Sally's life partner. Such a public acknowledgment would have been unthinkable a year earlier. "I am now the most relaxed inside than I've ever been," she tells me. "I can breathe better; I can look people straight in the eye without blinking; I am free because I don't have a secret anymore and because I no longer have to lie, which goes against my nature and beliefs. I owe that to Sally," she adds, thanking the woman who, in death, gave her permission to be herself in life.

Tam has also found a new closeness with Joyce, who knows the unbearable grief of burying a daughter. "I guess had I known that Sally was going to leave prematurely, I'd have spent more time with her," Joyce wrote to Tam. "I still howl occasionally, and shed a tear. Guess I did know for a year or so, but was in denial. You're a fine substitute, and I mean that in the nicest sense." She signed it, "Love from jr."

Joyce is still petitioning to get women out of prison. She tells me, "I think the gay thing is very secondary to who Sally was."

Bear says, "hugs are more common now" in the Ride family. And they have a new generation to practice on: In April 2013, Rowan Scott was born to Bear's son, Whit, and his wife, Claire. Rowan is Sally's first great-nephew. His dad was a toddler when he watched Aunt Sally's launch at the Cape; at her tree planting ceremony in Houston, Whit shot the video tribute from the other women of NASA.

ASTRONAUT

As for me, I'm still composing questions that I'll never get to ask, fully aware that the answers remain elusive. The dots don't all connect in Sally Ride's life. Still, in the course of writing this book I rediscovered my friend: at one level, the same funny, playful, smart, focused physicist-with-the-touch-of-a-poet I'd known for years. At another, the intensely private woman with the odd but loving childhood who had missed out on, or purposely avoided, sharing her feelings about so many things. I am sorry that I didn't—still don't—know exactly what she thought she had to protect. I ache that her efforts to make social change through science couldn't always ease her own way. And that our society often makes it so difficult for people to be who they are. But the enduring love of family and close friends is a testament to her full and happy life.

In so many ways, her integrity is intact, as constant as the principles that guided her. The teamwork she learned on the tennis court took her to orbit and helped create a company; her commitment to science— what *is*, not what we *want* things to be—informed both her research and her NASA investigations, as well as her steadfast aversion to hogwash; her decision not to dwell on the past—to move on when things don't work out—likely saved her a fortune in further psychotherapy bills. And her ability to recognize and grab hold of "your basic once-in-a-lifetime opportunity" made her own lifetime a legend. Sally didn't invent the occasion of her celebrity, but she rose to meet it with uncommon dignity and passion, elevating her achievement to the impetus for a national agenda. She taught us that our home planet is as exotic as any distant point in the cosmos, that you can fly high without ever leaving Earth.

In 1987, in her first assessment of the future of NASA—that bold assignment for a thirty-five-year-old—Sally concluded the proposal for a lunar base this way: "This initiative," she wrote, "would push back frontiers, not to achieve a blaze of glory, but to explore, to understand, to learn, and to develop . . ." Sally achieved her blaze of glory but never burned out. She moved on—to explore the possibilities, to understand the problems, to learn the best solutions and to develop the means to motivate new generations. Unwilling to be trapped in the symbolism of her feminist breakthrough, she invited everyone else to come along for the journey, to make our world livelier, more accessible, more exciting; to make its future more promising. Who was Sally Ride? A California girl who wanted to save the planet. An introvert whose radiant spirit pulled her into public service. An academic who could explain raindrops to college students and the wonders of weightlessness to a room full of little girls. Her optimism is also her legacy. She translated the dazzling reality that she saw from space into a beam of encouragement for the rest of us on Earth: "The stars don't look bigger, but they do look brighter."

Just before she got ill, Sally was asked if she wanted to fly in space again, the way John Glenn, at seventy-seven, had traveled on the shuttle's ninety-fifth mission in 1998, making the astronaut and former senator the oldest human to go into orbit. "If they can fly an old man, they can fly an old woman," Sally said, with a sly smile. At the time, she was fifty-nine. A few years earlier she had told me, "Yeah, I would go up in a second. But would I train for a year? No!" Sally was still setting her own rules. "I'd like to live my life and then give NASA a call."

Flying in space was neither her childhood goal nor her adult commitment. But having done it twice, she cherished the adventure. Her life reminds us that whatever our own personal limits, there's something out there grander than we can measure, more marvelous than we can imagine; something just waiting to be explored.

She felt the lure again on October 7, 2009, Astronomy Night at the White House, a star-gazing party for local youngsters attended by the entire Obama family on the South Lawn. More than a quarter century after she'd shot into space, Sally gamely donned her flight jacket and warmly answered questions from kids. One pressed the right button.

"What is your favorite planet?"

"Mars. It's the planet I can imagine visiting one day, standing on, driving a rover around the surface, exploring its canyons, exploring its volcanoes, and then, most important, looking for evidence of past or current life. If there is life on a location other than Earth, Mars is a good candidate."

She'd made the same exotic promise—or was it a challenge?—to youngsters across America over the years, passing the baton and leaning forward with a smile when she often said, "You and I will both see people set foot on Mars. The people in this room are just the right age to be the first to land. Who knows? It might be one of you. And that will be cool. That'll be very cool."

Once, she paused to dream. "Wish it would've been me."

So do I.

ACKNOWLEDGMENTS

I first want to thank Tam O'Shaughnessy for wisely recognizing the need for this book and for sharing, without reservation, her memories about her life with Sally. Tam allowed me to roam freely through Sally's personal and professional papers and *objets*, and she encouraged friends and colleagues to speak candidly about their own reminiscences. Talking about oneself and one's love is never easy; doing it while mourning is unthinkable. Tam never hesitated to help, with essential and thoughtful details about so many moments to which only she was a witness. That is equally true for the entire family. I am very grateful to Bear Ride, whose childhood recollections, good humor and sensible counsel (along with stacks of youthful correspondence) provided invaluable insights about her big sister. Joyce Ride tolerated endless questions (to which she shares the same allergy as Sally) with the wit she bequeathed to both of her daughters. As the only member of the Ride family without a doctorate, Joyce remains, as Bear and Sally used to joke, the wisest of them all.

Thanks also to Sally's old friends and loves, especially John Tompkins, Molly Tyson, Bill Colson and Steve Hawley, for frankness and sensitivity. Susan Okie was exceptionally generous with early memories and journalistic notes. Janet Mennie Schroeder provided vital letters. Billie Jean King took time from her very busy life to share key recollections. Kay Loveland lent her expertise as a psychologist and as a confidant during Tam and Sally's relationship.

At NASA, I am grateful for the openness of so many of Sally's friends and onetime colleagues. Special thanks for enduring repeated interrogations to Bob Crippen, Rick Hauck, George Abbey, Carolyn Huntoon, Rhea Seddon, Anna Fisher, Kathryn Sullivan, Duane Ross, Ellen Baker and Marsha Ivins. And again, to Steve Hawley. Alan Ladwig's long and unique relationship with Sally was matched only by his candor and enthusiasm in retelling the stories. Jennifer Ross-Nazzal at NASA's JSC Oral History Project helped guide me through a precious set of records. Thanks to Joe Allen for the connection. My old friends Dick Truly and Gene Cernan were also more than accommodating. In addition: Jody Russell from the JSC Media Resource Center for patiently and consistently digging up images; Margaret Weitekamp and Valerie Neal at the Smithsonian National Air and Space Museum for a personal tour and historical perspective; and Air Force General (Ret.) Don Kutyna for Sally's role during the Rogers Commission.

Sally's colleagues from Sally Ride Science have provided critical insights into her commitment to the next generation. In particular: SRS co-founders Karen Flammer (whose parsing of Sally's physics notes and lectures also helped me understand what I managed to avoid in college) and Terry McEntee, a sane and solid presence who knew her boss-turned-friend like no other. Maria Zuber walked me through her close collaboration with Sally during MoonKAM and other projects.

From her high school classmates to her physics students to her oncologists, everyone I interviewed contributed pieces to complete the picture of Sally's life. Institutional help came from the UCSD Alumni Office (Raymond Hardie), Swarthmore College Communications Office (Celina De Leon), Stanford University News Service (Regina Kammer).

Esther Newberg is the very best kind of literary agent and friend: she is, simply, always there. At Simon & Schuster, I am privileged to have worked with Alice Mayhew, whose sense of history immediately led her to grasp the importance of getting Sally's life between covers. Thanks to the entire team from Jonathan Karp to Jonathan Cox, Jackie Seow, Joy O'Meara, Eric Rayman and Julia Prosser.

The usual set of pals put me up and/or put up with me during the writing and kept the secrets, notably: Ellen Goodman, Michele Lee, Susan and Andy Hilford, Lois Dubin, Nola Safro.

Finally, posthumous thanks to my friend Sally Ride, whose can-do spirit and nonstop feminism took us along with her in June 1983, making our own impossible dreams seem more likely. She, and we, deserved more time.

Sources

INTERVIEWS (CONDUCTED JULY 2012–AUGUST 2013)

George Abbey, Barbara Adachi, David Anton, Norman Augustine, Wanda Austin, Susie Bachtel, Mike Baine, Ellen Baker, Barbara Barrett, Craig Barrett, Lindsay Beaven, Cathy Benko, Dori Berinstein, Guy Bluford, David Borhman, Diane Bowen, Andrew Bridges, Ed Buckbee, Adam Burgasser, Rain Burns, Dixon Butler, Michael Cassutt, Andrew Chaikin, Mary Cleave, Chelsea Clinton, Michael Coats, Kenneth Cohen, Cady Coleman, Eileen Collins, Bill Colson, Craig Covault, Ed Crawley, Bob Crippen, Sherri Davis, Alphonso Diaz, Angela Phillips Diaz, Toni DiMartino-Stebich, Sid Drell, Tracy Caldwell Dyson, Judith Estrin, John Fabian, Paul Fanta, Anna Fisher, Karen Flammer, Francis French, Robert Frosch, Lori Garver, James Garvin, Harold W. Gehman Jr., Jack Gibbons, Robert "Hoot" Gibson, Don Gips, Tamas Gombosi, Al Gore, Ann Gould, Dick Gould, Jan Graham, Whitney Grant, Gerry Griffin, Todd Halvorson, Fred Hargadon, Deborah Schneider Harrington, Hugh Harris, Myra Hart, Rick Hauck, Steve Hawley, Frances Hellman, Dave Hilmers, John Holdren, Harry Holloway, Paul Hoversten, Scott Hubbard, Frank Hughes, Carolyn Huntoon, Marsha Ivins, Harriett Jenkins, Jim Jensen, Dana Kadison, Billie Jean King, Jim Kohlenberger, Don Kutyna, Alan Ladwig, Wendy Lawrence, Shelly Lazarus, Ann Lebedeff, David Leestma, Paula Levin, George Lewis, John Logsdon, Alann Lopes, Alan Lovelace, Kay Loveland, Jim Lovell, Andrew Lowy, Allan McDonald, Maleah Grover McKay, Shirley Malcom, Lauren Martin, Lynn Martin, Jon McBride, Dan McCleese, Terry McEntee, Lucy McFadden, Pamela Melroy, James Middleton, Barbara Mikulski, Debbie Millman, Don Mizell, Quentin Mommaerts, Brian Muirhead, Valerie Neal, George "Pinky" Nelson, Grenn Nemhauser, Nichelle Nichols, John Niehoff, Teri Niehoff, Rick Nygren, Bryan O'Connor, James Oberg, Miles O'Brien, Ellen Ochoa, Susan Okie, Marilyn Ortiz, Tam O'Shaughnessy, Carolyn Porco, William Powers, Lisa Reed, Condoleezza Rice, Joanna Rice, Bear Ride, Joyce Ride, Steve Riley, Bob Rose, Duane Ross, Jennifer Ross-Nazal, Kate Rubins, Emily Sachar, Genesis Santos, Patricia Santy, Janet Mennie Schroeder, Whit Scott, Rhea Seddon, Asif Siddiqi, Richard Somerville, Gloria Steinem, Nicolle Stott, Kathryn Sullivan, Jane Swift, Richard Teets,

Norman Thagard, John Tompkins, John Townsend, Richard Truly, Molly Tyson, Diane Vaughan, Jesco von Puttkamer, Edina Weinstein, Brenda Wilson, Stephanie Wilson, Maria Zuber.

SELECTED BIBLIOGRAPHY
Most of the print, video, audio and electronic sources I accessed are cited in the Notes, by chapter. Those listed here were consulted more often.

BOOKS AND PUBLISHED REPORTS

Allen, Joseph P. *Entering Space: An Astronaut's Odyssey*. New York: Stewart, Tabori & Chang, 1984.

Atkinson, Joseph D. Jr., and Jay M. Shafritz. *The Real Stuff: A History of NASA's Astronaut Recruitment Program*. Foreword by Alan B. Shepard and Guion S. Bluford Jr. New York: Praeger Publishers (Praeger Scientific Studies/Praeger Scientific), 1985.

Cernan, Eugene, with Don Davis. *The Last Man on the Moon: Astronaut Eugene Cernan and America's Race in Space*. New York: St. Martin's Griffin, 2000.

Cooper, Henry S. F. Jr., *Before Lift-off: The Making of a Space Shuttle Crew*. Baltimore and London: Johns Hopkins University Press, 1987.

Foster, Amy E. *Integrating Women into the Astronaut Corps: Politics and Logistics at NASA, 1972–2004*. Baltimore: Johns Hopkins University Press, 2011.

Hansen, James R. *First Man: The Life of Neil A. Armstrong*. New York: Simon & Schuster, 2005.

Henley, John A., editor. Contributors: William David Lindsay Ride, Annabel Anderson, Maureen McMahon Clinton. *The Ride Connexion*. Melbourne: Javelin Books Pty Limited, 2008.

Kevles, Bettyann Holtzmann. *Almost Heaven: The Story of Women in Space*. Cambridge, Mass., London, England: MIT Press. 2006.

McDougall, Walter A. *The Heavens and the Earth*. New York: Basic Books, 1985.

Mullane, Mike. *Riding Rockets: The Outrageous Tales of a Space Shuttle Astronaut*. New York: Scribner, 2006.

Ride, Sally K. *Leadership and America's Future in Space: A Report to the Administrator* ("The Ride Report"). Published by NASA, August 1987.

Ride, Sally, with Susan Okie. *To Space & Back*. New York: Lothrop, Lee & Shepard Books, 1986.

Ride, Sally, and Tam O'Shaughnessy. *Exploring Our Solar System*. New York: Crown Publishers, 2003.

———. *Mission Planet Earth*. New York: Flash Point, Roaring Book Press, 2009.

———. *Mission Save the Planet*. New York: Flash Point, Roaring Book Press, 2009.

———. *The Mystery of Mars*. New York: Crown Publishers, 2009.

———. *The Third Planet: Exploring the Earth from Space*. New York: Crown Publishers, 1994.

———. *Voyager: An Adventure to the Edge of the Solar System*. New York: Crown Publishers,1992.

Rossiter, Margaret. *Women Scientists in America: Before Affirmative Action, 1940–1972*. Baltimore: Johns Hopkins University Press, 1995.

Santy, Patricia. *Choosing the Right Stuff: The Psychological Selection of Astronauts and Cosmonauts*. Westport, Conn., London: Praeger, 1994.

Seeking a Human Spaceflight Program Worthy of a Great Nation. Review of U.S. Human Spaceflight Plans Committee (Augustine Committee), Washington, DC, 2009.

Weitekamp, Margaret A. *Right Stuff, Wrong Sex: America's First Women in Space Program*. Baltimore & London: Johns Hopkins University Press, 2004.

MAGAZINE AND NEWSPAPER ARTICLES:

D.R., "Sally Ride: Astronaut and Now Author." *Publishers Weekly*. November 28, 1986.

Halvorson, Todd. "America's First Female Astronaut Speaks." *Florida Today*, June 17, 2008.

Laytner, Ron, and Donald McLachlan. "Ride, Sally Ride: Her Place Is in Space." *Chicago Tribune*, April 24, 1983.

Lewis, George N., Sally K. Ride, and John S. Townsend. "Dispelling Myths About Verification of Sea-Launched Cruise Missiles." *Science* 246 (November 10, 1989).

Okie, Susan. "At Home, Space Art and Trivia Tests." *Washington Post*, May 9, 1983.

———. "Cool Hand Sally Shows NASA Right Stuff." *Washington Post*, May 10, 1985.

———. "Fame Finds Astronaut Determined to Ignore It." *Washington Post*, May 8, 1983.

———. "Friend Charts Her Path to Space," *Washington Post*, May 8, 1983.

———. "Historic Ride: NASA's Ad Gave Physicist Wings." *Washington Post*, May 9, 1983.

———. "Simulated Flights Prepare Crew for the Real Thing." *Washington Post*. May 11, 1983.

Ride, Sally. "Flying Through a Neon Tube," *Los Angeles Times*. February 4, 2003.

———. "Single Room, Earth View." *Air & Space Magazine*. April/May 1986, 14–16. Reprinted July 2012.

———. "The Ninth Amendment: Where No American Woman Has Gone Before." In *American Perspectives: Ten Unique Pieces Offering Personal Insights into the Bill of Rights*. Undated publication (probably 2000) from now-defunct website Mightywords.com, Mighty Words (Hereafter, Ninth Amendment).

Sanborn, Sara. "Sally Ride: The Making of an Astronaut." *Ms.* January 1983.

Sherr, Lynn. "A Commanding Position." *Ms.* July/August 1998.

———. "A Mission to Planet Earth." *Ms.* July/August 1987.

———. "Remembering Judy." *Ms.* June 1986.

Temkin, Steven Allan. "The Father of Sally Ride, America's First Woman Astronaut, Talks About His Daughter." *Los Angeles Times* Syndicate, 1983.

Tyson, Molly, unpublished notes.

Tyson, Molly, "Women in Outer Space." *womenSports*, February 1978.

Williams, Janis. "Make Way for the Ladies in Space." *Saturday Evening Post*. September 1982, 42.

VIDEOS, SPEECHES, BROADCAST/CABLE
SEGMENTS, ONLINE ARTICLES AND POSTS

"A Moment in Time: Conversations with Legendary Women," with Gloria Steinem; DVD, disc 3, interview with SKR conducted in August 1983 (Steinem).

"Futures of Women in Science," SKR interview with Dr. Sue Ritter. Washington State University, Washington State University, 1980 (WSU).

"Intimate Portrait: Sally Ride," Lifetime, August 23, 1999 (Lifetime).

Johnson Space Center Oral History Project: series of interviews with various astronauts accessed at http://www.jsc.nasa.gov/history/oral_histories/oral_histories.htm. Identified in Notes by name of astronaut (Oral History).

"Sally Ride Interview," Academy of Achievement, June 2, 2006.

"Sally Ride on Greater Boston," Interview by Emily Rooney conducted at WGBH 2002, September, 2002.

"Sally Ride: 25 Years Later," NASA JPL video, California Institute of Technology, July 22, 2008 (JPL 2008).

Sally Ride: "Reach for the Stars." Regents Lecture, University of California, Berkeley. February 7, 2011 (UC-Berkeley).

SKR Film Interview by NASA, May 1983.

SKR Interview by PBS/*Nova*, 1984.

SKR lecture at University of Kansas, 1978 (KU).

Sherr, Lynn. Various filmed or taped interviews with SKR for ABC News from January 1981 through January 2008.

Texas Monthly Talks. KLRU-TV, June 16, 2010.

NOTES

INTRODUCTION

Interviews with Tam O'Shaughnessy, Bear Ride, Joyce Ride, Marilyn Ortiz, Genesis Santos, Maria Zuber, K. C. Cole, Susan Okie, Mike Baine, Valerie Neal, Leesa Hubbard. Fifth grade class at Reverend Dr. Ercel Webb Elementary School (PS 22), Jersey City, New Jersey; author interview with SKR for ABC News aired in several different formats, May–June 1983; some ABC video courtesy Eric Strauss; some of my reminiscences of Sally have appeared in slightly different form in my memoir, *Outside the Box* (Rodale, 2006) and in "Lynn Sherr: Sally Ride's Historic and Trailblazing Life as an Astronaut," posted on *The Daily Beast*, July 24, 2012; Linda Voss, "With Sally Ride," *Aerospace America*, August 2003; D.R., "Sally Ride: Astronaut and Now Author," *Publishers Weekly*, November 28, 1986; Steven Allan Temkin, "The Father of Sally Ride, America's First Woman Astronaut, Talks About His Daughter," *Los Angeles Times* Syndicate, 1983; STS-7 Pre-flight press conference, May 24, 1983; Mary Delach Leonard, "Ride, Sally Ride; Questions from Kids, Aspiring Astronauts Continue to Inspire the First American Woman in Space," *St. Louis Post-Dispatch*, April 28, 2003; "Sally Saves the Alphabet" storyboard, courtesy Tam O'Shaughnessy; David Lim, "Remembering Sally Ride," *The Harvard Westlake Chronicle*, September 5, 2012,

CHAPTER 1: CALIFORNIA GIRL

Roots: Interviews with Carolyn Huntoon, Joyce Ride, Bear Ride. H. H. Arnold-Bemrose, *Derbyshire* (Cambridge: Cambridge University Press, 1910); Henley, 17–30, 227–235; Joyce Ride's family background courtesy Mary Olson and Bear Ride; Dale Ride family scrapbooks courtesy Bear Ride.

Childhood: Interviews with Bear Ride, Joyce Ride. Steinem; Okie, "Friend Charts . . ."; Joyce Ride email to Tam O'Shaughnessy, August 31, 2012; Janet Wiscombe, "Private Property: Ask Sally Ride About Her Research. Or her Program to Revolutionize Science Education in America. But Skip the Queries on the Glory of Space Travel, and Don't Even Think About Anything Personal," *Los Angeles Times Magazine*, August 29,

1999; Jerry Adler, "Sally Ride: Ready for Liftoff," *Newsweek*, June 13, 1983; SKR personal papers; Lifetime.

Van Nuys: Interviews with Bear Ride, Joyce Ride, Tam O'Shaughnessy. T. J. Simers, "Quest for an Edge Leads to Wizard of Westwood," *Los Angeles Times*, March 18, 2003; Joyce Ride in ad for Peer, The Project on Equal Education Rights, a project of the NOW Legal Defense and Education Fund, in *Time*, August 6, 1984; Frank Finch, "LA Beats Giants on Neal Homer," *Los Angeles Times*, July 21, 1959; SKR personal papers; Academy of Achievement.

Europe: Interviews with Joyce Ride, Bear Ride. SKR letters to grandparents, September 1960–Spring 1961; SKR personal papers.

Encino: Interviews with Bear Ride, Joyce Ride, Tam O'Shaughnessy, Karen Flammer, Ann Lebedeff, Whitney Grant. SKR to Grap, April 30, 1961, SKR personal papers; SKR interview with Tom Brokaw, NBC News, June 1983; Steinem; Del Jones, "Ride Urges Emphasis on Math, Science Studies," *USA Today*, March 19, 2006; Astronomy Night at the White House, October 7, 2009; Carole Agus, "Sally Ride: First of a New Breed," *Boston Globe*, December 26, 1982; Penelope McMillan, "Astronaut Sally Ride—a Life of Drive, Achievement," *Los Angeles Times*, June 17, 1983; Beverly Beyette, "Sports Special; She Was Queen for a Day," *Boston Globe*, June 27, 1983; Adler; SKR personal papers.

Westlake: Interviews with Bear Ride, Joyce Ride, Susan Okie, Edina Weinstein, Janet Mennie Schroeder, Dana Kadison, Deborah Schneider Harrington, Maleah Grover McKay, Whitney Grant, Ann Lebedeff, Terry McEntee. *Vox Puellarum* (Westlake Yearbook) 1968 (copies from SKR and courtesy Susan Okie); SKR personal papers; SKR letter to Janet Mennie Schroeder, November 22, 1969; Steinem; SKR, "Great Science Education Starts with Inspired Teachers," posted at Mashable.com, May 8, 2012; Sara Sanborn, "Sally Ride: The Making of an Astronaut," *Ms.*, January 1983; Lifetime; Jones; SKR to John Tompkins, September 23, 1970.

College Bound: Interviews with Susan Okie, Fred Hargadon. Hargadon to Dale Ride, May 7, 1968, SKR personal papers.

CHAPTER 2: 40–LOVE, SALLY

Swarthmore: Interviews with Susan Okie, Janet Mennie Schroeder, Tam O'Shaughnessy, Fred Hargadon, Don Mizell, Sherri Davis. "Tennis, Astrophysics Keep Miss Ride Busy," *Delaware County (Pa.) Daily Times*, November 21, 1969; SKR to Mennie Schroeder, June 1968; Molly Tyson, "Space Age Computing," *Popular Computing*, June 1968; SKR to Mennie Schroeder, August 1, 1968; SKR to Mennie Schroeder, October 1, 1968; SKR to Joyce Ride, November 1969; SKR to Bear Ride et al., Fall 1969; SKR to family, Fall 1969; SKR transcripts from Swarthmore College; SKR to Mennie Schroeder, October 1969; SKR to Mennie Schroeder, April 1969; SKR to Andersons, Fall 1969; SKR to family, February 1969; Swarthmore College *Bulletin*, supplement to July 1969; SKR to family, probably February 1969; "Sally Ride Wins Net Title at Bryn Mawr by 6–1, 6–1," *New York Times*, May 5, 1969; Laytner; SKR to Joyce Ride, mid-November 1969; SKR to Bear Ride, December 1969; Academy of Achievement.

UCLA: Interviews with Joyce Ride, Bear Ride, Sherri Davis, John Tompkins, Fred Hargadon. SKR to Tompkins, August 31, 1970; Susan Cohen, "No Fears Yet, Says Woman Space Candidate," *San Jose Sunday Mercury News*, February 5, 1978; Lifetime; Temkin; SKR UCLA transcript; SKR to Mennie Schroeder, December 21, 1970; "Protvino, World of High Energies," *Soviet Life*, October 1971, 29–31; SKR to Tompkins, September 23, 1970; SKR to Tompkins, September 25, 1970. In this letter, Sally's excitement was also reflected in the wording of her return address: "A Stanford Student."

Stanford: Interviews with John Tompkins, Craig Barrett, Frances Hellman, Steve Hawley, Tam O'Shaughnessy, Bill Colson, Karen Flammer, David Bohrman. Statistics on women in physics from American Physical Society: APS/Source: IPEDS Completion Survey & NSF–NIH Survey of Graduate Students & Postdoctorates in Science and Engineering; Stanford commencement records and Physics Department statistics courtesy University Archives, Aimee Morgan, assistant university archivist; Lifetime; SKR Stanford University transcripts; SKR personal papers.

Molly: Interviews with Molly Tyson, Anne Gould. SKR to Mennie Schroeder, December 21, 1970; re: pomegranates: Sally spelled it "pomgranites"; Terrie McDonald, "Women's Athletics Challenged," *Stanford Daily*, c. 1972; Tyson, *womenSports*; SKR to Tompkins, October 28, 1970; Graham, http://www.crankyfitness.com/2012/07/remembering-sally-ride.html; SKR to Tompkins, November 10, 1970.

John: Interviews with John Tompkins, Bear Ride. SKR to Tompkins, November 1970; SKR to Tompkins, August 15, 1971.

Molly and Sally: Interviews with Molly Tyson, Rain Burns, Bear Ride, Gordon Kent, Jan Graham, Billie Jean King. Gerard Koskovich, "Private Lives, Public Struggles," *Stanford Magazine*, June 1993, courtesy Pamela Gorelow; Okie, "Fame Finds . . ."; SKR personal papers; SKR to Tompkins, November 1970; SKR to Tompkins, August 15, 1972; King to SKR, pre-June 1983.

Bill: Interviews with Bill Colson, Molly Tyson, Richard Teets, Tam O'Shaughnessy. Okie, "Fame"; Steinem; SKR, "The Ninth . . ."; Will Nixon, "NASA to Recruit Women," *Stanford Daily*, January 12, 1977, courtesy Margaret Rawson. Although Sally often attributed her application to a NASA recruitment ad that she saw on a Tuesday, she apparently misremembered that it was this article, published on a Monday.

CHAPTER 3: WAIT!

Sputnik: Interviews with Bear Ride. Cartoon by Jeff Parker, © *Florida Today* and *Fort Myers News-Press*, Caglecartoons.com; Sherr, *Outside the Box*; President Dwight D. Eisenhower, in response to a question from reporter May Craig, at White House press conference, October 9, 1957; "Johnson's Talk to Democratic Senators," *Washington Post*, January 8, 1958; Weitekamp, 33.

The Right Stuff: NASA Mercury Seven press conference, April 9, 1959; Tom Wolfe, *The Right Stuff*, New York: Farrar, Straus and Giroux, 1979, 279; JFK press conference, April 12, 1962; JFK speech at Rice University, September 12, 1962; JFK to Congress, May 25, 1961; LBJ to American College Public Relations Association in Chicago, June 25, 1963; JFK at remarks dedicating Aerospace Medical Health Center, San Antonio, November 21, 1963; NASA Mercury 7 press conference, April 9, 1959; Donald G. Cooley, "Portrait of the Ideal Space Man," *New York Times*, March 23, 1958; "Invitation to Apply for Position of Research Astronaut-Candidate," December 22, 1958.

Astronettes: Interviews with Margaret Weitekamp, Valerie Neal, Eileen Collins, Carolyn Huntoon, Hariett Jenkins. Weitekamp's *Right Stuff, Wrong Sex* is the most comprehensive of a number of recent books retelling the story of the pilots she calls "The Lovelace Women." Weitekamp (136–137) unearthed the LBJ letter from the LBJ Library in Austin, a superb job of reporting that brought this critical piece of paper to light. Lyndon B. Johnson Presidential Library, Austin Texas, Vice Presidential Papers. Weitekamp was also the first to report on the Carpenter memo (dated March 14, 1962) from the LBJ Library, Vice Presidential Papers. Carpenter later discussed the incident with author Martha Ackmann, who writes that she suggested, "Perhaps Johnson thought starting a woman's program would jeopardize the whole works," in *The Mercury 13: The True Story of Thirteen Women and the Dream of Space Flight* (New York, Random House, 2003), 148; Jerri Sloan Truhill in "Rocket Girls and Astro-nettes," radio show from Soundprint and Richard Paul, Public Radio Exchange, Cambridge, Massachusetts, February 22, 2010; "Qualifications for Astronauts," Hearings before the Special Subcommittee on the Selection of Astronauts of the Committee on Science and Astronautics, US House of Representatives, 87th Congress, Second Session, July 17 and 18, 1962 [No. 9], Washington: 1962, U.S. Government Printing Office; "2 Women in 175 Who Want to Get into Space," UPI story in *Chicago Tribune*, July 7, 1963; Jennifer Ross-Nazzal, Shannon Lucid, Helen Lane, "NASA Reflects America's Changing Opportunities; NASA Impacts US Culture," in *Wings in Orbit, Scientific and Engineering Legacies of the Space Shuttle, 1971–2010*, Wayne Hale, Executive Editor, Johnson Space Center and Government Printing Office, 2011; Trubatch in Jack Anderson, "Would-be Astronauts: Legion of Angry Women," *Parade*, November 19, 1967; Lindsay Anderberg, Polytechnic Institute of NYU; "First Soviet Spacewoman Also Topic of Sexist Cant," AP story quoting earlier AP dispatch about Tereshkova's flight and citing *Wisconsin State Journal* (Madison) editorial, *Lakeland Ledger*, June 19, 1983; "She Orbits over the Sex Barrier," *Life*, June 28, 1963; "A Mrs. in the Missile," *Los Angeles Times*, September 7, 1958; "The Lady Wants to Orbit," *Look*, February 2, 1960, 112, produced by Ben Kocivar; "Lucy Becomes an Astronaut," *The Lucy Show*, November 1962; Dorothy Roe, "Would-Be Astronettes Should Consider Problems, Space Travel Might Be a Bit Rough," *Orlando Sentinel*, 1965; NBC News, August 25, 1965; Cernan, 82; Abigail Trafford, "The Code of the Warriors," *Washington Post*, July 14, 1992; Marcia Dunn, Associated Press, "Pioneer 'Astronautrix' Aims

High," *Los Angeles Times*, July 26, 1998; Weitekamp, 3; "NASA's Support of Women and Girls," Pursuant to Executive Order 13506 Establishing The White House Council on Women and Girls, July 31, 2009.

Progress: Ruth Bates Harris, Samuel Lynn and Joseph M. Hogan to NASA administrator Fletcher, September 20, 1973; Jack Anderson, "White House Kept Lid on Nixon Home Costs," *Rome* (NY) *News-Tribune*, November 6, 1973; Kim McQuaid, "Racism, Sexism, and Space Ventures: Civil Rights at NASA in the Nixon Era and Beyond," in *Societal Impact of Spaceflight*, Steven J. Dick, Roger D. Launius, editors, NASA Office of External Relations, History Division, 2007; Senator James Abourezk in NASA's Equal Employment Opportunity Program Hearing, ninety-third Congress, second session, January 24, 1974, 46; Kevles, 51.

Shuttle: Interviews with John Logsdon, George Abbey, Michael Cassutt. Nixon on January 5, 1972, http://www.jsc.nasa.gov/history/suddenly_tomorrow/chapters/Chpt12 .pdf; Allen, 90.

Mission Specialist: Interviews with Duane Ross, Carolyn Huntoon, Nichelle Nichols. "NASA to Recruit Space Shuttle Astronauts," Release No. 76–44, July 8, 1976, JSC.

The Application: Interviews with Alan Ladwig, Molly Tyson. Laytner; SKR to author, 1981; SKR personal papers; SKR NASA materials courtesy Johnson Space Center, NASA; WSU.

The Process: Interviews with Duane Ross, George Abbey, Carolyn Huntoon, Alan Ladwig, Molly Tyson. Atkinson 153, 167; NASA News Release 78–03, January 16, 1978; SKR application courtesy NASA; Tyson, *womenSports*.

The Interview: Interviews with Susan Okie, Duane Ross, George Abbey, Carolyn Huntoon, Bear Ride, Steve Hawley, Rhea Seddon, NASA to SKR September 29, 1977; Okie, "NASA's Appeal . . ."; SKR Medical records courtesy NASA; SKR to Tompkins, October 18, 1970; Erica Goode, "Wanted in Space: Gregarious Loners Who Take Risks, Cautiously," *New York Times*, February 11, 2003; Tyson, notes; Atkinson, 215.

The Wait: Interviews with Susan Okie, Molly Tyson, Carolyn Porco, Bill Colson, Janet Mennie Schroeder, Edina Weinstein, George Abbey, Carolyn Huntoon, Robert Frosch, Duane Ross. Sanborn; Cohen; Tyson notes; Lifetime; SKR to Okie, November/December 1977.

The Phone Call: Interviews with Susan Okie, Bear Ride, Joyce Ride, George Abbey, Bill Colson. Lifetime; Dave Ansley, "Physics Graduate Student Chosen for Astronaut Team," *Stanford Daily*, January 17, 1987; Ansley, "New Woman Astronaut Gets Instant Fame," *Stanford Daily*, January 31, 1978; Scott Herhold, "Central Coast Scientists on Astronaut List," *San Jose Mercury News*, January 17, 1978; SKR Oral History 1; Cohen; SKR interview by NASA; NASA press conference January 16, 1978, at DC HQ; NASA press conference February 1, 1978, JSC, Houston; Tyson, notes.

CHAPTER 4: THIRTY-FIVE NEW GUYS

Reporting for Duty: Interviews with Hoot Gibson, Rick Hauck, Anna Fisher, Mike Coats, Bill Colson, Bill Powers, Carolyn Huntoon. SKR Oral History 1; "NASA Selects 35 Astronaut Candidates," Release No. 78-03, January 16, 1978; Mullane, 29; Thomas O'Toole, "The New Spacemen—and Women," *Washington Post*, January 17, 1978; Richard Richards, from whose JSC Oral History this is adapted, was actually in the astronaut class of 1980, but the problem was endemic; Norman Mailer, "Part II: The Psychology of Astronauts," *Life*, November 14, 1969; Sherr, *Outside the Box*; Sanborn; salary information courtesy Duane Ross, NASA, JSC; Tyson notes; WSU; Donna Miskin, "Women and Minorities Star in the New Astronaut Class," *Washington Star*, November 19, 1978; UC-Berkeley speech.

Flying: Interviews with Rick Hauck, Jon McBride, Steve Hawley, John Fabian, Norm Thagard, Anna Fisher, Rhea Seddon; Kathryn Sullivan. PBS; KU; Tyson notes; SKR to author in interview for ABC News, 1983; Bailey Morris, "Woman Astronaut Prepares for Space," *Washington Star*, June 22, 1979; SKR personal papers; Laytner; *Time*, August 14, 1978; Peter Gwynne with Holly Morris, "Sextet for Space," *Newsweek*, August 14, 1978.

The Women: Interviews with Kathryn Sullivan, Carolyn Huntoon, Rhea Seddon, Anna Fisher, Margaret Weitekamp, Bill Colson, Andrew Chaikin, Joe Allen, Ellen Baker. Nicholas C. Chriss, *Los Angeles* Times, July 11, 1978; Mullane, 29; Kathryn Sullivan JSC Oral History; Carpenter to National Women's Conference, November 19, 1977; "Not Such a Long Way, Baby," *Washington Post*, August 4, 1969; Tyson, notes; Terry McGuire in Susan Witty, "Our First Women in Space," *Geo*, September 1982; SKR Oral History; Gabriel H. Gluck, "Space Pioneer Urges Girls to Reach for the Stars," *Newark Star-Ledger*, May 5, 2002; Academy of Achievement; Andrew Chaikin, "Science & Technology: Women's Specialty: the real-Life Sciences," *Working Woman*. November–December 1996; SKR to Chaikin, August 22, 1996, courtesy Chaikin; Jerry L. Ross, *Spacewalker: My Journey in Space and Faith as NASA's Record-Setting Frequent Flyer* (West Lafayette, Ind.: Purdue University Press, 2013), 103; Henry Hartsfield at Presidential Commission on the Space Shuttle Challenger Accident, April 3, 1986.

Flying the Arm: Interviews with George Abbey, Jim Middleton, Bob Crippen, John Fabian, Bill Colson, Bob Rose;. SKR Oral History; SKR personal papers; Sanborn; WSU; Rhea Seddon Oral History.

Happy Hours, Happy Days: Interviews with Steve Hawley, Rick Hauck, Bill Colson, Molly Tyson, Marsha Ivins, Ellen Baker, Steve Riley, Hoot Gibson. Tyson notes; Cernan to LS on ABC News, August 30, 1983; SKR audio reflections,1983; Okie "Fame Finds . . ."; Santy, xv; Bob Ward, *The Light Stuff: Space Humor—from Sputnik to Shuttle* (Huntsville, Ala.: Jester Books, 1982), 80; Sanborn.

Steve: Interviews with Steve Hawley, Billie Jean King; Lifetime.

Back in Space: Interview with Mike Coats. SKR to LS, 1981; Crippen to LS, March 1981.

CapCom: Interviews with Richard Truly. SKR to LS, 1983; SKR to *Columbia* crew, STS-2 mission, November 12–13, 1981; SKR to Al Dale for ABC News, 1980.

CHAPTER 5: FIRST

Get Ready . . . : Interviews with George Abbey, Bob Crippen, Richard Truly, Hoot Gibson, Steve Hawley, Rhea Seddon, Kathryn Sullivan, Carolyn Huntoon. SKR to author, 1983; Frederic Golden, Guy Bluford, "Sally's Joy Ride into the Sky." *Time*, June 13, 1983; Abbey to author for ABC News, 1983; Ride, "Ninth Amendment"; Okie, "Cool Hand . . ."; Lifetime; SKR Oral History; Norman Mailer, *Of a Fire on the Moon* (New York: Little Brown, 1970), 44; Hauck to author for ABC News, 1981; Bob Crippen Oral History; Prime Crew press conference, April 29, 1982; Schlafly cartoon by Judge, 1982, © Field Syndicate; Tyson, notes.

. . . Get set . . . : Interviews with Norm Thagard, Bob Crippen, Rick Hauck, John Fabian, Susan Okie, Frank Hughes. Texas Monthly Talks; Sanborn; SKR to Brokaw, NBC News, 1983.

Time Out: Interviews with Steve Hawley, Bear Ride, Joyce Ride, Susan Okie, George Abbey, Carolyn Huntoon. *Los Angeles Times*, August 13, 1982; *Bryan* (Ohio) *Times*, August 24, 1982; *New York Times*, August 15, 1982; Paul Sweeney, "Sally Ride—'Super Woman,'" *Boston Globe*, May 29, 1983; Okie, "At Home . . ."; Hawley on *Today*, January 16, 1985, videotape courtesy Maureen Fitzgerald, David Corvo; Temkin; SKR on *Today*, January 16, 1985; Wiscombe; C-SPAN Video Library, US Senate session, June 2, 1986; Paul Recer, "Sally Ride's Space Flight Is 'Natural Progression,'" AP, *St. Louis Post-Dispatch*, June 12, 1983.

Anatomy Lessons: Interviews with George Abbey, Bob Crippen, Ellen Baker, Anna Fisher, Mary Cleave, Rhea Seddon, Kathryn Sullivan, Carolyn Huntoon. Seddon Oral History; Kevles, 12; Sullivan Oral History; Dr. Edgar Berman, 1970, to Rep. Patsy Mink, Democratic Party's Committee on National Priorities; Tyson notes; SKR Oral History; "3 Russians on Soyuz Return After 8 Days in Space," *New York Times*, August 8, 1992.

The Press, the Pressure: Interviews with Bob Crippen, Rick Hauck, Steve Hawley. Sanborn; Preflight press conference, May 24, 1983; Olive Talley, "Women Ready for Last Frontier," United Press International, in *Los Angeles Times*, June 5, 1983; *Life* to NASA April 1 and April 4, 1983; William H. Gregory, "Promoting the Shuttle" (editorial), *Aviation Week & Space Technology*, June 20, 1983; SKR to Brokaw, NBC News, 1983; Kathleen Hendrix, "Astronaut Sally Ride: The Sky May Not Be Her Limit," *Los Angeles Times*, May 13, 1982; Steinem; SKR to author, 1983; Temkin; Ninth Amendment; Carson on *The Tonight Show*, May 13, 1983; Miss Piggy to SKR, June 17, 1983; Miss Baker to SKR, June 1983.

KSC: Interviews with Ellen Baker, Bear Ride, Molly Tyson, George Abbey, Carolyn Huntoon, Anna Fisher. Ninth Amendment; SKR personal papers; SKR to Colson, October 1982; Tyson *womenSports*; SKR audio reflections, 1983.

Go!: Interviews with Rick Hauck, John Fabian, Norm Thagard, Bob Crippen, Hugh Harris, Lifetime; JPL; Kevin Panik; "Ninth Amendment"; SKR audio reflections, 1983; SKR Oral History; "For Ride's Family, a Day to Be Proud," AP story in *Boston Globe*, June 19, 1983; "Shuttle-Crazy Crowd Cries, 'Ride, Sally Ride,' " *New York Times*, June 18, 1983; size of crowd courtesy Hugh Harris via Brevard County Sheriff's Office.

Sally's Ride: Interviews with John Fabian, Bob Crippen, Rick Hauck, Norm Thagard, Steve Hawley, Andrew Chaikin, SKR audio reflections 1983; SKR personal papers; SKR Oral History. In a number of interviews, including her JSC Oral History, Sally said that during ascent, she forced herself to call out, "Roll Program." In fact, it was Crippen who called out "Roll Program" (it was always the commander's job); Sally, like all flight engineers, actually called out "LVLH," as reported here. She confirms that in her audio reflections. I speculate that she changed the facts when talking to the public to avoid having to explain LVLH, a complicated setting that was critical to maintaining the Shuttle's proper attitude. It wasn't the first, and wouldn't be the last time Sally fudged the facts in the interest, most likely, of avoiding confusion; Fabian Oral History; UC-Berkeley speech; Ride, "Single Room . . ."; JPL; Ride, *Mission Planet . . .* ; Academy of Achievement; Jeff Gill, *The Gainesville* (Florida) *Times*, November 18, 2005; "Ninth Amendment."

Homeward Bound: Interviews with Mary Cleave, Joyce Ride, Bear Ride, John Fabian. Lovell to Mike Collins, July 24, 1969.

CHAPTER 6: REENTRY

Welcome Home!: Interviews with Steve Hawley, Todd Halvorson, Ellen Baker, Kathryn Sullivan. Mailer, *Life*, 45; SKR Oral History; Halvorson 2008; "No White Roses for a Crew Lady," AP story in *Washington Post*, June 26, 1983; "Ninth Amendment"; Sullivan Oral History.

On the Road: Interviews with John Fabian, Norm Thagard, Steve Hawley, Bob Crippen, Deborah Schneider Harrington, Francis French, Susan Okie, Tam O'Shaughnessy, Carolyn Huntoon. *The* (Myrtle Beach) *Sun-News*, August 14, 1983; John Balzar, "Capitol Goes into Orbit for 'Sally Ride Day,' " *Los Angeles Times*, August 16, 1983; SKR to Scott Zachek, STARLOG, August 1985; *Washington Post*, July 13, 1983; Fabian Oral History; Barbara Gamarekian, "500 at NASA Museum Honor the Challenger Crew," *New York Times*, July 20, 1983; Steinem; Elizabeth Bumiller, "Sally Ride and the Bahrain Shuttle; Three Lives on the Day of a State Dinner," *Washington Post*, July 20, 1983; Joseph Trento and Susan B. Trento, "Why Challenger Was Doomed," *Los Angeles Times*, January 18, 1987; Tim O'Brien, "NASA Official Fights Ouster," *Washington Post*, October 29, 1973; John Noble Wilford, "Jane Fonda Chides the White House," *New York Times*, October 18, 1983; SKR personal papers; *Report of the Special Subcommittee*, 1962; Kathryn Holub, "Now She Shuttles Between Speeches," *Philadelphia Inquirer*, August 22, 1983; Judith Gaines, "In this Corner: Sally Ride's Next Orbit," *The Boston Globe*, June 30, 1983; song with 1983 lyrics courtesy Sally Ride Elementary, Woodlands, Texas.

Thanks for the Memories: Interviews with Gerry Griffin, Bob Crippen, Steve Hawley, Molly Tyson, Rain Burns, Bill Colson. SKR personal papers.

Intrigue in Budapest: Interviews with Rick Hauck, Steve Hawley, Tamas Gombosi, Dr. Harry Atkinson in *London Times*, August 6, 2012; SKR audio reflections, 1983; Hauck Oral History.

Inspiration: Interview with Barbara Barrett. SKR to author, 2008; Bruce Newman, "Being First: The Pride and Pressure of Breaking Barriers," *San Jose Mercury News*, October 9, 2008; Ellen Goodman, "The Future of a 'First Woman,'" *Washington Post*, June 25, 1983. © 1983 The Boston Globe Newspaper Company; "Ninth Amendment"; Ferraro to SKR June 22, 1984; Ferraro at Democratic National Convention, July 19, 1984; *Omni* magazine poll, November 1984; Ferraro, with Linda Bird Francke, *My Story* (New York: Bantam Books, 1985), 293.

Back to Work: Interviews with Steve Hawley, Bob Crippen, Dave Leestma, Kathryn Sullivan, Jon McBride, Rhea Seddon, Dave Hilmers. *USA Today*, July 31, 1984; Air-to-ground communication during mission, April 1985; Cooper, 209; "Ferraro, Ride: Women Still Face Career Barriers," *Orlando Sentinel*, June 29, 1985.

CHAPTER 7: EXPLOSIONS

Tam: Interviews with Tam O'Shaughnessy, Lindsey Beaven, Kay Loveland, Steve Hawley. Gerald Martin, *Gabriel García Márquez: A Life* (New York: Random House, 2009), 199; Bud Collins posting on his Facebook page, July 2012.

Victory Laps: Interviews with Steve Hawley. SKR to crew of STS-61B, November 1985; Steinem to SKR August 26, 1983 from SKR personal papers; "Sally Ride Opposed to 'Star Wars' Plan," UPI story in *Reading Eagle*, January 15, 1985; author application for Journalist-in-Space program.

***Challenger*:** Lifetime; SKR Oral History; Texas Monthly Talks.

The Rogers Commission: Interviews with Don Kutyna, Craig Covault, Allan McDonald, Tam O'Shaughnessy. SKR personal papers; Hearings of the Presidential Commission on the Space Shuttle Challenger Accident, February 11, 1986; SKR to Chaikin, August 22, 1996; Hearings, February 14, 1986; SKR to author for ABC News, March 6, 1986; Hearings, February 14, 1986; in Allan McDonald's book (McDonald, Allan J., with James R. Hansen, *Truth, Lies, and O-Rings: Inside the Space Shuttle Challenger Disaster* [Gainesville, Florida: University Press of Florida, 2009], 187), he adds that Sally said, "God, that took a lot of guts"; Hauck to author, 1988; SKR Oral History; SKR to Chaikin.

Split: Interviews with Steve Hawley.

CHAPTER 8: NEW TERRITORY

NASA Headquarters: Interviews with Alan Ladwig, Carolyn Huntoon, John Niehoff, Dixon Butler, Al Diaz, James Garvin, Brian Muirhead, Susan Okie. SKR Oral

History; Sherr, "A Mission . . ."; SKR personal papers; *Publisher's Weekly*; Denise Kalette, "Rare Visit with Sally Ride," *USA Today*, October 24, 1986; *Today* Show, NBC, October 14, 1986; SKR to UC-Irvine, October 3, 1986.

DCA-ATL-DCA: Interviews with Tam O'Shaughnessy.

The Ride Report: Interviews with Alan Ladwig, Terri Niehoff, Al Diaz, Dixon Butler, Al Gore, Barbara Mikulski, Craig Covault. Ride, *Leadership . . .* ; Craig Covault, "Ride Panel Calls for Aggressive Action to Assert US Leadership in Space," *Aviation Week & Space Technology*, August 24, 1987.

Done: Interviews with Alan Ladwig, Tam O'Shaughnessy, Steve Hawley. "Our Future in Space," *Los Angeles Times*, August 30, 1987; Michael Specter, "Astronaut Sally Ride to Leave NASA," *Washington Post*, May 27, 1987; NASA News Release no. 87–84, May 26, 1987, 2:00 p.m., "Astronaut Ride Will Leave NASA for Stanford University."

CHAPTER 9: DOWN TO EARTH

Arms and the Woman: Interviews with Sid Drell, Condoleezza Rice, George Lewis, John Townsend, Rodger Payne. SKR to Kyra Phillips, CNN, 2008; Voss; "Ex-Astronaut Sally Ride Shuns the Hoopla—and the Money," unsigned wire story from NASA HQ file, September 14, 1987; Diane Lederman, "Astronaut Hails Pioneer Spirit," *Holyoke Transcript-Telegram*, January 15, 1985; presentation of October 20, 1987, posted on Duck of Minerva site, and quoted courtesy Rodger Payne; Dawn Levy, "Sally Ride Speaks on the Tactical Role of Space and War," *Stanford Report*. April 17, 2003; Peter M. Banks and Ride, Sally K., "Soviets in Space," *Scientific American* 260(2), February 1989.

University of California, San Diego: Interviews with Tam O'Shaughnessy, Bear Ride, Joyce Ride, Steve Hawley, Kay Loveland, Billie Jean King, Grenn Nemhauser, Lindsey Beaven, Terry McEntee. Patrick McDonnell, "Astronaut Ride to Pursue Dual Interests at UCSD," *Los Angeles Times*, June 17, 1989; Kathy Sawyer, "Former Astronauts Flying High in New Jobs," *Washington Post*, June 17, 1989; Lee Dembart, "Being Female Is Not Significant, Astronaut Says," *Los Angeles Times*, May 25, 1983. Sally certainly meant what she said to Dembart but might have quarreled with the unintended implications of the headline; SKR on *Today* Show, May 12, 1983.

Professor: Interviews with Richard Somerville, Terry McEtee, Karen Flammer, Lauren Martin, Bear Ride, Joanna Rice, Mike Baine. Halvorson; SKR personal papers; CAPE reviews courtesy Martha Carbajal, CAPE Director, UCSD.

Inside the Beltway: Interviews with Rick Hauck, Richard Somerville, Alan Ladwig, Carolyn Huntoon, John Holdren, Susie Bachtel, Shirley Malcom, Brian Muirhead, Angela Phillips Diaz, Jack Gibbons, Al Gore, Jim Kohlenberger, Lori Garver, "Ride Backed," *USA Today*, March 9, 1989; Vincent DelGiudice, UPI, March 8, 1989; Mikulski to SKR, February 8, 1989; *Presidential Commission on the Assignment of Women in the Armed Forces (1991–1993); Statements and Testimony Submitted to Commissioners*; cartoon by Summers in *The Berkshire Eagle*, February 29, 1984; SKR to Mark Gearan, Alexis Herman, December 14, 1992.

EarthKAM: Interviews with Karen Flammer, Diane Bowen, Ed Buckbee, Chelsea Clinton, Dan McCleese, Tam O'Shaughnessy. SKR Oral History; JPL video re: KidSat; JPL 2008; Esther Newberg to Marian Wright Edelman, May 28, 1987; Eric Esary, Sally K. Ride, and Phillip Sprangle, "Nonlinear Thomson Scattering of Intense Laser Pulses from Beams and Plasmas," *Physical Review E*, October 1993; SKR to author, 1994.

The Speech: Interviews with Richard Somerville, Terry McEntee, Karen Flammer, Susan Okie, Tam O'Shaughnessy. SKR personal papers; SKR to Dorothy Briley, June 2, 1989.

Space.com: Interviews with Alan Ladwig, Andrew Chaikin, Mitchell Cannold, Dori Berinstein, Emily Sachar, Todd Halvorson, Toni DiMartino-Stebish, Tam O'Shaughnessy. James McWilliams, "Ride Tells Campers NASA Has 'No Issue' with Gender," *Huntsville Times*, October 30, 1999, account of SKR October 29 speech at Space Camp.

CHAPTER 10: SALLY RIDE SCIENCE

CEO: Interviews with Karen Flammer, Terry McEntee, Alann Lopes, Tam O'Shaughnessy, Billie Jean King, Myra Hart, Judith Estrin, Jane Swift. Donna Dubinsky; K. C. Cole, "35 Who Made a Difference: Sally Ride," *Smithsonian*, November 2005; *A Nation at Risk: The Imperative for Educational Reform*, A Report to the Nation and the Secretary of Education by the National Commission on Excellence in Education, April 1983; *Rising Above the Gathering Storm: Energizing and Employing America for a Brighter Economic Future* (Washington, DC: The National Academies Press, 2007); Stephanie Steinberg, "Astronaut Sally Ride Aims to Make Kids Starry-eyed," *USA Today*, August 2, 2010; SKR Oral History; Bell, N. (2010). *Graduate Enrollment and Degrees: 1999 to 2009*. Washington, DC: Council of Graduate Schools, © 2010 Council of Graduate Schools, Washington, DC; "Ride, Sally, Ride: 1st Female US Astronaut on Why Science Is Cool," *Inventors Digest*, November 2009; SKR personal papers; Texas Monthly Talks.

Making Science Fun: Interviews with Bear Ride, Tam O'Shaughnessy, Terry McEntee, Toni DiMartino-Stebich, Maria Zuber, Mike Coats. SKR to Tompkins, July 24, 1970; SKR at Lehigh Zoellner Arts Center lecture, April 8, 2008.

Headwinds: Interviews with Cathy Benko, Barbara Adachi, K. C. Cole, Shirley Malcom, Lucy McFadden, Tam O'Shaughnessy, Shelly Lazarus, Lynn Martin. SKR to Deloitte Women's Initiative Partner Conference, San Diego, November 2006; Jones; UC-Berkeley speech; Summers remarks at NBER Conference on Diversifying the Science & Engineering Workforce, January 14, 2005.

The Company: Interviews with Terry McEntee, Craig Covault, Tam O'Shaughnessy, Ken Cohen, Dori Berinstein, Leesa Hubbard, Sandy Antalis, Brenda Wilson, Meredith Manning, Maria Zuber. SKR to McEntee, November 10, 2000; Cindy Chang, "Ride into Sciences: Former Astronaut Challenges Young Women," *Pasadena Star-News*, March 20, 2005; *Some Assembly Required*.

MoonKAM: Interviews with Maria Zuber, Marilyn Ortiz, Julie Miller, Jane Swift, Deborah Schneider Harrington, Maleah Grover McKay, Toni DiMartino-Stebich, Francis French; Ros Krasny, "First American Woman in Space Promotes Careers in Science," *Reuters Life!* (Reuters.com), March 10, 2010; Marcia Dunn, "Sally Ride Reflects on Latest Pioneer," *The Bergen Record*, July 26, 1999, and Dunn, "Sally Ride Hears Echoes in Columbia Disaster," *Los Angeles Times*, June 15, 2003; Texas Monthly Talks.

CHAPTER 11: DUTY CALLS

Columbia: **Another Horrible Day:** Interviews with Bear Ride, Harold Gehman, Lisa Reed, Diane Vaughan, Todd Halvorson. Andrea Siedsma, "Down to Earth: Sally Ride's Next Launch," *The T Sector: Everything Tech San Diego*, April 2001; Ride, "Neon"; Nancy Imperiale, "Sally Ride Tells Girls to Keep Looking Toward Stars," *Knight Ridder Tribune Business News*, February 3, 2003; JFK press conference, May 5, 1961; SKR to CNN, February 2, 2003; Leonard; SKR to CAIB press briefing, April 8, 2003, Houston; Halvorson, *Florida Today*, May 21, 2003; *Columbia Accident Investigation Board Report*, August 2003; SKR to author, 2005; SKR email to Gehman et al., July 13, 2003; SKR personal papers; Claudia Dreifus, "A Conversation with Sally Ride: Painful Questions from an Ex-Astronaut," *New York Times*, August 26, 2003.

Back to the Future: Interviews with Lori Garver, Don Gips, Craig Barrett, Norm Augustine, Wanda Austin, John Holdren, John Logsdon, Austin Carr, "What Sally Ride Did for STEM Education," *Fast Company*, 2010; SKR to author, June 15, 2009; Armstrong, Cernan, Lovell, "Is Obama Grounding JFK's Space Legacy?" *USA Today*, May 25, 2011.

CHAPTER 12: THE SECRET

Interviews with Tam O'Shaughnessy, Kay Loveland, Billie Jean King, Joyce Ride, Bear Ride, Susan Okie, Bill Colson, Ann Lebedeff, Paula Levin, Brenda Wilson, Karen Flammer, Terry McEntee. *Publishers Weekly*; Bear Ride Pilgrim Place/Andiron Talk, March 3, 2010; *Touched by an Angel*, "Godspeed," episode 526, May 23, 1999; Office Depot commercial, 2002; Vuitton commercial, 2009; SKR to author, June 15, 2009.

CHAPTER 13: A VERY PRIVATE THING

Diagnosis, Treatment, Surgery, Decline, Grace: Interviews with Bear Ride, Tam O'Shaughnessy, Paul Fanta, Andrew Lowy, Karen Flammer, Terry McEntee, Barbara Adachi, Lynn Martin, Maria Zuber, Wanda Austin, Joyce Ride, Whit Scott. SKR medical records courtesy Dr. Paul Fanta; SKR personal papers; SKR to author, April 11, 2012.

Out: Patricia Santy, Harry Holloway, Hoot Gibson, Rhea Seddon, Kathryn Sullivan, Paula Levin, Terry McEntee. Bil Browning blog; "bystander" blogger, July 2012;

"Not everything is about sex," September 20, 2012; poster "Tara Li" on Bad Astronomy, July 23, 2012; letter to Andrew Sullivan.com, July 25, 2012; Santy.

Stardust: Interviews with Bear Ride, Tam O'Shaughnessy. "Physics" quote from Wernher von Braun, "Why I Believe in Immortality."

CHAPTER 14: IMPACT

Moonprints: Interviews with Maria Zuber, Bear Ride, Alan Ladwig, Joyce Ride. Impact Site location courtesy Ralph Roncoli, GRAIL Mission Design manager, JPL.

Earthworks: Interviews with Barbara Mikulski, Tam O'Shaughnessy, Frances Hellman, Christian Harrison, Craig Barrett, Steve Hawley, Bear Ride, Cady Coleman, Ellen Ochoa, Billie Jean King, Kate Rubins, Pamela Melroy, Anna Fisher, Rhea Seddon. Statistics for Sally Ride Science courtesy SRS; Joe Hansen, "A Is for Astronaut, H Is for Hero," itsokaytobesmart.com; Amy Mainzer in Thomas H. Maugh II, "Sally Ride Dies at 61," *Los Angeles Times*, July 23, 2010; various blog posts on NASA website; quotes from Whit Scott's video of the female astronauts courtesy Dottie Metcalf-Lindenburger, Tracy Caldwell Dyson, Whit Scott; Sherr, "Remembering . . ."

Lost in Space: Interviews with Kathryn Sullivan, Frank Hughes, Bob Crippen, Frances Hellman, Wanda Austin. Duke, Cunningham, Cernan at "Pioneers of Space," National Museum of Naval Aviation, Naval Air Station, Pensacola, Florida, December 15, 2012; UC-Berkeley speech.

Out and About: Interviews with Steve Riley, Tam O'Shaughnessy, Joyce Ride, Bear Ride, Whit Scott.

Astronaut: *The Ride Report;* "Sally Ride Interview," Scholastic.com, November 20, 1998; Texas Monthly Talks; SKR to author, January 29, 2005; Molly McGinn, "Sally Ride Brings Cary into Her Orbit," *The News & Observer* (Raleigh, North Carolina), February 2, 2000; Ride, *Leadership* . . . 55; Astronomy Night . . . ; Leonard.

INDEX

Page numbers in *italics* refer to illustrations.

Photo Credits

Numbers in *italics* refer to book pages; numbers in roman type refer to images in the photo insert.

NASA: Front cover, *81, 167, 215, 230, 278,* 23, 24, 25, 26, 27, 31, 32, 33, 35, 36, 38, 39, 40, 41, 42, 46, 47, 49, 56

© Randy G. Taylor: Back cover, *x,* 34, 37

Courtesy Ride family: *30,* 1, 2, 3, 4, 5, 6, 7, 8, 9, 10, 12, 13, 16, 19, 22

Courtesy John Tompkins: *1*

Lyndon Baines Johnson to James E. Webb, March 15, 1962, unmailed letter, Lyndon Baines Johnson Presidential Library, Austin, Texas. Memo says "Science/Space" file, image courtesy Margaret Weitekamp: *69*

The Stanford Daily © 2012 The Stanford Daily, Inc. All rights reserved. Reprinted with permission: *80*

Sally K. Ride personal papers, courtesy Tam O'Shaughnessy: *93, 96, 126*

Courtesy Kay Loveland: *193, 288*

Courtesy Sally Ride Science: *261,* 52, 53

Courtesy Tam O'Shaughnessy: *301*

Courtesy NASA/JPL-Caltech: *320*

Courtesy Dana Kadison: 11

Courtesy Swarthmore College: 14

AP Images: 43, 44, 48

Courtesy Molly Tyson: 15, 17 (Joyce Tyson)

Chuck Painter/Stanford News Service: 18

Courtesy Bill Colson: 20

San Francisco Examiner, courtesy of The Bancroft Library, University of California, Berkeley: 21

Courtesy Hoot Gibson: 28, 29

© Bettmann/CORBIS: 30

Sesame Street photo courtesy Sesame Workshop New York, New York, © Sesame Workshop. Sesame Street® and associated characters, trademarks and design elements are owned and licensed by Sesame Workshop. All rights reserved: 44

Courtesy Tamas Gombosi: 45

Courtesy Ronald Reagan Library: 50

Courtesy The White House, official White House photo: 51

Dominic Hart, NASA/Ames: 54

Bill Hrybyk, NASA/GFSC: 55

Every effort has been made to track down sources and obtain copyright permission. If you believe your name has been inadvertently omitted, please contact the author in care of the publisher.

About the Author

An award-winning ABC-TV News correspondent for more than thirty years, specializing in politics, social change and investigative reports, Lynn Sherr also anchored and reported on NASA's space shuttle program from its inception through the *Challenger* explosion. Her friendship with Sally Ride lasted long beyond that. Sherr was one of forty semifinalists in NASA's Journalist-in-Space competition, which was ultimately disbanded. Today she lives in New York and freelances on a variety of platforms. Among her bestselling books: *SWIM: Why We Love the Water; Outside the Box: A Memoir; America the Beautiful: The Stirring True Story Behind Our Nation's Favorite Song; Tall Blondes: A Book About Giraffes*; and *Failure Is Impossible: Susan B. Anthony in Her Own Words.* You can contact her at SallyRideBio@gmail.com or follow her on Twitter @LynnSherr.